T0345033

The U.S. National Income and Product Accounts

Studies in Income and Wealth
Volume 47

National Bureau of Economic Research
Conference on Research in Income and Wealth

The U.S. National Income and Product Accounts: Selected Topics

Edited by   Murray F. Foss

The University of Chicago Press

Chicago and London

MURRAY F. FOSS is Visiting Scholar at the American Enterprise Institute. He is the author of *Changes in the Workweek of Fixed
Capital* and (with Gary Fromm and Irving Rottenberg) *Measurement of Business Inventories.*

The University of Chicago Press, Chicago 60637
The University of Chicago Press, Ltd., London

Library of Congress Cataloging in Publication Data
Main entry under title:
The U.S. national income and product accounts.

(NBER studies in income and wealth; v. 47)
Papers presented at the Income and Wealth Conference held
May 3–4, 1979 in Washington, D.C.
Bibliography: p.
Includes index.
1. National income—United States—Accounting—
Congresses. I. Foss, Murray F. II. Income and
Wealth Conference (1979 : Washington, D.C.)
III. Title: United States national income and prod-
uct accounts. IV. Series.
HC106.3.C714   vol. 47 [HC110.I5]   330s   82–11081
ISBN 0–226–25728–2   [339.373]

Contents

Prefatory Note

This volume contains the papers presented at the Conference on National Income and Product Accounts of the United States held in Washington, D.C., on 3 and 4 May 1979. Funds for the Conference on Research in Income and Wealth are provided to the National Bureau of Economic Research by the National Science Foundation; we are indebted for its support. We also thank Murray F. Foss, who served as chairman of the conference and editor of this volume.

Introduction

Murray F. Foss

This volume, the forty-seventh in the National Bureau of Economic Research series on Research in Income and Wealth, contains papers, discussions of papers, and a round-table session that constituted the Income and Wealth Conference held in Washington, D.C., on May 3 and 4, 1979. The conference dealt with selected aspects of the U.S. National Income and Product Accounts, specifically, concepts, problems of deflation and the treatment of quality change in price indexes, and source data.

A conference on the national accounts, a topic proposed by the Executive Committee in late 1977, poses unusual problems these days because the accounts serve many different purposes, which in turn define many different constituencies among economists, economic statisticians, and other users. Some emphasize theory, while others stress numbers. Some place the greatest emphasis on the quarter-by-quarter tracking of economic activity and on business-cycle developments, others on the long-term growth of output and productivity, while still others are concerned with the scope and structure or composition of income and output at a point in time and over time. The several conferences on the national accounts as such have tended to stress—but not exclusively—concepts and structure (see Studies in Income and Wealth 1937, 1938, 1943, 1947, 1957b, 1958). But even though the underlying conceptual basis must always remain high on what might be called the national accounts agenda, it is no less important to recognize the vast growth of the accounts—since the early postwar years—in size and richness of detail, in frequency of appearance, and especially in usage. Although we probably need not be concerned with the economic implications of the fact that GNP is now

Murray F. Foss is currently a Visiting Scholar at the American Enterprise Institute for Public Policy Research.

a household term, it is of economic significance that the national accounts are at the heart of the enormous body of information used by business, government, research organizations, and economists generally for macroeconomic intelligence and analysis. Much of this is employed as an aid in the making of decisions that may have a profound effect on demand, output, and the rate of inflation. Yet there has never been a conference devoted to the accounts as a system of information pertaining to the behavior of the economy, especially in the short run. This informational aspect was a major focus of the May 1979 conference and explains the emphasis of the conference on source data and the need for data improvement.

Another major focus of the present volume is the problem of deflation—adjusting current dollar figures for price change—which has taken on added importance as the rate of inflation has accelerated. Users of the U.S. accounts have long had product data in constant dollars, but in practice such estimates frequently played a role subsidiary to the current-dollar estimates so long as the rate of inflation was low. That has long since ceased to be the case. Nominal GNP must now share center stage with real GNP and the rate of inflation. Both producers and users of the accounts are now forced to pay close attention to a wide variety of deflation problems that were often only of limited interest. One of these is the treatment of quality change. This is not a new problem to these conferences; it was discussed by Denison (1957) in volume 19 in connection with the measurement of capital, and in volume 28 by Griliches (1964) and by Jaszi, Denison, and Grove (1964), but it has taken on new importance in an era of national concern over energy and inflation, and it is a problem over which economists remain divided regarding proper treatment.

The conference started off with a session devoted to conceptual issues, which consisted of one paper by Richard Ruggles, and a second by Franklin Fisher and Karl Shell that the authors subsequently withdrew. The Ruggles paper, the opening paper in this volume, consists of three parts. The first is a history of the accounts since the early World War II period, which uses as points of reference major conferences and reviews that have focused on the accounts. Ruggles's historical approach is extremely useful for highlighting major issues as well as for explaining how the accounts evolved. The second discusses new developments, in which Ruggles takes up sectoring, nonmarket estimates and imputations, and the integration of financial transactions and balance sheets with the national accounts. The third part is a special appendix in which Ruggles offers an alternative approach to the treatment of insurance, pensions, and interest consistent with his "transactor's" approach to the accounts. He also presents household balance sheets for the postwar years with detailed breakdowns for tangible and financial assets.

Although there are a number of points of specific disagreement, Helen Stone Tice, the discussant, agrees with the general thrust of Ruggles's proposals. Beyond this she expresses the wish that Ruggles had spent more time than he chose to spend on certain issues that have come up in the past and that remain unresolved or "tabled." One of these is whether the accounts should be measuring welfare as "*the* primary or at least *a* primary aggregate" (my emphasis). The Bureau of Economic Analysis (BEA), of course, has always been very careful to point out that GNP measures output and not welfare, although the two concepts may be and frequently are closely associated. Tice brings up a topic that is of continuing interest, although one might argue that this interest has varied and may be somewhat less today than it was a decade ago when it was discussed at the Princeton Conference (Studies in Income and Wealth 1973, vol. 38). There will always be disagreement about what should be *the* primary measure because individuals differ in their views about what is most important in a society. Disagreements about *a* measure of welfare that might be included as part of the accounts will revolve around the ability of national income accountants to measure things that are not now measured.

Measurability is especially pertinent to a second issue, namely, whether nonmarket activities should be included in output, that is, whether output should be defined to include market transactions only. This was also discussed extensively at the Princeton Conference (Studies in Income and Wealth 1973, vol. 38). In this respect, BEA has already undertaken a number of studies dealing with nonmarket measures. One provides estimates of the services of the stock of durable goods held by persons, while another deals with the estimated value of government-owned capital (Katz and Peskin 1980; Musgrave 1980).

The third issue is whether capital gains and losses should be included in income. This is an old and difficult topic that has taken on new significance as the rate of inflation has increased. Although Ruggles does not deal with conceptual issues underlying capital gains, he does provide detailed data on revaluations in presenting estimates of changes in household balance sheets.

The second session was devoted to deflation, a main aspect of which concerns quality change. Although the problem of quality change is not a new one in economic measurement and has come up in a number of Income and Wealth Conferences in the past quarter century or so, there has been no resolution of opposing views. One view is that quality change is measured by cost to the producer, while others maintain that utility to the purchaser is the proper criterion. A new view is that both criteria are correct in principle, depending on whether the item in question is an output or an input. This volume contains four papers dealing in whole or in part with the quality change issue. Triplett's paper is concerned exclusively with theoretical aspects and might be read first for seeing the main conceptual problems. Gordon presents an alternative approach to the treatment of quality change that is used by BEA and that is illustrated in the Ziemer-Galbraith paper on government defense purchases. Early and Sinclair tell how the government has handled the quality change issue for a major price index.

John F. Early and James H. Sinclair of the Bureau of Labor Statistics present detailed information on how BLS has actually made allowance for quality change in calculating the Producer Price Index (PPI). Once BLS has determined that a specification change has occurred for an item being priced in the PPI, in practice this change may be handled in one of several ways. (1) When there are no data available for making an *explicit* quality adjustment (the majority of cases), one of two options is employed. (*a*) Where quality change is deemed "small" (according to procedures adopted on a product-by-product basis), it is neglected. This leads to the so-called direct price comparison. Direct comparison means that all of the observed price change will be recorded as pure price change, with no allowance for quality change. (*b*) On the other hand, if the BLS finds that the quality change is greater than the cutoff value and therefore cannot be ignored, this leads to the PPI linking procedure. This will show no price change over the month in which the changed item was introduced into the index. Obviously, by calling all of the observed price change quality change, the BLS misses any pure price change that may have accompanied the introduction of a changed item. (2) In some cases, BLS obtains the cost of the specification change from the manufacturer who provides the price data to the BLS, and uses cost as an explicit quality adjustment. Where used for an input price index, cost data supplied by a manufacturer are always regarded as an approximation to the user-value data that are considered theoretically appropriate for the index, on the grounds that in equilibrium the marginal cost of any change will approximate its incremental value to the user.

In 1976, BLS obtained more than 108,000 monthly price quotations for calculating the PPI, of which 455 represented specification changes that BLS treated with one of the procedures mentioned above. A special analysis of six categories of commodities for the years 1970–77 failed to reveal any cyclical patterns in the BLS treatment of specification change. And a detailed analysis of one item—construction cranes—by means of an alternative approach, namely, through hedonic indexes, suggests that if there is a bias in the BLS technique the bias is quite small.

Although the number of specification changes may appear small for an entire year, the authors note that many commodities are products of farms and mines and are not subject to specification change. Also capital equipment items may go for many years without change, and the BLS practice of pricing large-volume items tends to exclude goods subject to frequent specification change. In his discussion Griliches characterizes the number of specification changes found by BLS as extremely low and criticizes the authors for not having taken independent steps to determine if indeed there is some kind of downward bias on the part of BLS in the uncovering of specification change. Griliches's suggestion for an independent check is a good one. To do it properly probably requires much careful work, mainly in the field, at considerable cost, but the problem is important enough to warrant the effort.

Richard C. Ziemer and Karl D. Galbraith present results of BEA's new study of deflated defense purchases, a topic that is interesting not only because it poses difficult analytical and statistical problems but also because very recently the federal budget has reflected defense policy objectives that have been stated in terms of increases in real defense outlays.

Quality change is an important aspect of defense purchases of major items like aircraft. For these BEA has adopted the same conventions in deflating as it uses elsewhere in the GNP. When a change in specifications takes place, such as occurs with the introduction of a new weapons system, BEA values the change by the cost to the defense producers rather than by the usefulness to the Defense Department (DOD). Consequently, looking at defense purchases deflated in the BEA fashion may or may not tell anything about how much "firepower" the Pentagon has purchased; the figures will ordinarily be silent on this score. However, as a measure of resource use and of how much defense purchases may be impinging on total output, the meaning of this approach is free of ambiguity.

Another feature of the Ziemer-Galbraith study is their comparison of the price behavior of defense items with comparable items priced in the PPI. Their general position is that market conditions underlying the two sets of prices are so different that PPIs, which specifically exclude sales to the military, ought not be used to deflate defense purchases. Marilyn E. Manser, the discussant, felt that the authors should have been more systematic in making these comparisons, which Manser considers very useful. Apparently the authors did not have time for detailed analysis of these comparisons, so these ought to be viewed as the start of what could be a fruitful investigation.

Although the authors do not make this point, it is entirely possible that the DOD price data are a more accurate reflection of general market conditions than the PPI and perhaps should be used for civilian as well as military purposes. Among other things, there is a suggestion that some of the DOD series are more cyclically sensitive than their PPI counterparts. For example, DOD prices of men's apparel peaked in the fourth quarter of 1974, fell sharply until the third quarter of 1975, and did not regain their earlier peak until the fourth quarter of 1977. By way of contrast, the

PPI apparel items fell very little in the 1974–75 recession, and by the fourth quarter of 1977 were 18% above the fourth quarter of 1974 levels. The Ziemer-Galbraith paper by implication raises the question of whether prices are better measured from the seller's side or from the buyer's side.

The treatment of quality change in the making of index numbers is of special interest in an era of sharply higher energy prices. Robert J. Gordon's paper is concerned with quality change as it relates to the price of capital goods, specifically, how changes in maintenance and operating costs brought about by technical change affect the measurement of prices of commercial aircraft.

In the past, most empirical work on quality change has concentrated mainly on dimensional or performance aspects—a truck is a five-ton truck or a crane has a two-ton lifting capacity. The typical problem facing the maker of index numbers arises when the manufacturer indicates that he is dropping one line of his product for which he is substituting a new and improved line, say, a bigger truck or a crane with greater capacity. Technical change, however, can also take the form of products with reduced operating costs as noted in the Stigler Report of 1961 (Price Statistics Review Committee 1961) and by Denison in his 1957 paper.

The quality change issue is an important one in national income accounting. Denison's 1957 paper ("Theoretical Aspects of Quality Change, Capital Consumption and Net Capital Formation," in vol. 19 of the Income and Wealth Series), in which he considered alternative ways of treating quality change in capital goods, could serve as a reflection of BEA's position on this subject. The producer of national income accounts wants a theoretically precise definition of national income or net national product. For this he must know the circumstances under which capital will be kept intact, since the notion of keeping capital intact underlies the concept of income. To measure net capital formation he must have measures of additions to the capital stock (gross capital formation) and subtractions from it (depreciation and discards) that can be combined, and this requires magnitudes expressed in terms of the same prices. The problem of obtaining appropriate price indexes is especially difficult in capital goods because of quality change.

In the Denison view capital goods are considered equal in quality if they have the same cost in a given year, and not necessarily if they make the same contribution to production. With this criterion used for price indexes and deflation, the value of today's stock of capital goods in base period prices is what it would have cost to produce those same goods in the base period. Today's additions to the capital stock expressed in base year costs are what it would have cost in the base year to acquire the resources used to make today's additions. Similar considerations hold for deletions from the stock.

The approach that measures quality change by the specific contribution a capital good makes to production is viewed by Denison as an alternative that also has validity from a theoretical point of view, but one that is impractical and therefore to be rejected. The national income investigator cannot possibly have the required data for such a calculation. Only the user of the capital good would have the requisite information, and even the user would be confronted by practical difficulties in implementing this approach.

Gordon believes that many regulated industries provide information that can be used to evaluate quality change. In an industry like commercial aircraft, detailed information is available on costs associated with the shift, say, from turboprops to jets and among various vintages of jets. Gordon concludes that, when the savings in operating costs of the airlines are accounted for, the price of new aircraft declined at an annual rate of 7.5% from 1957 to 1971 instead of increasing by 2.6% per year as shown in official figures. Gordon feels that his approach has considerable potential to the extent that similar information is available in other regulated industries, which, it may be noted, account for a sizable share of business fixed capital.

In his comment on the Gordon paper, Triplett raises the issue of whether fuel savings from more fuel-efficient aircraft should enter a measure of airline costs in the form of an adjustment to aircraft prices. He concedes, however, that in a fixed-weight price index quantities cannot adjust, so the Gordon estimate gives an overall measure of input costs to the airline industry that moves in the right direction.

At the conference much of the discussion of Gordon's paper concerned its theoretical section. Triplett sketched an alternative conceptual approach to the problem of evaluating quality change in price indexes, which is incorporated in expanded form in the volume.

Triplett has extended the usual theories of price and quantity indexes, which deal with price and quantities of *goods*, to *characteristics* of goods. This is because in Triplett's view the quality of goods can be thought of in terms of specific characteristics, like the speed of a machine or its, say, lifting capacity. In his view, quality can be thought of quantities (in a vector) of characteristics, that is, quality change is intrinsically quantifiable. Also, following Fisher and Shell, Triplett uses a framework that distinguishes between input price indexes and output price indexes, except that the indexes refer to characteristics rather than to goods in each case. With an input price index, when relative input prices change and substitutions of one input for another are possible, the theoretically correct measurement of the price change requires that production in the industry using the inputs be held constant. When a quality change adjustment must be made, use of the criterion *contribution to output* or *value to the user* of the input assures that the inputs correspond to points on the same production isoquant. When dealing with output price indexes, however, the appropriate criterion for measuring price change is keeping resources constant. Given constant endowments of the factor inputs, as relative output prices change the mix of outputs can vary along a production possibility curve. For making a quality change adjustment in output prices, use of resource cost as the criterion assures that numerator and denominator of a price index correspond to points on the same production possibility curve.

For many purposes distinguishing between input prices and output prices is important; it clears up many theoretical problems that otherwise seem to require contradictory solutions. It is important to keep in mind, however, that there is a big gap between Triplett's pure theory and its implementation. For example, Triplett's theory requires that goods be defined in terms of characteristics, but that may prove quite difficult. Also, practical considerations dictate the use of fixed weighted indexes, which are inherently biased in terms of economy theory, but that does not mean that there has been no progress in measurement or that measurement should cease. And whether one uses a resource-cost or user-value criterion, actual data for making quality change adjustments are without question not easily obtained.

The remainder of the conference was concerned for the most part with data problems and consisted of a round-table discussion, an econometric study of data revisions, and critiques of a report on the source data used for the calculation of the national accounts. The round-table session was designed to elicit views from prominent users of the accounts. In this regard, it could be viewed as a replay—on a much smaller scale—of the papers prepared for the fiftieth anniversary of the *Survey of Current Business* in July 1971 (*Survey of Current Business* 1971, vol. 51). Given the many changes over the decade—the expanded utilization of the accounts, the growth of short-term econometric models, the increased rate of inflation, the "stagflation," and the decreased self-assurance among macroeconomists at least—the round-table session was well worthwhile.

All of the users in the panel had extensive experience with the accounts. Each panelist was free to choose his subject matter but each was requested to discuss the accounts in the light of his special experience. Each was asked also to submit a very short written statement, which is reproduced in the volume along with some of the subsequent verbatim discussion, which has been very slightly edited.

The two models builders expressed rather different points of view. Lawrence Klein of Wharton presented a list—a "wish list" as he called it—that gave considerable emphasis to issues raised in Klein's presidential address before the American Economic Association in December 1977 (see Klein 1978). He wants to analyze inflation in a more satisfactory fashion and consequently wants more frequent and timely input-output tables, which would provide a much more detailed breakdown of costs than is ordinarily available from, say, census sources.

Otto Eckstein of Data Resources, Inc., expressed the view that national income economists devote too much time to national income concepts and not enough time to the statistics. Eckstein is less concerned with what the accounts ought to measure and more concerned with the accounts as a body of information. He probably reflected the sentiments of the very large and growing number of economists who are engaged in assessing current economic conditions and in making short-run forecasts of the economy for their employers or clients and who are mainly concerned with an accurate portrayal of history, especially very recent history, like the latest three months or the last year or two.

Eckstein feels that series which represent little more than the filling of gaps in coverage or series that are guessed at in order to bring about conceptual completeness have little information content. He cites the inventory valuation adjustment (IVA) as an example of the latter. Few would disagree that the inventory valuation adjustment is subject to a considerable estimating error, especially quarterly. But BEA has always shown the IVA explicitly and anyone who prefers book profits to the national income accounts (NIA) version can always subtract the IVA from the NIA figure to arrive at the book figure. One would think, however, that the NIA version of inventory change or profits has much more information than the book figures. The same is true of the capital consumption adjustment, which Eckstein also singles out for criticism.

Speaking about his role as a policy advisor, Alan Greenspan focused on the importance of very up-to-date statistics as an aid in assessing current economic activity and the near-term outlook. He gave an example of using weekly data for appraising the business outlook in late 1974–early 1975 and deplored the discontinuance of weekly series on retail trade that he found especially useful at that time. That points up a continuing problem, namely, accuracy versus timeliness, a subject discussed at greater length in the session on the Creamer Report. Here it is worth noting that the amount of quarterly detail now shown in the accounts has expanded considerably over the years. The amount of industry detail has also expanded. Denison criticized changes in industry classifications made by the federal government in the Standard Industrial Classification, since the logic of the changes is often not clear and the changes themselves obstruct long-term industry comparisons. The issue raised by Denison, whose main interests have been in long-run change, is a nettlesome one. In making classification changes the government apparently gives considerable weight to industry requests, which have been heavily influenced by shorter-run considerations of sales and marketing.

Some statistical and conceptual issues that arise in an era of inflation were the focus of remarks by the late Arthur M. Okun. He noted that in principle there are two basic ways to measure real output—direct measurement (as is done, e.g., for most series of the Federal Reserve Index of Industrial Production), and by dividing a series measured in current dollars by a price index. In practice BEA uses the latter technique for much of what it does because most goods are too complex to be measured directly in terms of physical quantities. But the greater the volatility of price behavior, the more difficult the deflation, especially when the price data are collected quite independently of the dollar series that must be deflated, like retail sales, manufacturers' shipments, etc. This is partly because the federal statistical system is decentralized and the agency responsible for the collection of price data (the Bureau of Labor Statistics) is different from the agency responsible for collection of sales data (the Bureau of the Census). Okun put in a plea for more physical volume data, partly to supplement estimates derived through deflation and particularly to use as a check against possible bias in the deflation procedure (see also Usher 1975).

Okun also raised some conceptual points, the most important of which dealt with inflation adjustments. He asked whether the IVA should be applied to book profits alone, as is now done, or to the sum of book profits and corporate interest paid. He favored the latter, since both stocks and bonds are used to finance capital formation. The bond purchaser makes his purchase with the expectation of a certain rate of inflation. If he is wrong, he bears the real risk. To apply an inflation adjustment solely to stockholders is potentially misleading.

Anyone with only a slight familiarity with the accounts has to contend with frequent revisions in the data. For most regular users the revisions are an annoyance, but most persons recognize that revisions are the price that must be paid for more accurate information. The important issue is whether the revisions make a difference. One way to test this is through an econometric model. The paper by Grimm and Hirsch discusses how the statistical revisions published by BEA in January 1976—a so-called benchmark revision—affected the structure of the BEA econometric model, and how the revisions affected projections of key variables like GNP, real GNP, the rate of inflation, and the unemployment rate.

One of the main findings of the Grimm-Hirsch paper was that even though statistical revisions were responsible for some large revisions in individual structural parameters, basic properties of the model were not changed very much. Early quarter multipliers were little changed as a result of the revisions. Thus if one is interested in the overall behavior of the economy the revisions are of no crucial importance; if interest centers on industry detail, however, the story is quite different. Grimm and Hirsch also found that revisions helped predictive accuracy to some extent as a result of better measures of initial conditions, exogenous variables, and revised estimates of parameters. But forecasts of the 1974–75 recession, improved or not, were poor, a verdict that few forecasters of any type—econometric or judgmental—can escape.

The final session of the conference was devoted to source data. Although use of the national accounts has grown enormously in the past several decades, the underlying data and the estimation techniques employed by BEA have never been the exclusive subject of a detailed study. In this regard the report of the Advisory Committee on Gross National Product Data Improvement—the Creamer Report—breaks new ground in its examination of the statistical bases of the accounts and in its extensive recommendations for improvement (see U.S. Department of Commerce 1977).

The session was made up of several short papers, each of which was designed to give a critical evaluation of major parts of the report and which are answered by the late Daniel Creamer, chairman, and some members of his committee. Morris Cohen was asked to provide an overview of the entire report and to look at it from the point of view of the business cycle. The relevant question for the business cycle is how well the report treats the statistical problems of measuring and analyzing the cyclical behavior of the economy as seen in the accounts. Ronald E. Kutscher discusses how well the report treats the statistical problems of measuring and analyzing long-term growth, as BEA defines output. The qualification is important since alternative concepts of output were not the subject of this session. Albert Rees looks at the report's treatment of the statistical problem of deflation—in practical terms, the BLS price indexes and BEA's use of them in deflation. Finally, John A. Gorman examines the chapter dealing with the flow-of-funds accounts. The program committee also thought it appropriate to invite comment from the Bureau of Economic Analysis; this appears in the remarks of Robert P. Parker, chief of BEA's National Income and Wealth Division.

When we focus on the business cycle we are focusing on the quarterly statistics in the national accounts. These are the statistics that receive the most publicity in the news media and consequently have the greatest effect on perceptions of what is happening in the economy. They are figures that businessmen and government officials use most in making short-run policy decisions. In fact, the Creamer Committee came into being because economic policymakers in the early 1970s felt that the quarterly figures were not giving a reliable portrayal of economic developments.

Morris Cohen felt that the periodic benchmarking has tended to have a dampening effect on cyclical movements, a charge that Rosanne Cole illustrates very nicely in her rebuttal. But where Cohen held that some of the business cycle has been lost—an opinion shared to some extent by

Otto Eckstein in his remarks in the round-table session—Cole felt that the revisions are clearly closer to the truth. If there had been a discussion of how basic census series are revised, one could see that the revision technique—which tends to be linear adjustments—must have this effect. No doubt that on average this does yield the best results and has the virtue of being easy to carry out, but it does not necessarily give the most accurate portrayal of cyclical movements. From a business-cycle point of view it would seem desirable to collect not only annual data, say, in the Annual Survey of Manufactures, but monthly data as well for certain important series.

There are a host of problems associated with the deflation of current dollar magnitudes by price indexes. Estimates of real output can be no better than the prices used for deflation. One of the most important recommendations by the Creamer Committee is that the BLS base its PPI on shipment prices. Since BLS prices are now a mixture of prices in shipments and prices in new orders, this recommendation, which BLS is now implementing, should greatly aid the process of deflation. In this connection it is worth noting that Albert Rees raises the question of whether prices in shipments will provide an accurate portrayal of current market developments. For evaluating current market conditions one would want a price at which new orders are taken, but since new orders are not encompassed in the national accounts the Creamer Committe did not address itself to this question. It seems fairly clear, however, that an index based exclusively on shipments will lag behind current market developments, and the lag will vary over the cycle. Both types of prices are needed, since both objectives of price measurement—market evaluation and deflation—are important.

Ronald E. Kutscher's remarks were concerned with long-term growth. BEA conducts a major overhaul of the accounts at infrequent intervals in the so-called benchmark revisions. The benchmarking, and the comparison with existing levels of product and income extrapolated from the last benchmark, are done in terms of current-dollar measures, for which a considerable amount of new statistical material, like the quinquennial economic censuses, becomes available. But one of the most important questions one really wants answered in comparing two periods separated by five years or more is how well the published figures have tracked the rate of growth in real output. That question can be answered only partially in the sense that the set of prices used by BEA for preparing final estimates of deflated output is little different from the set of prices used for the preliminary estimates. In comparing the change in GNP between benchmark years with previously published data, the absence of error in current-dollar terms strictly speaking says nothing about the components of change, since there may be offsetting errors in the underlying real output and price components.

In his discussion of chapter 9 of the Creamer Report, John A. Gorman called attention to the large differences that exist between personal saving as measured in the national accounts and as measured in the flow-of-funds accounts. The two are equivalent conceptually but are derived from different statistical sources. One thing they have in common is that both estimates are derived as residuals. Gorman noted that from 1968 to 1978 the level of personal saving from the flow-of-funds series is much higher than that from the national accounts: moreover, on two occasions the two series show year-to-year changes that differ in direction. Even when they do agree in direction there are three instances where the differences in movement are greater than one-half of 1%.

Gorman made comments on all nine recommendations in this chapter and noted that only one would help reduce the discrepancy between the two personal saving rates. In response, Stephen Taylor remarked that, since all household items in the flow-of-funds are derived as residuals from information pertaining to other groups in the economy, any improvement in this nonhousehold information is bound to have a beneficial effect on the estimate of personal saving.

Robert P. Parker of BEA called attention to the fact that many of the recommendations made by the Creamer Committee had already been put into effect, while other recommendations were in the process of being implemented. In addition, among other things, Parker told of efforts BEA has made to engage in discussions with official bodies of the public accounting profession in order to make known the special needs of the national accounts. One can see great mutual benefit from such discussions if they materialize.

References

Denison, Edward F. 1957. Theoretical aspects of quality change, capital consumption, and net capital formation. In *Problems of capital formation: concepts, measurement, and controlling factors*, pp. 215–61. Studies in Income and Wealth, vol. 19. Princeton, N.J.: Princeton University Press for the National Bureau of Economic Research.

Griliches, Zvi. 1964. Notes on the measurement of price and quality changes. In *Models of Income Determination*. Studies in Income and Wealth, vol. 28. Princeton, N.J.: Princeton University Press for the National Bureau of Economic Research.

Jaszi, George; Denison, Edward F.; and Grove, Ernest W. Comment on Griliches's Notes on the measurement of price and quality changes. In *Models of Income Determination*. Studies in Income and Wealth, vol. 28. Princeton, N.J.: Princeton University Press for the National Bureau of Economic Research.

Katz, Arnold J., and Peskin, Janice. 1980. The value of services provided by the stock of consumer durables, 1947–77: an opportunity cost measure. *Survey of Current Business* 60 (July): 22–31.

Klein, L. R. 1978. The supply side. *American Economic Review* 68 (March): 1–7.

Musgrave, John C. 1980. Government-owned capital in the United States, 1925–79. *Survey of Current Business* 60, no. 3: 33–43.

Price Statistics Review Committee. 1961. *The Price Statistics of the Federal Government.* New York: National Bureau of Economic Research.

Studies in Income and Wealth. 1937, vol. 1. New York: National Bureau of Economic Research.

————. 1938, vol. 2.

————. 1943, vol. 6.

————. 1947, vol. 10.

————. 1957a, vol. 19. *Problems of capital formation: concepts, measurement, and controlling factors.*

————. 1957b, vol. 20. *Problems in the international comparison of economic accounts.* Princeton, N.J.: Princeton University Press for the National Bureau of Economic Research.

————. 1958, vol. 22. *A critique of the United States income and product accounts.* Princeton, N.J.: Princeton University Press for the National Bureau of Economic Research.

————. 1964, vol. 28. *Models of income determination.* Princeton, N.J.: Princeton University Press for the National Bureau of Economic Research.

————. 1973, vol. 38. *The measurement of economic and social performance.*

Survey of Current Business. 1971, vol. 51, no. 7 (July): pt. II. *The economic accounts of the United States: retrospect and prospect.*

United States. Department of Commerce. Office of Federal Statistical Policy and Standards. 1977. *Gross national product data improvement project report.* Report of the Advisory Committee on Gross National Product Data Improvement. (A preliminary report appeared in October 1977. The final report was published in 1979.)

Usher, Dan. 1975. Measuring real consumption from quantity data, Canada, 1935–1968. In Nestor E. Terleckyj, ed., *Household production and consumption*, pp. 585–642. Studies in Income and Wealth, vol. 40. New York: Columbia University Press for the National Bureau of Economic Research.

1 The United States National Income Accounts, 1947–1977: Their Conceptual Basis and Evolution

Richard Ruggles

1.1 Introduction

The national income accounts for the United States and their statistical implementation represent one of the major achievements in economics in the twentieth century. The design of the national income accounting system has been a cumulative development, which has been responsive both to the concepts embodied in modern economic theory and to the policy needs for information about the operation of the economic system. The implementation of the national income accounts in the form of a reliable and consistent set of statistical estimates represents an outstanding accomplishment on the part of those who have been engaged in this work over the last half century.

The purpose of this paper is to examine the national income accounting system of the United States and to show how the system has evolved since it was first put in place in 1947. It is hoped that this examination will lead to a better understanding of how the present system came into being and why it has the characteristics it does. The examination will focus on the major conceptual issues that have arisen in connection with the establishment of the national income accounting system and its subsequent revisions, and it is in this context that questions will be raised about the problem areas that remain to be solved and the directions future developments may take.

The U.S. national income accounting system has been characterized by relative stability and continuity. The process of change has been gradual and evolutionary, and, when changes were made that seriously affected the comparability of data over time, the Bureau of Economic Analysis (BEA) has taken care to provide complete revisions which in all cases

Richard Ruggles is Stanley R. Resor Professor of Economics at Yale University.

have covered the period since 1947 and usually have provided data back to 1929. Nevertheless, it is not feasible in a short paper to discuss chronologically all of the specific conceptual, methodological, classification, and statistical changes that have been made, as they are far too numerous. Instead, the approach taken by this paper will be to review the accounts at the points when major revisions were made by BEA or its predecessor organizations. This will provide cross-sectional views of what the national income accounting system was like in certain benchmark periods.

Similarly, it is neither possible nor desirable to attempt to cover the whole body of national income accounting literature written in the last 30 years. Instead, this paper will focus only on work that is directly related to the U.S. national income accounts and so can provide the basis for analyzing the central conceptual issues involved. Specifically, the documents that will be covered are (1) the 1951 and 1954 supplements to the *Survey of Current Business*, which presented in the fullest detail the sources and methods employed in preparing the U.S. national income accounts; (2) the proceedings of the 1955 Conference on Income and Wealth, published as *A Critique of the United States Income and Product Accounts* (Studies in Income and Wealth, 1958, vol. 22); (3) the Report of the National Accounts Review Committee, published in *Hearings before the Joint Economic Committee* in 1957; (4) the proceedings of the 1969 Conference on Income and Wealth, published as *The Measurement of Economic and Social Performance* (Studies in Income and Wealth, 1973, vol. 38); and (5) the fiftieth anniversary issue of the *Survey of Current Business*, titled *The Economic Accounts of the United States, Retrospect and Prospect* (July 1971, vol. 51, no. 7, pt. II).

In addition to examining the U.S. national income accounts and discussions directly relating to them, it will also be useful to compare and contrast the U.S. accounts with the United Nations System of National Accounts (SNA). The SNA currently serves as the basis for national income accounting in a considerable number of countries, and the differences between the U.N. system and that of the United States can illuminate some of the major conceptual issues involved in national income accounting.

Finally, it will be useful to examine the U.S. national income accounts in the light of related statistical work currently under way in the BEA and other statistical agencies. This, together with the earlier discussions of conceptual issues, will lead to some conclusions as to the possible directions future developments might take.

1.2 The Major Conceptual Issues and the Evolution of the U.S. National Income Accounts

1.2.1 The Pre-1947 Period

Although the first national income accounting system for the United States was published by the Department of Commerce in 1947, official estimates of the national income and its components had been made by the Department of Commerce since the mid-1930s. The process by which the national income estimates developed into a national income accounting system has been well described by Carol Carson (1975). When the Department of Commerce with the assistance of Simon Kuznets first produced national income estimates in 1934, attention was focused on national income produced and national income paid out. National income produced referred to the net product of the national economy, and national income paid out referred to the compensation in money or kind paid for efforts in producing the net product. There was no sectoring of the economy, and emphasis was placed on the estimation of total national income, which was primarily used as an indicator or barometer of economic activity. What was also missing in these early measurements was the expenditure breakdown of national product. As Carson has noted, however, the origin of the expenditure breakdown in the United States predates the Keynesian model of income determination (i.e., $Y = C + I$). As early as 1932 Clark Warburton was working on the estimation of consumption and capital formation, and in 1934 he published a table on the composition and value of gross national product in which consumer goods and capital goods were shown. This was the first use of the concept of gross national product. Kuznets in 1933 was also working on estimates of gross capital formation and consumers' outlay through a commodity flow approach. Finally, Lauchlin Currie at the Federal Reserve Board (FRB) was in 1934 working on the concept of pump-priming deficit and using this to analyze the net contribution of government to national buying power. At this time, however, there was still no consideration of sectors of the economy, and it is undoubtedly true that the subsequent development of the Keynesian framework had a considerable impact on the direction of the work during the latter part of the 1930s.

But, as Carson pointed out, it was the mobilization for World War II and the consequent demand for data relating to the economy as a whole that was primarily responsible for shaping the accounts. The central questions posed by the war were how much defense output could be produced and what impact defense production would have upon the economy as a whole. Answering such questions required analysis of total resource availabilities and of the income generated by the increasing production in relation to the availability of consumer goods. For example, the inflationary gap analysis of the Tax Research Division of the Treasury Department required information on how much income would be generated and how much of this income consumers could be expected to spend on available consumer goods. The emphasis thus shifted away from the earlier focus on national income aggregates to the estimation of how income was generated, received, and spent by various sectors of the economy.

At the same time, during World War II, similar developments were taking place in England. Richard Stone was developing a national income accounting system for the United Kingdom, and the White Papers in which this work was reported were available in the United States. During 1944, meetings between U.S., British, and Canadian experts were held to compare conceptual and statistical problems in national income estimation. In 1945, a group of experts on national income was convened by the League of Nations, and for this meeting Richard Stone drafted a national income accounting system which served as the basis for future international developments. By the end of the war, the stage was thus set for the emergence of a full-fledged set of U.S. national accounts.

1.2.2   The 1947 National Income Accounts

The first U.S. national income accounting system was published in the July 1947 supplement to the *Survey of Current Business*. The presentation was designed to accomplish three objectives: "(1) to complete the setting up of the whole body of national income statistics as an interrelated and consistent system of national economic accounts, (2) to improve the statistical procedures used in estimating all the series and to base them on the latest source data, and (3) to incorporate a number of changes in the basic aggregates so as to achieve more generally useful and clear-cut definitions of national income and national product." The system of accounts consisted of an overall account for the national economy, together with accounts for major sectors which would permit the tracing of various flows from one account to another. These accounts are shown below in Exhibit 1, tables I–VI.

Table I is the summary income and product account for the nation. It is a summary account in that it brings together in a single account the current transactions recorded in the sector accounts of businesses, consumers, and government. In drawing up the national income and product account, some difficult and controversial decisions had to be made regarding the activities that were to be considered economic production or income. Government interest, the services of housewives, and income from illegal activities were all excluded from national income and product. On the other hand, certain imputed items of income in kind were included, such as the rental value of owner-occupied housing and banking services rendered to persons without explicit payment.

Table II shows the income and product account for the business sector of the economy. In essence this table is a consolidated profit and loss statement for current business operations. The business sector covers all firms, organizations, and institutions that produce goods and services for sale at a price intended at least to approximate the cost of production. Mutual financial institutions, cooperatives, nonprofit organizations serving business, owner-occupied houses, and government enterprises were all included in the business sector.

Table III is a receipts and expenditures account for the government sector. It covers the consolidated general government operations of federal, state, and local governments, including social insurance funds and the purchases of government enterprises on capital account, together with their net interest payments and operating surplus or deficit.

Table IV presents the foreign account, which shows the transactions of the rest of the world with domestic businesses, persons, and government, on a net basis.

Table V, the personal income and expenditure account, includes not only individuals in their capacity as income receivers but also the income and expenditures of nonprofit institutions serving households, and of private trust funds and private pension and welfare funds. It should be noted that transfers among these different groups, for example, between households and nonprofit institutions, pension funds, etc., all consolidate out.

Finally, table VI is a consolidated gross saving and investment account. It was pointed out that this account was presented on a consolidated basis because the data necessary for a complete accounting structure had not yet been developed. A logical and useful extension of the national accounting system, it was agreed, would be the construction of corresponding asset and liability accounts for each sector.

This system of six basic accounts not only showed how the different sectors were interrelated and fitted into the total economy, but it also provided a framework for the extensive and detailed data generated by the Department of Commerce. By making relationships among the transaction flows explicit, and by providing control totals, the accounting system reduced the voluminous detail of the national income statistics to intelligible proportions. The 1947 supplement contained 37 tables of annual data for the years 1929–46. Tables were given for each side of the six accounts, and often more detail was provided than was shown in the accounts themselves. For example, the tables relating to the rest of the world grossed up the net purchases from the United States to show both exports and imports. Some of the tables gave breakdowns of individual items in the accounts. Personal consumption expenditures were shown by type of product for 12 categories. Detail was provided on construction activity and producers' durable equipment by type. Information on the performance of different industries and their contribution to national output was provided through industrial breakdowns of specific components of national income originating and of employment, for major industry groups and for subindustries at the two-digit level.

Supplementary tables were also developed on a variety of topics. Among these were reconciliation accounts, which showed the relationship between the saving figures in the national accounts and the Securities and Exchange Commission data on liquid saving, and the relationship between corporate profits derived from corporate tax returns and the corporate profits concept in the national income accounts. Data were provided for monetary and imputed interest, showing the derivation of the net interest concept in the national accounts. A table was provided giving the major items of personal income and consumptive expenditures in kind.

In addition to the annual data, a set of eight tables gave quarterly data for the major national income aggregates and their components, including national income, gross national product, and personal income, together with a table showing the relation among these concepts. Finally, monthly data were given for personal income by type of payment.

1.2.3   The 1951 and 1954 National Income Supplements to the *Survey of Current Business*

In both 1951 and 1954, the *Survey of Current Business* published *National Income* supplements that contained (1) a fuller explanation of the national income accounting system, (2) a description of the sources and methods used in constructing the estimates, and (3) a full set of revised statistical data for all 48 tables contained in the 1947 accounts. There were no substantive revisions of the national accounting system in either 1951 or 1954, but in 1951 supplementary tables on gross national product in constant dollars together with the implicit price deflators for the years 1929–50 were added. This type of information was formally integrated into the standard tables of national income statistics in the 1954 edition.

Both the 1951 and 1954 supplements were extremely important in providing the user public with a better understanding of the concepts involved in national income accounting and the methods of statistical estimation employed. In large part the widespread acceptance which the national income accounts achieved during the 1950s can be attributed to the comprehensive and detailed work that went into these supplements.

In explaining the accounts, major emphasis was placed on what at the time was considered to be the fundamental concept of national income accounting, namely, the concept of factor cost. The concept of factor cost was considered basic to the definition of national income and product, since the output of the nation (national product) was the result of the services rendered by the agents of production (labor, capital, entre-preneurial ability, and natural resources used in the production process) that cooperated in the creation of that output. At the same time these services, valued in the market by their earnings, constituted national income. Furthermore, such a measure of the services rendered by pro-ductive agents was viewed as of central importance for studies of resource allocation. Thus it would be important to know the incomes of various factors of production used in each industry in order to be able to compare the relative importance of different industries, or to provide information about the relative amounts of factors of production available for alloca-tion to various uses, or to assess the relative importance of labor and property factors in the outputs of various industries.

It was recognized that the factors of production were not precisely defined in economic theory but to some extent had to be formulated with reference to the problem at hand. It was agreed, for example, that factor cost would not serve the intended purposes when factor returns were distorted by a temporary or permanent nontransferability of factors to other uses, or when they were affected by monopoly or by imperfect competition. It was further admitted that property income was only tenuously related to the measure of the contribution of property and enterprise needed for problems involving resource allocation, because it included a residual share (profits) which fluctuated widely over the busi-ness cycle. In spite of these difficulties and limitations, however, it was concluded that the idea of factor cost was of fundamental importance in economic analysis, and national income defined as the aggregate of factor earnings was the only general measure by which the idea could be quantified.

The factor cost concept had direct implications for the measurement of one of the central elements of property income, namely, interest, in the national accounts. Since interest could be both received and paid out by business, the Department of Commerce showed net interest paid as an element of factor cost. But this raised several problems. In the case of financial institutions, the amount of interest received generally exceeded the amount of interest paid out, so that net interest paid out by financial institutions was negative. In order to avoid showing negative output for financial institutions, it was considered that an imputation should be made to quantify the banking services that financial institutions were providing free to their depositors in exchange for the use of their funds. On the product side, the imputation would be recorded as a sale of banking services, and on the factor cost side it would be reported as imputed interest paid. It was recognized that the treatment of interest and the banking imputation might be criticized as "unduly complex and more specifically as based on certain assumptions of doubtful validity." In particular, the appropriate allocation of banking services was difficult, but it was thought that, all things considered, it was the most satisfactory procedure devised so far.

There were, also, other difficulties connected with the net interest component. Interest paid by the government, it was argued, should be excluded from the measure of output, since it was not considered to arise from current production. This meant that government interest payments, unlike wage payments to government employees, were not considered to be factor costs but rather were classed as transfers.

The treatment of life insurance and pensions also involved special considerations. In the case of life insurance, it was argued that the standard national income and product classifications broke down owing to its combined saving and insurance functions, and imputations were therefore required. In the treatment adopted, claims and premiums were disregarded, and the property income of life insurance companies that was withheld from policy holders was treated as if it had been actually disbursed in the current period. This item of property income became imputed interest in the net interest component of income. Finally, life insurance companies were regarded as implicitly charging policy holders for their services, and an imputation equal to their operating expenses was entered to make this charge explicit: in the business account, under sales to persons and in the personal income account, as a consumption expenditure. As a result of all these actions, life insurance companies were in effect treated as individuals rather than businesses. Claims and premiums were canceled out as though they were transfers among individuals, and the increase in life insurance reserves and retained income was treated as part of personal saving.

Private pensions were also integrated into the personal income account. Employers' contributions to private pension funds were included in the "other labor income" of employees as if they had actually been received. Employee contributions to private pension funds were ignored, and neither the benefits paid out by private pension funds nor the reserves and income retained by such funds were explicitly shown in the accounts. Changes in private pension reserves and retained income would thus be reflected automatically as part of personal saving. The procedures followed for social security contributions were different, of course, since these were consolidated with the government sector. Any difference between social security contributions and benefits paid out was reflected in the government surplus or deficit rather than in personal saving.

1.2.4   The 1955 Critique of the U.S. Income and Product Accounts

The 1955 Conference on Income and Wealth was devoted to an extensive and detailed examination of the U.S. national income accounting system established in 1947. The participants in the conference had available to them not only the excellent statements on concepts, sources, and methods in the *National Income* supplements to the *Survey of Current Business* but also a major paper by George Jaszi, "The Conceptual Basis of the Accounts."

In his paper, Jaszi not only laid out the rationale of the U.S. national income accounting concepts but he also raised questions that he felt had not been satisfactorily resolved. His discussion of accounting design in terms of sectoring and types of account was particularly illuminating. He pointed out that the principle of sectoring had not been clearly established and contained ambiguities. Although sectors are usually thought to reflect institutional groupings, functional considerations are generally also involved. Thus although businesses, households, and governments are different kinds of institutions, they also involve different functions, and there is a tendency to define institutions in terms of the functions in which they engage. The conflict between institutional and functional sectoring is particularly apparent in the case of unincorporated enterprises. The U.S. national income accounts split the owner of an unincorporated enterprise into a business transactor with respect to his production, and a household transactor with respect to his income, expenditures, and saving. This has suggested to some national accountants that it would be desirable to set up different types of accounts to show production, appropriation, and saving and investment for each sector. Although Jaszi considered this possibility, he rejected it, since he concluded that introducing additional accounts and transferring subtotals from one account to another served only to make the accounting structure more complicated without increasing its information content.

Instead of increasing the complexity of the accounting structure, Jaszi proposed a revision of the 1947 six-account system into a simpler five-account system in which the business sector account would be consolidated with the national income and product account. The simpler version, he thought, would lose no useful information, and a number of inconsequential flows required to articulate the business sector with other sectors would be eliminated. Jaszi also thought it would be desirable to deconsolidate the saving and investment account to show separate accounts for nonfinancial corporations, financial intermediaries, persons, government, and international transactors. He recognized the desirability of measuring government and consumer capital formation, estimating the stock of government and consumer durables, providing better estimates of replacement cost depreciation, and obtaining information on capital gains and losses. Thus it is apparent that in 1955 Jaszi viewed the national income accounting system as the core of an extended and integrated system of economic accounts.

It was, however, the more traditional issues of national income accounting that occupied most of the attention of the conference and generated the most heated discussions. The issues that attracted the most attention were factor cost measurement, the controversy about intermediate output of government, and the treatment of interest, all of which centered about the correct measurement of output. Most of the participants were supportive of the concepts and procedures used by the Department of Commerce, but many were disturbed by the lack of symmetry between the treatment of consumer interest and government interest. No clear conclusions emerged on these topics, except the reaffirmation that the correct measurement of national income at factor cost was still considered to be of central importance.

1.2.5   The Report of the National Accounts Review Committee (1957)

In 1956, the Office of Statistical Standards of the Bureau of the Budget requested that the National Bureau of Economic Research form a National Accounts Review Committee to (1) provide a review and evaluation of the national income and related accounts, and (2) devise a program for improving the accounts. To a major extent, this committee based its work on Jaszi's paper for the 1955 Conference on Income and Wealth, and expanded on his view of the national income accounts as the central core of a more general national economic accounting system. They endorsed Jaszi's proposal for the five-account system, and urged the development of a more comprehensive system of economic accounts in which input-output, flow of funds, balance of payments accounts, and national balance sheets would be fully integrated with the national income accounts.

The committee also urged substantial expansion of the information on the government sector in the national income accounts. At the time the accounts contained only one account for general government. Although this account contained separate information for federal and state and local governments, it did not link the federal receipts and expenditures with the federal budget or show federal expenditures by function and program. The committee urged that such information be provided. With respect to government interest payments, the report considered that the treatment of government interest as a transfer payment could be justified for interest on the war debt. Once the war was over, payments to holders of war bonds, like payments to war veterans, were made for a service in a period of the past, and there was no counterpart in the production during the years when the payments were actually made. But for debt used to finance tangible assets which contribute their services to production during the period when interest is paid, the committee thought that the case was different. Since most state and local debt is of this type, state and local government interest should be included in total output.

In connection with its report the committee sent out questionnaires to business, labor, and academic economists (but not to economists in the federal government) inquiring what they wanted in the national accounts. The responses to this questionnaire were very interesting. Highest priority was given to the development of quarterly estimates of GNP at constant prices. Additional items listed in order of frequency of citation were (*a*) addition of information on the stock of consumer durables; (*b*) reconciliation of consolidated government receipts and expenditures of the federal government as shown in the national income and product accounts with the conventional and cash budget figures; (*c*) classification of government purchases of goods and services into current and capital expenditures, a distinction essential for the estimation of government saving and investment; (*d*) separation of nonprofit institutions and a few other groups now lumped together with households into the personal sector; (*e*) quarterly estimates of personal saving on a balance sheet basis, that is, as the result of independently estimated changes in the different types of assets and liabilities of households; (*f*) estimates of personal income in constant dollars; and (*g*) estimation of gross national product and its principal components on a monthly basis. These results suggest that what users wanted were more frequent reporting of figures useful for monitoring and analyzing the state of the business cycle, and more detailed information on the government sector and consumer durables.

Between the 1955 Conference on Income and Wealth and the 1957 Report of the National Accounts Review Committee, there was thus a shift in emphasis in the discussions on national income. The 1955 conference concentrated on the question of the proper measurement of national income. The discussion in the National Accounts Review Committee was centered around questions of how the existing national income accounting system should be expanded and integrated with other kinds of economic data and how it could better serve the needs of users. The concern, in other words, was no longer with the definition of the aggregates but with the data system as a whole.

1.2.6   The 1958 and 1965 Revisions of the National Income Accounts

In 1958 the Department of Commerce published *U.S. Income and Output*, a supplement to the *Survey of Current Business*, which for the first time since 1947 made significant changes in the national income accounting system and added very substantially to the information contained in the system. A new five-account system of summary accounts was adopted, which eliminated the business sector account in its entirety and dropped the subtotals showing income originating from the current accounts for government and households. The objective of removing this detail from the summary accounts was to display the broad measures and their interrelationships that had been found to be analytically most useful. The institutional structure of productive activity stressed in the 1947 accounts was no longer shown in the summary accounts, but it was felt that the gain in simplicity and in aptness for other principal uses more than outweighed this reduction in detail. The 1958 accounting system is shown in Exhibit 2, tables I–V.

Although the form of the summary accounts was altered, the basic accounting structure that lay behind the accounts remained essentially the same as before. But the new accounting system constituted a somewhat better framework for fleshing out the accounts in greater detail and for presenting new kinds of information in a way that was fitted into the framework of the five-account system. A number of new kinds of information were introduced.

In the national income and product account, increased emphasis was placed on constant-dollar measurements. As had been suggested by the National Accounts Review Committee, quarterly estimates were provided of gross national product in constant dollars. The loss of information resulting from the omission of the business sector from the summary accounts was more than made up by increased information in the detailed tables on the legal forms of organization of producing entities.

The government sector provided a completely new breakdown of government expenditures by type and function for the federal and state and local governments. Furthermore, federal government receipts and expenditures were reconciled with the federal budget, so that the user of national accounts could trace the exact differences between the budget figures and the national accounts.

The foreign sector transactions were expanded in detail and directly tied in with the balance of payments. A new table on U.S. government net foreign assistance and balance of payments capital account were also provided.

With respect to personal income, data were provided on the distribution of income by size and by region. The size distribution, furthermore, was broken down in terms of nonfarm families, farm families, and unattached individuals. Monthly data on personal income by type of payment was also added. Finally, substantially more detail was given for consumer expenditures in constant dollars.

The savings and investment information was also expanded. A table showing expenditures on new plant and equipment by industry was provided, and the net stocks of structures and equipment and inventories for manufacturing, developed by the perpetual inventory method, were introduced. Finally depreciation was given for corporate and noncorporate business by industry.

In brief, the 1958 revision represented a substantial increase in the amount of information contained in the national accounts, and this was accomplished in a systematic and orderly manner by fitting it into a simpler and more general framework. While to some degree this revision may have reflected the recommendations of the National Accounts Review Committee, in view of the timing of the publication in relation to the committee's report it is apparent that many of the changes contained in the 1958 revision must have been well under way before the committee finished its work.

Perhaps one of the more revealing sections in the report on the 1958 revision was that on directions of future research, which laid out in some detail the future plan of work of the National Income Division. It was stated that future development would be in the direction of deconsolidating the consolidated saving and investment account into sets of saving and investment accounts, or sources and uses of funds, for major economic groups. These proposed accounts would show transactions in financial assets and liabilities among domestic groups in relation to real changes in saving and investment. They would be drawn up for individuals, government, nonfinancial corporations, and financial institutions. In discussing future plans, the specific problems involved in classification of both financial and tangible assets and the need to develop measures of capital consumption were recognized.

With respect to the personal sector of the economy, which still included nonprofit institutions and private pension and welfare funds, it was recognized that separate information on each of these entities would be desirable. In addition, it was suggested that it would be useful to split up the personal saving and investment account by major types of families, for example, farm proprietors, nonfarm entrepreneurs, and wage and salary earners.

For the government sector, more work was planned on extending the functional breakdown of government expenditures, introducing more object-class details of expenditure and developing new information on the changes in financial assets and liabilities associated with the government surplus and deficit, this last bringing together information on inventories, public construction, realty holdings, and purchases and stocks of durable equipment. Finally, more information was planned on the interrelationships among different governmental units.

Although some increase in regional work was planned, it was to be limited to states and standard metropolitan statistical areas (SMSAs). It was argued that disaggregation to the county level was beyond the resources of the Office of Business Economics (OBE).

One of the more interesting proposed extensions was the work planned in the field of income distribution. Here it was proposed that better information on the distribution of income could be obtained by the integration of data from federal individual income tax returns with data from census and other sample field surveys, with the results adjusted to control totals based on OBE measures of personal income. Although it is apparent that at that time this was conceived of primarily as bringing together various tabulations, it was pointed out that effective use of tax return data would require matching studies to relate the income of sample consumer units to the tax returns they filed, so that distributions of tax return income could be converted to a family income basis. It was also suggested that the Internal Revenue Service (IRS) audit studies could be used to correct underreporting of income to tax authorities. Further suggestions included using field surveys of consumer expenditures to provide information on taxes, consumption, and saving by income group.

Finally, a program was laid out in the area of analyzing industry sales and purchases to determine direct industry sales in final markets and their interrelation with the network of other industry sales and purchases. In effect, what was being proposed was an approach to input-output.

After the 1958 revision, the next major revision occurred in 1965. The main purpose of this revision was statistical, and constituted comprehensive benchmark revisions centering around the incorporation of the 1958 economic censuses into the national income and product estimates. Since the 1958 revision, the OBE had taken over the work on input-output, and had produced for the year 1958 an input-output table that was integrated with the national income accounts. Aside from this major accomplishment, however, the 1965 revision indicated only modest progress on the ambitious program that had been laid out in 1958. Improved information was made available on the reconciliation of the government national income and product accounts to the consolidated budget. Better information was also provided on the nonmarket imputations contained in the accounts. Tables were added on gross corporate product and gross automobile product. Additional detail was provided on personal consumption expenditures in constant dollars. On the other hand, some of the tables that had previously been published were omitted, on the ground that new work in the areas concerned was in progress; these included the tables on expenditures on new plant and equipment, on sources and uses of corporate funds, on the size distribution of income, and on investment, depreciation, and capital stocks in manufacturing establishments.

In terms of conceptual changes, the 1965 revision was not very significant. The major change was the exclusion of interest paid by consumers from production. This was done in order to treat interest paid by consumers in the same way as interest paid by the government, and it was justified on the same grounds. It was noted that the treatment of both of these items was somewhat controversial, but on balance considerations seemed to favor the change that was made. The new procedure was one that was recommended by the United Nations and used by most countries, and reflected that U.N. view that payments of interest were not payments for services but distribution of income.

1.2.7   The United Nations System of National Accounts

After the 1947 League of Nations work by Richard Stone mentioned above, the Organization for European Economic Cooperation and later the United Nations both developed similar systems of national accounts which they proposed for international use. In July 1953 the United Nations published *A System of National Accounts and Supporting Tables* (series F, no. 2, referred to hereafter as SNA). This first version of SNA bore a strong resemblance to the five-account system adopted by the United States in 1958. The most obvious difference was that in the SNA, instead of a single national income and product account, there were two accounts, one of which derived gross domestic product and the second national income. The U.S. national income and product account was merely a consolidation of these two accounts. As with the U.S. system, current income accounts were provided for households including non-profit institutions and for general government. A rest-of-the-world account was also provided in both systems. One other difference between the U.S. and U.N. systems was that the SNA made provision for rudimentary capital reconciliation accounts for each sector, whereas the U.S. accounts employed only a consolidated gross saving and investment account for all sectors.

In the mid-1960s, however, a major revision of SNA was undertaken, and in 1968 a new *System of National Accounts* (series F, no 2, rev. 3) was published. The new system was substantially and radically different from both the earlier United Nations system and the system being used by the United States. It was viewed by its originators as providing a comprehensive framework for all of economic accounting, and it stressed the integration of the national income accounts with input-output, financial transactions, capital stocks, and balance sheets.

The revised SNA cast the accounting system into the form of a matrix, in which each row and column pair represented the two sides of an account. The theoretical scheme is shown in Exhibit 3, together with a list of entries. It should be noted that the entries shown in Exhibit 3 do not represent single aggregate transaction flows; rather they represent sub-matrices of transactions cross-classified by the categories indicated for the individual rows and columns. The matrix classifies entries into (1) opening assets, (2) production, (3) consumption, (4) accumulation, (5) rest-of-the-world transactions (current and capital), (6) revaluations, and (7) closing assets.

In addition to the matrix, the SNA also contained a proposed standard accounting structure and a large number of supporting and supplementary tables. The theoretical matrix was intended to be a quite general, flexible instrument from which many different specific applications could be drawn. The accounts shown in the 1968 SNA book represented one such specific application, but it was recognized that others were equally possible. The accounts were not, and were not intended to be, an isomorphic transformation of the matrix. The accounts were viewed as mainly of pedagogical use; the supporting and supplementary tables were meant to carry the burden of statistical presentation of data.

The basic structure of the new SNA introduced a number of new features. Some of the accounts were considered to be transaction accounts, since they brought together transactions of a given kind even when engaged in by different transactors. Other accounts were transactor accounts, since they brought together the transactions of specific economic units. In dealing with transactors, a further distinction was made. It was recognized that economic units could be grouped according to either the nature of their activities or their institutional form. For the activity (or industry) classification of transactors, which could be implemented most easily by using economic units defined on an establishment basis (plants, stores, and the like), only production and capital formation accounts were provided. In contrast, the institutional classification required economic units classified by their legal form of organization and could be implemented most easily with enterprise-based data. For institutional transactors, only income and outlay, capital finance, and balance sheet accounts were provided.

To establish links among the different principles of classification and sectoring employed, dummy transformation accounts were used extensively. Thus, for example, the link between commodities and industry activities for input-output purposes was accomplished through "make-and-use" matrices, showing, respectively, commodities originating in different industries and commodities used by different industries. Similar dummy accounts were used to link the establishment-based production data (classified by industry) and the enterprise-based income and outlay data (classified by institutional form). The dummy transformation account technique was intended to avoid the necessity for certain cross-tabulations that were regarded as statistically difficult and conceptually questionable. But, by the same token, it resulted in the loss of some important kinds of information. Thus, no information was given on the sources and uses of funds of industrial sectors, and conversely for institutional sectors no information was given on production activity. Capital formation by institutional sector was considered only in its financial aspects and was not given by type of asset.

Thus, although the matrix approach was quite general and did achieve the integration of all of the different forms of economic accounting into a single system, it did so at the cost of considerable complexity. The simple overview of the operation of the system was lost, and certain types of information, such as corporate profits by industry, or wages by legal form of organization, were eliminated from the system. The multiplicity of accounts, and the many minor flows given prominence in them, resulted in a system of gothic elaboration, in which the relation between the U.N. National Accounts Questionnaire and the basic SNA structure was not readily apparent to the user.

Since its introduction the new SNA has been adopted in part by a great many countries but in its entirety by almost none. The main summary accounts on gross domestic product and national disposable income and the income and outlay accounts for government and households, which closely resemble both the old SNA and the U.S. system, are widely implemented. For input-output analysis, make-and-use matrices are increasingly being adopted. Also, there is increasing interest among developed countries in the capital finance accounts, which show changes in financial assets and liabilities. On the other hand, the principle of dual sectoring with its accompanying dummy transformation accounts has not been widely followed. In general, countries seem to prefer a combination of institutional and industrial sectoring for both production and income and outlay information—not because the difficulties SNA sought to avoid are not recognized but because the information is useful and needed. For example, the European Community has developed the European System of Accounts, an adaptation of SNA that in essence provides full sets of accounts for both institutional sectors and industry branches.

Athough the United States was initially represented on the Expert Group charged with drawing up the revised SNA, as the system developed it became evident that the direction in which it was going was quite different from that considered to be appropriate for the future development of the U.S. system. In terms of the actual design of the U.S. accounts, the revised SNA has to date had little impact. Like most countries, however, the U.S. does provide information in SNA form in response to the U.N. National Accounts Questionnaire. The U.N. work has, furthermore, had more impact on concepts and definitions, as was noted above in connection with consumer interest.

1.2.8   The 1971 Conference on Income and Wealth

The 1971 Conference on Income and Wealth was concerned with the adequacy of the national income accounts for measuring economic and social performance. A number of participants at this conference expressed the view that the conference was in fact a continuation of the controversies and issues discussed at the 1955 conference. In some degree this was correct. The problem of distinguishing between intermediate and final product, for example, the question as to whether certain government expenditures were final product or merely intermediate goods, was raised and discussed at both conferences. There were, however, very marked differences even in the discussion of this topic. The 1955 conference had viewed national income almost entirely from the point of view of factor cost. But in the 1971 conference factor cost was not even mentioned, and the discussion focused on the product side of the accounts.

More importantly, however, the major thrust of the 1971 conference was that a number of kinds of important and useful information were missing from the accounts and that these should be taken into account in the measurement of economic and social performance. It was argued that many nonmarket activities such as housewives' services, other household activity, and even leisure were extremely important for the evaluation of social performance and should be reflected in the national accounts. The need to establish capital accounts for consumers and government, and to impute the services of these assets, was pointed out. Intangible capital relating to research and development and to human capital provided by education, child rearing, and to skills obtained on the job was also emphasized. Direct consumption provided by business, such as television, expense account living, and other amenities provided by employers to their employees or to the general public, needed to be considered. One of the problems leading to the most discussion was that of the environment. It was generally agreed that such environmental considerations as the quality of the air and water were important and that expenditures on improving the environment or preventing its further deterioration should not be ignored in the national accounts. There was no general agreement on whether these expenditures constituted intermediate or final products, but there was consensus that both environmental costs and environmental benefits should be reflected in the accounts.

There was also considerable discussion on the question of whether present methods of valuing goods at either market price or cost of production were appropriate in all uses. This question was raised particularly in connection with measuring government output, where those receiving the service might attach a value that is either more or less than cost. It was emphasized that the valuation in such cases might depend upon the distribution of the good or service, some recipients valuing it differently from others. Finally, the problem of quality change was recognized, and the value of hedonic measures in this connection was discussed.

What emerged very clearly from this conference was that many users considered that the present emphasis of the national income and product accounts on market transactions led to a perspective that was too narrow for the measurement of economic and social performance. It was cogently argued that additional information was required on nonmarket activity, on the services of consumer and government durables and intangible investment, and on environmental costs and benefits. It was also clear, however, that such extensions to the national income accounting framework involved imputations, the valuation of which was highly controversial and in many cases could only yield an order of magnitude. Those who used the national accounts for the analysis of economic activity in the short run, with a focus on inflation, the business cycle, and fiscal policy felt that the inclusion of such imputations would lessen the usefulness of the accounts. No satisfactory resolution of these conflicting objectives emerged.

1.2.9 The Economic Accounts of the United States: Retrospect and Prospect (1971)

At about the same time as the 1971 Conference on Income and Wealth, the Department of Commerce published a commemorative issue of the *Survey of Current Business* on its fiftieth anniversary, in which 43 contributors wrote individual articles about the national income accounts and offered suggestions for changes and additions.

In general, the contributors expressed their satisfaction with the present form of the national income accounts and the basic conceptual treatment of the flows. Although there was some reflection of the views expressed in the 1971 Conference on Income and Wealth, these were in general muted and more than balanced by those contributors who thought that the major function of the national income accounts should be to provide information for short-run analysis of the economy. In particular, some contributors did urge better information in the area of pollution costs and the environment, but many more were concerned with more timely and frequent publication of series that would be useful in forecasting or understanding current economic conditions. The view was expressed by some that the present accounts should not be tampered with, since they were currently performing a useful and important function. Aside from imputations, however, there were some concrete suggestions in specific areas. For example, a number of contributors were interested in seeing an expansion of the information on international transactions, citing the need for more detailed information on multinational corporations and on the bilateral dealings between the United States and specific countries and regions. In the area of input-output, it was suggested that it would be useful to adopt the SNA treatment, including make-and-use matrices. Probably the most frequent request for new information was for the extension of the national income accounting system into balance sheets containing information on capital stocks, not only for business but also for households and government.

As in the case of the 1955 Conference on Income and Wealth, George Jaszi closed the fiftieth anniversary volume with a review of all of the contributions. Although he noted resource constraints in a number of areas, he agreed that it would be desirable to construct balance sheets and to provide information on consumer and government durables. With respect to imputations, he noted that some were included in the accounts even in their present form and considered that some limited additions might be useful, but he warned that extensive imputation could destroy the value of the system and that restraint should be used in adding further imputations to the accounts. He specifically rejected the notion that welfare criteria should be allowed to alter the measure of gross national product. With respect to the design of the accounting structure and sectoring, Jaszi indicated general support for a system based upon record-ing the transactions of individual transactors in the accounts, with the objective of obtaining a meaningful summary picture of the economic process, and emphasized the importance of providing such an overview of the economy. He specifically rejected building the accounts on a dual sectoring principle (industries and institutions), and questioned the use-fulness of elaborate matrix presentations of the accounts.

1.2.10   The 1975 Revision

The 1975 revision again was primarily statistical. The unusual size of the revisions was due in part to the length of the period—encompassing two economic censuses instead of one—which had elapsed since the last benchmark revision in 1965, and in part to the severe inflation and other economic changes which had made the task of estimating the national income accounts more difficult.

The only major conceptual change introduced in the 1975 revision was the shift of capital consumption measurement to an economic rather than a book value basis. The new measure of capital consumption involved two changes. First, the service lives of assets were changed from those permitted in the tax regulations to lives which more accurately reflect actual practice. Second, depreciation was valued at market rather than at historical cost. The difference between the book value of depreciation charged by enterprises and the replacement cost depreciation shown in the national accounts was shown as a capital consumption valuation adjustment which, like the inventory valuation adjustment, became an adjustment to the book value of enterprise profits. There were also other minor conceptual changes, among them the treatment of mobile homes and the purchase of consumer durables by landlords. Some new tables and series were provided. Greater detail was introduced in the constant-dollar data, and for a number of series constant-dollar figures were shown for the first time on a quarterly as well as on an annual basis.

1.2.11   Current Activities Related to National Income Accounting

There are several activities now under way that are not yet reflected in the most recent published form of the U.S. national income accounts but are directly related and can be expected at some future time to be integrated with them. These are (1) the development of capital stock estimates for structures and durables of business, government, and households; (2) the estimation of the size distribution of income for families; and (3) the development of measures of nonmarket activity within the framework of the accounts.

For more than a decade BEA has been in the process of developing estimates of capital stock based on the perpetual inventory technique. The first report on such estimates was published in the December 1966 issue of the *Survey of Current Business*, and since then at irregular intervals articles providing an increasing amount of information on the stocks of structures and durables in both current and constant prices have appeared. These estimates are directly related to the national income accounts, since they are based upon the data in the accounts relating to purchases of structures and durables and to capital consumption. But because the national income accounts have not been extended to comprehend balance sheets, the capital stock data do not formally constitute a part of the national income accounting system. The Federal Reserve Board more recently has used the BEA estimates of capital stocks of structures and durables in conjunction with their own financial asset and liability data to produce balance sheets for enterprises and households.

With respect to the size distribution of income, the present methodology follows the lines suggested in the 1958 *U.S. Income and Output* supplement, using data from IRS individual tax returns in conjunction with sample surveys collected by the Bureau of the Census. However, the current work involves matching and merging of computer files of microdata, using techniques of both exact and statistical matching of records that were not foreseen in 1958. An article on the size distribution of income for the years 1964, 1970, and 1971 was published in the *Survey of Current Business* in October 1974, and at present work is continuing on more recent size distribution estimates. Although the size distribution estimates are closely tied to and aligned with the national income estimates of personal income, major conceptual differences remain which prevent the size distribution work from fitting neatly within the national income accounts.

Finally, BEA has established a new program to develop measures of nonmarket activity within the framework of GNP accounts. In part this work is a response to the emphasis put on this topic at the 1971 Conference on Income and Wealth, but it also reflects the strong interest in environmental studies within the Department of Commerce. The federal government's concern with the measurement of the costs of pollution control and environmental damage has stimulated work in this area. BEA's current program, however, includes not only environmental questions but also (1) time spent in nonmarket work and leisure, (2) the services of consumer durables, and (3) the services of government capital. The close relationship to the national income accounting system in this work is stressed, but as yet it has not been formally integrated.

1.3 Directions for Future Development

National income estimation in the United States had its roots in the neoclassical concept of the factors of production, and initially it focused primarily on the measurement of net income and resource allocation. The policy needs arising from the depression of the 1930s and World War II changed the focus to short-run macroeconomic analysis and resulted in a national income accounting system emphasizing the interrelationships among the sectors of the economy. It was in this context that the concept of gross national product came to dominate the earlier concept of national income, and the concern shifted from accurate measurement of specific aggregates to the analysis of market transactions and transfers among businesses, government, and households.

Although more than 30 years have passed since the U.S. national income accounting system was established, its basic structure has remained essentially unchanged. What has occurred instead is a continual improvement in the quantity and quality of the information provided. By and large, most users of the national income accounts are well satisfied with what the present system offers, and there are few who would wish to see radical changes made. This does not mean, however, that there is no room for further development in the U.S. national income accounts. Rather, it suggests that desired changes can probably be accommodated within the existing framework.

In the review of the discussions of conceptual issues over the past 30 years, four general topics stand out as areas where further work is called for. These are (1) the sectoring, subsectoring, and the structure of the accounts; (2) the treatment of nonmarket activities and imputations; (3) the basic accounting principles underlying the recording of transactions in the accounts; and (4) the integration of financial transactions and balance sheets with the national income accounts. Each of these topics will be examined briefly in the following sections of this paper.

1.3.1 Sectoring and the Structure of the Accounts

Although this topic is central to national income accounting and has important implications for its future development, it has not engendered very much explicit discussion. The original 1947 six-account system recognized business, government, households, and the rest of the world as the four primary sectors. In 1958 the system was reduced to five accounts, the business sector being consolidated with the national income and product account and not shown explicitly as a separate sector. This was done to reduce the number of minor and inconsequential flows in the accounts and to display the major flows in the economy more prominently and simply. The five-account system has continued unchanged to the present day and has served very well as the framework for the ever-expanding national income accounting statistics. It has successfully provided the kind of overview that was intended.

The dual sectoring of production accounts by industry, on the one hand, and income and outlay accounts by institutional sectors, on the other, employed in the United Nations SNA has been rejected by BEA on the grounds that it does not provide for certain kinds of information now included in the U.S. accounts, such as corporate profits by industry and compensation of employees by legal form of organization. Furthermore, the U.S. statistics also provide a useful breakdown of industries within legal form of organization, a type of information that is automatically ruled out of the SNA.

However, some difficulties are encountered with the present system of sectoring. One set of problems concerns the personal income sector and raises specific questions as to the criteria on which sectoring should be based. As was noted in discussing the work on the size distribution of income, there is a lack of correspondence between the definition of the personal income sector, which includes nonprofit institutions, and the size distribution income concepts, which refer only to families and individuals. This problem has been recognized by BEA from time to time, when they have recommended subsectoring the personal income account so as to separate nonprofit institutions from households. The original argument for including nonprofit institutions in the personal sector rested on the fact that these institutions are final consumers, as well as on the pragmatic ground of ease of statistical estimation. While it is true, as Jaszi pointed out, that institutional groupings often are based upon such functional characteristics, it does not seem in this case that it is appropriate to combine nonprofit institutions and households in the same sectoral grouping. Behaviorally, the difference between an individual household and a nonprofit organization, such as a university or hospital employing a large staff, is very substantial indeed. For many purposes it would be much more appropriate to group together nonprofit organizations and profit-making organizations in such fields as education and health.

Sectors should be drawn up on the basis of two criteria: (1) the behavioral and decision-making processes underlying a sector's activity, and (2) the types and sources of information that are available relating to the transactors included in a sector. The accounts for a sector should be thought of as a consolidation or combination of the accounts of reporting units within the sector. For each sector, it should be possible to conceive of a microdata set of homogeneous units which, when aggregated, would yield the sector account. Thus, it should be conceptually and statistically possible to relate sample surveys of households to the aggregate data shown in the household sector account.

In terms of these criteria it is evident that the personal income sector should be recast as a household sector, including all the families and individuals in the nation but excluding enterprise-like organizations such as nonprofit institutions. This not only would permit better analysis of household behavior, it also would make it possible to use microdata for subsectoring the household sector into various social and demographic groupings. The benefits of the integration of microdata with national accounts do not, of course, all accrue to the national accounts. Micro-data, based as they often are upon surveys, often contain substantial reporting biases which can only be discovered when they are matched against control totals obtained from other sources, such as are found in the national accounts.

In this connection, it is also necessary to consider the classifications of transactions employed in the accounts. It is unfortunate that at present the national accounts do not reflect in the detail of personal consumption expenditures the same classifications employed in the consumer expenditure surveys. If the national accounts and the consumer expenditure surveys were integrated around the same classification system, it would become possible to relate the expenditure pattern of different subsectors of the household sector to the total changes shown in the national accounts.

Shifting to a household sectoring, besides improving the integration of data, would also make possible a better integration of micro- and macroanalysis. In recent years there has been more and more interest in analyzing problems that require closely related micro- and macrodata. Thus, for example, the analysis of such questions as health delivery systems, social security, and welfare reform requires examination of transactions information in the context of other nontransactions data in the household, such as household composition and the age, sex, race, and employment status of its members. These problems are being analyzed increasingly through microanalytic simulation techniques using large microdata sets aligned with the national accounts. It is important that future efforts to construct important microdata sets, such as the Survey of Income and Program Participation currently in process, be conceptually and statistically integrated with the national income accounts; and, conversely, the national income accounts in the future will have to take these bodies of data into account, both in the sectoring of the economy and in the classification of transactions within sectors.

A second set of sectoring problems centers around the business or enterprise sector. Such a sector is of course still implicit in the U.S. accounts even though it is not shown explicitly. In order to provide a more disaggregated view of output, prices, employment, and productivity it would be useful to formalize the sectoring and subsectoring of enterprises. The precise subsectoring chosen should depend on behavioral homogeneity, the kinds of data available, and analytic interest.

The same principles of sectoring noted above in connection with the household sector are applicable to the enterprise sector and its main subsectors. It should be possible to conceive of a microdata set of relatively homogeneous reporting units that would add up to the total for the sector or subsector. In many cases, microdata sets may be available from administrative, tax, or regulatory records. For example, it may be possible to identify a utility subsector for which appropriate current accounts and balance sheets can be obtained for the individual reporting units. Although in some cases privacy restrictions may limit the use of individual records, in other cases much of the data is either of a public nature or can be provided in a form that would not involve disclosure.

In addition to accounts based on systematic and comprehensive sectoring and subsectoring of transactors, it may also be useful to develop special key sector or satellite accounts of either transactors or special groupings of transactions. For example, at the present time the U.S. national income accounts contain an account for the gross output and income from housing, and it may be desirable to develop special accounts dealing with energy. Such supplementary or satellite accounts need not necessarily be fully articulated with other sector or subsector accounts, but they should, of course, be consistent with and logically fit into the national accounting system.

With respect to the structure of accounts for sectors and subsectors, U.S. practice departs significantly, as was indicated above, from international recommendations, and it is appropriate to consider whether the international recommendations have merit. For the most part, the data do exist to construct the production accounts, appropriation accounts, capital accumulation accounts, capital finance accounts, reconciliation accounts, and balance sheets that SNA calls for. But such an approach seems to have little to recommend it. The multiplicity of accounts seems designed only to derive subtotals, and it results in much duplication and loss of the comprehensive overview of the accounting system in a maze of detail. It seems more appropriate to move in the reverse direction, dividing the accounts for sectors into just two categories, current and capital. If this were done, the current accounts would show current receipts and outlays, and the capital accounts would show balance sheets and the related capital transactions and revaluations. As Jaszi has suggested, there is no need to enforce the same format on the accounts for different sectors. It is appropriate to organize the current account for business enterprises around the concept of gross product (or value added), whereas the current account for government can appropriately be centered around government revenue and that for households around household income.

1.3.2 Nonmarket Activity and Imputations

The topic of nonmarket activity and imputation is, of course, as old as the history of national income measurement. The paradox of the man who marries his housekeeper is an old, old problem. The 1947 U.S. national accounts explicitly excluded such imputations as the services of housewives and illegal activities from the measure of national income, but a limited number of imputations considered to constitute a part of output were recognized. These were the imputed rental income of owner-occupied housing, the value of food and fuel consumed on farms, the value of food and clothing provided to the military, and banking services rendered without payment to depositors. In total, these imputations accounted, in 1947, for about 5% of GNP.

In the years since 1947, the topic of imputations has repeatedly been discussed. The 1955 Conference on Income and Wealth considered it in the context of the derivation of the national income aggregates. Much attention was given to the banking imputation, and general support was expressed for imputations relating to income in kind and owner-occupied housing. There were even some proposals that imputations should be made for the services of both consumer and government durables. But the possibility of imputations beyond the established production boundaries was not seriously considered. In contrast, the 1971 conference took a broader view of nonmarket activity and imputations in the context of measuring economic well-being and economic and social performance. Participants were no longer concerned only with imputations falling within the production boundary; they focused instead on the welfare of individuals. Questions discussed included human and other intangible capital and the flow of services it generated, the measurement of disamenities, and environmental costs and benefits. Contributors to the fiftieth anniversary volume were generally more conventional in approach, but some support was expressed for extending imputations into such areas as pollution, the environment, and nonmarket activity in the household. Despite this long discussion, however, the imputations in the national accounts still remain essentially as they were in 1947. At the present time they constitute approximately 8% of GNP, the rise since 1946 being attributable mainly to the increased importance of the imputation for owner-occupied housing.

Furthermore, despite all the discussion about imputations, it has never clearly been established just what the term is meant to cover. Owner-occupied housing, payments in kind, and the services of financial intermediaries are fairly self-evident—or, at any rate, users of the accounts are accustomed to them. But in the process of constructing national income accounts there are many instances of estimates which do not reflect market transactions and so involve some element of imputation. One of the most obvious of these arises in estimating capital consumption allowances. To the extent that capital consumption allowances are recorded as accounting entries in the books of enterprises, it can be argued that they do represent market transactions. But a number of adjustments are made to the recorded book values in order to convert them to economic depreciation and to include such elements as accidental damage to fixed capital. In a similar manner, an inventory valuation adjustment is introduced in order to exclude the effect of changes in the price of inventories from the current value of output. Most of these adjustments can be excluded from the category of imputations on the ground that they result from employing standard accounting rules to correct the accounts of enterprises, even when they involve introducing entries into the accounts where no such entries exist or are contemplated by the individual economic units. Thus capital consumption allowances are estimated for small businesses which may not actually charge any depreciation at all. Capital consumption allowances for owner-occupied housing depart further from recorded transactions. Such adjustments and corrections are useful and in some cases necessary. But care should be exercised to preserve to the fullest extent possible the information on the market realities as they exist in the records of the transactors, separately from the adjustments. BEA to date has by and large followed this principle, explicitly showing the capital consumption and inventory valuation adjustments in the accounts.

But it is not such imputations to correct and adjust accounting flows that generally result in controversy. Rather, it is the imputations that range beyond the traditional limit of what is considered to be output that give rise to problems. The 1971 conference considered nonmarket extensions of the accounts (1) for the study of long-term growth or changes, (2) for the analysis of the structure of the economy at a given point in time, and (3) for policy purposes relating to important social and economic questions. For the study of economic growth over long periods of time, information was needed on the change in the amount of leisure, the change in nonmarket activities, the services of consumer and government durables, the incidence of regrettable necessities in the system, and the amount of environmental disamenities. Quantitative estimates of the impact of all of these had been made and used by some researchers to adjust GNP. In order to analyze the structure of the economy at a given point in time, imputations taking into account the time-use patterns of households, the services of intangible capital, and the benefits provided by employers to employees were considered important. For the formulation and evaluation of economic and social policy, another set of imputations was relevant, including imputations relating to pollution abatement costs and benefits, and imputations reflecting the distribution of health and welfare benefits and their relation to the distribution of income and tax payments. Such imputations, however, go far beyond the aggregate imputations contemplated for adjusting national income and gross national product. They involve attribution of the imputations to income groups or to specific individuals. Where the imputations involve public goods, the attribution would be both conceptually and statistically difficult, if not impossible.

This discussion served mainly to emphasize that, unlike transactions data, there is no well-defined universe of nonmarket activities and imputations to be covered. The set of all possible imputations is unbounded. The only criterion that can be employed is whether the imputations are considered to be useful and necessary for the particular purpose at hand. In the fiftieth anniversary volume, Jaszi compared imputations to additions made to a house to adapt it to the needs of a particular family. He suggested that the additions may lack architectural unity, because they are shaped to the needs of the time and the resources available. This is indeed an apt comparison, especially when one reflects that in the case of the U.S. accounts no additions have been made since the original building was set up in 1947. Jaszi foresaw, however, that some limited additional imputation might prove to be useful in the future.

Whatever decision is made with regard to extending the imputations in the national accounts, it is important that the imputations that are made be shown clearly and explicitly. BEA now provides a supplementary table showing all the imputations that are made in the national accounts, but in the main accounts the imputations are combined with market transactions. As long as imputations have been relatively minor, this has not been a matter of central concern. However, if imputations are extended into such areas as nonmarket household activity or even to the services of consumer and government durables, their magnitude could swamp the market transactions data in the accounts, and for many of these kinds of imputations, estimates for monthly, quarterly, or in some cases even annual periods are not feasible or required.

Furthermore, for many of the imputations the problem of valuation is so serious that combining them with market transactions would introduce a factor of extreme arbitrariness. There are some cases where the valuation problem is relatively simple, as in the use of the rental value of equivalent space for owner-occupied housing. But in cases such as the value of leisure, the problem is not only difficult but essentially insoluble: one must decide whether the leisure of the wealthy is worth more than the leisure of the poor. For public goods, it is not at all clear whether the imputation should be based on the cost of providing the good or on the benefits to the recipient. For example, if the audience for public television doubles without any increase in the cost of providing the television service, has the output of public television services to households increased? Similarly, should food stamps be valued at their cost to the government, or at the value attached to them by the recipients? It is unfortunately true that no clear-cut principles have been established that will solve the valuation problems for all imputations.

For all of these reasons, an explicit separation of market transactions from imputations in the national accounts would seem highly desirable. One way of doing this would be to show market transactions separately from the imputations made in each sector account. It should be recognized, however, that imputations alone cannot meet the information needs for measuring economic and social performance. As some of the contributors to the fiftieth anniversary volume pointed out, no amount of imputation can convert a one-dimensional summary measure such as the GNP into an adequate or appropriate measure of social welfare. The problem is rather one of achieving an integration of macro- and micro-analysis using economic accounting data in conjunction with social and demographic nontransactions data. As has already been emphasized, a rapidly emerging tool for accomplishing such integration is the construction of microdata sets, containing social, demographic, and geographic data as well as economic data, to underlie the sector and subsector accounts.

1.3.3   The Recording of Transactions in the National Accounts

In the section of this paper on sectoring and the structure of the accounts, it was proposed that sectors and subsectors should be so defined that their accounts could be conceived of as the combination or consolidation of the accounts of a relatively homogeneous set of reporting units. This means that transactions recorded in the accounts for a sector or subsector should directly correspond to the transactions recorded for individual transactors. This principle was put forward (1) to make the sector and subsector accounts more faithfully reflect the economic behavior and decision making of the transactors; (2) to ensure a direct correspondence between the aggregated data in the sector and subsector accounts and the data in the microdata sets of transactors; and (3) to permit a better integration of macro- and microanalysis, making use of social, demographic, and other nontransactions data relating to transactor units in conjunction with transactions data.

Most users of the U.S. national income accounts view the flows shown in the accounts as reflecting actual transactions. In many instances this is correct, but in a substantial number of cases there are significant differences between the treatment in the national accounts and that which would appear in the accounts of transactors. This is especially true with respect to transactions dealing with insurance, pensions, and interest. It is not appropriate at this juncture to discuss in detail precisely how a "transactor" approach to the recording of these transactions would differ from conventional national income accounting practices, but for those interested in this topic such a discussion is provided in Appendix A. For the present purpose, however, it is important to recognize that the aggregate view of transaction flows in the national income accounts should bear a direct and recognizable relation to the transactions as they are recorded in the accounts of individual transactors.

1.3.4   A Current Account for the Household Sector

The application of these principles for sectoring and recording transactions would result in a major reconfiguration of the national income accounts. Before going on to the discussion of the fourth topic listed above, therefore, it will be useful to summarize the impact of the principles discussed so far on the current transaction accounts.

An example of the current receipts and outlay account for a redefined household sector and its relation to the Personal Income Account of BEA is given in Exhibit 4. Current accounts for the household sector for the years 1947–80 are given in table 1.A.1 of Appendix B. Exhibit 4 shows explicitly the relation between the major income and expenditure flows as they now appear in the BEA Personal Income Account and similar flows in the redefined Household Current Income and Expenditure Account. A discussion of the differences between these flows will indicate the general nature of the changes that have been made.

The removal of nonprofit institutions from the personal income sector in order to restrict the sector to households will of course affect most of the income and expenditure flows. In the Personal Income Account, nonprofit institutions receive property income from enterprises and transfer payments from the government, and their expenditures are included in consumption expenditures. Furthermore, in the Personal Income Account the inclusion of nonprofit institutions with households means that the transfers between households and nonprofit institutions are consolidated out of the account. When nonprofit institutions are excluded from the household sector, it is necessary to show explicitly the contributions households make to charitable and religious organizations.

In the Personal Income Account, employees receive wages and salaries and other income paid by employers. Part of this income is paid in kind (food and clothing provided by the military) and part is withheld by employers for health and welfare contributions. Although the withheld health and welfare contributions are costs to employers, they do not represent actual receipts by households. Although imputing pay in kind is reasonable, imputing the value of health and welfare contributions or benefits to employees poses difficult conceptual and statistical problems. Even individual recipients themselves may be quite unaware of the actual magnitudes involved. While individuals may receive the benefits, the actual payments go to doctors and hospitals, and the specific individual may not know what the costs are.

Furthermore, what is being provided to employees by their employers is really the health insurance, which assures them of health care when and if they need it. To impute actual medical costs to individual patients would distort the distribution of income in a quite unrealistic way, since the very high cost of medical care of those who are seriously ill would immediately put them into a very high income bracket: the poor would never get sick. Health insurance and health care should represent final consumption output, but its direct allocation to specific individual households does not seem to be any more justified than the imputation to individual households of other public goods such as education, the use of highways, and public libraries. For this reason it seems appropriate to treat employee health benefits as part of consumption provided by enterprises which, like government consumption, increases the welfare of households in general but cannot be allocated to specific individuals.

A different treatment is given to pension benefits, which are direct cash payments to individuals. Unlike the current practice in the Personal Income Account, these payments should not be netted with pension contributions but rather should be recorded as actual transfer payments by businesses or pension funds to individuals. It would also be appropriate, if information were available, to impute to individuals any change in the cash surrender value of pensions or life insurance resulting from employers' contributions. Other changes in life insurance and pension reserves, however, should not be treated as part of household income, on the grounds that households do not have access to this income and are in fact not even aware of its magnitude. Therefore, unlike the treatment in the Personal Income Account, these reserves would be excluded from the saving of households.

Rental income in the Personal Income Account, of course, includes an imputation for the rental income of owner-occupied housing. In the Household Sector Account, however, since market transactions are separated from imputations, rental income is reduced by this amount, and the rental income of owner-occupied housing appears as a nonmarket transaction.

Interest income in the Personal Income Account includes an imputation for the services of financial intermediaries. Since this is a nonmarket transaction, it has been excluded from interest income in the Household Sector Account, but it has not been included in imputed income received by households on the grounds that the allocation of banking services to individual households is both conceptually and statistically weak. To base the imputation solely on the size of bank deposits and to neglect banking services provided to borrowers is not readily defensible in a period when banks charge for their services, on the one hand, and pay interest on their depositors' accounts, on the other. Thus, like other unallocable items, the services of financial intermediaries are considered to be part of consumption provided by enterprises.

With respect to transfers, it has already been noted that private pensions paid to households are included as part of household income, whereas in the Personal Income Account they are netted against pension contributions. In addition, the transfers recorded in the Personal Income Account as government transfers for hospital and supplementary medical insurance (medicare) have been removed, on the same grounds that private health benefits were removed. Such government programs do not result in increases in market income to individual households; rather they provide health services to the population just as education expenditures provide education services. Their allocation to individual households is no more justifiable than allocation of education or other services that are also provided to individuals.

In order to restrict the outlay side of the Household Sector Account to current transactions, it will be necessary to exclude expenditures on consumer durables and the change in household stocks of nondurables. Furthermore, the exclusion of the transactions of nonprofit institutions and of imputations from consumer expenditures means that in-kind consumption, expenditures of nonprofit institutions, imputed banking services, imputed housing services, and other benefits in kind must also be excluded. On the other hand, adopting a "transactor" approach means that the actual payments of mortgage interest and property taxes by owner occupiers should be included. Finally, since nonprofit institutions are no longer consolidated with households, it is necessary to show explicitly the gifts which households make to these institutions.

In summary, what this redefined Household Sector Account is designed to do is trace transaction flows as they occur in the economy, carrying out only those imputations which can be directly allocated to individual households. Where goods and services are consumed by households as a group but the allocation to individual households is conceptually or statistically difficult, these items are treated in the accounts as public goods, whether made available by enterprises or government. The recognition of enterprise consumption as analogous to government consumption reflects the increase in the extent to which people's lives depend upon the fringe benefits provided by the society. One of the major characteristics of fringe benefits is that they are provided to specific groups as a matter of right, and the benefits accruing to any individual do not necessarily correspond to the contributions which are deducted from his earnings. Inasmuch as the individual has relatively little control over either the contribution which is deducted, on the one hand, or the nature and availability of the fringe benefits themselves, on the other, it seems reasonable to treat them in a way that is directly analogous to the treatment of taxes and government expenditures.

This does not mean that individual analysts should not study the distribution of the benefits of different kinds of public goods among different types of individuals or groups. Such research is needed, but it raises major theoretical problems of tracing incidence, and from the point of view of the national accountant it should be considered to be in the realm of analysis rather than statistical compilation.

1.3.5 The Integration of Financial Transactions and Balance Sheets with the National Income Accounts

When the U.S. national income accounting system was first developed in 1947, it was noted that a gross saving and investment account was provided on a consolidated basis for the economy as a whole because the information necessary for a complete structure of saving and investment accounts had not as yet been developed. In Jaszi's discussion at the 1955 Conference on Income and Wealth, he proposed developing component saving and investment accounts for nonfinancial corporations, financial intermediaries, persons including unincorporated enterprises, government, and international transactions. In the Report of the National Accounts Review Committee in 1957, the integration of the flow of funds financial transactions and sector balance sheets with the national income accounts was identified as being of highest priority. In 1958 OBE repeated its plans to implement a deconsolidation of the saving and investment accounts to show transactions in financial assets and liabilities for different sectors of the economy and to integrate information on tangible investment and durable goods stocks including those of government and consumers. Again in 1971, both the Conference on Income and Wealth and the contributors to the fiftieth anniversary volume of the *Survey of Current Business* urged the integration of financial transactions and balance sheets with the national income accounts.

To some degree, work in this area has gone forward. BEA has been developing extensive information on the stocks of tangibles derived directly from the national income accounts by the perpetual inventory method. But no formal integration of this information with financial transactions or the national income accounts has emerged. Recently the Federal Reserve Board has produced balance sheets that include both BEA tangible stock estimates and FRB financial asset and liability estimates, integrated with the financial transactions in the flow of funds data. However, FRB does not provide balance sheets for the government sector, and since its major focus is on financial institutions the presentation does not provide for the nonfinancial sectors of the economy the kind of deconsolidated sector saving and investment accounts that were contemplated by BEA.

Certainly the idea of integrating financial transactions and balance sheets with the national income accounts is not just an idea whose time has come; history indicates that it came 30 years ago. What has prevented this development that is universally recognized as desirable from taking place? Primarily, as the original 1947 statement indicated, the problem has been one of obtaining the appropriate data. For most of the period under discussion, sufficient information was not available for either financial transactions or tangible investment. Over time, however, these data deficiencies have been remedied, and now it would be a practical undertaking to develop fully integrated capital transaction accounts and balance sheets through a marriage of the capital stock data produced by BEA and the financial transactions data produced by FRB.

In developing such integrated accounts, it is necessary to recognize that changes in balance sheet values occur not only as a result of actual transactions but also because of changes in the valuation of existing stocks. Thus, in using the perpetual inventory method for estimating the current value of the stock of a given tangible asset, account must be taken not only of the net purchases (i.e., purchases less sales) and capital consumption of the asset but also of the net revaluations of the existing stock due to price changes, capital losses, and retirements. For financial assets, capital consumption does not enter as an element of change, and for many financial assets and liabilities revaluation is not required in order to obtain current market values. While sector balance sheets, like sector income accounts, reflect current market values, it is of course also possible to show at least the tangible portion of the balance sheet in terms of constant dollars, or if desired to present the whole of the balance sheet in terms of the purchasing power of some base period.

1.3.6   Balance Sheets for the Household Sector

An example of the household sector balance sheet, in terms of the stock of assets and liabilities, capital transactions, and revaluations, is given in Exhibit 5, and household sector balance sheets for the years 1947–80 are given in Appendix B, table 1.A.2.

In Exhibit 5 the sector balance sheets appear both as opening balances at the beginning of the year and closing balances at the end of the year. This general approach is quite similar to that employed in the United Nations SNA. However, in this table the net current value of each tangible asset is explicitly derived from (1) original book value, (2) revaluations, and (3) capital consumption.

The first column shows the opening balance sheet. The gross stock at book value is obtained by adding up all net purchases for past periods, at the prices actually paid. To this gross stock at book value is added the cumulative revaluation needed to bring the past outlays to current market value. The book value of capital consumption as recorded in the accounting records, the capital consumption adjustment, and the revaluations that are introduced to convert this book value to current value economic depreciation are all shown explicitly. The net current market value for any tangible asset is obtained by subtracting the cumulative current value of capital consumption from the current value of gross stock. For financial assets, the cumulative book value of purchases plus the cumulative revaluation equals current market value.

The second column shows current year capital transactions: the net acquisitions (purchases less sales) of assets during the period and the capital consumption chargeable against the asset during the period. Both capital consumption at book value and its adjustment to the concept of economic depreciation are given. The difference between the net acquisitions of a given type of asset and its economic depreciation during the period is equal to net capital formation. For financial assets and liabilities, the capital transactions reflect the amount of the asset or liability acquired during the current period.

The column showing revaluations during the current period reflects primarily the effect of price changes during the period upon existing capital stock. However, the value of the capital stock also must be adjusted downward (negative revaluation) to reflect retirements as well as any loss in value due to accidents, fire, or unforeseen deterioration.

The closing balance shown in the final column can be obtained by adding each of the rows across the table, producing new values for each element. The origin of the net worth of a sector can be traced to revaluations and net savings, and the disposition of net saving can be broken down between net acquisitions of tangible and financial assets.

This presentation thus does provide a deconsolidation of the saving and investment account such as Jaszi recommended as early as 1955. It is directly linked with the current accounts through expenditures on structures and durable goods by households together with their gross saving, and it is derivable entirely from existing data. This same general framework could be used to present balance sheets and financial transactions for other sectors of the economy.

Exhibit 1. The 1947 U.S. National Income Accounting System

Table I **National Income and Product Account, 1939 ($Millions)**

Compensation of employees:		Personal consumption expenditures
Wages and salaries	45,745	Gross private domestic investment
Supplements	2,075	Net foreign investment
Income of unincorporated enterprises and inventory		Government purchases of goods and services
valuation adjustment	11,282	
Rental income of persons	3,465	
Corporate profits and inventory valuation adjustment:		
Corporate profits before tax:		
Corporate profits tax liability	1,462	
Corporate profits after tax:		
Dividends	3,796	
Undistributed profits	1,209	
Inventory valuation adjustment	−714	
Net interest	4,212	
National income	72,532	
Indirect business tax and nontax liability	9,365	
Business transfer payments	451	
Statistical discrepancy	462	
Less: Subsidies minus current surplus of government		
enterprises	485	
Charges against net national product	82,325	
Capital consumption allowances	8,101	
Charges against gross national product	90,426	Gross national product

Right-hand column values:

Personal consumption expenditures	67,466
Gross private domestic investment	9,004
Net foreign investment	888
Government purchases of goods and services	13,068
Gross national product	90,426

Table II   Consolidated Business Income and Product Account, 1939 ($Millions)

Compensation of employees:			Consolidated net sales:	
Wages and salaries:			To consumers	63,816
Disbursements	36,250		To government	5,375
Excess of accruals over disbursements	0		To business on capital account	8,563
Supplements:			To abroad	1,123
Employer contributions for social insurance	1,330		Change in inventories	441
Other labor income	431			
Income of unincorporated enterprises and inventory valuation adjustment	11,282			
Rental income of persons	3,465			
Corporate profits before tax and inventory valuation adjustment:				
Corporate profits before tax:	1,462			
Corporate profits tax liability				
Corporate profits after tax:				
Dividends	3,659			
Undistributed profits	1,162			
Inventory valuation adjustment	−714			
Net interest	3,284			
Income originating	61,611			
Indirect business tax and nontax liability	9,365			
Business transfer payments	451			
Statistical discrepancy	462			
Less: Subsidies minus current surplus of government enterprises	485			
Charges against net product	71,404			
Capital consumption allowances	7,914			
Charges against business gross product	79,318		Business gross product	79,318

Table III Consolidated Government Receipts and Expenditures Account, 1939 ($Millions)

Purchases of goods and services:			Personal tax and nontax receipts	2,440
Purchases of direct services:			Corporate profits tax accruals	1,462
Compensation of employees:			Indirect business tax and nontax accruals	9,365
Wages and salaries	7,343		Contributions for social insurance:	
Supplements:			Employee contributions	596
Employer contributions for social insurance	199		Employer contributions:	
Other labor income	87		Business	1,330
Income originating and net and gross product	7,629		Government	199
			Households and institutions	11
Net purchases from business	5,375		Deficit (+) or surplus (−) on income and product	
Net purchases from abroad	64		transactions	1,867
Transfer payments	2,512			
Net interest paid	1,205			
Subsidies minus current surplus of government enterprises	485			
Government expenditures	17,270		Government receipts and deficit	17,270

Table IV Rest of the World Account, 1939 ($Millions)

Net payments of factor income to the United States:		Net disinvestment in the United States 888
Wages and salaries	2	
Interest	127	
Dividends	137	
Branch profits	47	
Income originating and net and gross product	313	
Net purchases from the United States:		
From business	1,123	
From government	−64	
From persons	−484	
Net current payments to the United States	888	Net disinvestment in the United States 888

Table V   **Personal Income and Expenditure Account, 1939 ($Millions)**

Personal consumption expenditures:			Wage and salary receipts:	
Purchases of direct services:			Disbursements by:	
Compensation of employees:			Business	36,250
Wages and salaries paid	2,150		Government	7,343
Supplements paid:			Households and institutions	2,150
Employer contributions for social insurance	11		Rest of the world	2
Other labor income	17		Less: Employee contributions for social insurance	596
Interest paid	801		Other labor income:	
			Business	431
Income originating in and net product of households			Government	87
and institutions	2,979		Households and institutions	17
Institutional depreciation	187		Income of unincorporated enterprises and inventory	
			valuation adjustment	11,282
Gross product of households and institutions	3,166		Rental income of persons	3,465
			Dividends	3,796
Net purchases from business	63,816		Personal interest income	5,417
Net purchases from abroad	484		Government transfer payments	2,512
Personal tax and nontax payments	2,440		Business transfer payments	451
Personal saving	2,701			
Personal outlay and saving	72,607		Personal income	72,607

Table VI   Gross Savings and Investment Account, 1939 ($Millions)

Business purchases on capital account	8,563	Excess of wage accruals over disbursements	0
Change in business inventories	441	Undistributed corporate profits (domestic)	1,162
Net disinvestment in the United States by rest of world	888	Corporate inventory valuation adjustment	−714
Government deficit (+) or surplus (−) on income and product transactions	1,867	Statistical discrepancy	462
		Capital consumption allowances by private business	7,914
		Foreign branch profits (net)	47
		Institutional depreciation	187
		Personal saving	2,701
Gross investment and government deficit	11,759	Gross private saving	11,759

Exhibit 2. The 1958 U.S. National Income Accounting System

Table I National Income and Product Account, 1957[a] (**$Billions**)

Item		
1	Compensation of employees	254.6
2	Wages and salaries	238.1
3	Disbursements (II-7)	238.1
4	Excess of accruals over disbursements (V-11)	.0
5	Supplements	16.5
6	Employer contributions for social insurance (III-18)	7.6
7	Other labor income (II-11)	8.9
8	Proprietors' income (II-12)	43.0
9	Rental income of persons (II-15)	11.8
10	Corporate profits and inventory valuation adjustment	41.9
11	Profits before tax	43.4
12	Tax liability (III-15)	21.6
13	Profits after tax	21.8
14	Dividends (II-16)	12.4
15	Undistributed (V-12)	9.4
16	Inventory valuation adjustment (V-13)	-1.5
17	Net interest (II-18)	12.6
18	National income	364.0
19	Business transfer payments (II-21)	1.6
20	Indirect business tax and nontax liability (III-16)	37.6
21	Current surplus of government enterprises less subsidies (III-10)	-1.3
22	Capital consumption allowances (V-14)	37.7
23	Statistical discrepancy (V-16)	.7
	Gross national product	440.3

Item		
24	Personal consumption expenditures (II-2)	284.4
25	Gross private domestic investment (V-1)	65.3
26	Net exports of goods and services	4.9
27	Exports (IV-1)	26.0
28	Imports (IV-2)	21.0
29	Government purchases of goods and services (III-1)	85.7
	Gross national product	440.3

Table II Personal Income and Outlay Account, 1957[a] (\$Billions)

Item			Item		
1	Personal tax and nontax payments (III-12)	42.7	7	Wage and salary disbursements (I-3)	238.1
2	Personal consumption expenditures (I-24)	284.4	8	Manufacturing	80.6
3	Durable goods	39.9	9	Other private	117.4
4	Nondurable goods	138.0	10	Government	40.1
5	Services	106.5	11	Other labor income (I-7)	8.9
6	Personal saving (V-10)	20.7	12	Proprietors' income (I-8)	43.0
			13	Business and professional	31.4
			14	Farm	11.6
			15	Rental income of persons (I-9)	11.8
			16	Dividends (I-14)	12.4
			17	Personal interest income	18.8
			18	Net interest (I-17)	12.6
			19	Net interest paid by government (III-9)	6.2
			20	Transfer payments	21.5
			21	Business (I-19)	1.6
			22	Government (III-7)	19.9
			23	Personal contributions for social insurance (III-19)	−6.6
	Personal outlay and saving	347.9		Personal income	347.9

[a]Numbers in parentheses indicate accounts and items of counterentry in the accounts.

Table III   Government Receipts and Expenditures Account, 1957[a] ($Billions)

Item		
1 Purchases of goods and services (I-29)	85.7	
2 Federal	49.4	
3 National defense (less sales)	43.9	
4 Other	5.5	
5 State and local	36.3	
6 Transfer payments	21.3	
7 To persons (II-22)	19.9	
8 Foreign (IV-3)	1.5	
9 Net interest paid (II-19)	6.2	
10 Subsidies less current surplus of government enterprises (I-21)	1.3	
11 Surplus or deficit (−) on income and product account (V-15)	1.7	
Government expenditures and surplus	116.2	

Item		
12 Personal tax and nontax receipts (II-1)	42.7	
13 Federal	37.4	
14 State and local	5.4	
15 Corporate profits tax accruals (I-12)	21.6	
16 Indirect business tax and nontax accruals (I-20)	37.6	
17 Contributions for social insurance	14.2	
18 Employer (I-6)	7.6	
19 Personal (II-23)	6.6	
Government receipts	116.2	

[a]Numbers in parentheses indicate accounts and items of counterentry in the accounts.

Table IV **Foreign Transactions Account, 1957[a] ($Billions)**

Item		Item	
1 Exports of goods and services (I-27)	26.0	2 Imports of goods and services (I-28)	21.0
		3 Transfer payments from U. S. Government (III-8)	1.5
		4 Net foreign investment (V-9)	3.5
Receipts from abroad	26.0	Payments to abroad	26.0

[a]Numbers in parentheses indicate accounts and items of counterentry in the accounts.

Table V **Gross Saving and Investment Account, 1957[a] ($Billions)**

Item		Item	
1 Gross private domestic investment (I-25)	65.3	10 Personal saving (II-6)	20.7
2 New construction	36.5	11 Excess of wage accruals over disbursements (I-4)	.0
3 Residential nonfarm	17.0	12 Undistributed corporate profits (I-15)	9.4
4 Other	19.5	13 Corporate inventory valuation adjustment (I-16)	−1.5
5 Producers' durable equipment	27.9	14 Capital consumption allowances (I-22)	37.7
6 Change in business inventories	1.0	15 Government surplus or deficit (−) on income and product account (III-11)	1.7
7 Nonfarm	.2	16 Statistical discrepancy (I-23)	.7
8 Farm	.8		
9 Net foreign investment (IV-4)	3.5		
Gross investment	68.8	Gross saving and statistical discrepancy	68.8

[a]Numbers in parentheses indicate accounts and items of counterentry in the accounts.

Exhibit 3. The United Nations SNA Matrix

A Symbolic Table

	1	2	3	4	5	6	7	8	9	10
Opening assets										
1 Financial assets										
2 Net tangible assets										
Production										
Commodities										
3 Commodities, basic value					$T_{3.5}$	$T_{3.6}$	$T_{3.7}$	$T_{3.8}$		
4 Commodity taxes, net					$T_{4.5}$	$T_{4.6}$	$T_{4.7}$	$T_{4.8}$		
Activities										
5 Industries			$T_{5.3}$	$T_{5.4}$						
6 Producers of government services			$T_{6.3}$					$T_{6.8}$	$T_{6.9}$	
7 Private services: domestic service and producers of private n-p services			$T_{7.3}$					$T_{7.8}$		$T_{7.10}$
Consumption										
Expenditure										
8 Household goods and services										
9 Government purposes										
10 Purposes of private n-p bodies										
Income and outlay										
11 Value added			$T_{11.3}$	$T_{11.4}$	$T_{11.5}$	$T_{11.6}$	$T_{11.7}$			
12 Institutional sector of origin										
13 Form of income										
14 Institutional sector of receipt										
Accumulation										
Increase in stocks										
15 Industries										
16 Producers of government services										
Fixed capital formation										
17 Industries										
18 Producers of government services										
19 Producers of private nonprofit services to households										
Capital finance										
20 Industrial capital formation, land, etc.										
21 Capital transfers										
22 Financial assets										
23 Institutional sectors	$T_{23.1}$	$T_{23.2}$								
Rest of the world										
24 Current and capital transactions	$T_{24.1}$	$T_{24.2}$	$T_{24.3}$			$T_{24.6}$		$T_{24.8}$		
Revaluation										
25 Financial assets										
26 Net tangible assets										
Closing assets										
27 Financial assets										
28 Net tangible assets										

NOTE: The contents of the submatrices can be summarized as follows:

$T_{1.23}$ The holdings of financial assets by the institutional sectors at the beginning of the period of account.

$T_{1.24}$ The holdings of financial assets, issued by the country under study, by the rest of the world at the beginning ◂ the period of account.

$T_{2.23}$ The holdings of net tangible assets by the institutional sectors at the beginning of the period of account. Th resident economic agents from which the institutional sectors are built up hold between them all the tangib▸

11	12	13	14	15	16	17	18	19	20	21	22	23	24	25	26	27	28
												$T_{1.23}$	$T_{1.24}$				
												$T_{2.23}$					
				$T_{3.15}$	$T_{3.16}$	$T_{3.17}$	$T_{3.18}$	$T_{3.19}$					$T_{3.24}$				
				$T_{4.15}$		$T_{4.17}$	$T_{4.18}$	$T_{4.19}$					$T_{4.24}$				
			$T_{8.14}$										$T_{8.24}$				
			$T_{9.14}$														
			$T_{10.14}$														
												$T_{11.23}$					
$T_{12.11}$																	
	$T_{13.12}$		$T_{13.14}$										$T_{13.24}$				
$T_{14.11}$		$T_{14.13}$															
									$T_{15.20}$								
												$T_{16.23}$					
									$T_{17.20}$								
												$T_{18.23}$					
												$T_{19.23}$					
												$T_{20.23}$					
												$T_{22.23}$	$T_{22.24}$				
			$T_{23.14}$							$T_{23.21}$	$T_{23.22}$			$T_{23.25}$	$T_{23.26}$	$T_{23.27}$	$T_{23.28}$
		$T_{24.13}$								$T_{24.21}$	$T_{24.22}$		$T_{24.24}$	$T_{24.25}$	$T_{24.26}$	$T_{24.27}$	$T_{24.28}$
												$T_{25.23}$	$T_{25.24}$				
												$T_{26.23}$					
												$T_{27.23}$	$T_{27.24}$				
												$T_{28.23}$					

assets in the country in which they are resident; and, at the same time, the ownership of a tangible asset abroad is represented by the holding of a financial asset. As a consequence the rest of the world is not represented in the system as holding tangible assets.

$T_{3.5}$ The inputs of commodities, reckoned at basic values, into the productive activity of industries.

$T_{3.6}$ The inputs of commodities, reckoned at basic values, into the productive activity of the producers of government services.

(Table notes continue on following pages)

$T_{3.7}$	The inputs of commodities, reckoned at basic values, into the productive activity of producers of private nonprofit services to households. It is generally assumed that these inputs do not arise in the case of domestic services on an individual basis.
$T_{3.8}$	Commodities, reckoned at basic values, entering into the consumption expenditure in the domestic market of all households, whether resident or not.
$T_{3.15}$	Additions to the stocks of commodities, reckoned at basic values, held by industries.
$T_{3.16}$	Additions to the stocks of commodities, reckoned at basic values, held by the producers of government services.
$T_{3.17}$	Commodities, reckoned at basic values, entering into the gross fixed capital formation of industries.
$T_{3.18}$	Commodities, reckoned at basic values, entering into the gross fixed capital formation of the producers of government services.
$T_{3.19}$	Commodities, reckoned at basic values, entering into the gross fixed capital formation of the producers of private nonprofit services to households.
$T_{3.24}$	Exports of commodities reckoned at basic values.
$T_{4.5}$	Commodity taxes, net, on the commodity inputs into the productive activity of industries. The sum $T_{3.5} + T_{4.5}$ represents these commodity inputs reckoned at producers' values.
$T_{4.6}$	Commodity taxes, net, on the commodity inputs into the productive activity of producers of government services.
$T_{4.7}$	Commodity taxes, net, on the commodity inputs of producers of private nonprofit services to households.
$T_{4.8}$	Commodity taxes, net, on commodities entering into household consumption expenditure in the domestic market.
$T_{4.15}$	Commodity taxes, net, on the commodities entering into the stocks of industries.
$T_{4.17}$	Commodity taxes, net, on the commodities entering into the gross fixed capital formation of industries.
$T_{4.18}$	Commodity taxes, net, on the commodities entering into the capital formation of producers of government services.
$T_{4.19}$	Commodity taxes, net, on the commodities entering into the capital formation of producers of private nonprofit services to households.
$T_{4.24}$	Commodity taxes, net, on exports of commodities.
$T_{5.3}$	Commodity outputs, reckoned at basic values, of industries.
$T_{5.4}$	Commodity taxes, net, on the outputs of industries. The sum $T_{5.3} + T_{5.4}$ represents the commodity outputs of industries reckoned at producers' values.
$T_{6.3}$	Commodity outputs, reckoned at basic values, of the producers of government services.
$T_{6.8}$	Government services entering into household consumption expenditure in the domestic market.
$T_{6.9}$	Services produced for own use by government services.
$T_{7.3}$	Commodity outputs, reckoned at basic values, of producers of private nonprofit services to households.
$T_{7.8}$	Domestic services and private nonprofit services entering into household consumption expenditure in the domestic market.
$T_{7.10}$	Services produced for own use by private nonprofit services.
$T_{8.14}$	Final consumption expenditure on goods and services in the domestic market by resident households.
$T_{8.24}$	Final consumption expenditure on goods and services in the domestic market by nonresident households.
$T_{9.14}$	Final consumption expenditure by general government.
$T_{10.14}$	Final consumption expenditure by private nonprofit institutions.
$T_{11.3}$	Protective import duties.
$T_{11.4}$	Other import duties.
$T_{11.5}$	Values added, i.e., compensations of employees, operating surpluses, provisions for the consumption of fixed capital and indirect taxes, net, in the productive activity of industries.
$T_{11.6}$	Values added in the productive activity of the producers of government services.
$T_{11.7}$	Values added in the productive activity of domestic services and the producers of private nonprofit services to households.
$T_{11.23}$	The negative of charges for the consumption of fixed capital.
$T_{12.11}$	Compensation of employees and operating surpluses classified by institutional sectors of origin.
$T_{13.12}$	Compensations of employees and operating surpluses arising in institutional sectors classified by component forms of income. For example, compensation of employees is divided between wages and salaries on the one hand and employers' contributions to social security and private pension funds, etc., on the other.

$T_{13.14}$ Current income transfers, including transfers to property income, paid out by the institutional sectors (as sectors of receipt).

$T_{13.24}$ Current income transfers, including transfers of property income, paid out by the rest of the world.

$T_{14.11}$ Indirect taxes, net, paid to general government.

$T_{14.13}$ Gross receipts of income by the institutional sectors (as sectors of receipt).

$T_{15.20}$ Increases in stocks of industries.

$T_{16.23}$ The finance, provided by the capital finance account of general government, of the increase in stocks of producers of government services.

$T_{17.20}$ Total gross fixed capital formation of industries.

$T_{18.23}$ The finance, provided by the capital finance account of general government, of gross fixed capital formation undertaken by producers of government services.

$T_{19.23}$ The finance, provided by the capital finance account of private nonprofit institutions, of gross fixed capital formation undertaken by the producers of private nonprofit services to households.

$T_{20.23}$ The finance, provided by the capital finance accounts of the institutional sectors, of gross industrial capital formation (in stocks, and fixed assets) and the net purchases, by these sectors of land and intangible assets other than financial assets.

$T_{22.23}$ Net acquisitions of financial assets by the institutional sectors.

$T_{22.24}$ Net acquisitions of financial assets, issued by the country under study, by the rest of the world.

$T_{23.1}$ The holdings of financial liabilities by the institutional sectors at the beginning of the period of account.

$T_{23.2}$ The net worths of the institutional sectors at the beginning of the period account.

$T_{23.14}$ The saving of the institutional sectors.

$T_{23.21}$ Net receipts of capital transfers by the institutional sectors.

$T_{23.22}$ Net issues of financial liabilities by the institutional sectors.

$T_{23.25}$ Revaluations of financial liabilities held by the institutional sectors.

$T_{23.26}$ Revaluations of the net worths of the institutional sectors.

$T_{23.27}$ The holdings of financial liabilities by the institutional sectors at the end of the period of account.

$T_{23.28}$ The net worths of the institutional sectors at the end of the period of account.

$T_{24.1}$ Financial liabilities issued by the rest of the world and held by the institutional sectors at the beginning of the period of account.

$T_{24.2}$ The net worth of the rest of the world at the beginning of the period of account arising from its relationships with the country under study; that is to say, the negative of the rest of the world's net indebtedness to that country.

$T_{24.3}$ Imports of commodities reckoned at c.i.f. values.

$T_{24.6}$ Direct expenditure abroad on goods and services by the producers of government services.

$T_{24.8}$ Final consumption expenditure abroad by resident households.

$T_{24.13}$ Gross receipts of income (whether distributed factor income or other current transfers) by the rest of the world from the country under study.

$T_{24.21}$ Net receipts of capital transfers by the rest of the world.

$T_{24.22}$ Net issues of financial liabilities, taken up by the country under study, by the rest of the world.

$T_{24.24}$ The rest of the world's balance of payments on current account with the country under study.

$T_{24.25}$ Revaluations of financial liabilities issued by the rest of the world and held by the country under study.

$T_{24.26}$ Revaluation of the net worth of the rest of the world arising from its relationships with the country under study.

$T_{24.27}$ Financial liabilities issued by the rest of the world and held by the institutional sectors at the end of the period of account.

$T_{24.28}$ The net worth of the rest of the world at the end of the period arising from its relationships with the country under study.

$T_{25.23}$ Revaluations of financial assets held by the institutional sectors.

$T_{25.24}$ Revaluations of financial assets issued by the country under study and held by the rest of the world.

$T_{26.23}$ Revaluations of net tangible assets held by the institutional sectors.

$T_{27.23}$ The holdings of financial assets by the institutional sectors at the end of the period of account.

$T_{27.24}$ The holdings of financial assets, issued by the country under study, by the rest of the world at the end of the period of account.

$T_{28.23}$ The holdings of net tangible assets by the institutional sectors at the end of the period of account.

Exhibit 4

**Comparison of the BEA Personal Income Account
with the Household Sector Current Account for the Year 1969 ($Billions Current)**

	BEA Personal Outlays and Saving	Household Current Outlays and Saving
Expenditures on durables	85.7	
Expenditures on nondurables	247.8	238.5
Expenditures	244.8	244.8
Less: Increase in stocks		−6.3
In kind consumption	3.0	
Expenditures on services	248.2	
Household expenditures	147.8	147.8
Nonprofit expenditures	15.5	
Imputed banking services	9.8	
Imputed housing services	52.0	
Other benefits in kind	23.1	
Interest payments	15.6	31.0
Consumer debt interest	15.6	15.6
Mortgage interest		15.4

	BEA Personal Income	Household Current Income
Wages and salaries	515.7	513.0
Payments	513.0	513.0
Pay in kind	2.7	
Other labor income	28.5	
Fees and other pay	.5	
Other benefits	27.9	
Proprietor income	67.0	65.4
Money income	65.4	65.4
Imputed income	1.6	
Rental income	19.6	8.5
Paid to households	8.5	8.5
Imputed rent	11.1	

Tax payments	115.7	128.5
Income taxes	101.5	101.5
Property taxes	.8	13.6
Other taxes and nontaxes	13.4	13.4
Personal contributions for social insurance		26.2
Transfers paid	.9	14.2
Gifts to nonprofits		13.3
Transfers to abroad	.9	.9
Imputed outlays		149.0
Except owner-occupied housing		97.0
Owner-occupied housing		52.0
Gross household saving		129.5
Capital consumption allowances		59.4
Consumer durables		11.9
Owner-occupied housing		58.2
Net household saving		
Personal saving (BEA)	40.6	
Personal outlays and saving	754.7	
Total current outlays and saving		864.9

Interest income	61.1	38.5
Paid to households	38.5	38.5
Paid to nonprofits	1.2	
Imputed interest	21.4	21.4
Dividends	22.4	21.4
Paid to households	21.4	21.4
Paid to nonprofits	1.0	
Business transfers	2.8	2.8
Private pension payments	11.9	
Government transfers	63.8	54.4
Paid to households	54.4	54.4
Paid to nonprofits	2.9	
Benefits in kind	6.5	
Current market income	715.8	
Imputed gross income	149.0	
Except owner-occupied	97.0	
Owner-occupied gross income	52.0	
Less: Employee soc. sec.	26.2	
Personal income (BEA)	754.7	
Total current receipts	864.9	

Exhibit 5

Household Sector Balance Sheets ($Billions Current)

	Closing/ Opening Balance (1968/69)	Capital Trans- actions (1969)	Revalu- ations (1969)	Closing/ Opening Balance (1969/70)
Reproducible assets (net current value)	874.4	49.1	33.6	957.2
Residential structures (net current value)	482.9	16.5	26.9	526.3
Gross stock (book value)	450.5	28.4	−1.9	477.0
Plus: Revaluation	253.0		37.3	290.3
Equals: Gross stock (current value)	703.5	28.4	35.4	767.3
Less: Capital consump. (book value)	96.5	8.0	−1.1	103.4
Less: Cap. consump. revaluation	124.1	3.9	9.7	137.6
Consumer durables (net current value)	310.5	26.3	3.3	340.1
Gross stock (book value)	540.3	85.7	−46.9	579.1
Plus: Revaluation	24.5		11.4	36.0
Equals: Gross stock (current value)	564.8	85.7	−35.4	615.1
Less: Capital consump. (book value)	241.9	56.9	−42.1	256.7
Less: Capital consump. revaluation	12.4	2.5	3.4	18.3
Inventories	81.0	6.3	3.5	90.7
Land	133.6		8.8	142.3
Fixed claim assets	671.5	44.2		715.7
Currency and deposits	480.9	5.3		486.2
Currency and demand deposits	109.7	−4.5		105.2
Time and savings accounts	371.2	9.8		381.0
Government securities	105.8	28.1		133.9
U.S. Treasury issues	73.1	10.8		83.9
Agency issues	8.9	5.6		14.5
State + local obligations	23.8	11.7		35.5
Other fixed claim assets	84.8	10.7		95.5
Corporate + foreign bonds	3.5	3.2		6.7
Mortgages	44.6	2.1		46.7
Open market paper	10.1	5.3		15.4
Other financial assets	26.6	.1		26.7
Equities	1491.4	−6.6	−70.8	1414.1
Corporate stock	731.3	−11.5	−92.9	626.9
Farm business equity	195.9	−1.5	8.8	203.2
Noncorp. nonfarm equity	317.6	1.5	19.1	338.2
Pension & ins. (cash value)	108.4	4.9	−0.3	113.0
Estates and trusts	138.2		−5.5	132.8
Total assets	3170.9	86.7	−28.4	3229.2
Liabilities	424.6	30.3		454.9
Mortgages	257.7	18.6		276.3
Consumer credit	126.9	10.8		137.7
Bank loans, n.e.c.	4.7	1.0		5.7
Other liabilities	35.2	0.0		35.2
Net worth (balance sheet)	2746.4	56.3	−28.4	2774.3
Net saving (current acct.)		58.2		
Capital gains + stat. discrep.		−1.9		
Total liabilities + net worth	3170.9	86.7	−28.4	3229.2

Appendix A

Financial Intermediaries in the National Accounts

The treatment of financial intermediaries is one of the most controversial issues in national income accounting. Generally, the measurement of output of financial intermediaries has been based on the concept of factor cost, viewed as the contribution of the factors of production; it has also been influenced by a concept of material output derived from the classical view of production in Smith, Ricardo, and Marx. The approach has generally been of an aggregative nature, which either consolidates out of the system the financial transactions of the individual transactors or in some cases completely ignores them. In many cases, to the extent that the sales of financial intermediaries' services do not reflect factor costs, the market value of sales is not considered to be a correct measure of "output." The reconciliation of the receipts side of the account of financial intermediaries with the factor cost side is achieved by consolidating the receipts with claims or the transfers which financial intermediaries pay, and which in national income accounting terms are not considered to be part of output.

This national income accounting view is not fully consistent with the way transaction flows are viewed by individual transactors. If the macroeconomic accounting system is to correspond to the microeconomic accounting of individual transactor, it will be necessary, in a number of cases, to alter the treatment of financial transactions. This appendix examines, in some detail, the transactions relating to insurance, pensions, and interest, comparing their present treatment in the national income accounts with the way they would be recorded in individual transactor accounts.

Fire and Casualty Insurance

Fire and casualty insurance is purchased by businesses and households as protection against the possibility of loss. Premiums are paid to insurance companies, which in turn use these funds to pay the claims of the insured suffering casualty losses and to cover the costs and profits of the insurance business.

Purchases by Business

In the national accounts, the purchase of fire and casualty insurance by business is treated on a net basis (i.e., the claims paid to business are subtracted from the premiums paid by business). This net premium payment is, of course, by definition also equal to the costs and profits of the insurance companies. The fire and casualty losses are recorded in the national accounts as "accidental damage to fixed capital," and this is added to capital consumption allowances. Thus by understating the insurance premiums which business pays and equally overstating capital consumption, two wrongs come out with the correct profits.

In the actual accounts of businesses, these transactions would be recorded differently: (1) insurance premiums paid by business would be considered to be an intermediate cost of goods and services purchased from other enterprises and would not be netted against claims; (2) the claims received by business would be considered capital transactions offsetting the casualty losses, also considered capital in nature; and (3) no addition would be made to capital consumption allowances for accidental damage to fixed capital.

It is apparent that the present national income accounting treatment of insurance transactions would be quite inappropriate for the accounts of the individual transactor. If this treatment were used, businesses suffering no loss would record the cost of insurance as the premiums actually paid, but for those having a loss the cost in insurance would equal "net premiums," that is, premiums paid less claims received, and could be a sizable negative flow; at the same time the fire or casualty loss would appear as a large increase in capital consumption allowances. These distortions are due in part to the failure of the national income accounts to achieve a proper separation of current transactions from capital transactions, and in part to a willingness to deal with consolidated accounts for all businesses as a group.

If the transactor's approach to the recording of fire and casualty insurance transactions of business were adopted for the national income accounts, it would not alter the measurement of total GNP. However, it would result in a decline in the product originating in enterprises buying insurance, since the cost of insurance would be considered to be total premiums rather than net premiums. This decline would be exactly offset by an increase in product originating in the insurance sector. Claims paid out would reflect that portion of the insurance sector's output that is paid over to claimants much in the same way that dividends represent payment of profits to stockholders. The transactor approach has the advantage of recognizing at the microlevel that total premiums paid by a firm are a current cost of operation and that casualty losses and reimbursements are adjustments to the capital account and not to current accounts.

Purchases by Households

Household purchases of fire and casualty insurance are treated in the national accounts in a manner parallel to the treatment used for business. Households are considered to pay "net premiums" (i.e., total premiums paid minus claims received), which are by definition equal to the costs and profits of the insurance companies. However, from the transactor's point of view, it is the total premium that represents a consumer purchase, and again claims received are a capital transaction. The national income accounting approach, by combining a major capital receipt (claims received) with a relatively minor current outlay (premium paid), does violence to an individual household's account. It should be noted, however, that for the case of insurance purchased by households the adoption of the transactor approach would result in an increase in GNP, since now consumer purchases of goods and services will reflect total premiums rather than net premiums paid, and this increase will correspond to an increase in the measure of the output of the fire and casualty insurance companies serving households. From the point of view of opportunity cost and utility theory, such an increase is quite appropriate. What households are purchasing is protection against loss, and the cost of such protection for the individual transactor consists of the full premium payment and not the net premium.

Health Insurance

Health insurance premiums may be paid by employers as fringe benefits for their employees, or they may be paid by households directly. The benefits paid by health insurance companies may consist of either third-party payments to doctors and hospitals for the provision of health care to the beneficiaries, or they may be "sick-pay" benefits paid directly to beneficiaries.

Purchases by Business

In the case of health insurance provided by employers as a fringe benefit to their employees, the premiums paid by employers are considered to be "other labor income" received by employees in the national income accounts. On the outlay side of the personal income account, employees are then considered to purchase (1) the services of health insurance companies as measured by their costs and profits, and (2) medical care services as measured by the payments health insurance companies make to doctors and hospitals.

From the employee's point of view, this fringe benefit (health insurance) is not an actual payment of money income. It does not appear on the statement of income and withholding his employer gives him for tax purposes. In most cases employees are quite unaware of the amount of the premium the employer actually pays. Although this fringe benefit could be considered to be imputed income, for any specific employee its valuation poses serious problems; the proper value might bear little or no relation to the premiums paid by the employer. For example, families with more than one wage earner might have unnecessary double coverage. Presumably its value to a single person might be less than to a family. Young employees might value it less than older employees. There does not in fact seem to be more justification for making this imputation than for imputing a value for other fringe benefits, such as subsidized meals, parking, expense accounts, recreational facilities, and even pleasant working conditions.

With respect to the administrative costs of health insurance and the costs of medical care provided by doctors and hospitals, the treatment in the national income accounts, if used as a basis for allocation to individual households, would involve gross distortions of income and expenditures. For individuals who were not sick, the cost would reflect only the operating costs of the health insurance companies, and it would appear, contrary to fact, that these individuals receive more "other labor income" than they pay out in health insurance costs. For individuals who do receive medical care, it would appear that they spend on medical care more than they receive in other labor income.

If transactor recording were adopted, employers would be recorded as purchasing health insurance for their employees. This would be reported as health services that enterprises provide their employees as a fringe benefit but would not appear in the employees' account as money income. The health insurance industry in turn would be considered as purchasing health services from doctors and hospitals. From the point of view of GNP and product originating by industry, this treatment would be identical to the current national income accounting treatment. From an aggregative point of view, the difference between the two treatments lies solely in whether employers' health insurance contributions are recorded as other labor income received by individuals, and whether the cost of health insurance and medical care is recorded as actual expenditures paid by individuals.

Sick-Pay Benefits

Payments of sick pay by health insurance and workmen's compensation is handled in the national income accounts by considering employers' contributions to be other labor income, and considering the costs of health insurance companies and the costs of medical care to be consumer expenditures. The difference between the health contributions included in other labor income and the costs included in consumer expenditures is equal to (1) sick pay paid to individuals, and (2) the change in reserves of health insurers and workmen's compensation funds.

The national income accounting treatment contrasts with the transactor's recording, which would treat sick pay as an actual payment of income to individuals and would exclude from household income and saving the changes in the reserves of health insurance and workmen's compensation funds. Again the transactor approach to the recording of these transactions would not alter GNP but would alter household income, household saving, and changes in reserves held by business enterprises.

Purchases by Households

When health insurance is purchased by individuals, the total premium individuals actually pay are not recorded in the national accounts as consumer expenditures. Instead the consumer expenditure for health insurance is considered to consist of the costs and profits of the health insurers; the cost of the medical care individuals receive is entered as a separate consumer expenditure. The difference between the premiums actually paid and these two categories of costs represents, as indicated above, the sick pay which is returned to individuals and the change in the reserves of the health insurers.

A transactor recording would require considering the full premium payment as a consumer expenditure of those paying it, and the receipt of sick pay as income of those receiving it. On this basis of recording, the change in the reserves of health insurance companies would be recorded as a change in "income retained" by them rather than as saving by households.

As in the case of household purchases of fire and casualty insurance, this shift to a transactor basis of recording would result in an increase in GNP. The increase would be equal to the difference between the premiums paid by households and the costs and profits of health insurers and the costs of medical care; looked at in another way it will also be equal to sick pay and the change in the reserves of health insurers. Such an increase is justifiable, since the premiums paid by households represent a bona fide purchase of increased health security, which guarantees medical care and sick pay if and when required.

Life Insurance and Pensions

The treatment of life insurance and pensions in the national accounts follows the general approach described above for health insurance. If life insurance and pension contributions are made by an employer, these contributions are considered part of other labor income and are reflected in personal income. The costs and profits of life insurance companies are considered to measure the amount spent for life insurance and pensions, and the difference between the contributions included in other labor income and the costs of insurance included in consumer expenditures is equal to the life insurance benefits and pensions paid plus the change in the reserves of life insurance companies and pension funds.

Where an individual himself buys life insurance or contributes to pension funds, the premium he pays is not entered in the national accounts as an expenditure—only the costs and profits of the life insurance companies and pension funds are considered to be consumer expenditure. Thus in this case also the difference between the premiums actually paid and the costs charged as consumer expenditure equal the life insurance benefits and pensions paid and the change in the reserves of life insurance and pension funds.

In applying transactor criteria to the recording of life insurance and pension transactions, first it must be determined whether the transactions affect the balance sheet of the individual. In the case of term insurance or pension plans that are not vested, no cash surrender value or equity is built up for the individual. If an employer makes life insurance and pension contributions as part of other labor income, this is a fringe benefit. Those who do directly benefit in the current period are those who receive life insurance or pension payments. Life insurance benefits paid in a lump sum to heirs should be recorded in the capital accounts, together with other estate transfers. Life insurance annuities or pensions should be recorded as current income received by households. Individual purchases of term life insurance should be treated in the accounts like household purchases of other casualty insurance.

If life insurance and pension contributions result in an increase in the equity of individuals, this increase should be reflected in the balance sheets and current accounts of individual transactors. An increase in an individual's equity should be reflected in his balance sheet by an increase in the cash surrender value of his insurance and pension policies, but not by some pro rata share of the total reserves of life insurance and pension funds. Similarly, a portion of the premiums paid by individuals represents saving in the current income account of the individual, so that in fact the premium must be split into two elements, current insurance and saving. Aside from these considerations, the premiums paid for life insurance and pension funds and the benefits received should be recorded in transactor accounts as described for term life insurance.

In discussing pensions funds, the United Nations SNA proposes treating unfunded pension funds as if they were funded. This would involve imputing pension contributions for business and deducting them from profits. In effect, a dummy account for nonfunded pension funds would be set up showing the net cumulative imputed pension contributions and the unfunded pension liabilities and reserves. Although information on the liabilities of unfunded pensions is interesting and useful, it does not seem to be appropriate or realistic to treat such imputations as actual transactions.

Interest

There has been extensive and intensive discussion of the treatment of interest in the literature of national accounting, but at the present time there is surprisingly widespread consensus on how interest transactions should be handled in the measurement of the national income aggregates.

The "Net Interest" Approach

In the U.S. national income accounts the concept of net interest was developed to handle interest transactions. Interest received by business is netted against the interest payments which business makes, yielding their "net interest" payments. It is apparent that, if a business receives more interest than it pays out, this net interest flow will be negative.

Several different rationales can be offered in support of this approach. It can be argued that interest is a payment for a factor of production, and net interest represents the net amount of this factor used by business. It can also be argued, however, that interest payments are not factor payments but, like dividend payments, represent a transfer of the income earned by a business to those having a claim on it. According to this view, interest received by an enterprise is like dividends received by an enterprise; both types of receipts represent income derived from the productive activity of other enterprises. On this basis, the interest any given enterprise receives should be excluded from the measurement of its output (income originating), and this can best be accomplished by omitting the interest received from the product side of the account and subtracting it on the income side from interest paid.

For financial institutions where interest receipts exceed interest payments by substantial amounts, the BEA procedure results in negative product. As a consequence, it has been found useful to recognize that financial institutions provide their depositors with banking services instead of paying interest, and these services, in effect, constitute imputed interest payments. Such imputed interest payments are valued at the cost of providing banking services to depositors. Once such imputations are introduced as part of interest paid by financial institutions, the net interest approach results in an income-originating measurement for financial institutions, which is equal to their costs and profits.

The United Nations Approach

The United Nations SNA does not formally adopt a net interest approach, but because it separates production accounts from appropriation accounts the effect is the same. The production account for an enterprise shows on the product side the receipts from the sale of goods and services, and on the cost side the purchases of intermediate goods and services, capital consumption allowances, indirect taxes, compensation of employees, and operating surplus. The operating surplus is, of course, a residual reflecting the difference between sales receipts and the costs of sales. It represents that part of factor income which is carried over to the appropriation account and is available for further distribution as income payments.

In the appropriation account of the SNA, other property income received, such as dividends and interest, is added to the operating surplus to show the total amount of income available. The disbursements side of the appropriation account shows the actual payments made. In the measurement of output, these procedures have the same effect as the net interest approach used in the U.S. national income accounts, that is, interest received is excluded from the measurement of output.

Consumer Interest Payments

Despite the general consensus about the treatment of interest in the national accounts, present practices are at considerable variance with a transactor's approach to the recording of interest transactions in the accounts of households, enterprises, and government. For the household account, the present net interest treatment excludes consumer interest as an element of consumer expenditure, and treats it as a transfer. From the point of view of the individual doing the borrowing, however, it is apparent that a useful service is being purchased. In many consumer expenditures, interest charges are implicit in the higher prices merchants charge where easy credit or charge privileges are granted. But, paradoxically, if a consumer discovers that he can buy at a lower price and borrows to finance the purchase, the explicit interest charge is, in the national accounts, excluded from consumer expenditures. The exclusion of consumer interest payments from the purchase of goods and services is usually based on one or more of the following reasons. First, it may be argued that no productive resources are involved in the loaning of money, and interest payments are merely a transfer paid by the borrower to the lender. This argument rests in large part on the proposition that income should be measured in terms of the costs of the factors of production, and interest represents only a redistribution of income and is not in itself a factor of production. Second, it may be argued, from a similar but slightly different point of view that no real production has taken place and as a consequence there is no operating surplus out of which interest can be paid. Furthermore, since interest payments are considered transfers, payment of interest by consumers does not represent a purchase of goods and services. Finally, it is sometimes argued that the payment of consumer interest is "unproductive," much in the same sense that Adam Smith argued that the services of domestic servants were unproductive. This view is unquestionably related to the medieval view that moneylenders are engaged in a form of usury that exploits the misery of debtors.

From the point of view of the individual consumers, however, the ability to borrow money, thus making it possible to acquire goods and services, does represent an increase in utility. If market valuations and opportunity cost are to be used to represent the value of goods and services, there is no logical reason from the individual transactor's point of view to exclude consumer interest as a legitimate purchase.

Enterprise Interest Payments

In the transactor accounts for enterprises, it is of course not customary to subtract interest received from interest paid. In computing operating surplus an enterprise might exclude interest received, but this would be done to separate the normal business activity of the enterprise from its financial activities. For financial enterprises, where normal business activities are financial, it would be unreasonable to make such a separation.

From a transactor point of view, it would be most logical for enterprises to treat their interest transactions as they treat rental receipts and payments. On the receipts side of the account, receipts from rentals are treated as the sale of goods and services; and on the outlay side, payments for rentals are an intermediate cost of goods and services purchased from other enterprises. As a consequence of this treatment of rental receipts and payments, it has been necessary to introduce into the national income accounts a supplementary "rental income" industry to contain the rental payments made by enterprises to individuals or to enterprises not already classified in other industries. This rental industry does not, of course, include all rental payments, since many rent payments are made to enterprises in other industries. Nor does it reflect the actual use of buildings and equipment, since enterprises owning their own buildings and equipment do not make rental payments. For the rental industry, however, the gross rental payments received represent the value of their sales; after appropriate deductions are made for costs (including interest and taxes), the residual return appears in the national accounts as part of "rental income of persons."

This same treatment can also be applied to interest transactions. Interest received by enterprises would be considered to be a sale of goods and services, and, like rental payments, all interest paid by enterprises would be considered an intermediate purchase from other enterprises. Under such a treatment it would be necessary to introduce a supplementary "interest" industry which would be the recipient of interest payments made by enterprises to individuals or companies not already classified in other industries. The gross receipts or sales of this industry would be the interest payments they received, and any costs incurred in connection with the lending of such funds would be deducted before the payment of "interest income to persons."

It has been argued that one of the major reasons why interest should not be treated as a cost was that it would misrepresent the "true" measure of value added or income originating in an industry. This same reasoning has also been applied to the treatment of rental payments—that these also represent part of the income generated within the enterprise. While from a production function point of view it may often be useful to take into account "rented capital goods" as well as owned capital goods for analyzing capital coefficients, it does not follow that the national income accounts should be constructed solely with this criterion in mind. First, in operational terms it would be extremely difficult to reconstruct enterprise accounts so as to eliminate all rentals and/or purchases which represent the use of capital assets. If this were attempted, furthermore, it would of course be necessary to impute to the enterprises the cost of ownership, including such things as management, taxes, etc. In the case of rentals, such as communications or computer services which include highly sophisticated equipment together with software or other costs, the statistical estimation problems become unmanageable.

Furthermore, from the point of view of the enterprise as a profit-making institution, it is more reasonable to treat both interest and rental payments as intermediate costs of production rather than as part of income originating and/or profits. What gross product originating in an enterprise is supposed to represent is the value which is added to the contributions provided by other enterprises, and to deny that the provision of capital is a contribution is something that only a very conventional national accountant or a Marxist would dare to suggest.

The transactor approach to interest would alter the pattern of income originating in the national income accounts. It would reduce the gross product of the enterprises that borrow, and it would correspondingly increase the gross product of enterprises that lend. One of the major consequences of this change would be that the gross product of financial institutions, without any imputation for imputed interest, would be exactly equal to what is now computed using imputed interest. The reason for this is, of course, that this approach considers the interest received by financial intermediaries to be a sale of goods and services, and, on the cost side, interest paid is included as an intermediate cost. Such a treatment leaves compensation of employees, taxes, capital consumption, and profits in gross product originating. This does not necessarily mean that the imputation for banking services should be abandoned; it does mean, however, that it is not required for measuring the gross product in financial institutions and should be justified on grounds similar to imputations for such things as television, radio, and other media that are currently paid for largely by advertising expenditures but that do represent a useful product to consumers.

Government Interest Payments

The final problem with respect to interest transactions lies in the handling of government interest payments. The exclusion of government interest as payment for a productive service is an old and universal tradition in national income accounting. The original justifications were put forth in connection with the government war debt arising from World War I. It was felt that government debt incurred for a past war should not be considered output in later periods. The National Accounts Review Committee reviewed these arguments and generally supported them, but raised a question about the debts of state and local governments that have often been incurred for schools, sanitation systems, parks, roads, and public buildings. With respect to the U.S. national income accounts, it has also been argued that government durables are not considered to produce income, and, therefore, since there are no real capital services that provide income it would be inappropriate to count government interest.

Nevertheless, in a market economy it is appropriate to consider that services actually purchased represent output, even if they are in some sense wasted. Thus, one does not ask whether a government employee is really worth what he is paid; the fact that he is paid for a service is taken as an indication that the service exists. The difference between a transfer payment and the purchase of services rests on whether some service is performed, not whether the service is used. Thus, a pension paid to a soldier differs from current pay to a soldier in that no services are provided in the current period by the soldier receiving the pension whereas the current pay of the soldier represents services made available. Whether the services are in fact used is considered irrelevant.

From this point of view the holders of government bonds are providing services fully as much as if they had purchased corporate bonds, and government interest payments should be recorded as the purchase of such services. Since government debt is fungible, furthermore, it is not appropriate to distinguish between debt incurred for war purposes, for fiscal policy purposes, or the purchase of government durables. Those interested in measuring "real production" or "economic welfare" can impute any deduction they wish for what they consider to be the nonproductive use of government interest—or for that matter any other nonproductive use of resources.

Appendix B

Household Current Accounts and Balance Sheets, 1947–1980[1]

Table 1.A.1   Household Current Income and Outlay Account ($Billions)

	1947	1948	1949	1950	1951	1952	1953	1954	1955	1956	1957	1958	1959	1960	1961	1962	1963
Wages and Salaries Received	121.5	133.8	133.1	145.1	168.8	182.7	196.2	194.7	209.8	226.4	237.4	238.5	257.0	270.1	277.5	296.0	311.4
Enterprises	107.3	118.6	116.2	126.8	144.8	155.1	167.5	165.2	178.6	193.2	202.1	200.6	217.4	227.7	232.1	247.2	259.4
Government	14.1	15.2	16.8	18.2	23.9	27.5	28.7	29.3	31.0	33.1	35.1	37.7	39.5	42.3	45.2	48.7	51.8
Rest of the World	0.1	0.1	0.1	0.1	0.1	0.1	0.1	0.1	0.1	0.1	0.1	0.1	0.2	0.2	0.2	0.2	0.2
Interest Income	4.6	5.0	5.5	6.1	6.6	6.9	7.6	8.3	9.0	10.0	11.4	12.4	13.5	14.8	15.7	17.8	19.9
Proprietors' Income	33.8	38.5	34.3	36.6	41.1	41.3	39.8	39.4	41.3	42.3	43.7	46.1	46.1	45.8	47.0	48.4	48.9
Rental Income	3.9	4.2	4.1	4.6	4.8	5.0	5.2	5.2	5.3	5.5	5.8	6.2	6.2	6.3	6.4	6.6	6.8
Dividends Received	6.2	6.9	7.1	8.6	8.3	8.3	8.6	8.9	10.0	10.7	11.1	10.8	11.7	12.4	12.8	13.8	15.0
Transfers Received	11.5	11.1	12.3	15.9	13.5	14.3	15.4	17.8	19.2	20.8	24.0	28.8	30.0	32.3	36.7	38.0	40.5
Enterprises	0.7	0.8	0.9	1.9	2.2	2.4	2.7	2.9	3.2	3.7	4.2	4.6	5.1	5.7	6.2	6.8	7.5
Pensions & welfare payments	0.3	0.4	0.4	1.4	1.6	1.8	2.0	2.2	2.4	2.7	3.1	3.5	3.8	4.2	4.7	5.3	5.8
Bad debt adjustment	0.3	0.5	0.5	0.5	0.6	0.6	0.7	0.8	0.8	0.9	1.1	1.2	1.3	1.5	1.5	1.5	1.7
Government	10.8	10.2	11.3	14.0	11.3	11.9	12.7	14.9	16.0	17.1	19.9	24.1	24.9	26.7	30.4	31.2	32.9
Social insurance payments	0.5	0.6	0.7	1.0	1.9	2.2	3.0	3.6	4.9	5.7	7.3	8.5	10.2	11.1	12.6	14.3	15.2
Other payments	10.3	9.7	10.7	13.1	9.5	9.7	9.7	11.2	11.1	11.5	12.5	15.6	14.7	15.5	17.8	16.9	17.7
HOUSEHOLD CURRENT INCOME (Market Transactions)	181.4	199.5	196.4	216.9	243.2	258.4	272.8	274.3	294.5	315.8	333.4	342.7	364.6	381.8	396.1	420.7	442.5
Imputed Gross Income	25.9	29.4	32.8	38.6	46.1	51.3	55.7	62.0	66.1	72.4	77.0	83.1	87.4	90.2	93.8	95.9	101.4
Owner-Occupied Gross Income	6.9	7.8	8.9	10.1	11.6	13.3	15.2	17.0	18.6	20.2	21.9	23.8	25.8	27.9	30.0	32.3	34.3
Capital consumption	2.6	3.0	3.1	3.5	4.0	4.3	4.5	4.8	5.2	5.5	6.0	6.4	6.6	6.8	7.1	7.4	7.6
Net imputed services	4.3	4.8	5.8	6.6	7.6	9.0	10.7	12.2	13.4	14.7	15.9	17.4	19.2	21.1	22.9	24.9	26.7
Margins, Owner Built Houses	0.0	0.1	0.2	0.3	0.2	0.2	0.2	0.3	0.2	0.2	0.2	0.2	0.2	0.2	0.3	0.3	0.4
Durables Gross Income	17.3	19.7	22.3	26.9	32.9	36.5	39.1	43.7	46.4	51.1	54.1	58.3	60.7	61.5	62.9	62.8	66.2
Capital consumption	11.5	13.1	14.4	16.0	18.6	20.5	22.4	24.7	26.4	29.4	31.6	33.3	35.1	36.1	37.3	38.2	39.6
Net imputed services	5.9	6.6	7.9	10.9	14.3	16.0	16.7	19.0	20.0	21.7	22.5	25.0	25.6	25.5	25.6	24.6	26.6
Farm Income in Kind	1.7	1.8	1.4	1.3	1.4	1.3	1.2	1.0	0.9	0.9	0.8	0.8	0.7	0.6	0.6	0.5	0.5
HOUSEHOLD GROSS CURRENT INCOME (Market and Non-Market)	207.4	228.9	229.2	255.5	289.3	309.7	328.4	336.4	360.6	388.1	410.4	425.8	452.0	472.0	489.9	516.6	543.9

Current Consumption Expenditures	120.1	129.6	132.4	138.3	149.7	157.8	165.2	170.1	179.5	187.5	199.6	203.4	219.7	229.1	236.5	249.5	261.3
Non-Durable Goods	84.7	90.6	91.7	94.6	102.9	108.3	112.3	114.8	119.0	124.3	131.3	136.3	142.1	147.1	151.2	156.9	162.5
Enterprises	84.5	90.3	91.3	94.2	102.3	107.5	111.2	113.7	117.9	123.2	130.2	135.2	141.0	146.1	150.2	155.9	161.5
Rest of the world	0.2	0.3	0.4	0.3	0.6	0.8	1.1	1.1	1.1	1.1	1.1	1.1	1.1	1.1	1.0	1.0	1.0
Services	35.4	39.0	40.7	43.7	46.8	49.5	52.8	55.3	60.5	63.2	68.3	67.1	77.6	82.0	85.3	92.6	98.9
Enterprises	34.8	38.3	39.9	42.8	45.8	48.4	51.7	54.0	59.0	61.6	66.6	65.2	75.5	79.7	82.9	90.0	96.0
Rest of the world	0.6	0.7	0.8	0.9	0.9	1.0	1.2	1.3	1.5	1.6	1.7	1.9	2.1	2.3	2.3	2.6	2.8
Interest Payments	2.2	2.8	3.3	4.0	4.6	5.3	6.3	7.0	8.1	9.4	10.4	11.2	12.5	14.1	15.1	16.4	18.1
Tax Payments	22.7	22.4	20.1	22.4	30.9	36.2	38.0	35.2	38.5	43.3	46.4	46.6	50.8	55.7	57.9	63.2	67.3
Income Taxes	19.3	18.6	16.1	18.2	26.3	31.1	32.3	29.2	31.8	35.4	37.7	37.2	40.7	44.4	45.5	49.7	52.6
Estate and Gift Taxes	1.0	1.1	0.9	0.8	0.9	1.1	1.1	1.2	1.3	1.6	1.8	1.7	1.8	2.2	2.5	2.6	2.9
Property Taxes	1.5	1.6	1.8	2.0	2.2	2.5	2.8	3.0	3.4	3.9	4.3	4.8	5.3	5.9	6.4	7.0	7.7
Other Taxes and Non-Taxes	1.0	1.1	1.3	1.3	1.5	1.6	1.7	1.9	2.0	2.3	2.7	2.9	3.0	3.2	3.5	3.9	4.2
Personal Contrib. for Social Ins.	2.1	2.2	2.2	2.9	3.4	3.8	4.0	4.6	5.2	5.8	6.7	6.9	7.9	9.3	9.7	10.3	11.8
Transfers Paid	3.7	4.0	4.0	4.2	4.7	5.2	5.7	5.8	6.2	6.8	7.1	7.6	7.8	8.3	8.6	9.1	9.5
Contributions to Non-Profits	3.1	3.4	3.5	3.8	4.3	4.8	5.2	5.3	5.8	6.3	6.7	7.2	7.3	7.9	8.1	8.6	8.9
Transfers to R.O.W. (net)	0.7	0.7	0.5	0.4	0.4	0.4	0.5	0.5	0.4	0.5	0.5	0.4	0.4	0.4	0.4	0.5	0.6
Gross Saving	30.6	38.5	34.4	45.1	49.8	50.1	53.7	51.6	57.0	62.9	63.2	67.0	65.9	65.3	68.4	72.1	74.4
Capital Consumption Allowances	14.1	16.1	17.5	19.5	22.6	24.8	26.9	29.5	31.6	34.9	37.6	39.7	41.7	42.9	44.4	45.6	47.2
Owner-occupied houses	2.6	3.0	3.1	3.5	4.0	4.3	4.5	4.8	5.2	5.5	6.0	6.4	6.6	6.8	7.1	7.4	7.6
Durable goods	11.5	13.1	14.4	16.0	18.6	20.5	22.4	24.7	26.4	29.4	31.6	33.3	35.1	36.1	37.3	38.2	39.6
Net Saving	16.6	22.4	16.8	25.6	27.3	25.3	26.8	22.1	25.4	28.1	25.5	27.3	24.2	22.4	24.0	26.5	27.2
HOUSEHOLD CURRENT OUTLAYS AND GROSS SAVING (Market Transactions)	181.4	199.5	196.4	216.9	243.2	258.4	272.8	274.3	294.5	315.8	333.4	342.7	364.6	381.8	396.1	420.7	442.5
Imputed Gross Outlays	25.9	29.4	32.8	38.6	46.1	51.3	55.7	62.0	66.1	72.4	77.0	83.1	87.4	90.2	93.8	95.9	101.4
Owner-Occupied Housing	6.9	7.8	8.9	10.1	11.6	13.3	15.2	17.0	18.6	20.2	21.9	23.8	25.8	27.9	30.0	32.3	34.3
Margins, Owner Built Houses	0.0	0.1	0.2	0.3	0.2	0.2	0.2	0.3	0.2	0.2	0.2	0.2	0.2	0.2	0.3	0.3	0.4
Durables Consumed	17.3	19.7	22.3	26.9	32.9	36.5	39.1	43.7	46.4	51.1	54.1	58.3	60.7	61.5	62.9	62.8	66.2
Farm Income in Kind	1.7	1.8	1.4	1.3	1.4	1.3	1.2	1.0	0.9	0.9	0.8	0.8	0.7	0.6	0.6	0.5	0.5
HOUSEHOLD GROSS CURRENT OUTLAYS AND GROSS SAVING (Market and Non-Market)	207.4	228.9	229.2	255.5	289.3	309.7	328.4	336.4	360.6	388.1	410.4	425.8	452.0	472.0	489.9	516.6	543.9

[1]Appendix B reflects data that became available with the BEA benchmark revision of December 1980. Data from 1977 forward do not reflect July 1982 revisions.

Table 1.A.1   Household Current Income and Outlay Account ($Billions) (Continued)

	1964	1965	1966	1967	1968	1969	1970	1971	1972	1973	1974	1975	1976	1977	1978	1979	1980
Wages and Salaries Received	334.1	359.9	395.9	424.4	467.0	513.0	546.0	579.0	632.7	699.9	762.0	802.8	885.9	979.3	1100.4	1230.4	1337.6
Enterprises	277.7	299.1	327.6	348.7	382.1	420.2	443.2	467.2	510.7	568.6	621.4	648.6	720.7	802.1	908.2	1024.6	1116.4
Government	56.2	60.6	68.0	75.5	84.6	92.5	102.6	111.6	121.7	131.0	140.3	153.9	164.9	176.9	191.8	205.4	220.8
Rest of the World	0.2	0.2	0.2	0.2	0.2	0.2	0.3	0.3	0.3	0.3	0.3	0.4	0.4	0.4	0.4	0.4	0.4
Interest Income	22.4	25.1	28.0	30.4	33.6	38.5	44.1	48.2	52.1	61.7	74.1	79.1	86.2	98.1	109.7	135.4	165.5
Proprietors' Income	51.0	55.4	59.0	59.7	62.5	65.4	64.5	67.7	74.9	91.3	85.9	86.9	90.4	98.9	112.2	125.9	124.3
Rental Income	7.2	7.7	7.8	8.3	8.5	8.5	8.8	9.0	10.1	11.7	12.9	12.2	12.8	15.6	17.5	18.8	19.8
Dividends Received	16.7	18.4	18.7	19.4	21.0	21.4	21.1	21.5	23.1	25.3	27.6	28.4	34.7	36.8	41.0	46.2	51.8
Transfers Received	42.4	45.9	50.0	55.2	62.0	69.1	83.2	98.2	109.6	124.9	146.1	182.3	196.7	209.7	225.4	252.6	297.9
Enterprises	8.2	9.1	10.4	11.5	12.8	14.7	16.6	18.6	20.8	23.2	26.4	30.9	33.6	37.3	42.4	48.8	56.2
Pensions & welfare payments	6.3	7.0	8.1	9.2	10.4	11.9	13.3	15.1	17.0	18.9	21.8	24.7	27.2	30.6	35.3	41.0	47.4
Bad debt adjustment	1.9	2.0	2.2	2.3	2.4	2.8	3.3	3.6	3.9	4.3	4.6	6.2	6.4	6.6	7.1	7.9	8.9
Government	34.2	36.8	39.6	43.7	49.2	54.4	66.6	79.5	88.8	101.7	119.7	151.4	163.1	172.5	183.0	203.7	241.7
Social insurance payments	16.0	18.1	19.8	21.1	24.6	26.4	31.4	36.6	40.9	50.7	57.6	65.9	74.5	83.2	91.4	102.6	118.7
Other payments	18.1	18.8	19.8	22.6	24.6	28.0	35.2	42.9	47.8	51.0	62.1	85.5	88.6	89.2	91.6	101.2	123.0
HOUSEHOLD CURRENT INCOME (Market Transactions)	473.7	512.4	559.3	597.4	654.6	715.6	767.8	823.7	902.5	1014.8	1108.7	1191.8	1306.7	1438.5	1606.2	1809.3	1996.9
Imputed Gross Income	105.2	110.0	115.8	127.0	136.5	149.0	161.3	173.2	188.7	203.6	224.1	253.1	273.9	301.8	342.6	391.2	448.6
Owner-Occupied Gross Income	36.5	39.1	41.9	44.8	47.7	52.0	55.8	60.7	66.4	73.5	81.4	89.4	98.4	110.9	126.9	146.5	167.0
Capital consumption	8.0	8.4	9.0	9.7	10.6	11.9	12.8	14.1	16.3	18.0	20.8	23.2	25.7	30.0	35.0	40.9	45.9
Net imputed services	28.5	30.7	32.9	35.1	37.1	40.1	43.0	46.6	50.1	55.5	60.6	66.2	72.7	80.9	91.9	105.6	121.1
Margins, Owner Built Houses	0.4	0.4	0.3	0.4	0.4	0.4	0.4	0.5	0.6	0.7	0.7	0.7	1.1	1.5	1.7	1.9	2.1
Durables Gross Income	67.9	70.1	73.2	81.5	88.1	96.3	104.7	111.7	121.3	128.8	141.4	162.4	173.8	188.8	213.4	242.1	278.8
Capital consumption	41.4	42.8	44.9	49.0	53.5	59.4	65.2	70.7	76.5	82.9	93.1	105.7	116.9	128.6	143.1	159.9	180.8
Net imputed services	26.5	27.3	28.3	32.5	34.7	36.9	39.5	41.1	44.8	45.9	48.3	56.7	56.9	60.2	70.3	82.1	98.1
Farm Income in Kind	0.4	0.4	0.4	0.3	0.3	0.3	0.4	0.3	0.4	0.6	0.6	0.6	0.6	0.6	0.6	0.7	0.7
HOUSEHOLD GROSS CURRENT INCOME (Market and Non-Market)	578.8	622.4	675.1	724.4	791.2	864.9	929.1	996.9	1091.2	1218.4	1332.8	1445.0	1580.5	1740.3	1948.8	2200.5	2445.6

Current Consumption Expenditures	276.2	293.1	316.2	324.4	349.9	386.3	418.0	443.6	477.5	521.4	576.2	628.5	688.4	749.2	829.4	935.3	1052.7
Non-Durable Goods	170.8	182.3	196.8	205.5	221.8	238.5	258.3	270.7	289.8	319.5	360.3	394.3	426.8	462.1	508.8	579.1	654.1
Enterprises	169.7	181.0	195.4	203.9	220.0	236.7	256.2	268.6	287.9	317.8	358.7	392.8	425.4	460.6	507.1	577.4	652.3
Rest of the world	1.1	1.2	1.5	1.6	1.7	1.9	2.0	2.1	1.9	1.9	1.6	1.5	1.4	1.5	1.7	1.6	1.7
Services	105.4	110.8	119.4	118.9	128.2	147.8	159.7	172.9	187.6	201.9	215.9	234.2	261.6	287.1	320.6	356.2	398.6
Enterprises	102.4	107.5	115.8	114.7	124.0	143.1	154.3	167.0	180.8	194.5	207.7	225.4	252.2	276.8	309.2	343.6	384.5
Rest of the world	3.0	3.3	3.6	4.2	4.2	4.7	5.4	5.9	6.8	7.3	8.1	9.4	9.4	10.3	11.4	12.6	14.2
Interest Payments	20.2	22.3	24.1	25.4	27.7	31.0	33.4	36.6	41.3	47.6	53.4	56.8	63.6	75.0	90.4	107.9	125.6
Tax Payments	66.2	73.2	83.6	92.2	108.6	128.5	130.3	132.6	158.1	169.1	189.7	190.2	220.0	251.8	285.0	328.6	365.1
Income Taxes	50.0	55.5	64.0	70.6	84.6	101.5	100.0	98.3	120.2	128.6	147.0	143.6	168.3	193.6	225.0	264.5	296.0
Estate and Gift Taxes	3.3	3.6	3.9	4.0	4.1	4.6	4.8	5.8	6.8	6.6	6.3	6.4	7.2	9.3	7.2	7.6	8.8
Property Taxes	8.3	9.0	9.8	10.8	12.2	13.6	15.3	16.8	18.0	19.3	20.4	22.2	24.1	26.2	27.2	27.7	27.8
Other Taxes and Non-Taxes	4.6	5.1	5.9	6.7	7.8	8.8	10.2	11.7	13.2	14.6	16.1	17.9	20.4	22.7	25.6	28.8	32.6
Personal Contrib. for Social Ins.	12.6	13.3	17.8	20.6	22.9	26.2	27.9	30.7	34.4	42.6	47.9	50.4	55.5	61.1	69.6	80.6	87.9
Transfers Paid	10.2	10.7	11.3	12.2	13.3	14.2	15.1	16.1	18.0	21.6	23.3	25.1	27.5	30.2	33.6	37.5	41.1
Contributions to Non-Profits	9.5	10.0	10.6	11.3	12.5	13.3	14.0	15.0	16.9	20.4	22.3	24.2	26.6	29.3	32.8	36.5	39.9
Transfers to R.O.W. (net)	0.6	0.7	0.7	0.9	0.8	0.9	1.1	1.1	1.1	1.3	1.0	0.9	0.9	0.9	0.8	1.0	1.2
Gross Saving	88.3	99.9	106.3	122.6	132.2	129.5	143.2	164.1	173.1	212.5	218.2	240.8	251.6	271.2	298.1	319.4	324.5
Capital Consumption Allowances	49.4	51.2	53.9	58.7	64.1	71.3	78.0	84.8	92.8	100.9	113.9	128.9	142.6	158.6	178.1	200.8	226.7
Owner-occupied houses	8.0	8.4	9.0	9.7	10.6	11.9	12.8	14.1	16.3	18.0	20.8	23.2	25.7	30.0	35.0	40.9	45.9
Durable goods	41.4	42.8	44.9	49.0	53.5	59.4	65.2	70.7	76.5	82.9	93.1	105.7	116.9	128.6	143.1	159.9	180.8
Net Saving	38.8	48.6	52.5	63.9	68.1	58.2	65.1	79.3	80.3	111.6	104.3	111.9	109.0	112.6	120.1	118.6	97.9
HOUSEHOLD CURRENT OUTLAYS AND GROSS SAVING (Market Transactions)	473.7	512.4	559.3	597.4	654.6	715.8	767.8	823.7	902.5	1014.8	1108.7	1191.8	1306.7	1438.5	1606.2	1809.3	1996.9
Imputed Gross Outlays	105.2	110.0	115.8	127.0	136.5	149.0	161.3	173.2	188.7	203.6	224.1	253.1	273.9	301.8	342.6	391.2	448.6
Owner-Occupied Housing	36.5	39.1	41.9	44.8	47.7	52.0	55.8	60.7	66.4	73.5	81.4	89.4	98.4	110.9	126.9	146.5	167.0
Margins, Owner Built Houses	0.4	0.4	0.3	0.4	0.4	0.4	0.4	0.5	0.6	0.7	0.7	0.7	1.1	1.5	1.7	1.9	2.1
Durables Consumed	67.9	70.1	73.2	81.5	88.1	96.3	104.7	111.7	121.3	128.8	141.4	162.4	173.8	188.8	213.4	242.1	278.8
Farm Income in kind	0.4	0.4	0.4	0.3	0.3	0.3	0.4	0.3	0.4	0.6	0.6	0.6	0.6	0.6	0.6	0.7	0.7
HOUSEHOLD GROSS CURRENT OUTLAYS AND GROSS SAVING (Market and Non-Market)	578.8	622.4	675.1	724.4	791.2	864.9	929.1	996.9	1091.2	1218.4	1332.8	1445.0	1580.5	1740.3	1948.8	2200.5	2445.6

Table 1.A.2   Household Sector Capital Accounts

	End of Year Value 1946	Cap. Trans. Acct. (1947)	Revaluation Acct. (1947)	End of Year Value 1947	Cap. Trans. Acct. (1948)	Revaluation Acct. (1948)	End of Year Value 1948	Cap Trans. Acct. (1949)	Revaluation Acct. (1949)	End of Year Value 1949	Cap. Trans. Acct. (1950)	Revaluation Acct. (1950)	End of Year Value 1950	Cap. Trans. Acct. (1951)	Revaluation Acct. (1951)	End of Year Value 1951
REPRODUCIBLE ASSETS																
(net current value)	180.7	19.2	16.2	216.0	21.9	5.9	243.8	19.3	−5.4	257.7	28.2	15.9	301.8	24.2	12.7	338.7
Residential Structures	90.0	7.2	15.0	112.2	9.5	7.7	129.3	8.4	−3.9	133.8	12.9	11.4	158.1	10.9	8.4	177.5
Gross Stock (book value)	94.2		25.6	119.7		11.5	131.2		−7.6	123.6		17.4	140.9		11.9	152.8
Plus: Revaluation	66.1	9.8	−0.5	75.4	12.5	−0.2	87.7	11.5	−0.4	98.8	16.4	−0.4	114.9	14.9	−0.3	129.4
Equals: Gross Stock (current)	160.3	9.8	25.0	195.1	12.5	11.3	218.9	11.5	−8.0	222.4	16.4	17.0	255.8	14.9	11.5	282.3
Less: Capital Consump. (book)	22.4	1.1	−0.3	23.2	1.3	−0.3	24.1	1.5	−0.3	25.3	1.7	−0.4	26.6	1.9	−0.4	28.2
Cap. Consumption Reval.	47.9	1.5	10.4	59.8	1.7	3.9	65.5	1.6	−3.8	63.4	1.8	5.9	71.1	2.1	3.5	76.6
Consumer Durables	55.0	9.0	1.8	65.7	9.8	0.9	76.3	10.6	−0.5	86.5	14.8	2.3	103.6	11.3	4.6	119.4
Gross Stock (book value)	83.3	20.4	−6.4	97.3	22.9	−6.9	113.2	25.0	−7.3	130.9	30.8	−9.7	152.0	29.8	−9.6	172.2
Plus: Revaluation	40.5	4.7		45.2	3.3		48.5	−2.8		45.7	0.3		46.0	4.1		50.1
Equals: Gross Stock (current)	123.8	25.1	−6.4	142.5	26.2	−6.9	161.7	22.2	−7.3	176.6	31.1	−9.7	198.0	33.9	−9.6	222.3
Less: Capital Consump. (book)	40.8	3.5		44.3	4.5		48.8	5.5		54.3	5.3		59.6	7.3		66.9
Cap. Consumption Reval.	28.0	4.5		32.5	4.1		36.6	−0.8		35.8	−0.9		34.9	1.1		36.0
Inventories	35.7	3.0	−0.6	38.2	2.6	−2.7	38.1	0.3	−1.0	37.4	0.5	2.2	40.2	2.0	−0.3	41.9
LAND	12.2		2.3	14.5		1.3	15.8		0.8	16.5		3.7	20.3		1.7	22.0
FIXED CLAIM ASSETS	189.2	5.7	2.3	194.9	2.8	1.3	197.7	3.3	0.8	201.1	6.0	3.7	207.0	9.6	1.7	216.7
Deposits	114.5	2.0		116.4	−0.5		115.9	0.7		116.6	4.7		121.3	8.8		130.1
Currency & checkable dep.	58.7	−1.4		57.3	−2.7		54.6	−1.9		52.7	2.4		55.1	4.1		59.2
Small time & svgs. deposits	55.6	3.4		59.0	2.2		61.2	2.5		63.7	2.3		66.0	4.6		70.6
Large time deposits	0.1	−0.0		0.1	0.0		0.1	0.1		0.2	0.0		0.2	0.1		0.3
Money market fund shares	0.0	0.0		0.0	0.0		0.0	0.0		0.0	0.0		0.0	0.0		0.0
Credit Market Instruments	67.5	3.3		70.8	3.0		73.8	2.2		76.0	0.7		76.7	0.3		77.0
U.S. government securities	50.6	1.8		52.4	1.3		53.7	1.3		55.0	−0.0		55.0	−0.7		54.2
Treasury issues	50.5	1.8		52.3	1.2		53.5	1.3		54.8	0.0		54.8	−0.9		53.9
Savings bonds	44.2	2.1		46.2	1.6		47.8	1.5		49.3	0.3		49.6	−0.5		49.1
Other treasury	6.4	−0.3		6.1	−0.4		5.7	−0.1		5.5	−0.3		5.3	−0.4		4.8
Agency issues	0.0	0.1		0.1	0.1		0.2	−0.0		0.2	0.1		0.2	0.2		0.3
State and local obligations	3.0	0.2		3.2	0.5		3.8	0.4		4.1	0.1		4.3	0.1		4.4
Corporate and foreign bonds	1.2	−0.1		1.1	0.0		1.1	−0.2		0.9	0.0		0.9	−0.0		0.9
Mortgages	12.6	1.3		14.0	1.0		15.0	0.7		15.7	0.5		16.2	0.9		17.1
Open-market paper	0.1	0.0		0.1	0.1		0.2	0.0		0.2	0.1		0.3	0.1		0.4
Security Credit	0.7	0.0		0.7	0.0		0.7	0.0		0.7	0.3		1.0	−0.1		0.9
Other Fixed Claims	6.5	0.4		7.0	0.4		7.4	0.3		7.7	0.4		8.1	0.6		8.6

EQUITIES HELD	357.8	3.9	21.1	382.7	4.3	7.0	394.0	3.1	5.5	402.6	5.9	47.6	456.2	6.2	36.9	499.3
Corporate Stock	84.9	0.9	-2.7	83.1	-1.7	0.8	82.2	0.6	7.1	89.9	0.5	19.3	109.8	1.6	17.1	128.4
Non-Corp. Non-Farm Equity	125.6	0.6	15.6	141.8	7.9	1.3	151.0	0.2	-0.6	150.6	2.0	11.5	164.1	1.2	8.0	173.4
Farm Business Equity	79.8	-0.1	8.7	88.5	-1.8	2.5	89.1	-0.2	-2.0	86.9	0.9	13.8	101.5	1.0	8.5	111.1
Pension & Insur. (cash value)	35.1	2.3	0.0	37.4	-0.0	2.4	39.8	2.5	-0.0	42.3	2.5	0.0	44.8	2.4	-0.0	47.2
Estates and Trusts	32.5	0.2	-0.5	31.9	-0.1	0.0	31.8	0.0	1.0	32.9	0.0	3.0	35.9	0.0	3.3	39.1
TOTAL ASSETS	739.9	28.7	39.6	808.2	31.7	11.4	851.2	25.8	0.9	877.9	40.1	67.3	985.3	40.0	51.3	1076.6
FIXED CLAIM LIABILITIES	37.4	8.0		45.4	7.7		53.2	8.2		61.4	12.7		74.1	8.4		82.5
Credit Market Instruments	34.5	8.3		42.8	8.0		50.8	7.9		58.7	11.9		70.6	8.5		79.1
Home mortgages	21.6	4.7		26.3	4.6		30.9	4.4		35.3	6.7		42.0	6.6		48.6
Consumer credit	10.8	3.7		14.5	3.2		17.7	3.2		20.9	4.8		25.6	1.6		27.3
Installment	4.4	2.7		7.1	2.4		9.5	2.7		12.2	3.3		15.5	0.7		16.2
Other	6.3	1.0		7.4	0.8		8.2	0.5		8.6	1.5		10.1	0.9		11.0
Bank loans, n.e.c.	0.2	-0.1		0.1	0.0		0.1	0.0		0.1	0.2		0.4	0.0		0.4
Other loans	2.0	0.0		2.0	0.1		2.2	0.2		2.4	0.2		2.6	0.2		2.8
U.S. gov't. loans	0.0	0.0		0.0	0.0		0.0	0.0		0.0	0.0		0.0	0.0		0.0
Policy loans	2.0	0.0		2.0	0.1		2.2	0.2		2.4	0.2		2.6	0.2		2.8
Security Debt	2.2	-0.4		1.8	-0.3		1.5	0.3		1.8	0.7		2.5	-0.1		2.4
Other Fixed Claims	0.7	0.1		0.8	0.1		0.8	0.1		0.9	0.1		1.0	0.1		1.1
NET WORTH	702.5	20.7	39.6	762.7	23.9	11.4	798.0	17.6	0.9	816.5	27.4	67.3	911.2	31.6	51.3	994.1
Tangibles	192.9	19.2	18.5	230.5	21.9	7.0	259.5	19.3	-4.6	274.2	28.2	19.7	322.1	24.2	14.4	360.7
Equities	357.8	3.9	21.1	382.7	4.3	7.0	394.0	3.1	5.5	402.6	5.9	47.6	456.2	6.2	36.9	499.3
Net Financial Assets	151.8	-2.3	0.0	149.4	-2.3	-2.6	144.5	-4.8	0.0	139.7	-6.7	-0.1	132.9	1.2	0.0	134.1
TOTAL LIABILITIES & NET WORTH	739.9	28.7	39.6	808.2	31.7	11.4	851.2	25.8	0.9	877.9	40.1	67.3	985.3	40.0	51.3	1076.6
Addenda:																
Net Saving (balance sheet)		20.7			23.9			17.6			27.4			31.6		
Net Saving (current account)		16.6			22.4			16.8			25.6			27.3		
Capital Gains Dividends		0.0			0.0			0.0			0.1			0.1		
Residual Discrepancy		4.1			1.5			0.7			1.7			4.2		

Table 1.A.2   Household Sector Capital Accounts (Continued)

	End of Year Value 1951	Cap. Trans. Acct. (1952)	Reval-uation Acct. (1952)	End of Year Value 1952	Cap. Trans. Acct. (1953)	Reval-uation Acct. (1953)	End of Year Value 1953	Cap. Trans. Acct. (1954)	Reval-uation Acct. (1954)	End of Year Value 1954	Cap. Trans. Acct. (1955)	Reval-uation Acct. (1955)	End of Year Value 1955	Cap. Trans. Acct. (1956)	Reval-uation Acct. (1956)	End of Year Value 1956
REPRODUCIBLE ASSETS																
(net current value)	338.7	21.1	2.3	362.1	21.9	-0.9	383.0	19.7	0.3	403.0	28.7	2.8	434.4	23.8	9.8	468.1
Residential Structures	177.5	10.7	2.6	190.8	10.9	0.2	201.9	12.4	2.8	217.1	15.2	5.4	237.7	13.4	4.2	255.3
Gross Stock (book value)	129.4	15.0	-0.7	143.7	15.4	-0.5	158.6	17.2	-0.9	174.9	20.4	-0.9	194.4	18.9	-0.8	212.5
Plus: Revaluation	152.8		3.0	155.8		-1.0	154.8		3.4	158.2		7.1	165.3		5.2	170.5
Equals: Gross Stock (current)	282.3	15.0	2.3	299.6	15.4	-1.5	313.4	17.2	2.4	333.1	20.4	6.2	359.7	18.9	4.4	383.0
Less: Capital Consump. (book)	28.2	2.2	-0.4	30.0	2.4	-0.4	32.0	2.7	-0.4	34.3	3.0	-0.5	36.8	3.3	-0.5	39.6
Cap. Consumption Reval.	76.6	2.1	0.1	78.8	2.1	-1.4	79.5	2.1	0.1	81.7	2.2	1.2	85.2	2.2	0.7	88.0
Consumer Durables	119.4	8.6	0.8	128.8	10.1	-1.0	137.9	7.1	-2.3	142.7	12.2	-3.0	151.9	8.5	5.3	165.8
Gross Stock (book value)	172.2	29.1	-9.1	192.2	32.5	-10.5	214.2	31.8	-11.0	235.0	38.6	-16.0	257.7	37.9	-17.6	277.5
Plus: Revaluation	50.1		-3.9	46.2		-12.5	33.7		-9.9	23.8		-8.3	15.5		7.6	23.1
Equals: Gross Stock (current)	222.3	29.1	-13.1	238.3	32.5	-23.0	247.9	31.8	-20.8	258.9	38.6	-24.3	273.2	37.9	-10.0	301.1
Less: Capital Consump. (book)	66.9	17.7	-8.1	76.4	19.8	-9.9	86.3	22.6	-11.4	97.5	25.1	-14.8	107.8	27.9	-16.8	118.9
Cap. Consumption Reval.	36.0	2.9	-5.7	33.1	2.6	-12.1	23.6	2.1	-7.1	18.7	1.3	-6.5	13.4	1.5	1.4	16.3
Inventories	41.9	1.7	-1.1	42.5	0.8	-0.1	43.2	0.2	-0.2	43.2	1.3	0.3	44.8	1.9	0.3	46.9
LAND	22.0		2.7	24.7		2.8	27.4		3.3	30.7		6.7	37.4		6.6	44.0
FIXED CLAIM ASSETS	216.7	14.6		231.3	13.7		245.0	10.6		255.5	14.9		270.5	18.9		289.4
Deposits	130.1	9.8		139.9	9.4		149.3	11.1		160.4	8.8		169.2	11.4		180.5
Currency & checkable dep.	59.2	2.0		61.2	1.2		62.5	1.9		64.4	0.1		64.5	2.0		66.5
Small time & svgs. deposits	70.6	7.7		78.4	8.2		86.5	9.1		95.6	8.6		104.3	9.4		113.7
Large time deposits	0.3	0.1		0.4	-0.0		0.3	0.0		0.4	-0.0		0.4	-0.0		0.3
Money market fund shares	0.0	0.0		0.0	0.0		0.0	0.0		0.0	0.0		0.0	0.0		0.0
Credit Market Instruments	77.0	4.3		81.3	3.8		85.1	-1.2		83.8	5.8		89.6	7.3		96.9
U.S. government securities	54.2	2.1		56.3	1.6		57.9	-1.6		56.3	2.1		58.4	3.2		61.6
Treasury issues	53.9	2.1		56.0	1.8		57.8	-1.6		56.2	1.5		57.7	2.7		60.5
Savings bonds	49.1	0.1		49.2	0.2		49.4	0.6		50.0	0.3		50.2	-0.1		50.1
Other treasury	4.8	2.0		6.9	1.6		8.4	-2.2		6.2	1.3		7.5	2.8		10.3
Agency issues	0.3	-0.1		0.3	-0.2		0.1	0.1		0.1	0.5		0.6	0.5		1.1
State and local obligations	4.4	1.3		5.6	1.7		7.3	1.7		9.0	2.8		11.8	1.4		13.2
Corporate and foreign bonds	0.9	0.3		1.2	-0.7		0.5	-2.3		-1.8	-0.3		-2.1	1.0		-1.1
Mortgages	17.1	0.6		17.7	0.8		18.5	0.9		19.4	1.0		20.5	1.6		22.0
Open-market paper	0.4	0.4		0.5	0.4		0.8	0.0		0.9	0.2		1.1	0.0		1.2
Security Credit	0.9	-0.2		0.7	-0.0		0.7	0.3		1.0	-0.1		0.9	-0.0		0.9
Other Fixed Claims	8.6	0.7		9.4	0.5		9.9	0.4		10.3	0.5		10.7	0.3		11.0

EQUITIES HELD	499.3	5.1	12.3	516.6	4.5	−7.3	513.8	5.7	73.0	592.6	3.4	59.7	655.8	4.9	34.2	694.9
Corporate Stock	128.4	1.4	10.3	140.1	0.3	−7.4	133.0	4.1	58.8	195.8	1.1	41.9	238.8	1.2	14.0	254.0
Non-Corp. Non-Farm Equity	173.4	0.1	4.5	178.0	0.9	3.3	182.2	−1.1	4.2	185.3	0.1	8.8	194.2	2.3	9.9	206.4
Farm Business Equity	111.1	0.8	−3.0	108.9	0.6	−2.6	106.9	−0.0	1.3	108.2	−0.8	1.8	109.2	−1.6	8.8	116.4
Pension & Insur. (cash value)	47.2	2.7	0.0	49.9	2.8	0.0	52.7	2.9	0.0	55.5	2.9	0.1	58.6	3.0	0.0	61.6
Estates and Trusts	39.1		0.5	39.7		−0.6	39.1		8.7	47.8		7.2	55.0		1.5	56.5
TOTAL ASSETS	1076.6	40.8	17.2	1134.6	40.1	−5.4	1169.3	36.0	76.6	1281.9	47.0	69.2	1398.1	47.6	50.6	1496.4
FIXED CLAIM LIABILITIES	82.5	12.0		94.5	12.6		107.1	11.6		118.7	20.2		138.9	15.7		154.6
Credit Market Instruments	79.1	11.7		90.8	12.1		102.8	10.4		113.2	19.4		132.6	15.5		148.1
Home mortgages	48.6	6.2		54.8	7.6		62.5	8.7		71.1	12.2		83.3	11.2		94.5
Consumer credit	27.3	5.3		32.6	4.2		36.7	1.5		38.2	7.2		45.3	3.9		49.3
Installment	16.2	4.3		20.5	3.8		24.3	0.6		24.9	5.4		30.3	2.9		33.2
Other	11.0	1.0		12.1	0.4		12.5	0.8		13.3	1.8		15.1	1.0		16.1
Bank loans, n.e.c.	0.4	0.1		0.5	0.0		0.5	0.0		0.5	−0.2		0.3	0.1		0.4
Other loans	2.8	0.1		2.9	0.2		3.1	0.2		3.4	0.2		3.6	0.3		3.9
U.S. gov't. loans	0.0	0.0		0.0	0.0		0.0	0.0		0.0	0.0		0.1	0.0		0.1
Policy loans	2.8	0.1		2.9	0.2		3.1	0.2		3.4	0.2		3.5	0.3		3.8
Security Debt	2.4	0.2		2.6	0.5		3.0	1.1		4.1	0.7		4.8	−0.0		4.8
Other Fixed Claims	1.1	0.1		1.2	0.1		1.3	0.1		1.3	0.1		1.5	0.2		1.7
NET WORTH	994.1	28.8	17.2	1040.1	27.4	−5.4	1062.2	24.4	76.6	1163.2	26.8	69.2	1259.2	32.0	50.6	1341.8
Tangibles	360.7	21.1	5.0	386.7	21.9	1.9	410.5	19.7	3.6	433.7	28.7	9.5	471.9	23.8	16.4	512.1
Equities	499.3	5.1	12.3	516.6	4.5	−7.3	513.8	5.7	73.0	592.6	3.4	59.7	655.8	4.9	34.2	694.9
Net Financial Assets	134.1	2.7		136.8	1.0		137.8	−1.0		136.8	−5.2		131.6	3.2		134.8
TOTAL LIABILITIES & NET WORTH	1076.6	40.8	17.2	1134.6	40.1	−5.4	1169.3	36.0	76.6	1281.9	47.0	69.2	1398.1	47.6	50.6	1496.4
Addenda:																
Net Saving (balance sheet)		28.8			27.4			24.4			26.8			32.0		
Net Saving (current account)		25.3			26.8			22.1			25.4			28.1		
Capital Gains Dividends		0.1			0.1			0.1			0.2			0.3		
Residual Discrepancy		3.4			0.5			2.2			1.2			3.6		

Table 1.A.2 Household Sector Capital Accounts (Continued)

	End of Year Value 1956	Cap. Trans. Acct. (1957)	Revaluation Acct. (1957)	End of Year Value 1957	Cap. Trans. Acct. (1958)	Revaluation Acct. (1958)	End of Year Value 1958	Cap Trans. Acct. (1959)	Revaluation Acct. (1959)	End of Year Value 1959	Cap. Trans. Acct. (1960)	Revaluation Acct. (1960)	End of Year Value 1950	Cap. Trans. Acct. (1961)	Revaluation Acct. (1961)	End of Year Value 1961
REPRODUCIBLE ASSETS (net current value)	468.1	20.2	1.1	489.4	15.4	3.7	508.5	24.4	−0.5	532.4	21.5	−2.3	551.7	17.6	−2.3	567.0
Residential Structures	255.3	11.3	0.0	266.6	11.1	0.7	278.4	15.2	0.3	293.9	12.8	0.1	306.8	11.8	−0.3	318.3
Gross Stock (book value)	212.5	17.3	−0.6	229.2	17.5	−0.6	246.2	21.8	−1.2	266.8	19.6	−1.3	285.1	18.9	−1.3	302.7
Plus: Revaluation	170.5		−1.9	168.6		−1.2	167.4		−0.8	166.6		−0.7	165.9		−1.6	164.3
Equals: Gross Stock (current)	383.0	17.3	−2.5	397.8	17.5	−1.8	413.6	21.8	−2.0	433.4	19.6	−2.0	451.0	18.9	−2.8	467.0
Less: Capital Consump. (book)	39.6	3.6	−0.5	42.8	3.9	−0.5	46.2	4.3	−0.6	49.8	4.6	−0.6	53.8	4.9	−0.7	58.1
Cap. Consumption Reval.	88.0	2.4	−2.0	88.4	2.5	−1.9	89.0	2.3	−1.7	89.7	2.2	−1.7	90.4	2.2	−1.9	90.6
Consumer Durables	165.8	7.7	1.2	174.7	3.6	3.1	181.4	7.3	−0.9	187.9	7.0	−2.5	192.4	4.3	−1.7	195.0
Gross Stock (book value)	277.9	39.3	−19.3	298.0	36.8	−19.8	315.0	42.4	−23.7	333.7	43.1	−25.8	351.1	41.6	−27.6	365.1
Plus: Revaluation	23.1		1.6	24.7		4.8	29.6		−1.7	27.9		−4.9	23.0		−3.1	19.9
Equals: Gross Stock (current)	301.1	39.3	−17.7	322.7	36.8	−14.9	344.6	42.4	−25.4	361.6	43.1	−30.6	374.1	41.6	−30.7	384.4
Less: Capital Consump. (book)	118.9	29.5	−17.7	130.7	31.0	−18.2	143.5	32.5	−21.4	154.7	34.0	−23.6	165.0	35.5	−25.7	174.8
Cap. Consumption Reval.	16.3	2.1	−1.2	17.2	2.3	0.2	19.7	2.6	−3.2	19.1	2.1	−4.5	16.6	1.8	−3.3	15.1
Inventories	46.9	1.2	−0.1	48.1	0.7	−0.2	48.7	1.9	0.1	50.7	1.7	0.1	52.5	1.6	−0.3	53.7
LAND	44.0		4.6	48.6		6.1	54.7		9.8	64.5		2.6	67.0		5.4	72.4
FIXED CLAIM ASSETS	289.4	17.3		306.7	17.1		323.8	23.2		347.0	20.3		367.3	19.9		387.2
Deposits	180.5	11.1		191.7	15.9		207.6	14.0		221.6	13.6		235.2	16.8		251.9
Currency & checkable dep.	66.5	−0.8		65.8	2.1		67.9	2.8		70.6	1.6		72.2	−1.4		70.8
Small time & svgs. deposits	113.7	11.9		125.6	13.8		139.4	11.3		150.7	11.6		162.3	17.8		180.1
Large time deposits	0.3	−0.0		0.3	0.0		0.3	−0.0		0.3	0.4		0.7	0.4		1.1
Money market fund shares	0.0	0.0		0.0	0.0		0.0	0.0		0.0	0.0		0.0	0.0		0.0
Credit Market Instruments	96.9	5.9		102.8	0.7		103.5	9.0		112.4	6.1		118.5	2.6		121.2
U.S. government securities	61.6	2.2		63.8	−2.9		60.9	5.0		65.9	−0.5		65.4	0.7		66.1
Treasury issues	60.5	1.5		62.0	−2.3		59.7	3.3		62.9	0.2		63.1	0.9		64.0
Savings bonds	50.1	−1.9		48.2	−0.5		47.7	−1.8		45.9	−0.3		45.6	0.8		46.4
Other treasury	10.3	3.4		13.8	−1.8		12.0	5.0		17.0	0.4		17.4	0.1		17.6
Agency issues	1.1	0.7		1.8	−0.6		1.2	1.7		2.9	−0.6		2.3	−0.2		2.1
State and local obligations	13.2	1.0		14.2	0.7		14.8	2.7		17.6	2.5		20.1	0.3		20.3
Corporate and foreign bonds	−1.1	0.6		−0.4	0.6		0.2	0.1		0.3	−0.2		−1.4	−1.4		−1.4
Mortgages	22.0	2.0		24.0	2.4		26.4	2.0		28.4	2.6		31.0	2.9		34.0
Open-market paper	0.9	0.1		1.3	−0.1		1.1	−0.8		0.3	1.7		0.2	2.0		2.2
Security Credit	0.9	0.0		0.9	0.3		1.2	−0.2		1.0	2.0		1.1	0.1		1.2
Other Fixed Claims	11.0	0.3		11.3	0.3		11.6	0.4		12.0	0.5		12.4	0.4		12.9

	1	2	3	4	5	6	7	8	9	10	11	12	13	14	15	16
EQUITIES HELD	694.9	3.1	-28.7	669.3	12.0	115.8	797.1	1.0	42.1	840.2	1.1	5.6	846.9	7.7	110.9	965.5
Corporate Stock	254.0	-0.7	-32.7	220.6	7.3	86.1	314.0	-1.3	23.7	336.4	-2.1	-5.0	329.3	3.4	87.5	420.2
Non-Corp. Non-Farm Equity	206.4	2.0	0.7	209.1	2.0	6.2	217.2	1.4	6.0	224.7	1.3	6.6	232.6	2.4	3.9	238.8
Farm Business Equity	116.4	-0.9	8.2	123.8	-0.2	11.9	135.4	-2.4	5.3	138.3	-1.2	2.3	139.3	-1.3	5.7	143.7
Pension & Insur. (cash value)	61.6	2.6	-0.0	64.2	2.9	0.1	67.3	3.3	0.1	70.6	3.1	0.0	73.7	3.3	0.2	77.2
Estates and Trusts	56.5		-4.9	51.6		11.5	63.1		7.1	70.2		1.7	71.9		13.6	85.5
TOTAL ASSETS	1496.4	40.6	-23.0	1514.0	44.6	125.5	1684.1	48.6	51.3	1784.1	42.9	5.9	1832.8	45.3	114.0	1992.1
FIXED CLAIM LIABILITIES	154.6	11.8		166.4	12.2		178.6	22.2		200.7	16.9		217.7	17.2		234.9
Credit Market Instruments	148.1	12.1		160.2	10.9		171.1	21.9		193.0	16.9		209.9	15.7		225.6
Home mortgages	94.5	8.9		103.4	9.5		112.9	12.8		125.7	11.7		137.4	12.2		149.6
Consumer credit	49.3	2.9		52.2	0.5		52.7	8.0		60.7	4.4		65.1	2.5		67.6
Installment	33.2	2.3		35.4	-0.1		35.3	5.8		41.1	3.9		45.1	1.0		46.0
Other	16.1	0.7		16.7	0.6		17.4	2.3		19.6	0.4		20.1	1.6		21.6
Bank loans, n.e.c.	0.4	-0.2		0.2	0.4		0.7	0.5		1.2	0.0		1.2	0.3		1.4
Other loans	3.9	0.5		4.4	0.4		4.8	0.6		5.4	0.8		6.3	0.7		7.0
U.S. gov't. loans	0.1	0.1		0.2	0.1		0.3	0.1		0.4	0.2		0.6	0.2		0.7
Policy loans	3.8	0.4		4.2	0.4		4.5	0.5		5.0	0.7		5.7	0.6		6.2
Security Debt	4.8	-0.4		4.4	1.2		5.5	0.0		5.5	-0.1		5.4	1.3		6.7
Other Fixed Claims	1.7	0.2		1.8	0.1		2.0	0.2		2.2	0.2		2.4	0.1		2.5
NET WORTH	1341.8	28.8	-23.0	1347.6	32.4	125.5	1505.6	26.5	51.3	1583.3	26.0	5.9	1615.2	28.1	114.0	1757.2
Tangibles	512.1	20.2	5.7	538.0	15.4	9.8	563.2	24.4	9.2	596.9	21.5	0.3	618.7	17.6	3.1	639.4
Equities	694.9	3.1	-28.7	669.3	12.0	115.8	797.1	1.0	42.1	840.2	1.1	5.6	846.9	7.7	110.9	965.5
Net Financial Assets	134.8	5.5		140.3	5.0		145.3	1.0		146.3	3.3		149.6	2.7		152.3
TOTAL LIABILITIES & NET WORTH	1496.4	40.6	-23.0	1514.0	44.6	125.5	1684.1	48.6	51.3	1784.1	42.9	5.9	1832.8	45.3	114.0	1992.1
Addenda:																
Net Saving (balance sheet)		28.8			32.4			26.5			26.0			28.1		
Net Saving (current account)		25.5			27.3			24.2			22.4			24.0		
Capital Gains Dividends		0.3			0.3			0.4			0.4			0.5		
Residual Discrepancy		3.0			4.8			1.8			3.1			3.5		

Table 1.A.2 **Household Sector Capital Accounts (Continued)**

	End of Year Value 1961	Cap. Trans. Acct. (1962)	Reval-uation Acct. (1962)	End of Year Value 1962	Cap. Trans. Acct. (1963)	Reval-uation Acct. (1963)	End of Year Value 1963	Cap Trans. Acct. (1964)	Reval-uation Acct. (1964)	End of Year Value 1964	Cap. Trans. Acct. (1965)	Reval-uation Acct. (1965)	End of Year Value 1965	Cap. Trans. Acct. (1966)	Reval-uation Acct. (1966)	End of Year Value 1966
REPRODUCIBLE ASSETS																
(net current value)	567.0	23.6	-3.0	587.6	28.4	-8.3	607.7	33.4	3.9	645.0	38.8	-4.7	679.1	40.8	17.6	737.5
Residential Structures	318.3	12.8	0.1	331.2	14.5	-6.9	338.8	14.7	8.2	361.7	14.8	3.3	379.7	12.7	17.4	409.8
Gross Stock (book value)	302.7	20.2	-1.7	321.2	22.1	-1.9	341.5	22.7	-1.5	362.6	23.2	-1.6	384.3	21.7	-1.4	404.5
Plus: Revaluation	164.3		-0.5	163.9		-10.6	153.3		11.0	164.3		3.7	168.0		23.8	191.8
Equals: Gross Stock (current)	467.0	20.2	-2.2	485.1	22.1	-12.4	494.8	22.7	9.5	526.9	23.2	2.1	552.2	21.7	22.4	596.3
Less: Capital Consump. (book)	58.1	5.2	-0.7	62.6	5.6	-0.8	67.4	5.9	-0.8	72.6	6.3	-0.8	78.1	6.7	-0.9	83.9
Cap. Consumption Reval.	90.6	2.2	-1.6	91.2	2.0	-4.7	88.5	2.1	2.0	92.6	2.1	-0.3	94.4	2.3	6.0	102.6
Consumer Durables	195.0	8.5	-3.2	200.3	11.8	-1.5	210.6	15.0	-4.2	221.4	20.2	-8.4	233.1	23.1	-1.0	255.3
Gross Stock (book value)	365.1	46.7	-29.4	382.4	51.4	-31.8	402.0	56.4	-36.1	422.4	63.0	-37.9	447.5	68.0	-42.0	473.4
Plus: Revaluation	19.9		-5.1	14.7		-1.3	13.4		-4.9	8.6		-11.6	-3.0		4.5	1.4
Equals: Gross Stock (current)	384.9	46.7	-34.5	397.1	51.4	-33.1	415.5	56.4	-41.0	431.0	63.0	-49.5	444.5	68.0	-37.6	474.9
Less: Capital Consump. (book)	174.8	36.8	-27.0	184.6	38.6	-29.1	194.1	40.6	-33.0	201.7	42.9	-34.7	209.9	45.4	-38.3	217.0
Cap. Consumption Reval.	15.1	1.4	-4.3	12.2	1.1	-2.5	10.8	0.9	-3.8	7.9	-0.0	-6.4	1.4	-0.5	1.7	2.6
Inventories	53.7	2.2	0.1	56.1	2.1	0.2	58.3	3.7	-0.1	61.9	3.9	0.4	66.2	4.9	1.3	72.4
LAND	72.4		6.4	78.8		4.7	83.5		8.0	91.5		8.8	100.3		8.0	108.3
FIXED CLAIM ASSETS	387.2	28.2		415.3	29.2		444.5	38.6		483.1	40.2		523.3	36.4		559.7
Deposits	251.9	25.1		277.1	29.3		306.4	31.2		337.6	35.3		372.9	21.8		394.7
Currency & checkable dep.	70.8	-0.7		70.0	3.7		73.7	5.4		79.1	7.6		86.8	2.6		89.4
Small time & svgs. deposits	180.1	25.4		205.4	24.8		230.3	24.9		255.2	26.9		282.0	18.3		300.3
Large time deposits	1.1	0.5		1.6	0.8		2.4	0.8		3.3	0.8		4.1	0.9		5.0
Money market fund shares	0.0	0.0		0.0	0.0		0.0	0.0		0.0	0.0		0.0	0.0		0.0
Credit Market Instruments	121.2	2.7		123.8	-0.3		123.6	6.2		129.8	2.8		132.6	12.9		145.6
U.S. government securities	66.1	1.4		67.5	-4.6		62.9	3.2		66.2	1.2		67.4	6.0		73.4
Treasury issues	64.0	1.5		65.5	-4.3		61.1	2.4		63.5	0.2		63.7	1.6		65.3
Savings bonds	46.4	0.5		47.0	1.2		48.1	0.9		49.1	0.6		49.7	0.6		50.2
Other treasury	17.6	1.0		18.5	-5.5		13.0	1.5		14.4	-0.5		14.0	1.0		15.0
Agency issues	2.1	-0.0		2.0	-0.2		1.8	0.9		2.7	1.0		3.7	4.4		8.1
State and local obligations	20.3	-2.1		18.3	2.4		20.7	2.5		23.2	1.7		24.9	3.8		28.7
Corporate and foreign bonds	-1.4	0.5		-0.9	-0.8		-1.7	-1.8		-3.4	-0.9		-4.3	0.4		-3.9
Mortgages	34.0	2.2		36.2	1.4		37.7	1.4		39.1	-0.1		39.0	1.7		40.7
Open-market paper	2.2	0.5		2.7	1.2		3.9	0.9		4.8	0.8		5.6	1.0		6.7
Security Credit	1.2	0.0		1.2	-0.0		1.2	0.4		1.7	0.9		2.5	0.2		2.7
Other Fixed Claims	12.9	0.3		13.2	0.1		13.3	0.8		14.0	1.2		15.3	1.4		16.7

EQUITIES HELD	965.5	-3.3	-40.3	922.0	3.1	90.4	1015.5	6.8	61.3	1083.7	7.2	91.4	1182.3	0.9	-30.0	1153.2
Corporate Stock	420.2	-7.8	-51.4	361.0	-2.4	65.2	423.8	2.2	42.0	468.1	0.8	60.5	529.4	-5.5	-49.4	474.6
Non-Corp. Non-Farm Equity	238.8	2.1	5.6	246.5	3.4	1.5	251.4	2.6	7.3	261.3	3.4	7.5	272.3	4.2	12.3	288.8
Farm Business Equity	143.7	-1.1	6.0	148.6	-1.8	7.5	154.3	-2.2	7.5	159.6	-1.6	13.6	171.7	-2.4	9.2	178.5
Pension & Insur. (cash value)	77.2	3.6	-0.2	80.6	4.0	0.2	84.8	4.3	0.2	89.2	4.6	0.2	94.0	4.6	-0.2	98.4
Estates and Trusts	85.5		-0.3	85.2		16.0	101.2		4.2	105.4		9.5	115.0		-2.0	113.0
TOTAL ASSETS	1992.1	48.5	-36.9	2003.7	60.7	86.9	2151.2	78.8	73.2	2303.3	86.3	95.4	2485.0	78.0	-4.4	2558.6
FIXED CLAIM LIABILITIES	234.9	21.1		256.0	28.0		284.0	28.5		312.5	29.9		342.4	23.0		365.4
Credit Market Instruments	225.6	21.1		246.7	25.9		272.6	28.5		301.1	28.9		330.0	22.7		352.7
Home mortgages	149.6	14.1		163.7	16.2		179.9	17.5		197.4	17.0		214.4	14.2		228.5
Consumer credit	67.6	6.3		73.9	8.9		82.8	9.8		92.6	10.6		103.2	6.5		109.7
Installment	46.0	5.0		51.0	6.8		57.8	7.7		65.6	8.3		73.9	5.5		79.3
Other	21.6	1.3		22.9	2.1		25.0	2.0		27.0	2.3		29.3	1.1		30.4
Bank loans, n.e.c.	1.4	-0.1		1.3	0.1		1.4	0.5		2.0	0.5		2.5	0.0		2.5
Other loans	7.0	0.8		7.7	0.7		8.4	0.7		9.2	0.8		10.0	2.0		11.9
U.S. gov't. loans	0.7	0.2		1.0	0.2		1.2	0.2		1.4	0.2		1.6	0.5		2.1
Policy loans	6.2	0.5		6.8	0.5		7.2	0.5		7.8	0.6		8.3	1.5		9.8
Security Debt	6.7	-0.1		6.6	2.0		8.6	-0.2		8.4	0.7		9.1	-0.1		9.0
Other Fixed Claims	2.5	0.2		2.7	0.2		2.9	-0.2		3.0	0.3		3.3	0.4		3.7
NET WORTH	1757.2	27.4	-36.9	1747.7	32.6	86.9	1867.2	50.3	73.2	1990.8	56.3	95.4	2142.6	55.0	-4.4	2193.2
Tangibles	639.4	23.6	3.4	666.4	28.4	-3.6	691.2	33.4	11.9	736.5	38.8	4.0	779.4	40.8	25.6	845.7
Equities	965.5	-3.3	-40.3	922.0	3.1	90.4	1015.5	6.8	61.3	1083.7	7.2	91.4	1182.3	0.9	-30.0	1153.2
Net Financial Assets	152.3	7.1		159.4	1.1		160.5	10.1		170.6	10.3		180.9	13.4		194.3
TOTAL LIABILITIES & NET WORTH	1992.1	48.5	-36.9	2003.7	60.7	86.9	2151.2	78.8	73.2	2303.3	86.3	95.4	2485.0	78.0	-4.4	2558.6
Addenda:																
Net Saving (balance sheet)		27.4			32.6			50.3			56.3			55.0		
Net Saving (current account)		26.5			27.2			38.8			48.6			52.5		
Capital Gains Dividends		0.5			0.5			0.6			0.9			1.3		
Residual Discrepancy		0.4			5.0			10.9			6.8			1.2		

Table 1.A.2 Household Sector Capital Accounts (Continued)

	End of Year Value 1966	Cap. Trans. Acct. (1967)	Revaluation Acct. (1967)	End of Year Value 1967	Cap. Trans. Acct. (1968)	Revaluation Acct. (1968)	End of Year Value 1968	Cap Trans. Acct. (1969)	Revaluation Acct. (1969)	End of Year Value 1969	Cap. Trans. Acct. (1970)	Revaluation Acct. (1970)	End of Year Value 1970	Cap. Trans. Acct. (1971)	Revaluation Acct. (1971)	End of Year Value 1971
REPRODUCIBLE ASSETS (net current value)	737.5	37.7	13.6	788.7	49.1	36.6	874.4	49.1	33.6	957.2	39.7	29.4	1026.2	57.5	27.1	1110.9
Residential Structures	409.8	12.4	9.6	431.8	16.2	34.9	482.9	16.5	26.9	526.3	15.3	21.8	563.4	25.7	32.9	622.0
Gross Stock (book value)	404.5	22.1	-1.2	425.4	26.8	-1.7	450.5	28.4	-1.9	477.0	28.1	-2.3	502.8	39.8	-3.1	539.5
Plus: Revaluation	191.8		12.0	203.8		49.2	253.0		37.3	290.3		30.4	320.7		47.4	368.1
Equals: Gross Stock (current)	596.3	22.1	10.7	629.2	26.8	47.6	703.5	28.4	35.4	767.3	28.1	28.1	823.5	39.8	44.3	907.6
Less: Capital Consump. (book)	83.9	7.1	-1.0	90.0	7.5	-1.0	96.5	8.0	-1.1	103.4	8.6	-1.1	110.8	9.2	-1.1	118.9
Cap. Consumption Reval.	102.6	2.6	2.1	107.4	3.1	13.7	124.1	3.9	9.7	137.6	4.2	7.4	149.3	4.9	12.5	166.7
Consumer Durables	255.3	21.1	3.2	279.6	27.0	4.0	310.5	26.3	3.3	340.1	20.0	8.2	368.3	26.6	-4.9	390.0
Gross Stock (book value)	473.4	70.1	-41.4	502.1	80.5	-42.3	540.3	85.7	-46.9	579.1	85.2	-48.0	616.3	97.2	-51.5	662.1
Plus: Revaluation	1.4		10.8	12.2		12.3	24.5		11.4	36.0		19.8	55.8		-2.5	53.2
Equals: Gross Stock (current)	474.9	70.1	-30.6	514.3	80.5	-30.0	564.8	85.7	-35.4	615.1	85.2	-28.2	672.1	97.2	-54.0	715.3
Less: Capital Consump. (book)	217.0	48.8	-37.9	227.9	52.1	-38.1	241.9	56.9	-42.1	256.7	61.4	-43.3	274.8	65.3	-45.0	295.2
Cap. Consumption Reval.	2.6	0.2	4.1	6.9	1.4	4.1	12.4	2.5	3.4	18.3	3.8	6.8	29.0	5.4	-4.2	30.2
Inventories	72.4	4.2	0.7	77.3	6.0	-2.3	81.0	6.3	3.5	90.7	4.4	-0.6	94.5	5.2	-0.9	98.8
LAND	108.3		8.0	116.3		17.3	133.6		8.8	142.3		9.2	151.6		6.2	157.8
FIXED CLAIM ASSETS	559.7	52.8		612.5	59.1		671.5	44.2		715.7	53.5		769.2	71.1		840.3
Deposits	394.7	44.6		439.2	41.7		480.9	5.3		486.2	52.4		538.6	78.9		617.4
Currency & checkable dep.	89.4	9.6		99.0	10.7		109.7	-4.5		105.2	9.2		114.4	12.2		126.6
Small time & svgs. deposits	300.3	33.9		334.3	26.8		361.0	15.6		376.6	28.8		405.4	65.4		470.7
Large time deposits	5.0	1.0		5.9	4.2		10.2	-5.8		4.4	14.4		18.8	1.3		20.1
Money market fund shares	0.0	0.0		0.0	0.0		0.0	0.0		0.0	0.0		0.0	0.0		0.0
Credit Market Instruments	145.6	4.6		150.2	13.8		164.0	38.8		202.8	-0.3		202.5	-10.2		192.3
U.S. government securities	73.4	2.5		75.9	6.1		82.0	16.4		98.4	-5.2		93.3	-11.5		81.7
Treasury issues	65.3	2.5		67.8	5.3		73.1	10.8		83.9	-11.6		72.4	-7.6		64.8
Savings bonds	50.2	1.0		51.2	0.6		51.9	-0.1		51.8	0.3		52.1	2.3		54.4
Other treasury	15.0	1.6		16.6	4.6		21.3	10.9		32.2	-11.9		20.3	-9.9		10.3
Agency issues	8.1	-0.0		8.1	0.8		8.9	5.6		14.5	6.4		20.9	-3.9		17.0
State and local obligations	28.7	-2.5		26.3	-2.5		23.8	11.7		35.5	-1.8		33.6	-2.0		31.6
Corporate and foreign bonds	-3.9	2.1		-1.8	5.3		3.5	3.2		6.7	9.1		15.8	6.3		22.1
Mortgages	40.7	1.5		42.2	2.4		44.6	2.1		46.7	1.4		48.1	1.0		49.0
Open-market paper	6.7	0.9		7.6	2.5		10.1	5.3		15.4	-3.8		11.7	-3.8		7.9
Security Credit	2.7	2.2		4.9	2.1		7.0	-1.8		5.2	-0.9		4.4	0.5		4.9
Other Fixed Claims	16.7	1.4		18.1	1.5		19.6	1.9		21.5	2.3		23.8	1.9		25.7

	1	2	3	4	5	6	7	8	9	10	11	12	13	14	15	16
EQUITIES HELD	1153.2	13.2	154.3	1320.6	9.3	161.6	1491.4	-6.6	-70.8	1414.1	-0.9	13.0	1426.2	-6.7	150.9	1570.5
Corporate Stock	474.6	7.9	123.3	605.7	3.7	121.9	731.3	-11.5	-92.9	626.9	-5.3	-13.3	608.3	-9.8	91.6	690.0
Non-Corp. Non-Farm Equity	288.8	1.1	8.3	298.1	1.5	18.0	317.6	1.5	19.1	338.2	-0.4	18.1	355.8	-1.0	16.5	371.4
Farm Business Equity	178.5	-0.7	9.3	187.0	-0.5	9.4	195.9	-1.5	8.8	203.2	-0.5	5.5	208.2	-2.1	17.9	224.1
Pension & Insur. (cash value)	98.4	4.9	0.2	103.5	4.6	0.3	108.4	4.9	-0.3	113.0	5.3	0.1	118.4	6.2	0.7	125.3
Estates and Trusts	113.0	0.0	13.2	126.2	0.0	12.0	138.2	0.0	-5.5	132.8	0.0	2.6	135.4	0.0	24.2	159.7
TOTAL ASSETS	2558.6	103.6	175.9	2838.1	117.4	215.4	3170.9	86.7	-28.4	3229.2	92.3	51.6	3373.2	122.0	184.3	3679.4
FIXED CLAIM LIABILITIES	365.4	24.1		389.5	35.1		424.6	30.3		454.9	22.6		477.5	47.0		524.5
Credit Market Instruments	352.7	20.1		372.8	31.8		404.6	33.4		438.0	23.9		461.9	44.0		506.0
Home mortgages	228.5	12.4		240.9	16.8		257.7	18.6		276.3	14.1		290.4	26.2		316.7
Consumer credit	109.7	5.7		115.4	11.5		126.9	10.8		137.7	5.4		143.1	14.7		157.8
Installment	79.3	3.8		83.1	8.5		91.7	9.5		101.2	4.4		105.5	12.7		118.3
Other	30.4	1.9		32.3	3.0		35.3	1.3		36.6	1.0		37.6	2.0		39.5
Bank loans, n.e.c.	2.5	0.7		3.2	1.4		4.7	1.0		5.7	1.8		7.5	1.8		9.2
Other loans	11.9	1.3		13.3	2.1		15.3	3.0		18.3	2.6		20.9	1.4		22.3
U.S. gov't. loans	2.1	0.3		2.4	0.8		3.2	0.4		3.6	0.3		3.9	0.4		4.2
Policy loans	9.8	1.0		10.8	1.3		12.1	2.6		14.7	2.3		17.0	1.0		18.0
Security Debt	9.0	3.7		12.7	2.9		15.6	-3.4		12.2	-1.8		10.4	2.7		13.1
Other Fixed Claims	3.7	0.3		3.9	0.4		4.3	0.4		4.7	0.4		5.1	0.3		5.4
NET WORTH	2193.2	79.6	175.9	2448.6	82.3	215.4	2746.4	56.3	-28.4	2774.3	69.7	51.6	2895.7	75.0	184.3	3154.9
Tangibles	845.7	37.7	21.6	905.0	49.1	53.9	1008.0	49.1	42.4	1099.5	39.7	38.6	1177.8	57.5	33.3	1268.6
Equities	1153.2	13.2	154.3	1320.6	9.3	161.6	1491.4	-6.6	-70.8	1414.1	-0.9	13.0	1426.2	-6.7	150.9	1570.5
Net Financial Assets	194.3	28.7		223.0	24.0		247.0	13.8		260.8	30.9		291.7	24.1		315.8
TOTAL LIABILITIES & NET WORTH	2558.6	103.6	175.9	2838.1	117.4	215.4	3170.9	86.7	-28.4	3229.2	92.3	51.6	3373.2	122.0	184.3	3679.4
Addenda:																
Net Saving (balance sheet)		79.6			82.3			56.3			69.7			75.0		
Net Saving (current account)		63.9			68.1			58.2			65.1			79.3		
Capital Gains Dividends		1.7			2.5			2.5			0.9			0.8		
Residual Discrepancy		14.0			11.8			-4.4			3.7			-5.1		

Table 1.A.2   Household Sector Capital Accounts (Continued)

	End of Year Value 1971	Cap. Trans. Acct. (1972)	Reval-uation Acct. (1972)	End of Year Value 1972	Cap. Trans. Acct. (1973)	Reval-uation Acct. (1973)	End of Year Value 1973	Cap Trans. Acct. (1974)	Reval-uation Acct. (1974)	End of Year Value 1974	Cap. Trans. Acct. (1975)	Reval-uation Acct. (1975)	End of Year Value 1975	Cap. Trans. Acct. (1976)	Reval-uation Acct. (1976)	End of Year Value 1976
REPRODUCIBLE ASSETS																
(net current value)	1110.9	75.4	43.1	1229.3	84.8	87.5	1401.6	63.1	127.0	1591.7	57.4	74.8	1723.8	85.0	109.8	1918.7
Residential Structures	622.0	32.9	46.4	701.3	33.8	82.0	817.2	25.4	81.6	924.1	22.1	54.9	1001.1	34.8	98.1	1134.1
Gross Stock (book value)	539.5	49.2	−3.9	584.8	51.8	−4.4	632.2	46.2	−4.7	673.7	45.3	−5.5	713.6	60.5	−6.6	767.5
Plus: Revaluation	368.1		66.9	435.0		119.3	554.2		118.0	672.2		79.5	751.7		143.9	895.6
Equals: Gross Stock (current)	907.6	49.2	63.0	1019.8	51.8	114.8	1186.4	46.2	113.3	1345.9	45.3	74.1	1465.3	60.5	137.2	1663.0
Less: Capital Consump. (book)	118.9	10.0	−1.1	127.8	10.9	−1.2	137.5	11.8	−1.3	148.0	12.5	−1.9	158.7	13.4	−2.0	170.1
Cap. Consumption Reval.	166.7	6.3	17.6	190.7	7.1	34.0	231.7	9.0	33.0	273.8	10.7	21.0	305.5	13.4	41.1	358.9
Consumer Durables	390.0	34.6	−3.3	421.3	40.4	3.7	465.4	28.4	41.6	535.4	26.5	23.1	585.0	40.0	11.5	636.5
Gross Stock (book value)	662.1	111.1	−57.0	716.2	123.3	−59.9	779.7	121.5	−61.4	839.8	132.2	−65.5	906.4	156.8	−75.4	987.9
Plus: Revaluation	53.2		1.5	54.7		14.6	69.3		81.9	151.2		45.0	196.1		25.3	221.4
Equals: Gross Stock (current)	715.3	111.1	−55.5	770.9	123.3	−45.3	849.0	121.5	20.5	990.9	132.2	−20.6	1102.5	156.8	−50.1	1209.2
Less: Capital Consump. (book)	295.2	71.3	−49.6	316.9	77.4	−51.9	342.3	83.2	−53.0	372.5	89.5	−55.9	406.1	97.4	−62.7	440.7
Cap. Consumption Reval.	30.2	5.2	−2.6	32.8	5.6	2.9	41.3	9.9	31.8	83.0	16.2	12.2	111.5	19.5	1.1	132.0
Inventories	98.8	7.9	−0.0	106.7	10.6	1.8	119.1	9.3	3.8	132.1	8.8	−3.3	137.7	10.3	0.2	148.2
LAND	157.8		26.0	183.8		34.8	218.5		34.6	253.1		19.6	272.7		44.0	316.7
FIXED CLAIM ASSETS	840.3	99.6		939.9	114.0		1053.9	106.6		1160.6	122.6		1283.1	146.2		1429.3
Deposits	617.4	85.9		703.3	77.9		781.3	65.7		847.0	92.1		939.1	122.2		1061.3
Currency & checkable dep.	126.6	12.4		138.9	14.5		153.4	8.1		161.5	7.4		168.9	15.8		184.6
Small time & svgs. deposits	470.7	67.3		538.0	37.7		575.7	34.0		609.8	96.5		706.2	117.5		823.7
Large time deposits	20.1	6.2		26.3	25.8		52.1	21.3		73.4	−13.0		60.4	−11.0		49.3
Money market fund shares	0.0	0.0		0.0	0.0		0.0	2.4		2.4	1.3		3.7	−0.0		3.7
Credit Market Instruments	192.3	11.1		203.4	33.9		237.2	39.7		277.0	26.1		303.1	17.0		320.1
U.S. government securities	81.7	1.0		82.7	17.3		100.0	19.4		119.4	15.9		135.3	8.8		144.1
Treasury issues	64.8	3.6		68.4	15.5		83.9	14.8		98.7	16.9		115.6	4.5		120.2
Savings bonds	54.4	3.3		57.7	2.7		60.4	3.0		63.3	4.0		67.4	4.7		72.0
Other treasury	10.3	0.4		10.7	12.8		23.5	11.8		35.4	12.9		48.3	−0.1		48.2
Agency issues	17.0	−2.7		14.3	1.8		16.1	4.6		20.7	−1.1		19.7	4.2		23.9
State and local obligations	31.6	1.1		32.7	4.3		37.0	9.3		46.3	4.7		51.0	−1.5		49.5
Corporate and foreign bonds	22.1	4.4		26.5	−0.2		26.3	3.1		29.4	6.2		35.5	5.7		41.3
Mortgages	49.0	6.3		55.3	3.3		58.6	3.7		62.4	3.8		66.2	7.1		73.3
Open-market paper	7.9	−1.7		6.2	9.1		15.3	4.2		19.5	−4.4		15.1	−3.1		12.0
Security Credit	4.9	0.1		5.0	−0.2		4.9	−1.0		3.9	0.6		4.5	1.8		6.3
Other Fixed Claims	25.7	2.5		28.2	2.3		30.6	2.1		32.7	3.8		36.5	5.1		41.6

EQUITIES HELD	1570.5	-13.6	167.8	1724.7	-12.2	-42.0	1670.5	-2.2	-75.9	1592.4	10.6	237.8	1840.8	-9.5	235.0	2066.4
Corporate Stock	690.0	-14.9	70.8	745.9	-18.6	-159.0	568.3	-1.6	-164.5	402.3	6.1	126.0	534.4	-6.1	94.2	622.6
Non-Corp. Non-Farm Equity	371.4	-0.6	37.7	408.4	3.4	58.1	470.0	-0.4	78.3	547.8	-2.4	42.5	587.9	-3.2	60.1	644.7
Farm Business Equity	224.1	-4.6	34.8	254.3	-4.3	72.9	322.8	-6.9	39.9	355.8	-1.8	45.9	399.9	-8.8	52.1	443.2
Pension & Insur. (cash value)	125.3	6.6	1.0	132.9	7.4	-1.6	138.7	6.8	-1.6	143.9	8.7	1.1	153.7	8.7	0.8	163.2
Estates and Trusts	159.7		23.4	183.1		-12.5	170.6		-28.0	142.6		22.2	164.9		27.9	192.8
TOTAL ASSETS	3679.4	161.4	236.9	4077.7	186.6	80.2	4344.5	167.6	85.7	4597.8	190.5	332.2	5120.5	221.7	388.9	5731.2
FIXED CLAIM LIABILITIES	524.5		68.4	592.9		75.3	668.2		48.9	717.1		49.7	766.8		95.5	862.3
Credit Market Instruments	506.0		63.4	569.4		79.2	648.7		50.0	698.7		48.3	747.0		89.7	836.7
Home mortgages	316.7		41.4	358.0		47.3	405.3		35.2	440.5		38.0	478.6		61.5	540.1
Consumer credit	157.8		19.8	177.6		26.0	203.7		9.9	213.6		9.6	223.2		25.4	248.6
Installment	118.3		14.9	133.2		21.9	155.1		9.5	164.6		7.7	172.3		21.5	193.8
Other	39.5		4.9	44.5		4.1	48.6		0.4	49.0		1.9	50.9		3.9	54.8
Bank loans, n.e.c.	9.2		0.9	10.1		3.4	13.5		1.6	15.2		-1.5	13.7		1.0	14.6
Other loans	22.3		1.3	23.6		2.6	26.2		3.2	29.4		2.2	31.5		1.8	33.4
U.S. gov't. loans	4.2		0.4	4.6		0.3	5.0		0.5	5.5		0.5	6.0		0.5	6.5
Policy loans	18.0		0.9	19.0		2.2	21.2		2.7	23.9		1.6	25.5		1.4	26.9
Security Debt	13.1		4.4	17.5		-4.3	13.2		-1.8	11.4		0.7	12.1		5.1	17.2
Other Fixed Claims	5.4		0.5	6.0		0.4	6.4		0.7	7.1		0.7	7.7		0.6	8.4
NET WORTH	3154.9	93.0	236.9	3484.8	111.3	80.2	3676.3	118.7	85.7	3880.7	140.8	332.2	4353.7	126.3	388.9	4868.9
Tangibles	1268.6	75.4	69.1	1413.1	84.8	122.3	1620.1	63.1	161.6	1844.8	57.4	94.4	1996.6	85.0	153.9	2235.5
Equities	1570.5	-13.6	167.8	1724.7	-12.2	-42.0	1670.5	-2.2	-75.9	1592.4	10.6	237.8	1840.8	-9.5	235.0	2066.4
Net Financial Assets	315.8		31.2	347.0		38.7	385.7		57.7	443.4		72.9	516.3		50.7	567.0
TOTAL LIABILITIES & NET WORTH	3679.4	161.4	236.9	4077.7	186.6	80.2	4344.5	167.6	85.7	4597.8	190.5	332.2	5120.5	221.7	388.9	5731.2
Addenda:																
Net Saving (balance sheet)		93.0			111.3			118.7			140.8			126.3		
Net Saving (current account)		80.3			111.6			104.3			111.9			109.0		
Capital Gains Dividends		1.4			0.9			0.5			0.2			0.5		
Residual Discrepancy		11.3			-1.2			13.9			28.7			16.8		

Table 1.A.2   Household Sector Capital Accounts (Continued)

	End of Year Value 1976	Cap. Trans. Acct. (1977)	Reval-uation Acct. (1977)	End of Year Value 1977	Cap. Trans. Acct. (1978)	Reval-uation Acct. (1978)	End of Year Value 1978	Cap Trans. Acct. (1979)	Reval-uation Acct. (1979)	End of Year Value 1979	Cap. Trans. Acct. (1980)	Reval-uation Acct. (1980)	End of Year Value 1980
REPRODUCIBLE ASSETS (net current value)	1918.7	112.6	151.2	2182.5	129.7	237.8	2550.0	125.2	161.1	2836.3	83.1	256.8	3176.3
Residential Structures	1134.1	50.6	136.0	1320.6	58.0	207.1	1585.7	55.9	129.5	1771.1	37.2	158.5	1966.8
Gross Stock (book value)	767.5	80.6	−8.5	839.5	93.0	−10.6	921.9	96.8	−12.4	1006.4	83.1	−10.9	1078.6
Plus: Revaluation	895.6		200.3	1095.8		306.0	1401.8		192.7	1594.5		232.2	1826.7
Equals: Gross Stock (current)	1663.0	80.6	191.8	1935.4	93.0	295.4	2323.8	96.8	180.3	2600.8	83.1	221.3	2905.3
Less: Capital Consump. (book)	170.1	14.6	−2.2	182.5	16.0	−2.4	196.1	17.5	−2.7	211.0	19.0	−2.9	227.1
Cap. Consumption Reval.	358.9	15.4	58.0	432.2	19.0	90.7	541.9	23.4	53.5	618.8	26.9	65.8	711.5
Consumer Durables	636.5	50.2	15.6	702.3	56.3	28.8	787.4	52.4	34.6	874.4	31.1	89.7	995.1
Gross Stock (book value)	987.9	178.8	−84.4	1082.3	199.3	−89.8	1191.8	212.3	−96.7	1307.4	211.9	−103.7	1415.5
Plus: Revaluation	221.4		32.8	254.2		53.5	307.7		64.0	371.7		162.7	534.3
Equals: Gross Stock (current)	1209.2	178.8	−51.6	1336.5	199.3	−36.4	1499.4	212.3	−32.7	1679.0	211.9	59.0	1949.9
Less: Capital Consump. (book)	440.7	107.1	−69.8	478.0	117.5	−73.6	521.9	128.7	−77.7	572.8	140.2	−84.4	628.6
Cap. Consumption Reval.	132.0	21.5	2.7	156.3	25.6	8.4	190.2	31.2	10.4	231.8	40.6	53.7	326.1
Inventories	148.2	11.8	−0.4	159.6	15.4	1.8	176.9	16.9	−2.9	190.8	14.9	8.7	214.4
LAND	316.7		42.0	358.8		79.9	438.7		51.8	490.5		92.8	583.3
FIXED CLAIM ASSETS	1429.3	158.7		1588.1	189.4		1777.5	210.8		1988.3	205.4		2193.6
Deposits	1061.3	127.6		1189.0	128.9		1317.9	133.7		1451.6	175.0		1626.6
Currency & checkable dep.	184.6	20.6		205.2	22.3		227.5	22.8		250.3	15.3		265.6
Small time & svgs. deposits	823.7	94.4		918.0	63.2		981.3	60.9		1042.2	80.4		1122.7
Large time deposits	49.3	12.5		61.9	36.4		98.3	15.6		113.9	50.0		163.9
Money market fund shares	3.7	0.2		3.9	6.9		10.8	34.4		45.2	29.2		74.4
Credit Market Instruments	320.1	25.6		345.7	51.8		397.6	69.9		467.4	19.2		486.6
U.S. government securities	144.1	14.1		158.1	25.3		183.4	44.0		227.4	15.5		242.9
Treasury issues	120.2	9.2		129.4	17.7		147.0	22.8		169.8	5.8		175.6
Savings bonds	72.0	4.7		76.8	3.9		80.7	−0.8		79.9	−7.3		72.5
Other treasury	48.2	4.4		52.6	13.8		66.4	23.6		89.9	13.1		103.1
Agency issues	23.9	4.9		28.8	7.6		36.4	21.2		57.6	9.7		67.3
State and local obligations	49.5	−3.6		45.9	1.7		47.6	1.9		49.5	1.8		51.3
Corporate and foreign bonds	41.3	−5.0		36.3	−2.5		33.9	4.8		38.7	1.7		40.4
Mortgages	73.3	10.4		83.6	11.1		94.7	11.6		106.4	7.5		113.9
Open-market paper	12.0	9.7		21.7	16.3		38.0	7.5		45.4	−7.3		38.1
Security Credit	6.3	−1.0		5.3	2.6		7.9	0.6		8.5	4.1		12.6
Other Fixed Claims	41.6	6.4		48.0	6.1		54.1	6.6		60.7	7.1		67.8

EQUITIES HELD	2066.4	3.9	90.2	2160.5	4.5	234.9	2399.9	-10.0	376.2	2766.0	-5.1	520.1	3281.1
Corporate Stock	622.6	-0.1	-31.7	590.8	1.1	26.4	618.3	-13.7	141.3	745.9	-1.5	250.6	995.1
Non-Corp. Non-Farm Equity	644.7	-0.2	87.3	731.8	2.7	122.9	857.4	3.7	112.4	973.5	-1.7	147.7	1119.6
Farm Business Equity	443.2	-7.6	38.4	474.0	-11.5	80.5	543.1	-12.5	86.4	616.9	-14.4	68.8	671.4
Pension & Insur. (cash value)	163.2	11.7	-0.7	174.3	12.2	0.2	186.7	12.5	0.7	199.9	12.4	2.5	214.8
Estates and Trusts	192.8		-3.2	189.6		4.8	194.4		35.4	229.8		50.5	280.3
TOTAL ASSETS	5731.2	275.3	283.4	6289.8	323.6	552.6	7166.0	326.0	589.1	8081.1	283.4	869.7	9234.2
FIXED CLAIM LIABILITIES	862.3	140.5		1002.8	163.9		1166.6	169.6		1336.3	109.3		1445.6
Credit Market Instruments	836.7	138.3		975.0	161.5		1136.5	169.5		1305.9	103.1		1409.0
Home mortgages	540.1	93.0		633.1	107.6		740.6	115.9		856.5	83.8		940.4
Consumer credit	248.6	40.2		288.8	47.6		336.4	46.3		382.7	2.3		385.0
Installment	193.8	36.4		230.2	41.9		272.1	39.2		311.4	1.4		312.8
Other	54.8	3.7		58.6	5.7		64.3	7.1		71.3	0.9		72.2
Bank loans, n.e.c.	14.6	2.8		17.4	2.5		19.9	0.9		20.8	8.0		28.8
Other loans	33.4	2.3		35.7	3.8		39.5	6.4		45.9	8.9		54.8
U.S. gov't. loans	6.5	0.6		7.1	1.2		8.3	1.7		10.0	2.2		12.2
Policy loans	26.9	1.7		28.6	2.6		31.2	4.7		35.9	6.7		42.6
Security Debt	17.2	1.3		18.5	1.3		19.8	-1.2		18.6	5.0		23.7
Other Fixed Claims	8.4	0.9		9.3	1.1		10.3	1.3		11.7	1.2		12.9
NET WORTH	4868.9	134.8	283.4	5287.0	159.8	552.6	5999.3	156.4	589.1	6744.9	174.1	869.7	7788.6
Tangibles	2235.5	112.6	193.2	2541.3	129.7	317.7	2988.6	125.2	213.0	3326.8	83.1	349.6	3759.5
Equities	2066.4	3.9	90.2	2160.5	4.5	234.9	2399.9	-10.0	376.2	2766.0	-5.1	520.1	3281.1
Net Financial Assets	567.0	18.2		585.3	25.6		610.8	41.2		652.0	96.0		748.0
TOTAL LIABILITIES & NET WORTH	5731.2	275.3	283.4	6289.8	323.6	552.6	7166.0	326.0	589.1	8081.1	283.4	869.7	9234.2
Addenda:													
Net Saving (balance sheet)		134.8			159.8			156.4			174.1		
Net Saving (current account)		112.6			120.1			118.6			97.9		
Capital Gains Dividends		0.6			0.7			0.9			1.7		
Residual Discrepancy		21.5			39.0			36.9			74.5		

Reference

Carson, Carol S. 1975. "The History of the United States National Income and Product Accounts." *Review of Income and Wealth*, ser. 21, no. 2 (June).

Comment   Helen Stone Tice

Richard Ruggles's paper consists of three major parts. The first is a history of the United States national income and product accounts (NIPAs) including the various reviews of them since 1947. The second is a discussion of certain avenues of future development of the accounts now being explored at the Bureau of Economic Analysis (BEA) and elsewhere. The last, placed in an Appendix, is a discussion of Ruggles's "transactor approach" to the recording of entries in the accounts as it applies to the treatment of interest and of financial institutions. I shall discuss the paper's treatment of each of these and then mention a few topics to which I wish more attention had been devoted.

Since their introduction in 1947, in what is essentially their present form, the national income and product accounts have undergone four major revisions (1954, 1958, 1965, and 1976); they have produced one major methodological study in 1954 and several minor ones accompanying the various benchmark revisions; and they have been subjected to formal critical reviews on five occasions (National Accounts Review Committee in 1957, the Conference on Research in Income and Wealth in 1955 and 1971, the Creamer Committee in 1977, and the views solicited on the occasion of the fiftieth anniversary of the *Survey of Current Business* in 1971). Ruggles covers all of these with the exception of the Creamer Report; perhaps the latter is too empirical for the sort of systems approach that is clearly the author's intent, and in any case there will be more on this elsewhere in this volume. In addition, there is a brief discussion of the "new" United Nations System of National Accounts (SNA) about which the United States has had reservations since its inception, or at least since its last revision. These developments are discussed fairly and adequately. The author's intent in this section seems to have been to demonstrate, first, that the accounts have changed little since 1947 in any fundamental way; second, that other forms of national economic accounts have been integrated with the NIPA as time has passed; and third, that BEA and its predecessor agencies have acted

Helen Stone Tice is an economist with the Bureau of Economic Analysis.
The views expressed are those of the author and do not necessarily reflect the opinions of the Bureau of Economic Analysis or of any other members of its staff.

responsibly to take account of the suggestions for improvement in the estimates and in their presentation which have been made over the years. By and large it is a more compact treatment of this piece of history than are others covering the same events and, as such, should be useful to those wishing an overview of the accounts and their development.

The subheads under the section "Directions for Future Development" reflect many of the themes which have characterized Ruggles's work in the national accounts over the last two decades. One is a concern with presenting a tidy summary system of accounts as an organizing device for the supporting tables; the summary accounts should highlight important aggregates, be few in number, and be fully articulated. A second is an interest in integrated systems of accounts with easy interfaces between the NIPA and other accounting presentations with which no formal integration has taken place. A third is a concern with the use of microdata sets and their integration into the accounting framework. A final consideration is the usefulness of the accounting system and its way of organizing data for policy analysis and decision making. Most of these themes have recurred since the days of Ruggles and Ruggles's *National Income Accounts and Income Analysis* which introduced a generation of students to the accounts and what could be done with them. They appeared in *The Design of Economic Accounts* and in the paper given at the 1971 Princeton Conference of this organization. Ruggles's formal proposals in the current paper are four in number, but the amplification of the last of these in an Appendix is so extensive as almost to constitute a fifth topic.

The first proposal which Ruggles makes has to do with sectoring. He enunciates two bases for sectoring, namely, the behavioral and decision-making processes underlying the sector's activity, and the types and sources of information available about the transactors to be included there. Hence he purifies the household sector by removing the nonprofit institutions, thereby making the sector conceptually at least a consolidation of the microdata set underlying the work on the income-size distribution. Abandoning his position of 25 years ago when he successfully urged the elimination of the enterprise sector, he reintroduces it and puts the orphaned nonprofit institutions into it. He also recognizes that the enterprise sector will need some further subsectoring if it is to be really usable. Once again, all the data necessary for this redefinition were taken from the existing NIPA.

The second modification which Ruggles proposes has to do with the accommodation of estimates of the value of nonmarket activity and imputations. Ruggles proposes separating the market flows from the imputed ones, again illustrating the proposal with the household sector and again using existing BEA estimates.

The third section of the paper is a discussion of what he calls the transactor approach to the recording of transactions. By this he means that the income flows should appear in NIPA as they would appear in the accounts, of, or be viewed by, the parties actually involved in the transaction. The specific modifications occasioned by the adoption of the transactor approach consist of the transfer of employer contributions for health and welfare from other labor income to business consumption, the transfer of government health benefits from personal to public consumption, the inclusion of mortgage interest and property tax payments by owner occupiers, and the grossing up of insurance and pension premiums, with benefits entering as current or capital transfers. It has been the case for many financial institutions that output is low in the current system because of the netting involved in its measurement. In order to achieve the present BEA definition of income, insurance benefits are netted against premiums, and employer contributions to uninsured pension funds become a component of other labor income, while the benefits paid current retirees go unrecorded. In the business sector of the Ruggles system, value added would be shifted from the nonfinancial to the financial sector, and, in addition, the fact that households no longer offset benefits against their purchases from the finance and insurance sector would increase personal consumption expenditures (PCE) and hence output. In the case of interest, Ruggles proposes that the present group of enterprises treat interest paid as an intermediate purchase and interest received as income; the treatment parallels the current treatment of rent. Continuing this analogy, he creates an interest industry to collect and distribute the interest paid outside the enterprise sector. Interest paid on both consumer and government debt are, I believe, to be considered current purchases of goods and services in Ruggles's system.

The redefined household current account shown in Exhibit 4 differs from the present personal account as a result of the principles already discussed. It now includes the owner occupancy of dwellings, which is no longer an enterprise; it capitalizes consumer durables expenditures; it has nonprofit institutions deconsolidated and removed; it has the distinction between market and imputed transactions made more explicitly; and it embodies the transactor approach with respect to interest, pensions, and insurance. Ruggles's final proposal is the integration of financial transaction accounts and balance sheets with the NIPA. Here he demonstrates, using the household sector as an example, that by judicious recombination of data from the NIPA and the Federal Reserve Board's (FRB) flow-of-funds accounts one can produce a balance sheet with current account net saving being matched, apart from a statistical discrepancy, by that portion of the change in net worth due to transactions. The remainder of the change in net worth is, of course, due to revaluations. Rather than the proliferation of accounts for each sector recommended by international standards, he has only two accounts: a modified current account and the capital account. As I said, an example is given of these accounts for the household sector.

Several comments are in order here. First, I generally agree with the thrust of Ruggles's directions for the development of the accounts. However, it would be nice to see the whole scheme worked out in detail, as I trust we shall in due course, before deciding that it represents an unalloyed blessing. It is entirely possible that the modifications which work so nicely for the household sector will create difficulties elsewhere in the accounts. I am thinking particularly of the new enterprise account with its nonprofit sector, but the proposed treatment of pension funds and other intermediaries may present problems as well. Aside from these doubts, the household sector and the enterprise subsectors I find to be tremendously appealing. The existing personal sector is a repository for all manner of income and private final consumption items, with many internal transactions among the transactors which it contains consolidated out; it is often used, however, as though it did contain only households. The Ruggles households are true households, and this presentation will be much more useful, I think. On the other hand, there is to be a price in terms of the reintroduced enterprise sector whose usefulness is diluted because it now has nonprofit institutions. The accounts, like the nation, need an attic; perhaps we should bite the bullet and create a "junque" sector for things that must be in but do not quite fit anywhere else and do not have as complete a data base to support them. The flow of funds has long had such a transactions category, and it may be time for the NIPA to resort to such a device. To some extent, this will be taken care of by subsectoring, but if the enterprise sector is worth having at all it should be cleaner than it appears it will be in this system.

Second, I thoroughly applaud the emphasis on balance sheets and capital accounts. It has long seemed to me that our thinking about a number of issues—housing, energy, other natural resources, and other aspects of the environment, to name a few—would be much improved if the official statistics on the performance of the economy focused on other concepts in addition to the measure of current production that has served us so long and so well. If the household accounts presented are any indication of what is planned for the rest of the sectors, then, while the Ruggles system may not suffice for the sorts of financial analyses that one may be accustomed to carrying out using the flow of funds, this presentation could indeed make accessible to the NIPA user with little or no experience with financial flows and their analysis a set of information which he might otherwise ignore. The table shown in Exhibit 5 is a bit hard to follow, however, since it is not really self-explanatory, and the text does not offer much guidance here.

Third, while the simplicity of the two accounts per sector system is certainly appealing, it is not, as I have observed, a real substitute for the more detailed flow of funds presentation; the adjustments to the tangibles and the reconciliation between saving from the current account and the change in net worth seem murkier than they perhaps need to be.[1] The presentation, while useful pedagogically, is not terribly compact in relation to the amount of information which must be presented in the business of being a statistical office, and it does not really highlight either outside the context of the movement between balance sheets.

Fourth, the separation of the accounts into market and imputed transactions has much to recommend it. Although, as Ruggles points out, his examples involve only items presently included in BEA's published estimates, this regrouping allows for the inclusion of such other imputations as time and professional ingenuity permit. In addition, it offers the benefit of highlighting the *market economy*, which has a much better underlying data base, whose estimates generally require fewer assumptions, and which can be observed at greater than annual frequency for the most part. This would seem to be a much more useful indicator of current economic activity for business and other economic forecasters to track than GNP as presently defined, with its load of baggage, statistically weak and of indeterminate size, riding the ups and downs of the business cycle. At present the only imputations of any size are those involved in the purchase and use of owner-occupied housing, but the interest imputations are by no means trivial. Imputations have several characteristics which distinguish them from most other classes of estimates. For one thing, they are often based on assumptions whose validity is difficult if not impossible to verify; for another, they typically are based on data which are not reported with the same frequency as is much of the remaining data base; and finally, there are few if any cross-checks available in other reports of the same transactions. Thus, I again find Ruggles's proposal to differentiate between market and nonmarket activity quite congenial. He carries out this proposal with data already in the NIPA, but the framework could serve as well were housepersons' services and other new imputations to be brought into the accounts.

Fifth, as it affects the household account, the transactor approach has the unfortunate effect of fragmenting flows that once were shown all in one place, and there may be some loss in analytical usefulness as a result.[2] Without the rest of the accounts, however, it is not easy to say how severe this loss will be, since the effect of the distribution of former PCE health outlays among household, public, and business consumption cannot really be assessed without seeing the full system of accounts.

Sixth, with respect to the proposed treatment of intermediaries, I am generally sympathetic since I have long felt uncomfortable with the view of the financial sector implied by the traditional approach. I have some reservations, however, about the treatment which is proposed here. Insurance companies do look at underwriting income, and this focus is preserved in the present NIPA system by the net premium definition of output. I wonder, therefore, whether gross premiums are really the preferred measure in this case. Furthermore, while the text speaks of considering the casualty payments as capital transfers, I look in vain for such an entry or even a space for such an entry in the capital account presented. While it would be nice to incorporate the payments to current retirees into the accounts as current income, the proposed treatment would appear to have no means for accommodating the equities in future benefits represented by the assets of pension funds. I am sure that the valuation placed on future pension benefits by the recipients of employer contributions to these funds is unknown, but I do not believe that people make no allowance for such income streams in their current financial planning.

Finally, grossing up the interest flows has much to recommend it, so long as interest payments and receipts do not disappear from the accounts in some identifiable form. But are not dividends susceptible to the same treatment? In particular, the dividend income of pension funds presently contributes a large negative amount to both aggregate profits and the profits of financial institutions. The treatment of enterprise interest payments does not seem unreasonable at first sight, though the saving in the complexity of the system from the elimination of the banking imputation is offset by the need to create the interest sector; and the new treatment has some implications for the measurement of output in nonfinancial enterprises which many would consider unfortunate, to say the least. The treatment of consumer and government interest which he proposes—I think—bothers me because of the indeterminacy of income outside the business sector. However, the capitalization of automobiles and other consumer durables which he proposes would suggest a treatment not unlike that given owner-occupied housing. One might also invoke capital account considerations in the case of interest on the public debt, since the securities on which this interest is paid are freely substitutable for business issues in investors' portfolios. I think that these questions cannot be adequately resolved except in the context of the complete system, and I urge the author to develop his proposal more fully.

These are my major comments on what the paper contains. There are, however, a number of areas which could have been explored on this occasion but which the author chose to treat only in passing or not at all. I bring them up only to invite discussion. One of these is the matter of the relation between the underlying information system and the design of the accounts. This theme runs implicitly throughout the discussion of sectors as aggregations of the underlying microdata set, the discussion of the transactor approach to the recording of transactions, the interest in defining a pure household sector and some homogeneous subsectors of the business sector, etc. We have traditionally modified observed transactor records to fit a national accounting system constructed around the definitions of national income and national product. Ruggles's system goes more than a little way toward viewing the accounts as an organizing device for the data base. In particular, the "transactor" approach if carried to its logical conclusion could lead to a set of aggregates whose definitions, built up from below so to speak, are rather different from those now commonly in use. To cite one example, the view of interest as a payment for a service rather than a portion of the return to capital cannot help but affect the production account. The transactor approach would appear to imply a rather different concept of output from what we are used to since the interest treatment implies a business income which includes investment gains as well as operating income, and underwriting is no longer the sole focus of insurance companies in the accounts. I wish that Ruggles had treated these implications more explicitly.

I also wish that more attention had been devoted to some of the issues from the past which still remain unresolved. BEA's performance with respect to meeting the requests of users and critics for improved concepts, data, and procedures has been good, though there are those who may have thought it glacial at times. There are still, however, many areas on which there was never a clear victory for one side or the other but merely an agreement to table further discussion. One obvious example is the question of whether the primary or at least a primary aggregate should be a welfare measure. Another is the extent to which capital gains are a part of income which should be recognized in the accounts. A third might be the location of the boundary of production beyond the market. One can understand the author's reluctance to disturb old bones, but it is entirely possible that one would give a different answer today if asked to decide on certain matters than the answers given several decades ago. The establishment of BEA's new Environmental and Nonmarket Economics Division occurred when we recognized the need to supplement GNP for welfare purposes.

There is one Pandora's box which Ruggles with great wisdom chose not to open. I refer to the issue of the proper focus of the accounts. There has long been a recognition that the GNP is not the only measure which should be considered by the architects of domestic economic policy and their critics. The Princeton conference in 1971 considered extensions of the accounts in the field of welfare measurement; Eisner would wish to extend the accounts in addition to cover capital gains and losses; and he, Kendrick, and Juster would wish to add many more imputations to conventional measures of income and production.

Ruggles recognizes this need, as both his emphasis on the capital accounts and his restructuring of the current account to make room for more imputations indicate. He does not go so far as to suggest that perhaps a new primary aggregate is required, or that any grand restructuring of the accounting system is called for. This is probably wise, and, indeed, this whole paper is a model of tact and diplomacy in an area where there is still substantial disagreement. But while I commend Ruggles's diplomacy and low profile, it is an unfortunate fact of life that the way in which data are organized and presented determine the way in which they will be used by others. The creator of a table has some particular analytical cast of mind which he naturally hopes will be shared by others, and all too often users oblige him if only through inertia. However, in one area at least, BEA is being called upon to make some redefinitions; I refer to some recent criticisms that our interest and profits numbers are incorrectly measured in part because of our failure to take account of the effect of inflation on the real cost of principal repayment. If the critics are correct and our flows of returns to capital are misstated, then perhaps the accounts need more than just a tire patch at this juncture.

What Ruggles's scheme would suggest that we do is point analysts in the direction of the capital account as well as the current account; what a more ambitious prescription would have called for is a reopening of the whole question of the proper definition of income as it was left 30 years ago. The Ruggles system would allow a lot of experimentation, however, while preserving our familiar NIPA aggregates; indeed, had we had the revaluation accounts he proposes, the whole interest and profit controversy might never have arisen. The Ruggles system also has room to allow for a similar exploratory process in welfare measurement.

In closing, I would like to add that, although the author chose to hide some of the more radical notions in a deceptively smooth concoction, there is a lot to be thought about in this paper. I hope that Ruggles will forgive me for pointing out the extent to which he has inserted the camel's nose into the tent with these seemingly modest proposals.

Notes

1. This was much more of a problem in the earlier version of the paper; the present table is considerably cleaner.

2. Again, this was much more of a problem in the original version of the paper which distinguished between market and imputed taxes as well.

References

Juster, F. Thomas. 1973. A framework for the measurement of economic and social performance. In Milton Moss, ed., *The measurement of economic and social performance*, pp. 25–84. New York: Columbia University Press for the National Bureau of Economic Research.

Ruggles, Nancy D., and Ruggles, Richard. 1970. *The design of economic accounts*. New York: Columbia University Press for the National Bureau of Economic Research.

Ruggles, Richard, and Ruggles, Nancy D. 1956. *National income accounts and national income analysis*. 2d ed. New York: McGraw-Hill, 1956.

Ruggles, Richard, and Ruggles, Nancy D. 1973. A proposal for a system of economic and social accounts. In Milton Moss, ed., *The measurement of economic and social performance*, pp. 111–53. New York: Columbia University Press for the National Bureau of Economic Research.

Comment   John A. Gorman

Ruggles proposes to replace the treatment of business interest as a factor cost by treatment as a purchased service. In addition to transferring output from the nonfinancial industries to the financial industries, this proposal would remove the "lid" rule from the definition of output. The lid rule is that profits form a lid on business interest payments, so that payment of interest does not necessarily result in output. Thus, if interest paid by business changes without a similar change in the value of business production, there will be an offsetting change in profits, which will ensure that the sum of interest, profits, and other incomes originating in business correctly measures the contribution to production originating in the business sector.

We have applied the lid rule to exclude the public utility "allowance for funds used during construction" from our measures of investment, output, and profits for communication and electric and gas utilities. I think Ruggles should deal with the question of whether removing the lid rule for interest has implications for our measurement of investment, output, and profits in these industries. The amounts involved are not trivial; had the allowance for funds used during construction been included in the accounts for 1977; electric and gas utility investment would have been raised 10%, and gross product originating would have been increased 5%. Inclusion of the allowance for funds used during construction would have increased profits plus capital consumption allowances in the industry by 13%.

A second consequence of shifting from a factor cost treatment to a purchased service treatment of interest is that interest would be treated like rent: the amount of output represented by interest would be shown as originating in the lending industry rather than the borrowing industry. It should be noted that this treatment gives opposite results from the treatment of capital leases promulgated by the Financial Accounting Standards Board (FASB) which, if implemented in the national income and product accounts, would shift output from the industry owning the

John A. Gorman is assistant chief, National Income and Wealth Division, Bureau of Economic Analysis.

asset to the industry renting the asset. I am not recommending the adoption of the FASB proposal but am suggesting Ruggles might want to review his proposed treatment of interest in the light of the FASB proposal for rent.

2 Quality Adjustment in the Producer Price Indexes

John F. Early and James H. Sinclair

The Producer Price Indexes (PPI) (formerly called Wholesale Price Indexes) measure price change at the primary market level. They refer to prices received by mines, manufacturers, farmers, importers, and electric utilities for commodities at all stages of processing—crude, intermediate (or semifinished), and finished. The objective of the price indexes is to measure pure price change for a fixed production mix. In practice, the set of commodities cannot remain unchanged. Some commodities are discontinued. Others are modified. And new commodities are added to make the price set more representative of the current economy.

When one variety of a commodity is discontinued in the index and replaced with another variety, the pure theoretical structure of the index is violated. These substitutions are necessary, however, and it is the task of the index maker to make substitutions in a way that will distort as little as possible the measure of pure price change. This process of calculating the index across the discontinuity which results from substitution is usually called quality adjustment. The purposes of this paper are to (1) provide the conceptual background on the way quality adjustment is made in the PPI, (2) describe the methods currently used for quality adjustment, (3) analyze the practical results of the application of these methods, (4) explore other methods that may be available for quality adjustment, and (5) note some of the major improvements that have begun for these indexes.

2.1 The Conceptual Background

We do not propose to determine here what the proper theoretical treatment of quality change in the PPI is. That task is currently in process.

John F. Early is the former assistant commissioner for industrial prices, Division of Industrial Prices and Price Indexes, Bureau of Labor Statistics. James H. Sinclair is a senior economist within the Division of Industrial Prices and Price Indexes, Bureau of Labor Statistics.

We seek in this section to document the logic and model that underlie the current practice. The PPIs have suffered, to a degree, from the lack of a clear conceptual definition. They can be conceived as output price indexes from the farms, mines, and factories of the U.S. economy. They may also be viewed as input price indexes to personal consumption at the earliest stages of distribution. The current revision efforts will put an end to that confusion, but the focus here is on the existing data.

Since there are different implications for quality adjustment in these two concepts, the result has been a hybridized methodology for handling quality adjustment. In general, quality adjustment consists of three steps. The first is identifying the physical changes in the item being priced. The second is characterizing each change as an improvement, deterioration, or no change in quality. The third is evaluating each change in dollar terms. In the second step, each change is characterized according to its expected impact on consumer utility (for consumer goods) or producer productivity (for capital equipment). In the third, the differences in cost of production are used to value the changes. It is then argued that in equilibrium the change in production costs and the change in user utility will be equal. If production costs were lower than the price, then other producers would enter the market and drive the price down until it reached the level of cost. If production costs were higher than the price the user was willing to pay, then production of the change would cease.

An interesting anomaly occurs in this methodology when an improvement is made in a product at a lower cost. Quite clearly one cannot give an improvement a negative value. In such cases, the value of the quality change is assumed to be zero.

There has been one major departure from this standard methodology. Antipollution devices that are required by law have been treated per se as quality improvements, even though their previous availability as options may have demonstrated no significant value being placed on them by users. This decision was reached by the special Interagency Committee on the Treatment of Anti-Pollution Devices in Price and Quantity Indexes. The persuasive argument for them was that, by virtue of the government requirement for the device, it was being valued by fiat for the population as a whole at its cost of production.

2.2 Quality Adjustment Procedures

In calculating the change in production costs between two varieties of a product, companies are asked to supply for each change cost data which reflect the differences in the amounts and kinds of labor and material inputs used in the production of the two. The difference in cost should be based on the cost differences in inputs under the cost structure and technological regimen that existed at the time of the introduction of the new variety. The company's standard markup for return to investors and entrepreneurship is also included.

In some cases a new feature is added to an item when that feature has previously been available as an option. The value of such a feature is calculated as the weighted average of the producer's cost and the market price of the option. The market price is weighted by the installation rate of the option, and the producer's costs is weighted by the remainder.

Of course, not all physical changes are quality changes. Changes which are not related to the ability of the component or the item as a whole to perform its function better are not considered quality changes. In particular, changes for the sake of style, such as changes to automobile grill designs, are not considered to be quality changes.

In addition to the producer's cost procedures, two other methods are widely used for dealing with quality changes. The first is the link. In this method the new variety is brought into the index showing no price change from the previous month. The implication of the link procedure is that all the difference in price between the two varieties is due to quality change. It is used when producer-cost data are not available and there are substantial quality differences between the two varieties. It is also used when the changes between the two varieties are so great that a feature-by-feature cost comparison is either impossible or likely to be highly inaccurate. The link procedure, therefore, becomes the tool for introducing totally new products.

The second alternative to the producer-cost procedure is the direct comparison. In this procedure, the prices of the two varieties are directly compared, that is, the price change is equal to the difference between the observed prices. The implicit assumption is that the difference in quality between the two is zero. This method is used when producer cost data are not available for small physical changes.

There is a fourth method which could theoretically yield very good results. This is the overlap method. In this method, both varieties are priced in the same time period. The difference in the market price between the two can then be taken as the valuation of the quality difference. This method works well only if there is a previously stable relationship between the two prices. Normally, substitutions occur between subsequent models or versions of the same item. If any of the older models are still being sold, it is frequently at a discounted clearance price which distorts the market valuation of the quality change. (The reverse case of a premium for the discontinued model may also occur.) No identifiable cases of this procedure were discovered in the data examined later in this paper.

We can express the three procedures used for quality adjustment in symbolic notations as follows:

Let P_t = the price of the new variety at month t, P_{t-1} = the price of the old variety at month $t-1$, L_{t-1} = the link price of the new variety, Q_t = producer cost of the quality changes between the two varieties.

The ratio $P_t/(L_{t-1})$ is the relationship which is used in the calculation of the price index for month t. It is in the derivation of L_{t-1} that the three procedures differ from each other as follows: producer-cost method, $L_{t-1} = P_{t-1} + Q_t$; link method, $L_{t-1} = P_t$; direct comparison method, $L_{t-1} = P_{t-1}$.

It should be noted that, since Q_t is valued in dollars at time t, the formula for the producer-cost method will overstate the link price during a period of rising prices. Since we want to set $P_t(L_{t-1}) = (P_t - Q_t)(P_{t-1})$, the proper expression for the producer-cost method would be:

$$L_{t-1} = \frac{P_t}{(P_t - Q_t)} P_{t-1}.$$

This formula adjusts the $t-1$ price by the ratio of quality change rather than the dollar value. The improved formula is now being used in the PPIs, but for the period under study the first formula was used.

2.3 Results of Quality Adjustment in the PPI

During 1976 the Bureau of Labor Statistics (BLS) obtained more than 100,000 observations for the monthly calculation of the PPI. We have identified all cases of product substitution in the PPIs during 1976. There were 455 such cases, or slightly less than one-half of 1% of the total number of price observations, during the year. The following analysis is based on that set of substitutions. Further analysis is also presented for a subset of commodities covering the time span 1970–76.

In analyzing the results of the different methods, we have used the following two measures: pure price change (or price change), $(P_t/L_{t-1}-1) \times 100$; quality change, $(L_{t-1}/P_{t-1}-1) \times 100$.

In the producer's cost methodology, the observed percentage change in prices is factored into both a pure price change and a quality component. In the case of links to show no change, the pure price change is zero and the observed price change is implicitly set equal to the quality change. In the direct comparison cases the observed and pure price changes are equal and the quality change is zero. Tables 2.1–2.5 and figure 2.1 summarize the results of quality adjustment in 1976.

2.3.1 1976 Quality Adjustment Classifications

Out of the 108,756 price observations used in the PPI in 1976, there were 455 quality adjustments using one of the three quality adjustment methodologies. As table 2.1 shows, 129 were evaluated by producer-cost changes (28% of all quality adjustment in 1976), 184 were links to show no price change (40% of 1976 quality adjustments), and 142 were direct comparisons (31% of 1976 quality adjustments). Column 5 of table 2.1 shows quality adjustments of each PPI group as a percentage of total prices reported for that group in 1976. The producer cost methodology is perhaps the most interesting from a research point of view, since it incorporates a combination of both price and quality changes. Frequency distributions of quality and price changes by size of change are listed in tables 2.2 and 2.3, respectively. By glancing at table 2.1, one can see that the pattern of adjustments is not uniform among commodity groups. PPI group 14 (transportation equipment) stands out as having a large proportion of producer-cost observations (68%). This is partly a function of greater BLS emphasis in these industries as well as the reporters' willingness to provide cost breakouts on items that affect the performance or physical characteristics of these commodities.

Column 5 in table 2.1 reflects the number of annual quality adjustments as a percentage of all the prices reported to BLS for each commodity group during 1976. Four-tenths of 1% of these reported prices required some type of quality adjustment before they were used in calculation of the Producer Price Index. The high relative frequency of quality adjustments in transportation equipment can be traced to the annual model changes for automobiles and, to a lesser extent, for trucks. High relative frequencies for household durables reflect frequent model changes in appliances, while frequent style and construction changes in footwear account for the high rate among leather products. On the other hand, farm products, processed foods, fuels, and nonmetallic minerals are mostly highly homogeneous primary products that rarely, if ever, undergo any measurable quality shift.

The great majority of producer-cost quality adjustments fell in the 0%–10% range, with a few extreme quality adjustments in PPI groups 10, 11, and 12. Perhaps a more meaningful analysis involves a consideration of the direction of quality and price changes under the producer-cost methodology. In figure 2.1, all points that deviate from both the vertical and horizontal axes are producer-cost estimates of quality adjustments. (In fig. 2.1, 19% of all cases lie beyond the scale.)

It is apparent that the majority of changes occur in the price and quality increase quadrant ($+ +$). The price and quality decrease quadrant ($- -$) had the fewest (five) number of observations. The price decrease and quality increase quadrant ($- +$), that is, a better product with a pure price decrease, had 11 observations. Most of these cases either include an addition of the product or are an increase in the size or quantity.

On the other hand, the effects of price increase with quality decrease show up in 34 observations. Due to their large number they will not be listed individually. Out of the 39 observations, 18% were in group 11 (machinery and equipment), 13% in group 14 (transportation equip-

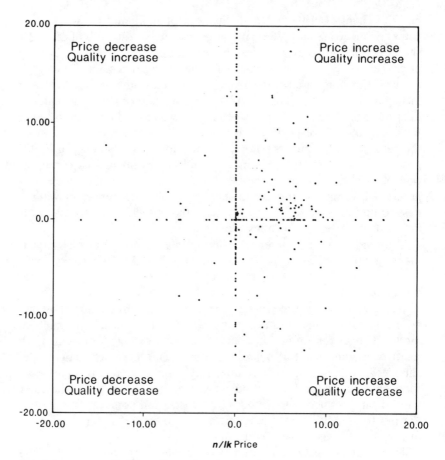

Fig. 2.1   Quality adjustment plot (vertical axis = all price change due to quality; other observations = change due to price and quality; horizontal axis = direct comparison = only price).

ment), and 6% in group 10 (metals and metal products). There were no extraordinary reasons for the producer-cost estimates of quality decline with price increase only that less was offered at a higher price (e.g., more expensive, smaller beer bottles, and thinner gauged, higher priced copper pipes).

Within the link-to-show-no-price-change area, the greatest number occurred in machinery and equipment (PPI group 11), furniture and household durables (PPI group 12), and metals and metal products (PPI group 10).

Table 2.4 breaks out the PPI classifications into negative and positive magnitudes of link-to-show-no-change quality adjustments. A little less than half of the link observations occurred in the ± 0%–9.9% range, but there was a considerable number of large price changes in the machinery and equipment section. Since on average this group is made up of very expensive commodities, one would think that the change in quality as a proportion of the absolute price change would be relatively small. As evidenced by table 2.4, there were 34 cases of quality change that were 30% or higher, some of them as large as 60%–80%. Changes this large almost inevitably are handled with the link-to-show-no-change technique.

The direct comparisons were fairly significant, accounting for 31% of all 1976 quality adjustments. It should be remembered that direct comparisons, by definition, reflect only price changes. Although quality changes may be associated with these price changes, no allowance is made for them because they cannot be identified explicitly. On average, these adjustments usually reflect "minor" specification changes, but there are 15 observations in table 2.5 that represent price changes above 20%, and two that are above 100%. Such large price changes at least suggest that they may include some quality change. As table 2.1 shows, PPI groups 10, 11, and 12 accounted for the major share of direct comparisons in 1976. These same three groups accounted for a similar share of the links. In PPI group 3 (textile products and apparel), most of the changes in specifications have resulted in direct comparisons. For these products the ability of BLS to obtain and use producer-cost adjustments for quality change has been limited.

Another point about table 2.5 to consider is that even the large number of zero price changes may be a result of either the proper handling of small specification changes or a price that is reported as unchanged that is really masking some sort of quality change. The observations under analysis in this paper are the results of changes in the detailed specifications of products. A decrease in quality could be masked by a seller offering a lower quality good at the same price. Conversely, quality improvements not matched with a price increase would tend to be hidden. The machinery group includes cases of this type embodying technological advances at lower costs. By way of contrast, the zero price changes in other groups, such as textiles, apparel, and leather, reflect style changes for the most part. There may have been a change in the detailed specification, but since the BLS procedure is to treat most style changes as not being quality changes, these changes were directly compared.

During 1976, less than one-half of 1% of the observed prices represented specification changes. Since price changes occur in less than one-third of the observations and since price change and specification change frequently occur together, the effect of quality adjustment is probably somewhat larger than this frequency alone might suggest. Nevertheless, the effects of the quality adjustment methodology are not likely to be very large in the short run. Even though the data shown in this section may seem low at first glance, the small number is consistent with a number of features of the index: (1) the large number of crude materials (cattle, natural gas, iron ore, etc.) do not undergo specification change, (2) capital equipment models change very infrequently—often going several years without change, (3) the current BLS practice of pricing volume sellers usually means that the items least likely to be dropped or radically changed are included in the index.

The exclusive use of the link-to-show-no-change methodology would clearly impart a downward bias to the price index. Similarly, the exclusive use of the direct comparison methodology would impart an upward bias. Since neither method predominates and since the size distribution of each is generally consistent with the assumptions on which it is based, these data provide no clue to the direction of any quality adjustment bias in the indexes.

2.3.2   1970–76 Quality Adjustment Classifications for 10 Selected Commodity Groups

This section focuses on changes over time in quality adjustment techniques used in the PPI. Ten specific groups of commodities were selected at the PPI subproduct (six-digit) level for the time-series study. They were selected after looking at a frequency distribution of the three types of quality changes for all PPI groups for 1976. Care was taken to incorporate each type of quality adjustment and several different commodities to see if the same distribution observed in 1976 held for earlier years. Because of time constraints and the difficulty of obtaining the original pricing forms, the time period under investigation was limited to the years from 1970 to 1976. Some data were missing for 1970 and 1974, which may result in an undercount of direct comparisons for those years.

Table 2.6 depicts the breakdown of the types of quality changes by specific years and the total number of prices reported for the same period. Even though the number of reported prices remained relatively stable for these groups over the seven-year period, the number of quality adjustments generally increased. It would certainly be unlikely that the number of actual product changes in the economy increased so greatly during the period, although the expanding government requirements for additional health, safety, and environmental design changes may have played a role. Some of the increased quality adjustment can be attributed to the greater resources that became available to the BLS program during these years; these were used in part to update and revise the items priced for the indexes. There is no clear evidence of either business cycle or price control effects on the frequency of substitution. Nor is there a clear trend in the relative use of each of the methods of adjustment.

Table 2.7 provides a summary of each of the 10 selected groups for the years 1970–76. Each of the three methods was used for quality adjustments within each of eight of the 10 groups. The method selected was usually the result of the type of change and the availability of data.

Women's footwear (PPI code 043201) is a commodity with frequent model changes. Fashion tends to dictate both the style and materials used in producing such goods. Quite often the new models are so radically different from previous models that comparisons have not been feasible. Most price changes associated with style changes in this group were also accompanied by quality change, so most of the quality adjustments in this group have been handled by a link-to-show-no-price-change, which is not entirely consistent with the general policy of not allowing quality adjustments for style changes. The overall frequency of quality change in this area is much lower than might be expected, since most of the shoes priced are very standard items not subject to style change. Even the more fashionable items are fixed as to material and method of construction.

During the 1972–75 period many changes took place in farm harvesting machinery (PPI code 111206) to meet federally mandated Occupational Safety and Health Administration (OSHA) requirements. A link-to-show-no-price-change was generally used by BLS for significant (i.e., large cost) changes of this type; most others were treated using the producer-cost methods. In PPI group 14 (transportation equipment), most legally required changes were valued at producer cost.

In PPI group 123101 (soft surface floor coverings), the lack of producer cost information and the dissimilarity between old and replacement models caused a large number of links. New carpets, with different blends, pile depth, etc., were introduced replacing discontinued carpets. Since it is difficult to make quality adjustments for such products, BLS resorted to the large number of links-to-show-no-price-change.

The transportation area (PPI group 141101, passenger cars; and 141102, motor trucks) quality adjustments were of the producer-cost variety. The isolated direct comparison cases were due to the lack of quality change information (generally imports of trucks produced by some individual companies). When a link-to-show-no-price-change occurred in passenger cars or motor trucks, it occurred because a brand new or radically altered model was introduced in the index.

Tables 2.8–2.10 contain frequency distributions by magnitude for each type of quality adjustment. The producer-cost quality adjustments were generally in the 0%–20% range, with the exception of PPI code 101501 (gray iron castings) of which four cases were in the 30% or higher category. Links-to-show-no-change, contained in table 2.9, were more dispersed across all percentage change categories, most notably among soft surface floor coverings. Direct comparisons showed up primarily in the 0%–10% range, with the exception of PPI code 114901 (valves and fittings).

2.4   Regression Techniques for Quality Adjustment of Crane Prices

There is a substantial and growing body of literature on the use of regression techniques to estimate the value of quality changes (Griliches 1971; Triplett 1971, 1975). The term "hedonic" is normally used in reference to this technique but carries no special implication for the theory behind its use. It is not the intention here to provide any special discussion of the technique. The results of our application of the technique to construction cranes will be reported as an example of how independent checks can be made on the quality adjustment in the indexes. Some discussion of the errors in hedonic estimates is provided.

The regression or hedonic technique of quality adjustment begins by transferring the analytical focus from the priced item as a single entity to the item as a collection of characteristics. Thus the price of an individual item (p) is viewed as being a function of the prices for each of its n characteristics (x_k). The x_k variables are either nominal dummy variables or continuous variables, such as physical performance characteristics. Each unit of each characteristic has an implicit price (b_k) associated with it. In linear form this becomes $p = b_o + b_1 x_1 + b_2 x_2 + \ldots b_n x_n$. The hedonic approach uses regression techniques to estimate the implicit characteristic prices of an item from the observed values for the price and characteristics of the item.

Most hedonic studies have used the data from which their regressions were estimated to then estimate a price index adjusted for quality change. In this study we have followed Triplett and McDonald (1977) and estimated the regression coefficients from a large, independent source of data, and then used the regression coefficients to quality adjust the actual prices used in calculating the corresponding PPIs. This approach permits one to identify the impact of the hedonic adjustment technique as compared to the standard methodology without statistical interference from the use of a different sample, and possibly even a different universe for estimating the index.

Construction cranes (hydraulic, crawler, and truck-mounted) were selected for this study because (1) relatively little work has been done in the capital goods area, (2) this is an important part of the PPI structure, (3) enough substitutions occurred over the 1971–77 period to make the effort fruitful, and (4) a good data source was available from which to estimate the regression coefficients.

2.4.1   Data Source

Since the PPI data were limited in the number of available models, the Equipment Guide Book Company "Green Guide" was used as the source of data to estimate the hedonic equation. This price book is widely used in the construction equipment industry. The Green Guide provides prices and summary specifications for a 10-year period. The prices are new manufacturers' list prices, f.o.b. factory, the same type used in the PPI for this product. Cranes are generally sold at list price with no discounts applicable. The same company produces specification data books that give detailed information on every crane produced. These data are in effect reproductions of manufacturers' specification sheets providing information on lifting capacities, overall dimensions, and performance capabilities.

The next task was to select the variables which might be price determining and to compile a cross-section data base that divided cranes into three distinct groups: hydraulic, crawler, and truck cranes. Initially it was thought these three divisions were homogeneous, but further along in the study hydraulic cranes were divided into self-propelled and carrier-mounted because of their heterogeneous nature. Care was taken in the compilation of the independent variables so there would be no proliferation of variables which potentially could cause double counting in the determination of quality characteristics, that is, those that are likely to be highly correlated with each other.

Theory is of no help in determining the best functional form for the regression equation. A simple criterion was used in which the proper functional form would be the one which maximizes the explanatory power of the regression equation (i.e., minimizes the unexplained variance or the residuals) while still satisfying the assumptions of the ordinary least-squares estimating procedure.

2.4.2 Determination of the Independent Variables

The crane characteristics used in the regression equation (independent variables) included both performance (e.g., lifting capacity and lifting speed) and dimensional (e.g., crane weight, length, and width) types. A large list of potential explanatory variables was compiled initially. A list of these variables, for each type of crane, can be seen in tables 2.11–2.13. All characteristics listed were regressed against the prices (and natural log of prices) for each crane.

Probably the most challenging data base, with reference to problems encountered, was that for hydraulic cranes. The dimensional characteristics (e.g., weight, height, length, width, etc.) were all insignificant, which means either they were not price determining or that their effect was included in the performance characteristics. The first problem with performance characteristics dealt with the choice of a lifting capacity characteristic for use in the equation: retracted or extended. When both characteristics were included in the equation the signs of the regression coefficients between boom extended and retracted lifting capacity were opposite. This problem is to be expected when two variables express the same function. The interrelationship (multicollinearity) was borne out by the simple correlation coefficients (see table 2.14). Lifting capacity (both retracted and extended, nos. 3 and 6, respectively, in table 2.14) seemed to be highly correlated with most of the other independent variables as well as with each other. The retracted boom lifting capacity variable explained approximately 97% of the variability in the dependent variable price. This was greater than the extended lifting capacity variable or any other independent variable.

The statistics on how much a crane can lift is a function, basically, of three parameters: radius (the number of feet the boom is extended from the center of rotation), angle, and height. The parameters were couched, however, in terms of safety standards applied by a trade association: the Power Crane Shovel Association (PCSA). The lifting capacity of an extended boom was expressed at a wide variety of radius, angle, and height values among the cranes. The retracted lifting capacity was always expressed with a constant value of radius or angle across all cranes.

Because the retracted lifting capacity variable provided both a more consistent measure and greater explanatory power, it was used in the equations.

Hydraulic cranes have a functional performance feature that is unique and differs from the other two data sets. Torque or horsepower mechanically drives a winch that lifts an object in crawler and truck cranes. However, hydraulic cranes lift an object from a position driven by hydraulic pressure derived from the horsepower of the engine. The hydraulic pump horsepower is more indicative of what the crane can lift than the engine horsepower. Consequently, a hydraulic pump horsepower variable was created to explain this performance function. Pump hydraulic horsepower is basically a function of the gallons per minute of hydraulic fluid that flows through the hydraulic lines, the pounds per square inch of fluid, and a horsepower constant. It turned out, however, to have low explanatory power.

One other problem encountered was that, although two cranes produced by one company had identical prices, one of the cranes had a one-ton greater lifting capacity. The problem seemed to be associated only with hydraulic cranes and was isolated. The company was contacted for an explanation, and its reply was that when there is so small a change in lifting capacity the only change required is an increase in the counterweight. If this were the case, the lifting capacity regression coefficient should be very small; in fact the exact opposite was true. Most other companies indicated, however, that even a small increase in lifting capacity could entail a change in the structure of the boom either by changing the gauge of the steel, by increasing the incidence of double welds, by adding more cross members, or by having stronger joint connections. Because this was an isolated case and the sample of hydraulic cranes was large (92 before it was further divided into carrier-mounted and self-propelled), its influence on the regression coefficients was probably minimal. However, this example does illustrate clearly that individual transactions may not conform to a rational model.

2.4.3 Estimating the Characteristic Price Equation

Cross-section regressions were run on all four data sets (self-propelled and carrier-mounted hydraulic cranes, truck cranes, and crawler cranes) using prices for 1976. The results can be seen in tables 2.15–2.18 for the final functional form in each case. It is possible that some of the price variation may be due to real or perceived differences among companies. These company effects were checked for each equation. First, company influences were investigated by inspecting the plot of regression residuals for each company. There were several marked differences in each data set that suggested one or two companies had consistently higher or lower prices (even though each crane had essentially the same characteristics) relative to the other companies in each data set. A more explicit investigation was needed to measure the "unexplained" company effects; consequently dummy variables were introduced into the regression equation for each company. When the regression coefficients were estimated, a Chow Test was administered to test the company effects against the previously selected characteristic coefficients (e.g., lifting capacity, horsepower, etc.). The F-ratio for crawler and truck cranes was greater than the F-critical ratio at .01; therefore, the regressions for crawler and truck cranes include the company effects. The significant company variables may have actually captured the effects of unmeasured characteristics such as durability of service. They may also have captured a type of brand identification effect. Since substitutions in the PPI are not made across companies, these variables will not affect directly the price index to be estimated using these equations. However, the magnitude of the other coefficients are changed as a result of introducing the dummies, and, therefore, the inclusion of these variables does not have an effect.

2.4.4 Selecting Functional Form

The best functional form was identified using the Box-Cox technique which standardizes the sum of squared residuals between the linear and log forms (Zarembka 1974). The linear form used price as the dependent variable; the semi-log used the natural logarithm of price as the dependent variable, and the double-log used the log of both the price and the independent variables, except the dummies, which remained linear. To determine the optimal functional form, the linear sum of squared residuals was standardized and compared to the unexplained variance of the log forms using the following standardization formula:

$$(1) \qquad c = \exp\left(\frac{-\Sigma \log Y_i}{n}\right),$$

(1.1) $(c^2) \cdot (\Sigma e_i^2 \text{ linear}) = \text{standardized residuals.}$

Also, to test for a significant difference between the three functional forms investigated (linear, semi-log, double-log), an ordinary χ^2 likelihood ratio test was used: the functional forms were significantly different from each other in all cases.

(1.2) $$\chi^2 = \frac{n}{2} \left| \ln \frac{c^2 \, \Sigma ei \text{ linear}}{\Sigma ei \text{ semi-log or double-log}} \right| .$$

As can be seen in table 2.19, the functional forms with their respective unexplained variance is presented. With the exception of self-propelled hydraulic cranes, in which the linear functional form was the most appropriate, the double-log was the functional form with the lowest sum of squared residuals after transformation for all the data sets.

2.4.5   Hedonic Quality Adjusted Price Indexes

The quality adjusted price changes for the substitutions in the crane indexes (point estimates) were calculated using the implicit prices as estimates of the specific characteristics of each of the four types of cranes. Quality adjusted price changes and confidence intervals to measure the degree of statistical error were calculated for each functional form (linear, semi-log, and log-log) in order to analyze the effect on the choice of functional form on the actual quality adjusted price changes. Only the best functional form was used to reestimate the price index. Since the coefficients for this project were based on 1976 observations, quality adjustments using the linear form for years other than 1976 must be adjusted by a price relative to correct for price changes from the data base period 1976. The coefficients for the other cases were expressed in percentage terms (log-log), therefore, no adjustment had to be made. The formula for the linear estimation of the quality adjusted link price is rather straightforward:

(2) $$\hat{P}_j = P_i + \sum_{k=1}^{n} \hat{b}_k \cdot \Delta x_k,$$

where $\hat{P}_j$ = quality adjusted link price for model j; P_i = previous month base price for model i; $\hat{b}_k$ = regression coefficients of characteristics k that changed in the commodity specification; $\Delta x_k = (x_{jk} - x_{ik})$, characteristic change from the old to the new model; and n = number of characteristics in the equation.

The confidence intervals for the estimated quality changes are:

(2.1) $$\hat{P}_{i \pm t_{\alpha/2}} \cdot \sqrt{S^2 \Delta x' (x'x)^{-1} \Delta x} \; ,$$

where S^2 = variance of regression equation, $x'x$ = cross product of observation matrix, $\hat{p}_j$ = quality adjusted price, $t_{\alpha/2}$ = Student's

t-statistic for a two-tailed distribution at the α confidence interval, and Δx = vector of characteristic changes from the old model to the new model.

When only one characteristic changes, (2.1) reduces to:

(2.2) $\hat{P}_{j \pm t_{\alpha/2}} \cdot S_{b_k} \cdot x_k$,

where S_{b_k} = standard error of the regression coefficient for characteristic in question.

However, when one goes from a linear distribution to a log-normal distribution, the expected value of the exponent is not the same as the exponent of the expected value; therefore, a correction factor must be used. For both the semi-log and double-log equations, the formula for the quality adjusted link price is:

(3) $\hat{P}_j = P_i \exp\left(\sum_k z_k b_k - 1/2 \, S^2 \, z'(x'x)^{-1} z\right),$

where b_k = the estimated coefficient of the kth characteristic, S = estimated standard error of the regression equation, $z_k = \ln(x_{jk}/x_{ik})$ if the independent variables (x's) are in the double-log form, and $z_k = (x_{jk} - x_{ik})$ if the independent variable are in the linear form.

If only one variable changes in the estimating equation, (3) becomes:

(3.1) $\hat{P} = P \exp\left(z_k b_k^{-1/2} S_{b_k}^2 Z_k^2\right),$

where S_{b_k} = standard error of regression coefficient.

The confidence interval for the calculated point estimate of quality adjusted price is:

(3.2) $P_\alpha = \hat{P} \exp\left(\pm \, U_{\alpha/2}\sqrt{S^2 z'(x'x)^{-1} z}\,\right),$

where U = critical value for the normal curve $\alpha/2$ distribution.

During the period for which data were available (1971–77), five specific cases of specification change occurred for cranes, all of which were evaluated using the producer-cost methodology. The net specification changes for each case are in table 2.20. In cases 4 and 5, even though there was a model substitution in which the new model was a more powerful crane, the Boom Swing Speed and the Boom Point Height decreased in value. The slowing of Boom Swing Speed is understandable, since a heavier boom structure may take more time to revolve. In the fifth case, the Boom Point Height was less for the new model.

Table 2.21 presents the results of recalculating quality adjusted prices for five cases. Column 1 (labeled Producer Cost) contains a measurement of quality adjustment, expressed in percentage terms, for the producer-cost methodology. Column 3 also measures quality change; however, in this column the link prices (L_{t-1}) are not derived from the producer-cost information but from the implicit prices estimated from the hedonic equation with the best functional form. Columns 2 and 4 contain confidence interval limits of these estimates. Columns 5, 6, and 7 show estimates for each functional form. By comparing column 1 with column 3, one can readily observe that relative to the hedonic approach the producer-cost methodology understates the quality change in cases 1, 2, and 4 that actually occurred during the measurement period. The opposite was true for cases 3 and 5. In case 1 the producer-cost evaluation of quality actually was within the 95% range of the hedonic quality adjustment. Further, it is interesting to note substantial differences in columns 5, 6, and 7 associated with different functional forms. In some cases the differences are large enough to alter the direction of difference from the producer cost method.

Table 2.22 depicts the differences between the index calculated with the producer-cost methodology and the revised index employing hedonic quality adjustments. The letters indicate when the actual quality change took place. This comparison brings out differences in both size and direction of change. The hedonic quality adjustments caused the range of the differences in the month of the change between the actual and revised indexes to be between −5.4% and +2.7%. However, one should keep in mind that this table represents the finest level of detail and consequently gives rise to the greatest quality differences between the two types of indexes. Note also the counteracting influences of cases 2 and 3 in 1976.

A more relevant yardstick for measuring the impact of substituting new quality adjustments based on the hedonic approach is to observe the impact of the quality adjustments on "all" cranes. What this implies is that we are including all different sizes and types of cranes that were included in the PPI. Table 2.23 reflects the influences of the five cases on the "all" cranes index. The percentage change from December 1970 to December 1977 between the original and revised index is very small indeed, only .11%. However, differences are somewhat larger during particular months or subperiods.

2.5 Quality Adjustment and the Revised PPIs

The study of quality adjustment in the crane indexes show a small, negative revision in the index when regression techniques are used for quality adjustment. While the average effect is a downward revision of the index, some observations were revised in each direction. A study of the refrigerator component of the PPI is the only other study that has used regression techniques to quality adjust the actual observations on which an official index is based. Triplett and McDonald (1977) found that the application of regression techniques produced an index that declined 23% over the 1960–72 period compared with a decline of 17% in the official index. Like our crane study, they found that the direction of revision was, on average, consistent with the hypothesis that there is a positive quality error in price indexes but that for individual observations and particular subperiods the reverse was true.

The variety of evidence examined in this paper suggests any quality error in the Producer Price Indexes is a very complex phenomenon with no clear evidence of overall magnitude or direction. We certainly do not wish to minimize the potential difficulties involved in providing proper quality adjustment. But such occurrences are infrequent in the index. They show a reasonable distribution of price and quality magnitudes. Hedonic techniques provide a useful check on the ongoing quality adjustment process but still seem to be too complex to be generally applicable in a production environment. The evidence in this paper is that the impact of a hedonic technique seems to be relatively small in the short run and variable over time in both size and direction. However, the evidence is too sparse to draw any general conclusions. Two interesting problems have been identified that will require further research: the relatively large statistical error in the hedonic estimates, and the sensitivity of the results to the selection of the functional form.

PPIs are currently undergoing a comprehensive revision. The first experimental results were released in August 1978, and the full results will be released on an industry-by-industry basis between January 1980 and April 1985. Some of the improvements being made by the revision include probability sampling, net output weighting, and better transaction prices. Also as part of this effort, more resources will be devoted to quality adjustment (Early 1978). Further research will be conducted on alternative methods for quality adjustment in an index-production environment. And appropriate theory and methods will be developed for measuring error from all sources, including quality adjustment. As part of the improved index system, a complete, automated file on all substitutions will be maintained, which will make possible a more complete and prompt analysis of the effects of substitutions on the indexes.

Table 2.1   **Classification of Quality Adjustments, PPI, 1976**

PPI Major Commodity Group	Total (1)	Producer Cost (2)	Link, No Change (3)	Direct Comparison (4)	Total Quality Adjustments as Percent of All Prices in Each Commodity Group in 1976[b] (5)
		Cases of Quality Adjustment as Percent of All Quality Adjustments[a]			
01. Farm products	0	0	0	0	0
02. Processed foods and feeds	1.32	.22	.44	.66	.07
03. Textile products and apparel	3.96	.66	.88	2.42	.34
04. Hides, skins, leather, and related products	2.64	.44	1.54	.66	1.04
05. Fuels and related products, and power	0	0	0	0	0
06. Chemicals and allied power	3.08	.44	.66	1.98	.12
07. Rubber and plastic products	2.64	.22	1.10	1.32	.28
08. Lumber and wood products	.44	0	.22	.22	.05
09. Pulp, paper, and allied products	2.20	0	1.10	1.10	.25
10. Metals and metal products	12.97	2.42	6.37	4.18	.38
11. Machinery and equipment	37.36	10.77	14.51	12.09	.49
12. Furniture and household durables	13.63	1.98	7.69	3.96	1.27
13. Nonmetallic mineral products	.44	.44	0	0	.05
14. Transportation equipment	14.73	9.89	3.08	1.76	2.38
15. Miscellaneous products	4.62	.88	2.86	.88	.44
	100.00	28.40	40.40	31.20	.40

[a]455 total cases.
[b]108,756 total price observations in 1976.

Table 2.2 **Frequency Distribution of Quality Change for Producer Cost Method, PPI, 1976**

PPI Code	0–9.9 +	0–9.9 −	10–19.9 +	10–19.9 −	20–29.9 +	20–29.9 −	30–39.9 +	30–39.9 −	40–49.9 +	40–49.9 −	50–99.9 +	50–99.9 −	>100 +	>100 +	Total
01															0
02			1												1
03	2	1													3
04															0
05															0
06	1	1													2
07				1											1
08															0
09															0
10	3	4			2			1			1				11
11	23	5	8	6					1			2	3		48
12	5	2				1							1		9
13		1											1		2
14	35	9			1		1		1			1			48
15	3					1									4
Total	72	23	8	10	4	1	1	1	0	0	0	1	3	5	129

Table 2.3 **Frequency Distribution of Pure Price Changes in Producer Cost Method, PPI, 1976**

PPI Code	0–9.9 +	0–9.9 −	10–19.9 +	10–19.9 −	20–29.9 +	20–29.9 −	30–39.9 +	30–39.9 −	40–49.9 +	40–49.9 −	50–99.9 +	50–99.9 −	>100 +	>100 −	Total
01															0
02		1													1
03	2	1													3
04															0
05															0
06	2														2
07	1														1
08															0
09															0
10	8	2	1												11
11	36	3	5				1					1			46
12	7	1			1										9
13	2														2
14	44	2	3			1									50
15	2	1		1											4
Total	104	11	9	1	1	1	1	0	0	0	0	1	0	0	129

Table 2.4   **Frequency Distribution of Links to Show No Price Change, PPI, 1976**

PPI Code	0–9.9 +	0–9.9 −	10–19.9 +	10–19.9 −	20–29.9 +	20–29.9 −	30–39.9 +	30–39.9 −	40–49.9 +	40–49.9 −	50–99.9 +	50–99.9 −	>100 +	Total
01														0
02		1									1			2
03	1	1	1		1									4
04	3	1	2				1							7
05														0
06		1	1				1							3
07	1	2		1					1					5
08													1	1
09	1	4												5
10	6	6	2	3	1	1	1	1	2	1		3	2	29
11	25	6	14	2	4	1	4	1	2	1	5		1	66
12	11	3	7	2	4	4	1	1	1			1		35
13														0
14	4	6			1	1						1	1	14
15	1	1	4	2		2		1				1	1	13
Total	54	31	32	10	10	9	5	7	5	3	6	6	6	184

Table 2.5   **Frequency Distribution of Price Change for Direct Comparisons, PPI, 1976**

PPI Code	0	0–9.9 +	0–9.9 −	10–19.9 +	10–19.9 −	20–29.9 +	20–29.9 −	30–39.9 +	30–39.9 −	40–49.9 +	40–49.9 −	50–99.9 +	50–99.9 −	>100 +	Total
01															0
02	3		1				1					1			6
03	11	2											1		14
04	1	2						1							4
05															0
06	5	1	1	1				1		1					10
07	1	2	1						1	1				1	7
08	2														2
09	2	2	1												5
10	11	8													19
11	28	5	5	4		3	1	2	1	1					50
12	12	3	2											1	18
13															0
14	4	4													8
15															0
Total	80	29	11	5		3	2	4	2	3		1	1	2	143

Table 2.6   **Classification of Quality Adjustments,
for Ten Selected Commodity Groups, PPI, 1970–1976**

Type of Quality Adjustment	Cases of Quality Adjustment Per Year						
	1976	1975	1974	1973	1972	1971	1970
Producer cost	45	59	40	54	23	4	27
Link	47	23	18	31	11	14	0
Direct comparison	16	0	6[a]	2	3	2	0[a]
Total no. cases per year	108	82	64[a]	87	37	20	27[a]
No. reported prices	4,128	4,224	4,284	4,284	4,284	4,272	[b]

[a]Some data not available.
[b]Comparable figures not available.

Table 2.7   **Cases of Quality Adjustment for Ten Selected
Commodity Groups, PPI, 1970–1976**

PPI Code	Number Producer Cost Adjustments	Number Link Adjustments	Number Direct Comparison Adjustments	Total Adjustments	Total Price Observations
043201 (women's and misses' footwear domestic)	2	16	2	20	1,848
101501 (gray iron castings)	12	8	2	22	7,092
104101 (builder's hardware)	1	15	5	21	3,648
111206 (harvesting machinery)	16	18	3	37	2,148
112802 (tractors, crawler type)	23	20	1	44	1,728
114901 (valves and fittings)	2	8	6	16	3,108
117837[a] (optoelectronic devices)	0	2	2	4	276
123101 (soft surface floor coverings)	0	31	4	35	2,748
141101 (passenger cars)	107	11	2	120	1,260
141102 (motor trucks)	89	15	2	106	1,620
Total	252	144	29	425	25,467

[a]Began in 1975.

Table 2.8   **Frequency Distribution of Change for Producers' Cost Method for Ten Selected Commodity Groups, PPI, 1970–1976**

PPI Code	0–9.9 +	0–9.9 −	10–19.9 +	10–19.9 −	20–29.9 +	20–29.9 −	30–39.9 +	30–39.9 −	40–49.9 +	40–49.9 −	50–99.9 +	50–99.9 −	>100 +	>100 −
Quality Change														
043201		2												
101501	4	2		1	1			1	1		2			
104101		1												
111206	14	1	1											
112802	13	4	1	3	2									
114901	1				1									
117837														
123101														
141101	87	14	3		2	1								
141102	68	13	7			1								
Total	187	37	12	4	6	2	0	1	1	0	2	0	0	0
Price Change														
043201	2													
101501	9	1	1		1									
104101			1	1										
111206	10	2	4											
112802	17	4	1											
114901			2			1								
117837														
123101														
141101	75	26	5		1									
141102	60	12	14		1				1					
Total	173	45	28	1	3	1	0	0	1	0	0	0	0	0

Note: Total observations = 252.

Table 2.9   Frequency Distribution of Links to Show No Change for Ten Selected Commodity Groups, PPI, 1970–1976

Percent Change

PPI Code	0–9.9 +	0–9.9 −	10–19.9 +	10–19.9 −	20–29.9 +	20–29.9 −	30–39.9 +	30–39.9 −	40–49.9 +	40–49.9 −	50–99.9 +	50–99.9 −	>100 +	>100 −
043201	9	1	5		1									
101501		1		1		1	2	1	2					
104101	2	1	1	3	1	1			1	1		3	1	
111206	11	2	2		2						1			
112802	12	2	2			1	1				1		1	
114901	1		3	1			1		1				1	
117837			1								1			
123101	6	4	4	3	5	1	1	1	2	1	1		2	
141101	7	3				1								
141102	13	2												
Total	61	16	18	8	9	5	5	2	6	2	4	3	5	0

Note: Total observations = 144.

Table 2.10   Frequency Distribution of Price Change for Direct Comparisons for Ten Selected Commodity Groups, PPI, 1970–1976

Percent Change

PPI Code	0–9.9 +	0–9.9 −	10–19.9 +	10–19.9 −	20–29.9 +	20–29.9 −	30–39.9 +	30–39.9 −	40–49.9 +	40–49.9 −	50–99.9 +	50–99.9 −	>100 +	>100 −
043201	2													
101501	2													
104101	5													
111206	2			1										
112802	1													
114901	1		2		2									
117837	2													
123101	2	2												
141101	2						1							
141102	2													
Total	21	2	2	1	2		1							

Note: Total observations = 29.

Table 2.11   **Independent Variables for the Hydraulic Crane Data Base[a]**

1. Crane type (carrier-mounted or self-propelled)
2. Boom retracted boom length
3. Boom retracted rated lifting capacity
4. Boom retracted at boom radius
5. Boom extended boom length
6. Boom extended rated lifting capacity
7. Boom extended at boom radius
8. Boom maximum angle
9. Boom maximum hook height
10. Maximum height at maximum weight
11. Boom topping speed
12. Boom swing speed
13. Hoist speed
14. Pump hydraulic horsepower
15. Outrigger type
16. Outrigger extended width
17. Crane engine type
18. Crane engine cylinders
19. Crane engine horsepower
20. Crane length
21. Crane height
22. Crane width
23. Crane wheel base
24. Crane gross weight
25. Crane maximum speed
26. Standard carrier engine type[a]
27. Standard carrier engine cylinder[a]
28. Standard crane engine horsepower[a]

[a]These characteristics referred to the carrier-mounted hydraulic crane. It was later decided that the hydraulic crane data base should be divided into carrier-mounted and self-propelled hydraulic cranes. In this way, the dummy variable "crane type" could be dropped.

Table 2.12   **Independent variables for the Truck Crane Data Base**

1. Boom length
2. Boom angle at minimum radius
3. Boom radius minimum
4. Boom lifting capacity minimum radius
5. Feet from hook point minimum radius
6. Minimum load line minimum radius
7. Boom radius maximum
8. Boom lifting capacity maximum radius
9. Feet from boom point maximum radius
10. Minimum load line maximum radius
11. Boom angle maximum radius
12. Maximum boom angle
13. Boom swing speed
14. Maximum single line hoist speed
15. Maximum single line pull main hoist
16. Crane engine type
17. Crane engine cylinders
18. Crane engine horsepower
19. Crane engine revolutions per minute
20. Standard carrier engine type
21. Standard carrier engine cylinders
22. Standard carrier engine horsepower
23. Carrier speed

Table 2.13   **Independent Variables for the Crawler Crane Data Base**

1. Boom maximum capacity
2. Boom on boom length
3. Boom at radius
4. Boom length
5. Maximum hoisting speed on single line
6. Boom type
7. Minimum boom length with type of boom top
8. Maximum boom length
9. Maximum fly-jib length
10. Crawler width retracted
11. Crawler width extended
12. Crawler pad width
13. Crawler pad length
14. Crawler weight
15. Ground bearing pressure
16. Cab height with crawlers
17. Total crane weight with boom and counter-weight
18. Counterweight
19. Tailswing radius
20. Cab length without counterweight
21. Cab width
22. Cab height without counterweight or crawlers
23. Crane engine type
24. Crane engine horsepower
25. Crane engine revolutions per minute
26. Crane engine drive
27. Crane maximum travel speed

Table 2.14   Simple Correlation Coefficients from Hydraulic Crane Data Base (Includes Both Self-Propelled and Carrier Mounted Cranes)

	(1)	(2)	(3)	(4)	(5)	(6)	(7)	(8)	(9)	(10)	(11)	(12)	(13)	(14)	(15)	(16)	(17)	(18)	(19)	(20)	(21)	(22)	(23)	(24)	(25)	(26)	(27)
1	1.000	.666	.687	.604	.738	.596	.476	.597	.735	.749	.651	.550	.606	.634	.795	.675	.048	.313	.311	.655	.592	.059	.099	.645	.814	.179	.991
2		1.000	.863	.979	.969	.943	.785	.976	.973	.962	.957	.941	.934	.916	.811	.978	.241	.842	.862	.995	.979	.206	.228	.918	.943	.094	.655
3			1.000	.795	.940	.819	.659	.784	.925	.925	.878	.714	.780	.861	.770	.876	.117	.742	.776	.855	.800	.154	.177	.918	.794	.059	.662
4				1.000	.992	.954	.791	.990	.932	.916	.930	.980	.947	.891	.755	.965	.327	.799	.871	.984	.994	.199	.217	.878	.941	.101	.597
5					1.000	.992	.758	.918	.997	.996	.916	.900	.900	.904	.843	.962	.198	.799	.810	.960	.925	.215	.241	.941	.925	.081	.722
6						1.000	.884	.944	.879	.882	.866	.900	.909	.881	.770	.949	.278	.842	.857	.949	.952	.164	.181	.869	.979	.096	.588
7							1.000	.779	.726	.751	.754	.766	.725	.901	.569	.768	.204	.675	.702	.781	.785	.161	.176	.711	.724	.067	.467
8								1.000	.779	.914	.924	.977	.942	.876	.748	.967	.382	.870	.869	.982	.995	.204	.222	.868	.949	.099	.590
9									1.000	.929	.929	.882	.911	.906	.845	.969	.211	.800	.817	.967	.945	.214	.238	.941	.940	.080	.721
10										1.000	.987	.944	.893	.898	.854	.960	.241	.781	.797	.955	.919	.215	.241	.947	.925	.084	.745
11											1.000	.941	.902	.892	.784	.938	.196	.806	.842	.952	.928	.189	.210	.911	.886	.084	.649
12												1.000	.945	.944	.701	.926	.358	.844	.835	.950	.977	.196	.212	.819	.904	.100	.548
13													1.000	.844	.714	.919	.262	.809	.814	.954	.949	.248	.245	.858	.889	.076	.592
14														1.000	.726	.905	.171	.767	.799	.907	.884	.195	.216	.882	.844	.072	.619
15															1.000	.835	.048	.577	.584	.801	.747	.216	.246	.800	.845	.144	.788
16																1.000	.292	.850	.856	.981	.969	.207	.229	.918	.947	.108	.666
17																	1.000	.454	.324	.274	.356	.246	.326	.970	.295	.154	.645
18																		1.000	.962	.851	.882	.214	.219	.805	.756	.180	.651
19																			1.000	.864	.984	.244	.250	.842	.712	.141	.621
20																				1.000	.984	.147	.157	.892	.942	.086	.645
21																					1.000	.201	.219	.880	.942	.104	.584
22																						1.000	.999	.464	.977	.091	.582
23																							1.000	.485	.941	.117	.641
24																								1.000	.842	.071	.625
25																									1.000	.176	.812
26																										1.000	.216
27																											1.000
28																											

Table 2.15   Self-Propelled Hydraulic Cranes
                       A. Linear Regression Coefficients

Quality Variables[a]	Coefficients	Standard Error	t-Statistics
Lifting capacity	2169.2600	201.0189	10.790
Maximum lifting height	31.2995	5.9601	5.251
Boom topping speed	287.6940	121.0072	2.377
Boom swing speed	9193.0200	1608.7750	5.714
Engine horsepower	34.2335	39.4713	0.867

**B. Linear Estimate of Intercept and Company Effects
from Self-Propelled Hydraulic Crane Regression**

Company[b]	Coefficients	Standard Error	t-Statistics
Intercept[c]	− 9255.4560	19826.890	− .4668
Bantam	81.2964	5825.198	.0140
Broderson	− 1671.6920	12078.040	− .1384
Bucyrus-Erie	10713.9900	7140.533	1.5000
Drott	11015.8100	5551.588	1.9840
Galion	14260.3400	9606.422	1.4840
Grove	2156.7110	4549.937	.4740
Hyster	2223.1710	7957.227	.2794
Lorain	2473.0400	7511.479	.3292
P and H	7965.3620	5154.097	1.5440
Pettibone	2367.5810	7340.416	.3225
Warner and Swasey	− 6406.1480	9418.650	− .6802

$R^2 = .94331$
Standard error of residual = 845.71
Sample size = 61

Crane price (dependent variable): mean = 111,227
Standard deviation = 62,406

[a]Estimated without company dummies which were, as a whole, insignificant.
[b]These companies were derived from the "Green Guide" and in no way reflect actual companies that are priced in the PPI.
[c]Austin-Western was included in the y-intercept.

Table 2.16   **Carrier-mounted Hydraulic Cranes**
A. Log-Log Regression Coefficients

Quality Variables[a]	Coefficients	Standard Error	t-Statistics
Lifting capacity	.3443582	.067681250	5.088
Maximum lifting height	.0003310	.000141158	2.346
Boom topping speed	.0136750	.005049586	2.708
Boom swing speed	.2141211	.022945020	9.332

B. Linear Estimate of Intercept and Company Effects
from Self-Propelled Hydraulic Crane Regression

Company[b]	Coefficients	Standard Error	t-Statistics
Intercept[c]	10.06874000	.31394700	32.070
Bantam	− .02443212	− .07376190	− .331
Bucyrus-Erie	.24878560	− .06548293	3.799
Drott	.06297117	.09278927	.679
Grove	− .03281932	.06307050	− .520
Link Belt (FMC)	.16683410	.10007760	1.667
Lorain	.14671190	.14406750	1.018
P and H	.08088108	.07017277	1.153
Pettibone	.07826455	.10504100	.745
Warner and Swasey	− .02088442	.07259642	− .228

The dependent variable is the natural logarithm price.

R^2 = .9820268
Standard error of residual = .0751401
Sample size = 31

Crane price (dependent variable): mean = 76,770
Standard deviation = 6,441

[a]Estimated without company dummies which were, as a whole, insignificant. Intercept data came from a different regression estimate.
[b]These companies were derived from the "Green Guide" and in no way reflect actual companies that are priced in the PPI.
[c]Austin-Western was included in the y-intercept.

Table 2.17 **Crawler Cranes**
A. Log-Log Regression Coefficients

Quality Variables	Coefficients	Standard Error	t-Statistics
Lifting capacity	.421730700	.0399051800	10.57
Maximum lifting height	.001109538	.0002065855	5.37
Engine horsepower	.001107087	.0003046310	3.63

B. Log-Log Estimate of Intercept and Company Effects
from Crawler Crane Regression

Company[a]	Coefficient	Standard Error	t-Statistics
Intercept[b]	6.3136880	.38374550	16.450
Bucyrus-Erie	.1209202	.05201461	2.330
Koehring	−.0169128	.06094477	−.278
Lima	.0033107	.06549748	.050
Link-Belt (FMC)	−.0253000	.04507097	−.455
Lorain	.2443997	.12301540	1.990
Manitowoc	−.1787732	.05913360	−3.020
Northwest	.5968208	.04105696	1.450
P and H	.0182433	.05508285	.331
Unit	.0035194	.12373360	.028

The dependent variable is the natural logarithm price.

$R^2 = .9761163$
Standard error of residual = .1139354
Sample size = 80

Crane price (dependent variable): mean = 226,080
Standard deviation = 154,189

[a]These companies were derived from the "Green Guide" and in no way reflect actual companies that are priced in the PPI.
[b]American was included in the y-intercept.

Table 2.18   **Truck Cranes**
A. Log-Log Regression Coefficients

Quality Variables	Coefficients	Standard Error	t-Statistics
Lifting capacity	.388152900	.0969392800	4.00
Maximum lifting height	.000974499	.0004301725	2.27
Engine horsepower	.001334569	.0006628524	2.01

B. Log-Log Estimate of Intercept and Company Effects
from Truck Crane Regression

Company[a]	Coefficient	Standard Error	t-Statistics
Intercept[b]	9.77262500	.43826080	22.300
Bantam	− .62374620	.16769490	− 3.720
Bucyrus-Erie	.21800800	.10344780	2.110
Lima	− .05877054	.08425340	− .689
Link-Belt (FMC)	− .25938990	.07657147	− 3.390
Lorain	.06346180	.07583306	.862
Manitowoc	.13640830	.17467810	.781
Northwest	− .13694970	.12073060	− 1.130
P and H	− .07919773	.08635810	− .917

The dependent variable is the natural logarithm of price.

R^2 = .9638091
Standard error or residual = .1700581
Sample size = 37

Crane price (dependent variable): mean = 247,203
Standard deviation = 138,920

[a]These companies were derived from the "Green Guide" and in no way reflect actual companies.
[b]American was included in the y-intercept.

138

Table 2.19   Testing for Best Functional Form
              Using Box-Cox Power Transformation Test[a]

Type of Crane	Standardized Sum of Squared Residuals
Hydraulic Cranes	
1. Self-propelled[b]	
Linear	.4973005
Semi-log	.7321062
Log-log	.5482269
2. Carrier-mounted	
Linear	.2030923
Semi-log	.1976967
Log-log	.1832833
Truck Cranes	
Linear	.9757013
Semi-log	1.7095040
Log-log	.9254327
Crawler Cranes	
Linear	2.2006408
Semi-log	2.6330330
Log-log	1.2611700

[a]A χ^2 test was used to test for a difference between all the functional forms. In all instances the χ^2 value was significant at .01 level.
[b]Notice the linear functional form had the smallest sum of squared residuals for "self-propelled" hydraulic cranes.

Table 2.20   Net Specification Changes from Old
              to New Model for Five Specific Cases

Case	Lifting Capacity (tons)	Boom Point Height (inches)	Boom Swing Speed (rpm)	Boom Topping Speed (sec)	Engine Horse-power
1[a]					+44
2[b]	+10	+120			+24
3[b]	+10	+ 96			
4[c]	+ 7	+102	−1		
5[c]	+ 5	− 16.25	+5	+1.5	

[a]Self-propelled hydraulic crane.
[b]Truck cranes.
[c]Carrier-mounted hydraulic cranes.

Table 2.21 **Quality Changes for Producer-Cost Methodology and Three Hedonic Function Forms (Percent)**

		Best Functional Form[a]			Point Estimate Other Functional Forms		
Case	(1) Producers Cost	(2) Lower Limit	(3) Point Estimate	(4) Upper Limit	(5) Linear	(6) Semi-Log	(7) Log-Log
1	1.30	−2.71	2.88	8.47	2.88[b]	3.81	.027
2	1.18	4.09	8.12	12.30	20.88	24.08	8.12[b]
3	10.43	3.36	6.69	10.13	18.50	20.19	6.69[b]
4	1.89	6.49	11.33	16.40	16.50	18.88	11.33[b]
5	30.26	8.75	11.68	14.69	21.78	11.17	11.68[b]

[a]The best functional form as determined by Box-Cox test.
[b]95% confidence interval.

Table 2.22   Actual and Hedonic Crane Index for Five Specific Cases

	January	February	March	April	May	June	July	August	September	October	November	December
Case 1 (self-propelled hydraulic)												
1971 actual index	119.6	119.6	119.6	119.6	119.6	119.6	119.6	119.6	119.6	119.6	119.6	119.6
1971 hedonic index	119.6	119.6	119.6	119.6	119.6	113.1[a]	113.1	113.1	113.1	113.1	113.1	113.1
Cases 2 and 3 (truck crane):												
1976 actual index	221.0	221.0	221.0	221.0	221.0	226.6	230.1	230.1	230.1	230.1	230.1	230.1
1976 hedonic index	221.0	221.0	221.0	221.0	221.0	226.6	230.1	230.1	232.6[a]	232.6	232.6	225.9[a]
Cases 4 and 5 (carrier-mounted hydraulic)												
1977 actual index	147.4	147.4	147.4	149.8	149.8	150.6	150.6	150.6	150.6	151.6	151.6	151.6
1977 hedonic index	147.4	147.4	147.4	159.0[a]	159.0	154.6[a]	154.6	154.6	154.6	155.6	155.6	155.6

[a]Month in which quality adjustment took place and implicit link price was substituted for producer-cost link price.

Table 2.23 "All" Cranes Index Original and Hedonic (1972 = 100)

	January	February	March	April	May	June	July	August	September	October	November	December
1971 original	94.2	94.2	94.2	94.3	94.4	94.4	96.6	96.6	96.6	96.9	96.6	96.4
1971 hedonic	94.2	94.2	94.2	94.3	94.4	94.2[a]	96.4	96.4	96.4	96.7	96.4	96.2
1972 original	97.5	98.8	98.8	98.8	98.8	99.3	99.3	99.4	99.4	99.4	100.0	100.0
1972 hedonic	97.4	98.7	98.7	98.7	98.7	99.2	99.2	99.3	99.3	99.3	99.9	99.9
1973 original	100.1	100.1	101.2	101.5	101.5	102.7	102.8	102.8	102.8	102.8	103.3	106.2
1973 hedonic	100.0	100.0	101.1	101.4	101.4	102.6	102.7	102.7	102.7	102.7	103.2	106.1
1974 original	106.2	107.1	108.2	110.6	114.5	115.3	119.8	121.9	125.1	126.8	129.2	133.1
1974 hedonic	106.1	107.0	108.1	110.5	114.4	115.2	119.7	121.8	125.0	126.7	129.1	133.0
1975 original	135.9	137.9	139.5	143.7	143.7	144.9	146.9	147.2	147.9	150.8	151.0	153.7
1975 hedonic	135.8	137.8	139.4	143.6	143.6	144.8	146.8	147.1	147.8	150.7	150.9	153.6
1976 original	153.7	153.8	153.8	153.8	154.2	156.0	157.8	158.3	159.0	159.6	159.7	159.9
1976 hedonic	153.6	153.7	153.7	153.7	154.1	155.9	157.7	158.2	159.2[a]	159.8	159.9	159.7[a]
1977 original	163.6	163.4	163.4	164.1	164.7	165.9	166.2	167.4	167.4	167.9	168.7	168.9
1977 hedonic	163.4	163.2	163.2	164.5[a]	165.3	165.8[a]	166.1	167.3	167.3	167.8	168.6	168.8

[a]Month in which actual quarter adjustment occurred for cranes under investigation.

References

Early, John F. 1978. Improving the measurement of Producer Price Change. *Monthly Labor Review 101 (April):* 7–15.

Griliches, Zvi, ed. 1971. *Price indexes and quality change.* Cambridge, Mass.: Harvard University Press.

Triplett, Jack E. 1971. *The theory of hedonic quality measurement and its use in price indexes.* Washington, D.C.: Bureau of Labor Statistics.

Triplett, Jack E. 1975. The measurement of inflation: a survey of research on the accuracy of price indexes. In Paul H. Earl, ed., *Analysis of inflation.* Lexington, Mass.: Lexington Books.

Triplett, Jack E., and McDonald, Richard J. 1977. Assessing the quality error in output measures: the case of refrigeration. In *Review of Income and Wealth.* Series 23, no. 2. (June), pp. 137–55.

Zarembka, Paul. 1974. Transformation of variables in econometrics. In Paul Zarembka, ed., *Frontiers in econometrics*, pp. 81–104. New York: Academic Press.

Comment   Zvi Griliches

The paper consists roughly of three parts: first, there are some introductory comments explaining the current philosophy of quality and adjustment in the PPI; second, there is a survey of the frequency and type of quality adjustment in 1976 and a more detailed listing of quality adjustments for 10 selected commodity groupings during the 1970–76 period; and, finally, there is a report on an exploratory hedonic regression study of power cranes. The three parts are only barely linked, and I shall comment on each of them separately.

The first section describes current practice in the PPI without necessarily endorsing it. The current practice is based on the assumption that quality change is to be valued by the difference in the cost of production that it induces. I have both conceptual and practical objections to this procedure. First, I believe this to be an inappropriate definition of quality change. The appropriate measure is one based on the utility to the purchaser of the item. I understand that one may use producer cost for lack of anything better or because of the unwillingness to enter the treacherous waters of utility estimation, but I do not understand its elevation to dogma, to the status of a "desirable" definition of such indexes. If such a procedure were followed consistently for all quality

Zvi Griliches is chairman of the Department of Economics, Harvard University, and research associate at the National Bureau of Economic Research.

changes, it would come close to abolishing this source of productivity growth by construction (except for differences between beginning and end period weights) since it would recognize only those changes in output per commodity unit (quality per model) in the producing industry which correspond to measurable changes in production costs. But then output per unit of input will not have changed. The argument that all this will work out in equilibrium does not wash as far as I am concerned. The essence of price and productivity measurement is the evaluation of transitions between equilibria. There are also problems with the empirical implementations of this notion. Conceptually, as far as I can tell, the relevant notion must be of *marginal* production costs. In practice they also include the "standard mark-up for return to investors and entrepreneurship." But that assumes away the possibility of price change that comes from the erosion of such margins over time.

Perhaps an example will help here. Imagine a change in Bayer Aspirin bottles from 50 to 75 pills per bottle and a change in price from 50 cents to 70 cents per bottle. If a true production cost notion were taken, one would use the information that marginal cost of an aspirin pill does not exceed .3 cent and that the difference in the bottle and associated transportation cost is not larger than 5 cents per bottle (all these numbers are, of course, invented but are illustrative of the right orders of magnitude). Thus the total production cost change per bottle due to the new package is $7.5 + 5 = 12.5$ cents, implying a 7.5 cents *increase* in the price of a bottle of aspirin. But the actual price per pill has come down (from 1 to .93 cent per pill). Obviously, the BLS will not use the above producer-cost calculation but will rather accept the pill as the relevant unit here. But how does it *know* that the pill *is* the relevant unit without an implicit utility analysis?

I have also a more mundane objection to the producer-cost concept. I believe that it leads to a too great reliance on crude accounting data provided by firms and to a serious downward bias in the index (for *those* items), since it has been in the interest of firms and industries to claim that various changes have been very costly. I do not believe that the BLS has adequate resources for checking and challenging such claims in appropriate detail.

The section on the actual prevalence of various adjustment practices is very valuable in what it describes but falls short of what I would have liked to see. There is no independent examination of a sample of cases to see how many changes were *not* identified and how many of the identified changes were treated correctly. That is, we do not learn anything directly about the *quality* of such quality adjustments. What we do learn indirectly is quite disturbing.

In 1976, out of 108,756 price observations, only 455 were *reported* as creating a comparison problem. The incidence appears to be very low. It implies that out of about 10,000 different commodities and varieties priced one encountered only 455 comparability problems during one year. Either many true comparability problems are not reported or the PPI by design excludes most of the rapidly changing commodity areas from its purview. I assume that both are true. Of those examined 31 percent were presumed not to show any quality change, while 40 percent were assumed to show no improvement in quality relative to price. The remaining 28 percent were adjusted using the producer-cost method with a preponderance of positive quality change estimates (91 out of 129). My guess is that in this period of inflation "quality change" is probably *overestimated* in a sector where it is measured by the producer-cost method and underestimated everywhere else.

Looking at table 2.1 we find most of the producer-cost valued-quality changes concentrated in the machinery and equipment and transportation equipment industries. In the latter industry, many of these changes arise from mandated changes in the products and probably represent a serious overestimate of such change from the user's point of view. Surely the recent laws have led to a significant increase in the cost of automobile ownership, per year or per passenger mile, which is not reflected adequately in the official indexes.

There are other disturbing aspects of these tables. More than half of the "links," of direct substitutions, involve changes in commodities which differ by more than 10 percent in their price. More than a quarter of all links differ by more than 20 percent in their prices. One wonders how comparable such links really are.

Looking at the more detailed data for the 1970–76 period for 10 detailed commodities the same kinds of questions arise. The bulk of the adjustments occur for passenger cars and trucks where the rate of adjustment is roughly on the order of one per model per year. Since the adjustments there are based primarily on producer-cost estimates, I suspect that they overestimate quality change in this particular time period. The other categories (e.g., tractors, valves, and builders hardware) exhibit a rather low rate of adjustment, implying that many changes in quality are not being caught by the current procedures.

The last section shows that it is easier to criticize the PPI than to propose effective alternatives. It presents estimates of hedonic price regressions for several types of power cranes and uses the estimated coefficients to adjust the actual price quotations in the PPI. Since these regressions are based on data for only one year, there is some doubt about the propriety of applying the estimated coefficients to the whole 1971–77 period. Moreover, the instability observed in the estimates of the various coefficients might have been alleviated by expanding the regression sample to cover more years. One can always test, later on, whether such pooling of observations over time is legitimate.

The resulting estimates are used to evaluate five cases of producer-cost adjustments. The individual estimates based on the hedonic regressions are subject to so much uncertainty, however, both because of sampling error and because of ignorance of the appropriate functional form, that little can be concluded from such a comparison. It appears that producer-cost adjustments *underestimate* slightly the quality change that occurred in these particular cases. There were, however, only five such specification changes for *all* crane models in the seven-year period that was examined by them. This is rather surprising and may indicate how little I know about cranes, but it also might lead one to wonder about the representativeness of the crane models being sampled by the PPI.

I learned a great deal from reading the Early-Sinclair paper, and I am grateful to the authors for providing all this information, even as I hanker for more. We need more such studies, however, before we can start generalizing about the role, magnitude, and direction of the "quality error in the PPI."

3   Deflation of Defense Purchases

Richard C. Ziemer and Karl D. Galbraith

3.1 Perspective

This paper discusses the deflation of federal government purchases that are classified as national defense in the national income and product accounts (NIPAs). The paper is divided into five sections. The first section, Perspective, reviews the relationship of national defense purchases in the NIPAs, the history of the deflation effort, the summary results, and their impact on the gross national product. The second section, Concepts, Measurements, and Problems, discusses the general approaches involved in developing price indexes for defense purchases. The third section, Specific Approaches to Defense Purchases, discusses the approaches taken in measuring the prices of four types of purchases: compensation, new aircraft and missiles, new ship construction, and military construction. These types are considered in detail because they are of considerable relative importance in defense purchases and presented significant measurement problems. The fourth section, Comparisons with Private Sector Measures of Price Change, compares price changes for defense purchases with those for similar goods purchased by the private sector. The fifth section, Future Plans, looks ahead at how the work can be extended to other types of government purchases.

3.1.1 Background

National defense purchases include Department of Defense (DOD) military functions, military assistance to other nations, atomic energy defense functions, stockpiling of strategic materials, and certain other small items. DOD military functions and military assistance to other

Richard C. Ziemer and Karl D. Galbraith are economists with the Bureau of Economic Analysis.

nations generally account for over 95% of total national defense purchases. The relationship of national defense purchases to GNP is shown in table 3.1.

Prior to the 1980 GNP benchmark, current-dollar estimates of national defense purchases appeared in the NIPAs, but constant-dollar estimates were not available. The primary reason for this was that price indexes applicable to national defense purchases had been lacking. The deflation of federal government purchases in the NIPAs had been carried out only for the total of defense and nondefense purchases. Of necessity, the Bureau of Economic Analysis (BEA) placed heavy reliance on component price indexes from the Producer Price Index (PPI), which excludes goods specific to the military, and the Consumer Price Index (CPI). While reliance on the use of the PPI and CPI was necessary and might be satisfactory for the total, BEA felt that it certainly would not be satisfactory at a more detailed level of government purchases, particularly for national defense purchases. Indeed, the lack of defense purchases in constant dollars had long been a serious shortcoming of the NIPAs.

Substantive work on developing constant-dollar estimates of defense purchases began in February 1973, when the BEA initiated a study, sponsored by the U.S. Arms Control and Disarmament Agency, to determine the requirements and the feasibility of measuring the prices of defense purchases (Commerce 1975) The study concluded that the application of standard pricing techniques to existing data taken from actual DOD transactions would allow the development of price indexes for purchases of goods and services related to the defense function. The study also concluded that such a measure could be constructed for defense purchases in constant dollars.

Subsequently, with the urging of the Joint Economic Committee of the U.S. Congress, and with the presentation of a proposal prepared by BEA in August 1975, DOD entered into an agreement with BEA to conduct research and develop measures for estimating defense purchases in constant dollars within the framework of the NIPAs, and to publish an official defense deflator. That study has now been completed. (Commerce 1979) These data have not only improved the accuracy of real GNP but they also make it easier for policymakers in government to measure the attainment of real growth objectives. The president, for example, recently established a real growth objective for the defense budget. Without appropriate measures of real defense purchases and of changes in the prices of defense purchases, the meeting of such an objective cannot be adequately assessed.

It should be noted that total DOD purchases as well as the estimates by major type of product shown in this paper differ from estimates of national defense purchases published in the *Survey of Current Business*. These differences arise from the somewhat different coverage of the two series as well as the use of more extensive information not earlier available. The data derived in this study were statistically integrated into the NIPAs at the time of the 1980 benchmark revision.

3.1.2 Summary Results

Table 3.2 provides summary measures of DOD purchases in current and constant dollars as well as implicit price deflators for major product types and for the total from 1972 to 1978. More detailed results, some of which are contained in Section 3.3, are available from BEA. The universe of DOD purchases was stratified into 26 categories and 87 relatively homogeneous subcategories. These subcategories and their relative importances are shown in Appendix B for 1972 and 1977. Table 3.3 shows how incorporation of the new DOD series would change various implicit price deflators (IPD).

3.2 Concepts, Measurements, and Problems

Current-dollar defense purchases consist of compensation of employees and goods and services purchased from the private sector and valued at market prices. Most but not all goods and services purchased for national defense are reasonably constant in quality over time and consequently are susceptible to the statistical methodologies associated with the price indexes published by the Bureau of Labor Statistics (BLS). Even major technological breakthroughs such as jet aircraft can be considered new products and can be introduced into price indexes with these statistical methodologies. Still, matching desired concepts with actual transactions involved the many problems associated with using data that have been created for purposes other than incorporation into the NIPAs.

A few measurement conventions are worth noting before specific pricing procedures are taken up. For many types of defense contracts the value of defense goods produced but not delivered is reflected as an increment in business inventories. When these goods are delivered to DOD there is an offsetting increase to national defense purchases such that GNP is not changed. Thus, to the extent that defense goods had entered private inventories, a current period delivery to DOD should have no current period effect on GNP as a whole because of the offsetting effects of the decrease in business inventories and the increase in national defense purchases. In principle, constant-dollar GNP as well as current-dollar GNP is to remain unchanged when defense goods are shipped from business inventories. The defense goods treated in such fashion are durable goods with long production times, such as aircraft and tanks, but ships and military construction are important exceptions.

Another measurement convention arising from the structure of the NIPAs distinguishes the value of transfer payments such as retirement pay from the current-dollar value of defense purchases. Transfer payments are considered financial flows that are additions to personal income and do not represent an increment to the value of current production.

The measurement of current-dollar defense purchases is also complicated because of numerous intra-DOD transactions that appear in DOD financial reports and would cause double counts in the NIPAs if not removed. Such transactions are consolidated into a single DOD financial statement so that only the value of transactions with the private sector and the compensation of employees enter the NIPAs.

3.2.1 Measurement of Price Change

The NIPAs concept of valuing purchases at market prices has been interpreted to mean transaction prices, that is, the price that was actually paid to a supplier for a specified good or service.

The measurement of price change for defense purchases as defined in the NIPAs is difficult for many reasons. One difficulty arises because many prices are frequently unknown, even after the good is delivered, because of cost-sharing agreements and disputed costs. In addition, at any point in time there exists an array of values to which the term "price" is or can be applied. There are list prices, order prices, shipment prices, fixed prices, escalated prices, and many other types (National Bureau of Economic Research 1961, pp. 32–34; Council on Wage and Price Stability 1977, pp. I-9–20; Department of Defense 1975, pp. 2C1–2C27). BEA has chosen to use those prices, by whatever name, which are closest to the price finally paid. For example, where a good is bought under a firm-fixed-price contract the contract prices could be used. However, if the contract had an escalator clause, then the escalated contract price finally paid by DOD would be used.

Another measurement problem of pricing goods arises from the need to price repetitive purchases, that is, a good with an identical physical specification purchased in different time periods. For many goods this is difficult because many types of available records do not separate recurring and nonrecurring components of a purchase. Nonrecurring components of a purchase might include technical drawings that will appear only in the initial purchase contract. These drawings could be priced as a separately specified item, or, alternatively, their value could be spread over all units made from those technical drawings. If such nonrecurring items are not excluded from contracts where a good with a fixed specification is being priced, they can seriously distort subsequent price change. Consequently, in order to price the identically specified good over time it is necessary to strip out such nonrecurring items from contracts.

Defense purchases are typically for components of a complete good. A round of ammunition, for example, may be purchased with separate contractors supplying the metal casing, fuse, powder, and assembly of the finished round. Virtually every durable good is bought in pieces that are provided to a prime contractor who assembles the components into a ship, tank, missile, or aircraft. In addition, a single contractor may have numerous contracts related to the assembled good, for example, for research and development, technical services, and production components. Each contract is considered by BEA as the basis for a separate transaction that is individually priced.

Many separable goods and services may be bought as part of one contract with one contractor, but not every item within a contract is necessarily priced by BEA. It is not possible or necessary to price every item within a contract, particularly if prices can be expected to move similarly. Therefore, prices were generally obtained for finished items that were separably specified within contracts. The number of pricing specifications that were directly priced is shown in Appendix C for each of the 26 categories into which DOD purchases were stratified.

3.2.2 Specification versus Functional Pricing

Specification pricing and functional pricing are the two major approaches to measuring price change (United Nations 1977, p. 11). Specification pricing, which conforms to other government statistics (e.g., PPI), is the general approach used to measure price change in the NIPAs.

Specification pricing defines a commodity by its physical characteristics; functional pricing, in contrast, defines a commodity by attributes that serve a particular purpose regardless of physical characteristics. What is a quantity change under the specification pricing approach will frequently be a price change under the functional approach.

A specification pricing approach was used to adjust for quality change in DOD purchases. It is similar to the technique used by the Bureau of Labor Statistics for the PPI and CPI (Commerce 1975, pp. 41 ff.). A change in specifications is the key to the determination of quality change; once the existence of quality change has been determined, it must be evaluated. The value of a quality change is defined as the production cost associated with the specification change. For example, if a combat boot is changed at some cost to make it waterproof, a changed specification, then the value of the quality change is defined as the cost of the specification change. In calculating the pure price change in combat boots, it is necessary to adjust for the improved quality. It is important to remember that the valuation of the quality change is based on the cost and not the usefulness of the quality change to the user.

"Costless quality change" is a special problem that was treated in this study with the traditional approach. If the quality of a good has improved but there is no associated change in factor cost, the valuation of the quality change is defined as zero. If the quality of an item has improved and the cost has decreased, the procedure is to treat the good as though no quality change had occurred. The price change is a simple comparison of prices. By making no quality adjustment and using the two unadjusted prices, a price decrease and unchanged quality are reflected.

3.2.3 Other Measurement Problems

Many measurement problems are of concern because the nature of actual purchases makes implementation of the concepts difficult. For example, in some cases quantities could not be associated with certain types of purchases, primarily because they were of a unique nature. The output of research and development purchases could not be specification priced in quantifiable units. Space satellites were another defense purchase that were not directly priced because rapid technological advances of satellites have brought about numerous physical differences that make specification pricing very difficult.

Another measurement problem arises because of what is known as the "warm production base" or purchase of readiness. Briefly, a warm production base reflects a situation where DOD buys a small quantity of a good from a contractor at an extremely high price in order to maintain a production capability in case the good is needed in large quantities in the future. Excess capacity in the aircraft industry has been the subject of a recent study and cited by some as an example of a "hidden" and pervasive warm production base (Department of Defense 1977b). This situation occurs principally, however, in the areas of unique defense goods. Identification of a readiness purchase is not always easy. They were not specifically identified and treated in this study.

The base year for price deflators in the accounts is 1972. However, the selection of this or any base period will present problems if all prices are not at equilibrium. Those prices that have not reached their equilibrium position are over- or underweighted relative to the prices that are at equilibrium in the base period. This problem is found in any statistical series but is accentuated in the case of new weapon system purchases. As production of a new system increases, these purchases generally experience sharp decreases in the quantity of labor inputs per unit and in output prices. That is, cost and price per unit display what is known as a learning curve. Any weapon system that is introduced during or slightly before the base period will be overweighted in the series because its base period price will be unusually high.

3.3 Specific Approaches to Defense Purchases

The universe of purchases was stratified into 26 categories and 87 relatively homogeneous subcategories. These subcategories and their relative importances are shown in Appendix B for 1972 and 1977. Various approaches to deflating these categories reflect the nature of the purchases, available information, and limits of measurement techniques. In order to illustrate a range of problems, results are discussed for five major items: aircraft, missiles, compensation of employees, ships, and military construction.

3.3.1   Aircraft

The aircraft subcategories discussed in this section are those relating to the separately purchased components of new aircraft procurements such as the airframe, engine, and electronic equipment.

The approach used to measure price change of new production aircraft was to use specification pricing techniques on components such as airframes and engines. Major components such as engines are usually purchased by DOD from separate contractors and are furnished to the airframe contractor for installation. Such components, plus the airframe and assembly, were separately priced to develop deflators for purchases of aircraft.

The three most important characteristics determining price change for military aircraft appear to be the number of years a particular model has been in production, the quantity produced in a fiscal year (including non-DOD, i.e., foreign military sales), and the specific component group (engines, electronics, etc.).

The age of an aircraft system influences price change because a "learning curve" dominates price behavior early in the life of a particular model or specification. The learning curve reflects the decreasing costs per unit of production associated with a repetitive operation as the operation is continued. These decreasing costs may apply to several inputs, but they are usually expressed in terms of manhours.

Learning curve theory is not new (Wright 1936). Basically, learning curve theory states that over a wide range of output marginal man-hour requirements per unit can be described by a straight line on log-log paper. Learning curves vary from aircraft to aircraft and from specification to specification.

As the number produced continues to rise, the rate of decline in unit costs will gradually diminish and the unit price approaches a constant. Regardless of the particular learning curve, by the time production reaches the one-hundredth unit, man-hour requirements per unit are nearly constant. This point can be reached by high production rates for a short period of time, or low production rates for a longer time. After this point, the price changes of labor and materials will ordinarily increase as inflation more than offsets the effect of increases in the productivity of labor.

The second characteristic affecting price change is the number of units ordered in a contract. Changes in the quantity of aircraft purchased in a contract have significant effects on unit prices, even if the quantity does not accrue to DOD. "There will be a savings on the order of $90 to $100 million to the U.S. Air Force fiscal year 1980 and fiscal year 1981 F-15 procurements if potential Foreign Military Sales to Israel and Saudi Arabia are consummated and current estimates of delivery schedules and buy quantities remain unchanged" (United States Senate 1978b, p. 4611). Low production rates are typical of current DOD aircraft procurements. Low production rates keep production lines going, avoid start-up and close-down costs, which can be substantial, and keep procurement costs within annual DOD budgets. On a unit cost basis, however, low production rates are costly and reduce possibilities for automation.

The third characteristic affecting price change is the specific component group, that is, airframe, engines, or electronics. Price changes of these major component groups differ because these components are produced with significantly different mixes of labor and capital equipment and reflect differential price movements in the mix of materials.

Direct consideration of these characteristics in the sample selection procedure could result in more efficient samples. However, it was easier to price more aircraft models than it was to develop an efficient sample.

New aircraft were initially stratified into air force, army, and navy purchases, and a sample (shown below) was systematically selected with probability proportional to the estimated value of deliveries. However, the sample is now judgmental and is virtually the universe of new aircraft purchases. Each new aircraft model entering production is added to the sample with certainty. The specifications selected for pricing within a new aircraft, such as the airframe, engines, and electrical equipment, generally account for most of the value of the system.

Air Force	Navy	Army
A-7D	A-4M	AH-1G/S
A-10A	A-6E	C-12A
C-5A	A-7E	CH-47A
C-12A	AH-1G/J/T	UH-1H
C-130E/H	E-2C	UH-60A
CH-47C	EA-6B	
E-3A	F-14A	
F-4E	P-3C	
F-5E	S-3A	
F-15A/B	UH-1N	
F-16A		
F-111D/F		
UH-1D/H		

The value of delivered aircraft, as required for the NIPAs, is not available from any known source. Therefore, the current-dollar value of new aircraft purchases was estimated for each quarter based upon the value of deliveries of the priced components (Commerce 1979, pp. 57–58).

A current-dollar value of deliveries was developed for each directly priced component from the product of delivered units times the component unit price. Within each system this value of deliveries was blown up to the total value of the system to account for any nonpriced components in that system. For systems not in the sample the value of deliveries was estimated as being proportional to those systems that were priced within the military service. Since most systems are included in the sample, the value of unpriced systems is very small relative to the total value of purchases for aircraft.

Aircraft components are frequently purchased at prices that are not fully known until the rewards, penalties, and engineering changes are determined and negotiated at contract completion. The prices generally used were ones which reflect the ultimate total payment by DOD for a good with a given physical specification. Estimated prices at completion were derived from data routinely found in contract control documentation and used whenever they were available. Although these prices at completion are only estimates at any point in time, they are frequently the best of the available prices because they reflect profit adjustments and contractual cost-sharing agreements.

A combination of reports was vital to ensuring that the values used to develop prices related to goods with the same physical specification. Estimated prices at completion were derived from Cost Performance Reports (CPR) after prorating cost sharings, profit, and overhead across the total contract. Cost Information Papers were then used to identify nonrecurring costs that are not shown in CPRs and which, if not removed, would distort the price change.

The previously described specification pricing approach was the basis for the quality adjustment guidelines applied to military aircraft. These guidelines are shown in Appendix D. The results of quality adjusting aircraft of the same model (e.g., A-10A) were surprisingly slight. While the number of engineering changes was great, especially for new models, most changes did not require quality adjustments and those that did made only a slight difference. It was found that most engineering changes did not involve a physical change to the specific item priced, or were undertaken to remedy a design defect, or were done at no change to the contract price. Contracts frequently had clauses that provide for changes at no additional cost if they were below a certain threshold, that is, $25,000. A great deal of the costs usually announced with engineering changes involved nonrecurring items that were not priced, that is, tooling, training, changes to technical manuals, special tools, and modification kits for aircraft already delivered. Such nonrecurring items were treated as separate purchases.

Although the values involved in quality adjusting an existing aircraft model were generally insignificant, when a new model replaces another the differences in costs are substantial. The process of introducing new aircraft involves a procedure known as linking.

Introducing the price of a new model is an extension of the quality adjustment problem that confronts all compilers of price indexes. The following discussion illustrates the methodology as it was applied to the linking of the F-15A to the F-4E.

The F-15 replaced the F-4. Often it is not clear what the new product is replacing, and this obviously can greatly complicate an attempt to link a new product to specific existing products. However, according to the DOD, "The F-15 is an advanced tactical fighter developed for the air superiority mission. It will replace the F-4 as the primary air superiority aircraft" (Department of Defense 1977a, p. 22).

The F-15 had a substantially higher cost, and the question arose as to how much of the higher cost represented quality improvement. The F-15 clearly outperforms the F-4. The F-15, for example, has a lighter basic takeoff weight, shorter takeoff distance, faster sea level rate of climb, quicker time to climb, quicker acceleration time, higher maximum ceiling, higher sustained load factor, slower approach speed. When there is a quality improvement at a higher cost, such as between the F-15 and F-4, then the correct procedure is to value the quality difference and link the two weapon systems, component by component. Linking allows only that part of price change not associated with quality change to be reflected as a price increase. The following is an example of linking in which prices that had been used in the past were quality adjusted so as to be comparable with current period prices. (This is called "back price" linking as distinct from "forward price" linking).

Time Period	Unadjusted Prices	Adjusted	
		Prices	Indexes
1	$5.00	(5.40)	100.0
2	5.00	(5.40)	100.00
3	5.60	5.60	103.7
4	5.88	5.88	108.9
5	5.88	5.88	108.9

Between periods 2 and 3 the unadjusted price increased 60 cents, with 20 cents judged to be a price increase and 40 cents attributed to quality change. Under the back price method of linking, the period 2 price is made $5.40 and the current price is left unchanged, so that between periods 2 and 3 only a 20-cent price increase is shown in the index.

The value of the quality difference between the F-15 and F-4 is defined as the difference in overlap prices in a particular time period. By valuing the difference in models, it is possible to relate the two specifications in terms of each other. These prices should reflect not only the same general price level but also the same relative position on the respective learning curves if serious problems are to be avoided. F-4Es had been delivered by the hundreds before the contract for the first F-15A was signed in 1972. The same point on the learning curve of the F-15A is the proper basis for overlap price measurement of the quality difference. However, in the absence of such an overlap, the one-hundredth unit of the new model was compared to one of the last units of the old model. Both models are represented by points where the learning curve has flattened and additional production is judged to have relatively little effect on the unit price change.

The overlap time period used for valuing the quality difference was taken to be the time at which the first production contract for an F-15 was signed. The F-4E price in the overlap period had the virtue of being an actual transaction price. The F-15A price, however, had to be derived from estimates of future production costs. This calculation was carried out with the DOD estimates of future program costs that are used for their own cost analyses and budgeting for the Congress. This was done for each component; in addition, the inflation factors built into the DOD estimates were removed. What remained is an estimated F-15A component specification price that represents a similar state of learning for the time period of the last F-4E.

The table below shows the airframe deflator for the F-4E and F-15A without adjustment for quality differences and with the adjustment. The Total columns are weighted averages of the F-4E and F-15A series using the quantity of airframes delivered in each year as weights. The index for the F-15A without quality adjustment is based on the functional pricing approach, that is, one F-15A is the same quantity of airframe as one F-4E. Because the initial F-15As that were delivered in 1974 were approximately 3½ times as expensive as the F-4Es, they enter with an index level of 433.3. Adjusting for quality by the procedures described above reduces the F-15A index to 296.8 in 1974. Approximately 40% of the difference in cost between F-4Es and F-15As in 1974 was considered a quality improvement, the remainder a price difference. It should be noted that the percentage decline in price for the F-15As from 1974 to 1977 is the same in both series and mostly represents movement along the learning curve.

Airframe Deflator (1972 = 100)

Year	Without Quality Adjustment			With Quality Adjustment		
	F-4E	F-15A	Total	F-4E	F-15A	Total
1972	100.0		100.0	100.0		100.0
1973	127.2		127.2	127.2		127.2
1974	126.1	433.3	330.9	126.1	296.8	253.3
1975	130.1	418.7	260.6	130.1	286.8	215.7
1976	134.7	329.3	285.4	134.7	225.5	210.4
1977		326.6	326.6		223.7	223.7
1978		334.9	334.9		229.4	229.4

The results of pricing new aircraft are shown in table 3.4. The pronounced contrasts between the IPD movements of navy and air force aircraft especially from 1972 to 1975 are the result of the introduction of new weapon systems. The navy IPDs declined because the first deliveries of the F-14A, S-3A, and E-2C happened to occur during the base year. This caused the base year prices for navy aircraft to be exceptionally high on average, because actual deliveries were those of aircraft produced early in their respective learning curves. This overstates the constant-dollar value of subsequent deliveries of F-14As, S-3As, and E-2Cs to the navy. The air force series, in contrast, had relatively low base year prices because only the older systems were still being delivered in 1972. Therefore, the air force aircraft index moved upward after 1972 when the first deliveries began of the F-15A and A-10A, which were high on their learning curves. The sharp changes in the IPDs for the air force in the fourth quarter of 1973 and navy in the second quarter of 1976 were caused by a change in the mix of deliveries of aircraft components with quite different price indexes.

3.3.2 Missiles

Missile series were developed using the same concepts and measurement conventions as aircraft. The sample selection shown below and the derivation of current-dollar estimates and prices were also similar. The missiles subcategories included in this section are for components of new missiles. The unit of purchase appropriate to measure the price change of missiles was determined by the contractual procedures used by DOD to purchase different missiles. Although some missiles are purchased as complete units, for example, army's Dragon and air force's Maverick, most missiles are purchased as components. These components, such as the missile body, guidance and control unit, and rocket motor are assembled into a final product by the main contractor or by a facility owned and operated by the federal government. In all cases, the particular items priced represented actual purchases from non-DOD sources.

Army and Marine Corps Missiles	ICBM and SLBM	Other Air Force Missiles	Other Navy Missiles
Chapparal	Minuteman	Maverick	Harpoon
Dragon	Poseidon	Shrike	Phoenix
Hawk	Trident	Sidewinder	Shrike
Lance		Sparrow	Sidewinder
Pershing		SRAM	Sparrow
Tow			Standard ER
			Standard MR

The implicit price deflators for missiles shown in table 5 were quite surprising. The army and marine corps missile series showed sharp declines, because early contracts of the Dragon and Tow systems had high base year prices similar to those of navy aircraft. However, the decline was further accentuated because of price competition for relatively large numbers of assembly-line production units. Normally the DOD buys from a single contractor, but DOD is sometimes able to seek a second source for missile production because the number of units involved is so much greater than for aircraft. The army realized large price saving on the Dragon as did the air force and navy on Sparrow missiles, because two contractors were competing for the production contracts. Thus, missile prices moved sharply downward because of both the effect of learning and competition.

3.3.3   Compensation

Compensation of civilian and military employees is the largest category of DOD purchases. It consists of wages, salaries, supplements, benefits, and payments in kind to DOD employees.

Purchases of compensation, like other goods and services, are specification priced. The units of compensation being purchased by the government are hours worked with specified characteristics. The characteristics of education and experience of the employee have been determined to be the major price-determining characteristics of employees in the U.S. economy. It should be noted that Denison (1974) also used sex of the employee as a price-determining characteristic, but this was not deemed necessary for federal government compensation because of the antidiscrimination policies in effect during the period under consideration. Any violations of these policies would represent misclassifications that were not identifiable in the data used. The correct base price measure then is the base period average compensation for each hour worked by individuals who are stratified by education and experience. Since current data on the education and experience of DOD employees are not available, proxy measures for these characteristics were developed through the use of Civil Service grade and step classifications.

The Civil Service classification system (and to a considerable extent the wage grade system for blue-collar workers) provides a built-in measure of these strata because requirements for each grade are based on the education or experience of the employee. In addition, promotions to steps within a grade reflect additional employee experience. "Grade creep," a gradual increase in the average grade of employees that is not commensurate with their education and experience represents an overstatement of employee "quality." However, no data were available on the extent of this or other misclassifications. This study adhered to the NIPA convention of making no adjustments for changes in employee productivity.

Employment data on civilian employees were available by grade and step for each time period. Data on hours worked were not available, so data on "weekly hours paid for" were substituted. These were applied to the employment data to generate the number of hours paid for in each quarter. Data were developed on the average hourly compensation by grade and step for the base period and were multiplied by the number of hours in each grade and step to develop the quarterly estimate of hours paid for valued at base period prices.

A similar but somewhat modified procedure was used for military personnel. Employment was stratified by rank and by years of service as a measure of education and experience. Adjustments were not made for average hours worked, since military personnel are considered to be on duty 24 hours a day, except during actual periods of leave.

Certain allowances (e.g., basic allowance for quarters, uniform and clothing allowance, family separation allowance) were treated as part of basic pay; changes in rates for these allowances appear as price changes. It was assumed that increases in these allowances do not relate to experience and education and, thus, do not reflect increased employee quality. Using this same assumption, the value of food and clothing furnished to employees were also treated as part of basic pay. However, certain types of pay (e.g., flight pay, jump pay) represent additional training or experience of the employee. These types of pay are deflated separately and added to real compensation to reflect the additional quality to DOD.

The military and civilian compensation IPDs are quite different (table 3.6). Although the military and general schedule (GS) civilians have been given the same basic salary increases, the total civilian IPDs increased more rapidly because of the impact of higher pay raises to "wage-board" or blue-collar workers. Wage-board workers are given increases on the basis of local wage surveys; this has resulted in substantially greater increases than those given to military personnel and GS civilians.

3.3.4   New Ship Construction

New ships, like other major weapon systems, are generally purchased as components. Major components, such as propulsion systems and electrical equipment, are often separately contracted for by the navy and delivered to a private shipyard for integration with the hull. The private shipyard constructs the hull, procures some equipment, and installs the government furnished equipment (GFE) to complete the ship for delivery to the navy.

Although purchases of GFE components were separately priced and deflated with standard techniques, ship construction at private shipyards was deflated with a method of pricing different from that used for the other weapon systems. Ship construction is included in the NIPAs on a work put-in-place rather than on a delivery basis, that is, work on ships is recorded on the books of contractors as sales as the work progresses. With other weapon systems involving lengthy production periods, the work done is charged to inventory, which is liquidated only when the completed item has been delivered.

Most attempts to develop prices for ship construction in the past have relied on an input approach. The input method has two drawbacks. First, since the output is not being measured, it is virtually impossible to measure the quality change in the product being produced. Second, any changes in productivity are difficult to measure and incorporate into the estimate of price change. In order to circumvent these problems the BEA decided to select the physical design of several ship models that were kept constant, that is, "frozen." The "frozen" physical design became the pricing specification that was repriced over time at shipyards. In this way the many engineering and design changes that occur during ship construction were assumed to experience the same price change as the basic design. The "frozen" ship approach overcame the drawbacks of a technique based on a fixed set and quantity of inputs. The problems of productivity change and capital/labor substitutions were overcome because the constant specifically defined output permitted variations in inputs.

The exact specification for a frozen ship was developed by BEA in conjunction with selected private shipyards to ensure that the data on labor hours, labor rates, materials, and overhead costs related to an appropriate design that could be reconstructed over time. The ship models whose designs were frozen were an attack submarine (SSN 688 class), surface combatants (FFG-7 class and DD-963 class), and support ship (auxiliary oiler). Once the basic hours, labor rates, materials, and overhead costs were developed for the frozen ship, these data were then reestimated in each succeeding time period to calculate price change for a fixed output.

Total labor hours changed as a result of skill levels at shipyards and the impact of regulations imposed by the Environmental Protection Administration (EPA), Occupational Safety and Health Administration (OSHA), and the navy. The overhead rates used were those prevailing in particular time periods at private shipyards for work on navy ships.

IPDs for materials actually purchased by shipyards for navy ships were not developed because similar materials were bought infrequently and to different specifications. Most material costs were associated with major equipment items such as propulsion turbines, reduction gears, and general classes of goods such as pumps. The contract prices that shipyards actually negotiated with producers of major pieces of equipment and the navy are frequently escalated by the movement of PPIs. Consequently, until a contract is renegotiated, the price change to DOD for many important pieces of equipment will be equal to the movement of particular PPIs. In these instances, weighting of PPIs provided the correct measurement of price change for these items to the shipyard.

A total frozen ship price should include not only the cost of labor, material, and overhead but also profits. Profit, however, relates to the completed ship, and the ship's actual price remains uncertain until delivery is made and the rewards, penalties, engineering changes, and any claims are settled. Moreover, the frozen ship methodology assumes that shipyards are compensated for their costs. If shipyards are not fully compensated because of disputes over cost-sharing or claims made at time of settlement, a frozen ship index will probably overstate the actual price change to the navy. The overstatement, however, relates only to the difference between reported shipyard ship construction costs and the amount paid under the navy contract including any claim settlement. If claims are not reflected in the frozen ship data, then the price change to the navy will be understated to the extent that final claims will be greater than anticipated. As a result of these considerations, no explicit incorporation of profit in frozen ship prices was made, and the direction of any measurement error is unclear at this time.

The price change for the ship category was the net result of significantly different deflators for new ship construction at shipyards and GFE as shown in table 3.7. The relatively low deflator for ship GFE is attributed to the high relative importance of electronic equipment. The prices of many pieces of electronic equipment have declined as a result of new technology and lower labor inputs. The upward price movement of new ship construction reflected declining productivity at several shipyards.

3.3.4   Military Construction

This category includes all construction purchased by the military services on contract from the military construction appropriation. Construction activities included in other categories are those performed in-house by DOD employees, government purchases of construction materials, family housing, and the construction portion of the Minuteman Force Modernization Program.

Purchases of construction in the NIPAs are recorded on a work put-in-place basis. Thus DOD is assumed to purchase the construction as it is performed, even though they do not take title until the contract is completed. During the period of construction, payments are made to the contractor on the basis of an estimate of work completed. While at any given time these payments will not exactly correspond to the total amount of work that has been completed, they are a good approximation.

The definition and measurement of an appropriate price for construction purchases poses many difficult problems. As was indicated in the pricing of ships, input pricing is generally considered to be unsatisfactory in that it does not allow for changes in the productivity of labor, capital/labor substitution, or output quality change.

An attempt was made to bypass these problems and directly price the unit of construction that was being purchased by DOD. The price per unit (i.e., square foot, linear foot, cubic yard, etc.) of a specified type of construction (e.g., barracks) was defined to be the appropriate market price of construction purchased by DOD. Generally, physical changes that were made during the construction period did not affect either the quality or function of the structure. This is because the approach of DOD to construction is to specify functional requirements rather than to enumerate detailed material or structural specifications. For example, the specifications for troop housing center around the number of bathrooms for each intended occupant and requirements such as soundproofing. Deviations from the basic physical specification which affected utilization, for example, a bathroom for every two occupants in place of one for every four, would require quality adjustment. The average unit price, therefore, accurately measures the purchase price of a particular construction type to DOD. The measure of price change derived from these data reflects any changes in productivity, capital/labor substitution, material substitution, etc., that occur during the construction period as well as changing profit margins.

It should be noted that the regional differences in factor costs for the same specification are considered price change to DOD. However, differences in construction performance requirements based on climate (e.g., a storage facility for JP-4 in Alaska vs. Southern California) were considered quality differences.

Generally construction was purchased on fixed-price contracts; therefore, the price was constant for each project through the duration of the construction period. Only changes to the work being performed or legal claims altered the price for a given project. Wherever feasible, the final price paid for a project was used. This price, calculated on a per unit basis, included all changes or modifications during the life of the project.

Military construction purchases were stratified into nine classes (see table 3.17). Reports on selected projects were not always available within these classes, and it was assumed that within each class the project prices moved similarly.

The number of units of construction (square feet or cubic yards) put-in-place per quarter was determined by dividing total units by the number of quarters between contract award and contract completion. In many cases, construction started or ended during a quarter rather than at the beginning or end. Therefore, the nearest one-third of a quarter was determined from the starting month, and quarter units were allocated for one-third or two-thirds of the total.

Expenditures by project were estimated by multiplying the total units put-in-place per quarter on the project by the unit price of the project. Total units per quarter and total current-dollar expenditures for that quarter were aggregated by class and divided to arrive at a weighted average price per quarter stated in dollars per unit put-in-place during that quarter. These average prices by class were used to develop price indexes and then to deflate the current-dollar estimates of the value of construction put-in-place.

Unit price differences relating to geographic area or to project size were assumed to be price differences and not unit quality differences. The concept of quality change used in construction may be illustrated by some specific examples. If the requirements for troop housing were changed from open dormitory sleeping facilities on each floor to private rooms for each occupant, a quality change occurred. If, however, brick exterior walls were used in one facility and concrete block with stucco walls were used in another, there would be no quality difference if both met construction standards with respect to load-bearing, sound-deadening, etc.

Table 3.8 shows implicit price deflators for military construction, which has just been discussed, as well as the somewhat more comprehensive category "structures."

3.4   Comparisons with Measures of Price Change in the Private Sector

In the short run, price changes of goods purchased by the DOD need not be the same as those for similar goods priced in the PPI. These potential differences provided one basis for BEA concern that use of PPIs might provide unreliable estimates of national defense purchases in constant dollars.

The DOD and government in general are considered by the private sector as a distinct market, with its own set of paperwork and special specifications, together with political and social overtones. Products may be similar, but they may be subject to different demands purchased in different lot sizes under different terms of sale and with different specifications as compared to those purchased in civilian markets. Therefore price change in this market may be quite different from the price change experience of the private marketplace. Although the price-determining forces in civilian and military markets are different in a number of respects, they are similar in other respects. For example, materials and labor are drawn from the same sources of supply, the composition of products is roughly the same, and manufacturers may use the same or similar capital equipment in the production of these products.

There has been little information available to test whether price indexes representing goods in civilian markets can be relied upon to represent price trends of articles purchased for military programs. There have been fewer doubts concerning goods like missiles and tanks, which have no civilian counterparts. The use of civilian market price trends for materials (steel, engines, chemicals, etc.) and labor rates as inputs were discussed earlier in the paper. So long as price trends of defense purchases had to be estimated through proxy indexes such as the PPI, which, by definition, excludes sales of unique military purchases, the questions remained largely unresolved. However, when the BEA began to construct price indexes for military purchases, the question could be answered at least in part.

The comparisons made herein are limited but indicate the nature of the problem. Comparisons are made between PPIs and DOD price indexes for petroleum products, citrus fruits, clothing, and hot rolled carbon steel; broader indexes are used for construction. The PPI has been the subject of numerous reviews (Stigler and Kindahl 1970; Council on Wage and Price Stability 1977). One conclusion of the COWPS report that the data reaffirm is that "the scope and coverage of the body of wholesale price data are not adequate for the uses made of the data."

The BEA IPDs are constructed by means of the Paasche formula—that is, weights for each current quarter are used in the calculation of the index change from the base period (1972) to the current period. The PPIs, on the other hand, utilize the Laspeyres formula whereby weights are fixed for relatively long periods of time (five or more years). In order to remove the effect of different price index formulas, the BEA indexes were recalculated at the lowest feasible level as Laspeyres indexes using fixed weights.

All of the price indexes in this section are fixed weighted by base period quantities, as is usual for the Laspeyres price index formulation used by the PPI. Other differences in the methods used by the PPI could not be adjusted for in the DOD data available for this paper. The PPI, for example, frequently uses price as of a single day of each month. The DOD data are generally an average of the transation prices for specification for an entire quarter. The PPI generally represents sellers' prices; the DOD data usually refer to buyers' prices. Further, the PPI makes the seller or buyer part of the pricing specification, that is, if company X provides a price for specification Y, the price of company X for Y is only compared to itself. In calculating transaction prices for DOD, the seller was not part of the pricing specification because the objective was to measure what DOD had to pay for the same specification in different time periods. The BEA indexes are developed quarterly. Since the PPIs are monthly, quarterly indexes for each commodity were computed as simple averages of the three monthly indexes and then put on the reference base of the corresponding BEA series. Despite these differences, a comparison with the PPI is made because they are the government statistics used to represent price change in the private sector, and historically they have been used implicitly to estimate national defense purchases, which are part of federal purchases in constant dollars in the published national income and product accounts.

3.4.1 Petroleum Products

Petroleum products are a major nondurable purchase of the DOD and an especially good series in the PPI, since petroleum prices were overhauled to reflect (recent upgrading that introduced direct pricing of) major market transactions of refiners. Regular gasoline, kerosene base jet fuel, and diesel fuel are purchased by the DOD and are also priced in the PPI. Each of these goods is rather homogeneous so that a comparison of the PPI and prices of defense purchases is greatly facilitated.

Price indexes and specifications are shown in tables 3.9 and 3.10, respectively. Figure 3.1 shows the price change for regular gasoline. The

Fig. 3.1   Comparison of price indexes for regular gasoline (July–September 1973 = 100.0)

indexes were put on a third quarter of 1973 (73-III) base because comparable data at this level of detail were not available for earlier periods.

The PPI data are collected as monthly sales (revenue and volume) for each of the Census Bureau regions for specified products from refiners and deep water terminal operators. The use of monthly sales data results in a one-month reporting lag to the BLS. This lag was removed in the comparisons. The PPI fixes the weight of these petroleum products below the product specification level, that is, each seller of these petroleum products has its weight fixed at a regional level regardless of actual sales in current time periods.

The DOD average specification price, in contrast, is a delivered price (the quotient of disbursements divided by delivered quantities) for the national stock number specification in each quarter. Available DOD data did not allow fixing weights at a regional and company level as is done in the PPI so that the effect of such weighting differences is unknown.

The price indexes for these petroleum products indicate that the price change to the DOD was much greater than it was to industrial and commercial consumers in the PPI.

The DOD began having problems obtaining bids for petroleum products as early as September 1972, a full year before the Arab embargo of October 1973. Growth of refinery capacity slowed in the United States during the late 1960s, in part from declines in domestic crude oil production capacity and environmental legislation. By late 1972, many domestic refiners no longer had surplus refining capacity. Quantities offered by domestic refiners to DOD for delivery in the first half of 1973 fell far below historic experience. Foreign offers did not exhibit a similar trend until the second half of 1973. As nonmilitary demand rose and surplus refining capacity diminished, price freeze regulations enacted in May 1973 froze price levels for petroleum products to the military at levels far below those in commercial markets (United States House 1974). Many contracts that had been negotiated at much higher prices for delivery beginning in July 1973 were faced with a government edict to roll prices back to the level in earlier contracts. Consequently, many suppliers exercised their legal right to refuse delivery, and DOD was forced to draw down their inventories. The embargo imposed by the Arab states in October 1973 further reduced supply, and DOD inventories dropped sharply. The inventory reductions halted in December 1973 as a result of temporary restrictions on consumption and increasing supply resulting from legislative allocations. DOD was then able to start rebuilding inventories, but at considerably higher prices than earlier.

Measures of price change say nothing about average prices. This fact is often forgotten and is especially revealing for these petroleum products. Average prices of regular gasoline sold to the DOD and commercial consumers appear below for 1973-III and 1978-IV in cents-per-gallon.

	73-III	78-IV	73-III/78-IV Difference
PPI	18.0	43.9	25.9
DOD	12.2	37.3	25.5

Both sets of prices exclude taxes and include transportation charges to the consumer which can change over time. The absolute difference in the price change of regular gasoline seems insignificant given the measurement differences of the two series. The DOD price index increased more than the PPI because its base period price was lower. The same absolute change, therefore, yields a greater percentage change to DOD.

Jet fuel purchased by DOD had a smaller price change than that reflected in the PPI. Both the airlines and the DOD are large consumers eagerly sought by refiners. JP-4 is a kerosene base jet fuel that is virtually the same as reflected in the PPI. JP-5 is a naptha base jet fuel which is made about equally from gasoline and kerosene components of crude petroleum and accounts for most of DOD jet fuel. JP-5 experienced price change less than that of the kerosene base jet fuel and greater than that for regular gasoline, which is what one would expect.

Average prices for jet fuel are shown below for 73-III and 78-IV in cents-per-gallon. Both series include some transportation charges and

	73-III	78-IV	Difference
PPI (kerosene base)	12.5	39.2	26.7
JP-4 (kerosene base)	13.2	38.7	25.5
JP-5 (naptha base)	14.2	39.5	25.3

exclude taxes. Despite the effect of different methodologies, a one-cent per gallon difference in price change for jet fuel is substantial. The impact of the price increase to DOD was reflected earlier because of the decline of surplus refining capacity and the frequency and method by which DOD solicits competitive bids. Some airlines were fortunate to have bought under multiyear contracts that resulted in lower average prices, even though surplus refining capacity was disappearing and petroleum exporting countries were setting higher crude oil prices.

Diesel fuel prices as shown in table 3.9 increased dramatically more to DOD than shown in the PPI. Prices in cents-per-gallon are shown below.

	73-III	78-IV	Difference
PPI	13.8	38.7	24.9
DOD	10.6	39.2	28.6

The absolute difference in price changes between PPI and DOD is significant and represents the loss of surplus refining capacity. The price-per-gallon differential in 78-IV is probably not significant. The DOD is no longer sought as a market to sell off production needed to keep refineries at full capacity.

3.4.2   Citrus Fruits

Citrus fruits have volatile price changes that are greatly influenced by the weather, season, and competitive markets.

The PPI prices reflect only the spot market prices in Chicago and New York. Prices are taken from trade publications on the Tuesday of the week containing the thirteenth of the month. The DOD price in contrast reflects both the spot and contract market throughout the United States. The DOD average price each quarter is a self-weighted average of prices paid in all geographical regions and types of transactions (spot, contract). The DOD price indexes are quarterly averages of the three months weighted by purchases in each month. The PPI quarterly average, in contrast, is an equally weighted average of spot market prices, for geographical points, on a single day. These differences in methods are significant because of the substantial swings in the price of these products over a three-month period. Price indexes and detailed specifications for citrus fruits are shown in tables 3.11 and 3.12, respectively.

Figure 3.2 shows the movement of the two composite price indexes over time. The long-term trend is clearly evident, and the short-run differences in the magnitudes of price change are significant. The use of PPIs would generally have understated constant-dollar citrus purchases because the price index is generally greater than that shown for DOD purchase prices.

3.4.3   Clothing

Comparisons for groups of clothing and footwear were made with similar PPI groupings. The composite indexes for men's apparel and footwear are shown on a fixed-weighted basis in table 3.13. The detailed specifications making up the two composite indexes are shown in table 3.14. Figure 3.3 shows the price change of men's footwear in the PPI and DOD.

An unpublished study by Allan Searle (1977) made an item-by-item comparison of DOD and PPI price indexes for similar clothing, textiles, and footwear. Searle found greater price dispersion of DOD apparel and footwear prices than was reflected in the PPI. He also found that substitution of DOD for PPI weights had no effect on PPIs. However, the substitution of PPI for DOD weights had an appreciable downward effect on the DOD indexes because of the impact of greater price dispersion of DOD items.

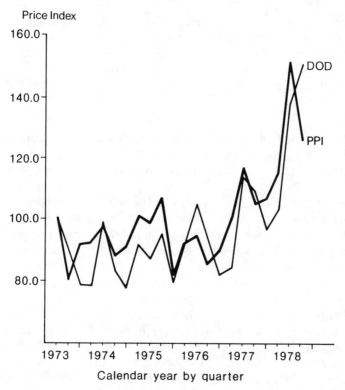

Price Index

Fig. 3.2   Comparison of price indexes for citrus fruit (July–September
                     1973 = 100.0)

Both the DOD and PPI indexes were put on a base of first quarter
1972 = 100 to make them comparable. No attempt was made to weight
similar specifications equally within the composites. Although the more
rapid rise of DOD clothing prices cannot be attributed to any one factor,
several influences were isolated. The DOD items frequently represented
the purchase of a service, for example, the materials were supplied by
DOD to the contractor who manufactured the shirt. The DOD series
would then have a higher labor component than the PPI price, which
includes the producers' cost of materials.

Another factor is that DOD is required to purchase combat boots
produced at certain federal prisons. In many cases, these prices were
higher than bid prices from private producers, which accelerated the
change in the price of footwear to DOD.

If composite PPI indexes were used to deflate defense purchases, they
would have overstated constant-dollar purchases of men's apparel in
almost every time period. Using proxy indexes for DOD clothing and

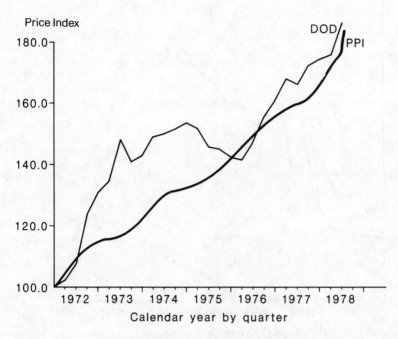

Fig. 3.3   Comparison of price indexes for men's footwear (January–March 1972 = 100.0)

footwear seems unlikely to provide a correct estimate of constant-dollar purchases or price change.

3.4.4 Hot Rolled Carbon Plate

Hot rolled carbon plate is purchased by the DOD under a variety of detailed specifications. These specifications are shown in table 3.15. The prices for these various specifications were converted to a price per ton, and then a weighted average price for delivered hot rolled carbon plate to DOD was calculated. The PPI is a list price less usual discounts. The price change to DOD is greater for most periods for which data were available, as shown by the indexes in table 3.16 and figure 3.4. The Cost of Living Council also found that average realized prices for hot rolled carbon sheets increased more than those shown by the PPI (Council on Wage and Price Stability 1977, p. IV–19).

Although the price change reflected in the DOD data is greater, the average price for 100 pounds was very similar in the base period (72-IV).

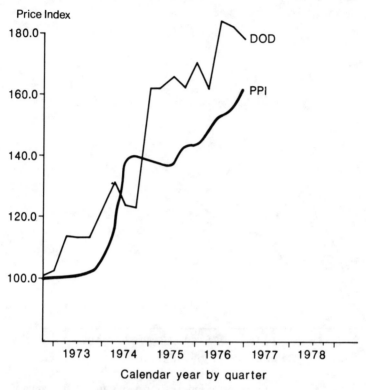

Fig. 3.4   Comparison of price indexes for hot rolled carbon plate (October–December 1972 = 100.0)

This is in sharp contrast to the petroleum products where base period average prices were significantly different. These average prices in dollars per 100 pounds are shown below for 1972-IV and 1977-I.

	PPI ($)	DOD ($)	Difference ($)
72-IV	8.657	8.578	.079
77-I	13.364	15.212	1.848

The increase in DOD average prices does not seem due to a change in mix, that is, to the use of several national stock numbers (NSN) or the method used to combine them. This is supported in that the only product to be delivered in both 72-IV and 77-I was NSN 9515–00–153–3310 and was close to the average. The differences appear more likely due to changes in discounts and extra charges which accompany changes in market conditions.

3.4.5 Construction

There is no reasonable comparison between the PPI and the DOD construction series. The PPI contains only price indexes of construction materials, while the DOD series includes the total construction cost (labor, materials, and overhead) and profit. There exist many other measures of price change for construction, most of which are based on input costs of materials and labor. The Engineering News Record Building Cost Index (ENR) is used by DOD as a guide in evaluating cost changes of military construction. The ENR index includes labor costs as well as materials costs (see table 3.17) but contains no adjustments for changes in labor productivity, competitive conditions, or other intangibles.

The ENR was rebased to 1972, and the DOD construction series was recalculated on a fixed-weight Laspeyres basis for comparison purposes (see fig. 3.5 and table 3.18). The two series show a remarkably similar trend over the entire period. There are, however, large differences in short-term changes, especially during 1973 and from mid-1977 to mid-1978.

3.4.6 Summary of Detailed Comparisons

Detailed comparisons of PPIs and DOD indexes have been made showing differences and similarities that are striking. The differences are short term, while the similarities are long term. The nature of the DOD market makes it likely that it will experience price changes that will be significantly different from these prevailing in the private sector. It seems obvious that the precision of short-term estimates of price change of defense purchases cannot be reliable unless actual DOD transactions are measured.

3.5. Future Plans

The direct pricing of DOD purchases for the purpose of deflating national defense in the NIPAs has just begun. A set of historical statistics has been prepared and is updated on an ongoing basis. These data were fully incorporated into the December 1980 benchmark revision of the NIPAs and are updated each quarter in the *Survey of Current Business*.

The program is unique in many respects. One aspect is the effort to extract information from massive amounts of data on actual transactions contained on computer tapes. Such an approach is quite different from the usual manner in which price indexes are compiled, and the price data base rapidly becomes too large to be individually handled and under-

Price Index

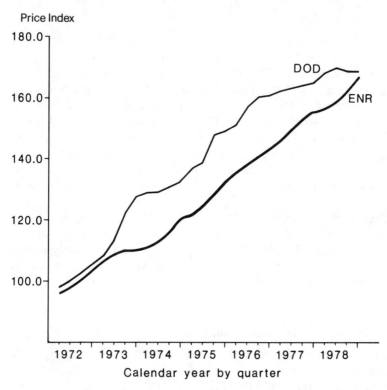

Fig. 3.5   Comparison of price indexes for construction (calendar year
1972 = 100.0)

stood. More reliance is placed on conventions and edit steps, which are
established to process data and reveal problems with the basic inputs.

Deflation of DOD purchases has been of primary interest in this
project. However, there is no reason why the rest of government (i.e.,
federal, state, and local) cannot be directly priced and deflated. There is
evidence that records or prices paid exist at all levels of government. Only
the lack of resources prevents the assembly of an appropriate data base.

Deflation at this time has been done primarily for the purpose of
deflating the NIPAs. Other users of statistics have interests that might be
better served by price indexes based on approaches other than specification pricing and aggregations other than the NIPAs. Aggregations by
appropriations or military force structures seem to have special appeal to
the DOD. The future may well inaugurate a time when the price index
techniques and principles will be known widely enough that individuals
and organizations will create their own measures in order to facilitate
their analysis. The Office of Management and Budget, for example,
could examine budgets with much greater sophistication if programs were
deflated by actual and not proxy measures of price change. The life cycle

costs of various programs (i.e., the research and development, production, and maintenance) could all be integrated and deflated to reveal the true price change and cost of existing and planned programs.

Individuals and organizations have relied too long on existing price indexes. Indexes based upon government documents are attractive because they impose no direct paperwork or reporting burden on the private sector. The knowledge and resources are already in place to create comprehensive price indexes relating to government activity.

Table 3.1   Relationship of National Defense Purchases to the GNP

	1972	1973	1974	1975	1976	1977	1978
				$Billions			
GNP	1185.9	1326.4	1434.2	1549.2	1718.0	1918.0	2156.1
Govt. purchases goods and services	253.1	270.4	304.1	339.9	362.1	394.5	432.6
Federal	101.7	102.0	111.0	122.7	129.2	143.9	153.4
National defense	73.1	72.8	77.0	83.0	86.0	93.3	100.0
				% GNP			
GNP	100.0	100.0	100.0	100.0	100.0	100.0	100.0
Govt. purchases goods and services	21.4	20.4	21.2	21.9	21.2	20.6	20.1
Federal	8.6	7.7	7.7	7.9	7.5	7.5	7.1
National defense	6.2	5.5	5.5	5.4	5.0	4.9	4.6

Table 3.2   **Department of Defense Purchases, NIPA Basis by Major Type of Product ($Millions)**

Calendar Year	Total Purchases	Durable Goods	Non-durable Goods	Services	Struc-tures	Compen-sation
			Current-Dollars			
1972	72,053	14,921	5,006	15,223	1,671	35,232
1973	72,743	14,350	4,663	16,005	1,987	35,738
1974	78,072	15,723	5,886	17,649	2,081	37,033
1975	81,288	17,360	5,454	17,266	2,166	39,042
1976	83,601	18,064	4,931	18,479	2,044	40,083
1977	90,700	20,873	5,643	20,107	2,088	42,009
1978[a]	98,126	22,873	6,160	21,826	2,098	45,169
			Constant 1972 Dollars			
1972	72,053	14,921	5,006	15,223	1,671	35,232
1973	68,268	13,938	4,107	15,115	1,773	33,335
1974	67,845	14,737	3,595	15,172	1,693	32,648
1975	65,259	15,113	2,941	13,214	1,655	32,336
1976	63,160	14,588	2,531	13,026	1,443	31,572
1977	63,925	15,443	2,646	13,051	1,396	31,389
1978[a]	64,593	15,665	2,649	13,331	1,302	31,646
			Implicit Price Deflators			
1972	100.00	100.0	100.0	100.0	100.0	100.0
1973	106.56	103.0	113.5	105.9	112.1	107.2
1974	115.07	104.7	163.7	116.3	122.9	113.4
1975	124.56	114.9	185.4	130.7	130.9	120.7
1976	132.36	123.8	194.8	141.9	141.7	127.0
1977	141.92	135.2	213.2	154.1	149.6	133.8
1978[a]	151.9	146.0	232.5	163.7	161.1	142.7

[a]Preliminary.

Table 3.3   Comparison of Published Implicit Price Deflators and New Estimates Incorporating DOD Data

	1973 Previously Published Estimate	1973 New Estimate	Difference	1974 Previously Published Estimate	1974 New Estimate	Difference	1975 Previously Published Estimate	1975 New Estimate	Difference
				Index Numbers, 1972 = 100.0					
GNP	105.80	105.86	.06	116.02	115.95	−.07	127.15	127.02	−.13
Govt. purchases goods and services	106.7	107.0	.3	117.5	117.1	−.4	128.9	128.3	−.6
Federal	105.8	106.6	.8	115.9	115.1	−.8	127.5	125.9	−1.6
Less compensation	104.0	105.4	1.4	119.0	117.1	−1.9	133.5	130.1	−3.4
				% Change from the Preceding Year					
GNP	5.8	5.9	.1	9.7	9.5	−.2	9.6	9.5	−.1
Govt. purchases goods and services	6.7	7.0	.3	10.1	9.4	−.7	9.7	9.6	−.1
Federal	5.8	6.6	.8	9.6	8.0	−1.6	10.0	9.4	−.6
Less compensation	4.0	5.4	1.4	14.4	11.1	−3.3	12.2	11.1	−1.1

	1976			1977			1978[a]		
	Previously Published Estimate	New Estimate	Difference	Previously Published Estimate	New Estimate	Difference	Previously Published Estimate	New Estimate	Difference
Index Numbers, 1972 = 100.0									
GNP	133.76	133.70	−.06	141.61	141.64	.03	152.09	152.07	−.02
Govt. purchases goods and services	136.8	136.5	−.3	146.3	146.5	.2	157.8	157.7	−.1
Federal	134.4	133.6	−.8	142.7	143.2	.5	153.3	153.0	−.3
Less compensation	140.3	138.7	−1.6	148.7	149.6	.9	160.8	160.2	−.6
% Change from the Preceding Year									
GNP	5.2	5.3	.1	5.9	5.9	0	7.4	7.3	−.1
Govt. purchases goods and services	6.1	6.4	.3	7.0	7.3	.3	7.9	7.6	−.3
Federal	5.4	6.1	.7	6.2	7.2	1.0	7.4	6.8	−.6
Less compensation	5.1	6.6	1.5	6.0	7.9	1.9	8.1	7.1	−1.0

Source: Bureau of Economic Analysis.
Note: All estimates are based on data prior to the 1980 GNP benchmark revision.
[a]Preliminary.

Table 3.4　　　　Implicit Price Deflators for DOD Purchases
of Aircraft (CY 1972 = 100)

Calendar Year/ Quarter	Total	New Army Aircraft	New Air Force Aircraft	New Navy and Marine Corps Aircraft
1972	100.0	100.0	100.0	100.0
1973	101.8	104.4	107.4	97.8
1974	97.6	116.0	113.4	87.9
1975	107.9	127.8	132.2	92.4
1976	117.5	144.4	135.2	102.7
1977	132.3	142.4	153.9	121.8
1978[a]	146.2	147.2	155.7	142.2
1972-I	96.2	98.7	91.1	99.4
II	101.9	99.9	104.6	100.1
III	100.7	99.9	101.9	100.1
IV	101.0	101.5	102.4	100.2
1973-I	102.5	101.8	105.3	101.0
II	103.2	104.7	110.0	102.0
III	104.1	107.5	113.6	99.7
IV	97.9	110.4	103.0	92.2
1974-I	99.6	113.2	115.6	93.2
II	97.9	116.1	109.7	89.7
III	98.7	118.8	110.8	90.5
IV	94.5	121.8	117.8	79.7
1975-I	104.5	124.6	132.2	89.4
II	105.9	127.4	138.5	89.3
III	111.3	127.5	134.4	95.2
IV	109.4	128.8	127.4	95.7
1976-I	117.3	136.7	127.5	99.7
II	119.6	144.8	139.3	102.9
III	116.3	154.1	139.3	103.2
IV	116.9	146.4	136.1	104.8
1977-I	123.9	142.3	145.6	113.5
II	132.3	141.9	155.0	122.4
III	133.6	142.2	151.2	123.5
IV	139.8	143.2	163.5	127.5
1978[a]-I	141.0	142.6	153.8	133.1
II	146.7	141.3	154.3	147.1
III	147.1	141.0	155.0	146.1
IV	149.4	157.4	158.6	142.1

Source: Bureau of Economic Analysis.
Note: The total for the aircraft category includes subcategories not shown separately for aircraft modifications, spare and repair parts, support equipment and facilities. Engineering services, other contractual services, and government-furnished materials are excluded from the aircraft category.
[a]Preliminary.

Table 3.5   Implicit Price Deflators for DOD Purchases of New Missiles
Systems Components, by Major Subcategory (CY 1972 = 100)

Calendar Year/ Quarter	Total	Army and Marine Corps Missiles	Air Force Other Missiles	Navy Other Missiles	Intercontinental and Submarine launched Ballistic Missiles
1972	100.0	100.0	100.0	100.0	100.0
1973	98.6	98.9	84.3	106.8	95.6
1974	96.0	90.1	69.8	106.5	98.3
1975	104.2	92.0	70.2	102.8	111.7
1976	115.3	74.9	80.9	128.0	141.0
1977	122.0	75.1	128.7	107.7	162.4
1978[a]	128.1	85.2	118.2	131.4	173.6
1972-I	100.5	105.1	102.6	104.6	100.5
II	100.3	98.2	102.7	105.0	100.2
III	100.4	98.8	100.9	105.3	100.1
IV	99.2	98.7	92.7	92.3	99.6
1973-I	99.6	98.6	93.3	95.4	99.3
II	98.9	100.8	93.3	104.0	95.1
III	99.4	99.7	87.0	107.7	92.3
IV	96.5	97.3	76.5	116.8	93.6
1974-I	92.9	89.5	71.1	92.5	97.4
II	93.3	90.2	71.1	94.5	97.3
III	97.1	88.7	69.9	110.4	97.5
IV	101.0	91.8	65.6	120.1	101.2
1975-I	102.5	94.1	64.7	89.4	109.8
II	101.0	92.4	67.9	97.8	110.0
III	106.9	100.4	74.4	109.1	112.6
IV	107.6	80.0	75.1	125.4	116.7
1976-I	114.4	71.0	83.0	148.6	135.7
II	115.3	66.3	81.4	163.0	140.2
III	117.4	85.4	79.4	118.3	142.2
IV	114.2	79.5	80.5	103.8	146.2
1977-I	116.4	72.0	127.7	104.7	152.6
II	123.1	77.2	126.9	104.7	160.0
III	120.5	74.1	127.2	107.0	165.1
IV	129.2	78.5	135.2	113.3	172.1
1978[a]-I	121.1	82.6	129.2	132.7	179.5
II	123.0	86.8	121.1	125.6	171.5
III	133.5	85.6	113.7	130.0	177.1
IV	134.2	85.3	115.1	137.8	167.1

Source: Bureau of Economic Analysis.
Note: The total for the missile category includes missile modifications, spare and repair parts, support equipment and facilities which are not shown separately. Engineering and other contractual services, components produced in industrially funded activities, and the construction portion of the Minuteman force modernization program are excluded from the missiles category.
[a]Preliminary.

Table 3.6   Implicit Price Deflators for Compensation of DOD
             Military and Civilian Personnel (CY 1972 = 100)

Calendar Year/ Quarter	Total	Military	Civilian
1972	100.0	100.0	100.0
1973	107.2	107.0	107.5
1974	113.4	113.1	114.1
1975	120.7	118.7	124.0
1976	127.0	123.7	132.2
1977	133.8	129.5	140.7
1978	142.6	137.3	151.0
1972-I	98.4	99.0	97.3
II	98.6	98.9	98.0
III	99.1	98.4	100.2
IV	104.1	103.7	104.6
1973-I	105.3	104.8	106.3
II	105.5	105.7	105.1
III	107.0	106.6	107.7
IV	111.1	111.1	111.0
1974-I	111.1	111.2	110.9
II	111.4	111.2	111.8
III	113.1	112.4	114.3
IV	118.2	117.5	119.3
1975-I	118.8	117.5	120.9
II	119.2	117.5	122.0
III	120.2	117.5	124.5
IV	124.8	122.3	128.7
1976-I	125.3	122.3	130.1
II	125.6	122.3	130.8
III	125.9	122.6	131.2
IV	131.0	127.5	136.7
1977-I	131.4	127.5	137.6
II	131.7	127.5	138.4
III	132.2	127.5	139.6
IV	140.0	135.4	147.4
1978[a]-I	140.5	135.4	148.6
II	140.8	135.7	148.8
III	141.0	135.6	149.5
IV	148.3	142.5	157.2

Source: Bureau of Economic Analysis.
[a]Preliminary.

Table 3.7   **Implicit Price Deflators
for DOD Purchases of Ships (CY 1972 = 100)**

Calendar Year/ Quarter	Ships	New Ship Construction at Private Shipyards	Government furnished Equipment for New Ship Construction
1972	100.0	100.0	100.0
1973	109.2	113.4	103.5
1974	125.5	133.2	113.4
1975	139.7	155.0	117.8
1976	146.1	165.7	118.9
1977	157.8	186.1	124.8
1978[a]	171.5	199.5	137.7
1972-I	99.7	99.7	99.8
II	100.1	100.0	100.1
III	100.1	100.1	100.0
IV	100.1	100.2	100.1
1973-I	106.5	111.7	99.5
II	107.9	113.0	101.3
III	111.1	114.0	106.5
IV	112.5	115.2	108.3
1974-I	117.7	123.1	109.8
II	122.0	127.8	112.5
III	128.7	138.8	113.2
IV	132.4	142.1	117.4
1975-I	134.9	150.2	113.2
II	137.9	152.4	116.9
III	143.2	157.7	121.9
IV	144.0	160.7	120.1
1976-I	143.3	160.8	118.0
II	145.7	161.8	121.5
III	146.8	166.1	118.0
IV	148.8	174.7	118.4
1977-I	155.3	184.4	122.1
II	160.9	185.5	130.7
III	156.1	186.3	121.7
IV	158.9	188.3	124.9
1978[a]-I	168.4	195.4	135.6
II	171.0	200.0	136.6
III	172.5	200.6	138.6
IV	173.9	201.7	140.0

Source: Bureau of Economic Analysis.
Note: The ship category also includes conversions at private shipyards and government-furnished equipment for conversions.
[a]Preliminary.

Table 3.8 **Implicit Price Deflators for DOD Purchases of Structures and Military Construction (CY 1972 = 100)**

Calendar Year/ Quarter	Structures	Military Construction
1972	100.0	100.0
1973	112.1	112.8
1974	123.0	124.0
1975	131.0	132.0
1976	143.8	144.1
1977	151.8	152.5
1978[a]	161.1	162.1
1972-I	98.0	97.2
II	98.7	98.3
III	101.6	102.3
IV	101.9	102.2
1973-I	104.6	104.7
II	108.4	108.6
III	115.4	116.0
IV	119.6	120.7
1974-I	124.1	126.0
II	124.9	126.4
III	126.7	127.5
IV	116.7	116.4
1975-I	120.9	121.5
II	129.4	129.7
III	137.3	137.7
IV	136.3	137.7
1976-I	139.4	139.7
II	145.8	146.3
III	146.1	146.5
IV	144.8	145.1
1977-I	136.9	136.8
II	158.8	160.4
III	155.5	156.2
IV	158.2	158.9
1978[a]-I	158.9	159.6
II	162.1	163.9
III	161.3	162.6
IV	162.1	162.2

Source: Bureau of Economic Analysis.
Note: Structures include, in addition to military construction, family housing, missile silos, and net purchases of existing structures.
[a]Preliminary.

Table 3.9   **Petroleum Products Comparisons (CY 1973-III = 100)**

Calendar Year/ Quarter	Regular Gasoline		Jet Fuel			Diesel Fuel	
	PPI	DOD	PPI	DOD (JP–4)	DOD (JP–5)	PPI	DOD
1973-III	100.0	100.0	100.0	100.0	100.0	100.0	100.0
IV	105.6	119.5	107.8	115.8	106.9	110.1	139.3
1974-I	133.7	237.3	132.6	198.8	183.4	156.0	248.3
II	160.6	230.4	165.2	207.1	204.2	189.4	250.9
III	176.4	248.2	190.0	245.4	227.0	210.2	272.0
IV	168.3	272.7	197.8	249.9	233.8	206.6	288.8
1975-I	169.6	286.3	205.5	237.2	227.5	203.8	290.0
II	179.0	289.1	218.2	234.8	226.7	206.1	289.4
III	201.6	289.5	230.0	240.9	220.1	219.5	307.1
IV	207.5	289.7	237.2	236.6	228.5	230.0	288.7
1976-I	201.0	304.2	245.6	239.2	230.8	234.1	300.3
II	198.3	313.3	240.7	237.3	221.0	230.5	306.2
III	215.5	308.6	240.9	241.5	227.2	234.4	298.1
IV	215.7	309.6	250.1	246.3	234.2	240.5	292.7
1977-I	213.2	319.8	262.8	250.6	243.3	254.3	299.9
II	223.6	321.7	276.7	263.5	252.3	266.3	321.5
III	228.5	321.4	283.3	270.3	256.7	268.3	337.7
IV	224.6	317.6	298.0	277.4	270.4	269.8	334.9
1978-I	222.0	309.6	305.2	283.9	268.1	272.8	345.3
II	225.1	330.2	308.6	282.6	267.7	270.8	338.6
III	238.8	327.9	312.9	286.1	273.0	271.0	341.8
IV	245.4	309.7	315.0	293.8	227.8	279.4	369.5

Source: Bureau of Economic Analysis.

Table 3.10 **Petroleum Product Specifications**

Regular gasoline
PPI
    PPI 05–71–02–03, gasoline, regular grade, monthly sales to commercial consumers
DOD
    NSN 9130–00–160–1818, gasoline, automotive, combat type I, MIL–G–3056, NATO code no. F–46, MG1
Jet fuel
PPI
    PPI 05–72–03–01, jet fuel, kerosene base, commercial type, monthly sales to airline industry, bonded fuel excluded
DOD (JP–4)
    NSN 9130–00–256–8613, turbine fuel, aviation, grade JP–4, (naptha base), MIL–T–5624
DOD (JP–5)
    NSN 9130–00–273–2379, turbine fuel, aviation, grade JP–5 (kerosene base), MIL–T–5624
Diesel fuel
PPI
    PPI 05–73–03–01, diesel fuel, no. 2 or standard diesel, monthly sales to large consumers
DOD
    NSN 9140–00–273–2377, diesel fuel, MIL–F–16884 (NATO symbol F–76)

Source: Bureau of Economic Analysis.

Table 3.11   **Citrus Fruits**

Calendar Year/ Quarter	Citrus Fruits		Grapefruit		Lemons		Oranges	
	DOD	PPI	DOD	PPI	DOD	PPI	DOD	PPI
1973-III	100.0	100.0	100.0	100.0	100.0	100.0	100.0	100.0
IV	86.7	80.0	66.8	74.4	95.0	77.6	93.1	91.2
1974-I	78.3	91.3	60.9	57.1	91.4	103.4	72.6	106.6
II	77.8	91.9	61.0	64.2	90.3	94.8	72.3	117.5
III	98.2	97.6	82.4	73.7	108.3	102.6	96.2	114.8
IV	82.7	87.6	63.8	62.3	89.8	91.1	90.1	109.3
1975-I	77.3	90.9	62.1	67.5	82.7	100.5	83.9	98.6
II	91.4	100.8	82.3	75.4	94.8	115.2	95.0	101.6
III	86.4	98.7	82.2	91.8	86.2	106.8	91.7	90.5
IV	94.3	106.8	112.5	61.9	93.2	135.0	75.8	102.6
1976-I	79.2	81.7	60.5	63.7	87.8	86.8	83.6	92.2
II	90.2	91.7	74.3	70.1	103.7	105.1	81.8	90.0
III	104.7	94.7	104.2	97.7	105.0	90.9	104.7	98.7
IV	94.2	84.4	86.5	76.3	90.8	85.2	109.7	91.9
1977-I	81.7	89.2	74.7	64.4	70.0	99.7	112.3	96.8
II	83.9	100.5	82.7	71.3	66.0	106.4	120.1	122.1
III	113.5	116.4	128.2	110.5	100.0	117.3	123.2	124.6
IV	108.8	104.3	88.6	79.7	104.0	83.0	140.9	173.7
1978-I	96.1	106.1	74.7	81.2	89.9	97.4	132.4	151.4
II	103.7	115.8	74.3	82.8	106.5	136.1	131.3	113.4
III	137.6	151.5	82.9	106.6	166.1	180.4	144.0	172.8
IV	150.5	125.5	126.4	122.2	144.2	95.9	190.0	187.7

Source: Bureau of Economic Analysis.

Table 3.12   **Citrus Fruit Specifications**

DOD
  NSN 8915–00–126–8804, oranges, fresh any variety except temple
  NSN 8915–00–582–4071, lemons, fresh
  NSN 8915–00–616–0198, grapefruit, fresh
PPI
  01–11–01–01, grapefruit, Florida, white, seedless, sizes 32, 36, 40, N.Y. Auction, 4/5
    bushel
  01–11–01–04, lemons, California, sizes 115, 140, 165, half box, Chicago Auction
    marted
  01–11–01–11, oranges, California, Naval or Valencia, sizes 88 and 113, half box,
    Chicago Auction market

Source: Bureau of Economic Analysis.

Table 3.13   **Men's Clothing and Footwear**

Calendar Year/ Quarter	Men's Apparel		Men's Footwear	
	DOD	PPI	DOD	PPI
1972-I	100.0	100.0	100.0	100.0
II	102.2	100.3	101.8	104.7
III	103.5	100.9	106.7	107.7
IV	104.7	102.1	122.3	110.8
1973-I	105.7	103.1	128.7	114.1
II	105.6	104.6	133.5	115.6
III	108.8	105.7	146.5	115.6
IV	121.2	108.6	139.4	118.3
1974-I	136.3	112.6	141.8	120.9
II	138.0	117.7	147.6	125.7
III	153.1	121.8	148.1	128.2
IV	164.8	124.5	150.8	130.8
1975-I	161.5	124.5	152.2	131.6
II	147.2	123.5	150.2	132.8
III	143.9	123.8	144.8	134.2
IV	145.3	126.5	144.5	136.9
1976-I	144.9	129.4	140.4	140.8
II	148.3	131.1	140.0	145.9
III	147.8	135.2	145.7	148.9
IV	154.9	138.6	154.5	150.8
1977-I	156.7	142.4	159.7	153.7
II	159.6	143.8	167.7	157.1
III	160.2	146.0	164.5	159.4
IV	167.3	147.2	171.8	161.7
1987-I	164.8	148.4	173.2	166.6
II	162.5	149.3	175.2	172.1
III	163.1	151.1	184.3	175.5
IV	163.8	154.0	185.1	183.2

Source: Bureau of Economic Analysis.

189

Table 3.14 **Men's Clothing and Footwear Specifications**

Men's Apparel

DOD
  NSN 8405–00–082–6609, trousers utility cotton sateen, OG–107
  MIL–T–833 k (class 1) dtd 11 Feb 71 and am. #2 dated 16 Feb 72
  NSN 8405–00–614–9938, shirt, utility, durable press, army shade 507
  NSN 8405–00–935–2714, trouser, mens, poly/wool, tropical blue shade 3346,
    type 1, class 5
  NSN 8415–00–163–7701, trouser, food handlers, cotton drill white
  NSN 8415–00–177–4834, cap, hot weather, OG–106
  NSN 8415–00–268–7871, gloves, leather, work, cream heavy M–1950
  NSN 8415–00–394–3598, trousers, flying men's, cotton warp and nylon filling
    oxford USAF shade 1509, sage green (modified F–18)
  NSN 8415–00–491–2679, coveralls, flying men's cotton
  NSN 8415–00–634–4794, gloves, shell, leather, black M–1949
  NSN 8415–00–753–6483, coveralls, cold weather mechanics
  NSN 8415–00–782–2916, cap, cold weather (A–2) navy
  NSN 8415–00–904–5134, undershirt, men's winter lightweight
  NSN 8420–00–166–5850, drawers, men's ctn thigh length white type 1, class 1
  NSN 8420–00–543–6643, undershirt, man's ctn, quarter sleeve
  NSN 8440–00–872–2171, socks, men's, ctn/nyl/wl, OG–408, stretch type, cush.
    sole 20%/30%/50%
PPI
  PPI 03–81–02 men's apparel[a]

Men's Footwear

DOD
  NSN 8430–00–554–4228, shoe, dress, men's, black, oxford
  NSN 8430–00–620–0520, shoe, service, chukka
  NSN 8430–00–782–3077, boot, combat, men's leather, DMS
PPI
  PPI 04–31 men's and boys' footwear[a]

Source: Bureau of Economic Analysis.
[a]These PPIs are based upon numerous eight-digit codes, roughly 18 for men's apparel and five for men's footwear in 1978. Prior to December 1977 there were about 27 eight-digit codes for men's apparel. The codes and their short descriptions can be seen in the appropriate monthly Bureau of Labor Statistics report for *Producers Prices and Price Indexes*.

Table 3.15   **Hot Rolled Carbon Plate Product Specifications**

DOD

NSN 9515–00–153–3183, steel plate, carbon, hot rolled, 10.2 lb/sq ft, 60 inches wide × 240 inches long, 1,020 lb/pm

NSN 9515–00–153–3185, same as 3184 except 348-inch width, 60 inch long and 10.2 lb/sq ft, 1,479 lb/pm

NSN 9515–00–153–3214, same as 3184 except 0.25 inch thick, 96 inches wide × 348 inches long, 2,368.6 lb/pm

NSN 9515–00–153–3223, same as 3184 except 15.30 lb/sq ft, 60 inches × 240 inches long, 1,530 lb/pm

NSN 9515–00–153–3224, same as 3184 except 15.3 lb/sq ft, 60 inches × 348 inches long, 0.375 inch thick, 2,218.5 lb/pm

NSN 9515–00–153–3236, same as 3184 except 0.500 inch thick, 60 inches wide × 240 inches long, 2,042 lb/pm

NSN 9515–00–153–3255, same as 3184 except 0.75 inch thick, 60 inches wide × 240 inches long, 3,060 lb/pm

NSN 9515–00–153–3262, same as 3184 except 35.7 lb/sq ft, 72 inches wide × 348 inches long, 6,212 lb/pm

NSN 9515–00–153–3264, same as 3184 except 1.0 inch thick, 60 inches wide × 240 inches long, 4,083 lb/pm

NSN 9515–00–153–3280, same as 3184 except 2.0 inches thick, 60 inches wide × 240 inches long, 8,167.6 lb/pm

NSN 9515–00–153–3310, same as 3184 except 0.375 inch thick, 72 inches wide × 240 inches long, 1,837 lb/pm

NSN 9515–00–153–3341, same as 3184, 30.6 lb/sq ft, 96 inches wide × 240 inches long, 4,896 lb/pm

PPI

10–13–02–61, hot rolled carbon steel sheets, commercial quality, cut lengths, .1271 inch minimum (TMW) × 48 inches wide × 120 inches long, cut edge, not pickled, base chemistry, base quantity (40,000 or over of an item) mill to user, f.o.b. mill.

Table 3.16   Hot Rolled Carbon Plate

Calendar Year/ Quarter	PPI	DOD
1972-IV	100.0	100.0
1973-I	100.0	101.3
II	100.0	112.5
III	100.0	112.5
IV	100.0	112.5
1974-I	105.3	120.3
II	115.5	131.9
III	139.3	123.4
IV	139.3	122.1
1975-I	138.9	161.1
II	136.6	161.7
III	135.8	164.4
IV	143.6	161.6
1976-I	143.6	168.7
II	146.4	161.5
III	152.1	182.3
IV	155.2	180.8
1977-I	161.3	177.3

Source: Bureau of Economic Analysis.

Table 3.17   Construction Specifications

DOD. The nine classes of construction which comprise military construction are:
1. Airfield pavements
2. Training facilities
3. Maintenance facilities
4. Covered storage facilities
5. Administrative buildings
6. Troop housing
7. Facilities for personnel support and services
8. Research, development, and test buildings
9. Roads and streets

ENR. The ENR is based on four specifications:
1. Structural steel shapes base mill price
2. Bulk portland cement, 20-city average
3. 2 × 2 lumber, 20-city average
4. Skilled labor, 20-city average

Source: Bureau of Economic Analysis.

Table 3.18   **Construction Comparisons (CY 1972 = 100)**

Calendar Year/ Quarter	DOD	ENR
1972	100.0	100.0
1973	116.8	108.5
1974	129.6	114.9
1975	142.2	124.5
1976	154.9	135.9
1977	162.2	147.3
1978	166.6	159.7
1972-I	96.9	96.9
II	97.8	99.0
III	102.1	101.0
IV	103.2	103.1
1973-I	106.5	106.2
II	112.9	108.5
III	121.0	109.1
IV	126.6	110.3
1974-I	128.4	110.1
II	128.3	113.0
III	129.6	118.0
IV	132.2	118.4
1975-I	137.3	119.9
II	138.2	122.8
III	145.7	126.5
IV	147.4	128.9
1976-I	149.0	130.7
II	154.1	133.7
III	158.3	138.2
IV	158.0	141.1
1977-I	160.7	142.8
II	162.4	144.1
III	162.6	148.8
IV	163.0	153.6
1978-I	169.3	154.1
II	165.6	157.1
III	165.5	162.8
IV	166.0	164.9

Source: Bureau of Economic Analysis.

Appendix A

Relation of Unified Budget Outlays to NIPA Purchases for DOD and MAP

The relationship between outlays in the unified budget and NIPA purchases is determined by the definition and magnitude of the adjustments made for coverage and timing. This reconciliation is shown in table 3.A.1 for fiscal year 1974.

Outlays require coverage adjustments for DOD outlays that are outside the scope of national defense purchases in the national accounts. These include net lending, payments to U.S. territories (geographical exclusions), foreign currency conversion, capital gains, land and netting

Table 3.A.1   **Relationship of DOD Outlays in Unified Budget and NIPA National Defense**

	Fiscal Year 1974
Unified Budget DOD and outlays of Military Assistance Programs (MAP)	78,445
Less:	
Net lending	251
Geographic exclusions	18
Foreign currency conversion	1
Capital gains	(4)
Land	20
Plus:	
Netting and grossing	29
Timing: Progress payments	291
Foreign military sales	534
Accounting adjustments	300
Equals NIPA DOD and MAP expenditures	78,813
Less:	
Grants-in-aid to state and local governments	180
Military retirement transfer payments	5,061
Transfers to foreigners	54
Net interest paid	40
Subsidies less surplus PXs and commissary	(142)
Equals NIPA DOD and MAP purchases	73,620
Plus:	
Social Security	60
Atomic Energy Activities	1,417
General Service Administration sales	(1,289)
Civil Service Commission	419
Special programs	(198)
Other agencies	32
Equals NIPA national defense purchases	74,061

Source: Bureau of Economic Analysis.

and grossing. Timing adjustments to outlays to reflect current purchases are largely for the increase in advances net of payables (i.e., progress payments), foreign military sales, accounting adjustments, and Military Assistance Programs (MAP).

DOD and MAP expenditures are further adjusted for transfer payments, which are not included in defense purchases in the NIPAs, by removing grants-in-aid to state and local governments, military retirement transfer payments, transfers to foreigners, net interest paid, and subsidies less current surplus of government enterprises (i.e., PXs and commissaries).

NIPA DOD and MAP purchases are also adjusted for activities of other federal agencies that are included in the definition of national defense purchases. These include atomic energy activities by the Department of Energy and sales by the General Service Administration. Small adjustments are also made for Social Security, Civil Service Commission, special programs, and other agencies.

Appendix B

**Defense Price Index: Relative Importance
of Purchases in Current Dollars**

	1972	1977
Total defense purchases	1.000	1.000
Compensation	.490	.465
Civilian	.180	.189
Military	.310	.276
Structures	.023	.023
Construction	.019	.025
Family housing construction	.002	.002
Family housing improvements and minor construction	.001	.001
Family housing maintenance	.002	.003
Military construction	.014	.018
Missile silos (force modernization program)	a	.001
Net purchases of existing structures	.004	− .002
Services	.211	.221
Communication services	.008	.007
Base communications	.002	.002
Communications services industrial fund	.004	.003
Postage	.002	.002
Depot maintenance	.015	.019
Air Force	.006	.004
Army	.002	.005
Navy	.007	.010
Installation support services	.002	.026
Contract operation installations	.002	.003

	1972	1977
Equipment maintenance	.005	.006
Housepeeking services	.007	.006
Maintenance, repairs and minor construction of real property	.005	.006
Rents	.002	.003
Training and education	.001	.002
Medical services	.005	.006
Other services	.029	.030
Automatic data processing contractual service	.003	.003
Automatic data processing leased equipment	.004	.003
Consulting, engineering, and technical services	.005	.004
Indirect hire	.011	.014
Miscellaneous services	.005	.004
Printing and reproduction	.001	.002
Research and development	.079	.081
Transportation of things	.024	.022
Air	.003	.001
Rail	.003	.003
Sea	.009	.006
Terminal services	.001	a
Truck	.008	.012
Travel and transportation of persons	.012	.015
Air	.006	.006
Bus	a	a
Rail	a	a
Reimbursable expenses	.006	.009
Utilities	.005	.010
Electricity	.004	.007
Gas	.001	.001
Sewage services	a	.001
Steam and hot water	a	a
Water	a	.001
Weapons services	.012	.005
Aircraft	.002	.003
Missiles	.009	.001
Ships	.001	.001
Durable goods	.203	.234
Aircraft	.081	.083
Air Force new aircraft	.031	.027
Army new aircraft	.002	a
Modification equipment, spares, and support equipment	.029	.029
Navy and Marine Corps new aircraft	.019	.027
Ammunition plant modernization	.002	.003
Communication and electronics equipment	.013	.015
Air Force	.003	.004
Army	.003	.004
Marine Corps	.001	a
Navy	.006	.007
Defense stock funds (durable goods)	.009	.013

	1972	1977
Industrial funds purchases (durable goods)	.007	.007
Military services stock funds (durable goods)	.015	.026
Air Force	.006	.008
Army	.005	.013
Navy	.004	.005
Missiles	.023	.024
Air Force other missiles, new missiles	.002	.002
Army and Marine Corps missiles, new missiles	.003	.004
ICBM/SLBM new missiles	.001	.004
Modification equipment, spares, and support equipment	.004	.004
Navy other missiles, new missiles	.010	.003
Satellites	.002	.002
Special activities	.001	.005
Other equipment	.018	.022
Air Force	.010	.012
Army	.002	.003
Marine Corps	.001	a
Navy	.005	.007
Ship construction	.025	.029
New ship construction	.014	.019
New ship GFE	.007	.009
Ship conversion	.003	.001
Ship conversion GFE	.001	a
Vehicles	.009	.012
Combat	.003	.007
Noncombat	.006	.005
Weapons	.001	a
Nondurable goods	.073	.057
Ammunition	.028	.011
Air Force	.009	.005
Marine Corps	.001	a
Navy	.005	.004
Defense stock funds (nondurable goods)	.004	.043
Bulk petroleum	.026	.029
Clothing and textiles	.004	.005
Other nondurables	.002	.003
Subsistence	.012	.006
Military services stock fund (nondurable goods)	.001	.001

[a] = less than .0005.

Appendix C

Number of Price Specifications by Category

Category	Number of Price Specifications
Aircraft	73
Ammunition	171
Communications	542
Compensation	4,332
Construction	201
Depot maintenance	450
Electronic equipment	890
Installation support services	50
Medical services	32
Missiles	104
Other equipment	377
Other services	72
Research and development	90
Ship construction	105
Stock funds: defense stock fund	1,200
Stock funds: military services	4,500
Transportation of things	99
Travel and transportation of persons	218
Utilities	124
Vehicles	20
Weapons	9
Total	13,659

Appendix D

Guidelines for Quality Adjusting Aircraft

Quality changes for which price adjustments were made include all physical changes that have cost and performance consequences.

Improved performance is recognized as an enhancement of the aircraft's mission, for example, close air support, electronic warfare, antisubmarine warfare. It assumes that expected or specified performance characteristics are associated with the physical configuration of aircraft in production. The remedy of unexpected physical defects is considered price increases and not quality improvements because production aircraft are expected to fit together properly and to work. Aircraft enter production after considerable research and development that includes full-scale development models and prototypes.

A. Quality adjustments are made for:
  1. Changes in design or materials which change the aircraft's
     a) Length of service
     b) Need for repairs
     c) Ease of repair
     d) Weight
     e) Quality of materials in relation to their function
  2. Changes in mechanical features that affect the aircraft's
     a) Overall operation
     b) Efficiency
     c) Ability of a component to perform
  3. Engineering changes that affect the aircraft's probability of mechanical failure with respect to particular systems
  4. Safety features, for example, better seat ejection systems
  5. Antipollution, noise abatement equipment, etc., installed for nonmilitary objectives
B. No quality adjustments are made for physical changes associated with
  1. Style
  2. Appearance
  3. Design solely to make the aircraft seem new or different
  4. Comfort
  5. Convenience
  6. Remedy of production compatability deficiencies
C. New technology may make it possible to achieve recognizably better quality at lower cost. No satisfactory technique has been developed for adjusting for quality change in such situations. Therefore, rather than reflect erroneous quality deterioration no adjustments were made. Prices before and after the change are directly compared in order to give at least partial credit for quality improvement.

References

Commerce. U.S. Department of Commerce. 1975. *Measuring price changes of military expenditures*. Washington, D.C.: Government Printing Office.

Commerce. U.S. Department of Commerce. 1979. *Price changes of defense purchases of the United States*. Washington, D.C.: Government Printing Office.

Council on Wage and Price Stability. Executive Office of the President's COWPS. 1977. *The wholesale price index: review and evaluation*. Washington, D.C.: Government Printing Office.

Denison, Edward F. 1974. *Accounting for United States economic growth 1929–1969*. Washington, D.C.: Brookings Institution.

Department of Defense. 1975. *Armed services procurement regulations.* Washington, D.C.: Government Printing Office.

———. 1977a. *Program acquisitions cost by weapon system, Department of Defense budget for fiscal year 1977.* Washington, D.C.: Government Printing Office.

———. Joint DOD Office of Management and Budget. *Aircraft Industry Capacity Study.* 1977b. Washington, D.C.: Government Printing Office.

National Bureau of Economic Research. Price Statistics Review Committee of NBER. 1961. *Price statistics of the federal government.* Washington, D.C.: Government Printing Office.

Searle, Allan. 1977. Clothing and textiles, comparison of military purchase price indexes with comparable market price trends. Unpublished study.

Stigler, George J., and Kindahl, James K. 1970. *The behavior of industrial prices.* NBER Ser. no. 90. New York: National Bureau of Economic Research.

United Nations. 1977. *Guidelines on principles of a system of price and quantity statistics.* New York: United Nations.

United States. Congress. House. Committee on Armed Services. 1974. *Department of Defense energy resources and requirements.* 93d Cong., 2d sess. 31 January; 4, 6, 25, 27 February; 8 March; 23 April; 7, 8, 16 May.

———. Senate. Committee on Armed Services. 1978a. *DOD authorization for appropriations for fiscal year 1977: hearing on S. 2571, part 6-tactical air.* 95th Cong., 2d sess., 3, 6, 8, 9, 15, and 16 March.

———. Senate. Committee on Armed Services. 1978b. *DOD authorization for appropriations for fiscal year 1977: hearing on S. 2571, part 7-tactical air.* 95th Cong., 2d sess., 5, 6, 12 April.

Wright, P. T. 1936. Factors affecting the cost of airplanes. *Journal of aeronautical sciences.* New York: Institute of Aeronautical Sciences.

Comment   Marilyn E. Manser

In their paper, Ziemer and Galbraith discuss the deflation of defense purchases. The recent publication of implicit price deflators (IPD) for Department of Defense (DOD) purchases of goods and services is the culmination of an effort which began in 1973. (Commerce 1979). A forthcoming article in the *Survey of Current Business* will present the IPD for all defense purchases based on these new price data, and they will be

Marilyn E. Manser is senior economist at Mathematica Policy Research, Inc.

fully incorporated into the national income and product accounts (NIPA) at the time of the next benchmark revision.

The importance to budget planning and to public policy debate of satisfactory constant-dollar measures of total government expenditures for various types of defense purchases needs no comment. A project similar to this one for nondefense purchases would clearly be desirable, and, as the authors note, it could be done in a manner similar to this one. But before doing so, attention should be paid to evaluating the results of this project.

By far the major portion of the Ziemer-Galbraith paper, specifically Sections 3.2 and 3.3, is devoted to summarizing the results of the project to develop deflators for defense purchases and to describing in detail the construction of the deflators for certain categories of defense expenditures. Much of this material is presented elsewhere (Commerce 1979) and will, it is hoped, be readily available from government sources to users of these deflators. It is useful that such extensive discussion of methodology and data has been provided by the Bureau of Economic Analysis (BEA) on these indexes; however, this conference paper would, in my opinion, have been more usefully devoted to comprehensive analysis of the importance of the various issues and problems noted below for the resulting measures.

The first thing to think about in assessing these new IPDs is what questions we want to ask about price increases for defense and how useful this new index is for answering them. Ideally, we might want to have a deflator for the output of national defense. Appropriately, constructing such an index was ruled out for the present because of the problems of measuring "national defense." Clearly, measuring the output of nondefense government goods would also be highly complex, and the approach taken here is consistent with the usual treatment of government in the NIPA.

The authors say that the results of this project are instead measures of the real volume of inputs used to provide national defense. That does seem to be an appropriate construct to measure for defense. The components of DOD purchases are labor compensation and material goods in various states of production (However, the theoretical construct that an implicit price deflator is generally taken to correspond to is *not* an input price index [Fisher and Shell 1972, pp. 49–59].)

Previous work on price measurement has identified a number of methodological and statistical problems. One methodological problem given a great deal of attention in previous work on price measurement is the choice of the form of the index. (Presumably, as has been done recently in the *Survey of Current Business* for the major category IPDs, alternative index formulations will eventually be presented for defense purchases.) Other major problems and issues concern choice of transaction versus list prices, sample selections, timing problems, quality change and introduction of new goods.[1] Choices that were employed in this project are described, but more discussion of their rationale and alternatives considered would have been useful. Choices made regarding use of specification pricing and treatment of quality change and introduction of new goods are akin to those used for the PPI. This effort to construct a deflator for DOD purchases attempts to obtain exclusively transaction prices. No consistent criteria for sample size were applied. Section 3.2 of this paper considered in detail the measurement of prices for five categories. For aircraft, missiles, and ship construction, the sample coverage of prices was extremely high. Thus, while there may be a problem of inefficiency, there is unlikely to be a problem of their being misrepresentative. For compensation, collection of wage data was comprehensive and straightforward. However, for construction, the price coverage was erratic.

The problems that arise with respect to aircraft and missiles, both of which are included in the NIPAs on a delivery basis, are similar to one another. The major conceptual problem arising here is the method of linking into the index a new aircraft or missile which is intended to replace an older type. The conceptually appropriate measure of the price of the old type to use for the link is the marginal cost of the last unit produced; the choice made here, to use "one of the last old aircraft model units," is therefore reasonable. In order for the state of technology to be comparable, the choice was made to price the new unit at the point at which the new learning curve reaches the flattening out stage; a reference or discussion in the paper to explain and justify the method used to establish the learning curve estimate used for new models would have been helpful.

It is well known that in price index construction the choice of the base year will generally affect the values. Here, for aircraft and missiles, the base year is especially important. This is because high base year prices that occur for items produced early in their respective learning curves can, as noted by the authors on page 152, cause the base year prices to be exceptionally high on average and thus to overstate the constant dollar value of subsequent deliveries of the item. It would have been useful if the authors could have included, in addition to their verbal discussion, some calculations of how different these price indexes would have been if (1) a different base year has been chosen, or (2) a different method of handling the problem had been adopted.

For the ship construction category, the approach taken is to pick a particular physical design of a ship and use it as the specification to reprice over time at shipyards. The nature of the item does seem to warrant a somewhat different treatment than that employed for aircraft and missiles, which are produced in larger quantities of identical products. Nonetheless, more frequent change of ship design than that mentioned— 10 years—would seem to be clearly desirable.

On the surface, the development of a price index for defense might be thought to entail special measurement problems and methodological issues only for those defense goods which have no counterpart in the civilian marketplace. Consequently, the authors' comparison in Section 3.4 of the IPD for selected DOD goods for which markets may be the same as for nondefense goods with what appears to be a corresponding PPI is very useful. (In fact, these comparisons are the major contribution of this paper, since the description of this new IPD series has been released elsewhere.)

For this purpose, the DOD price data are used to construct a Laspeyres index which is then compared to the PPI. Thus, the discrepancy caused by use of different index formulations is removed. It would also be interesting to see a comparison of the DOD Laspeyres index with the IPD, but the IPDs for the categories on which the DOD-PPI comparisons are made are not published separately in the BEA reports. (This raises the question of whether the DOD coverage for these categories is sufficient to make the comparisons undertaken in Section 3.4 statistically meaningful.)

Assuming that the indexes for these selected defense categories are statistically reliable, I would state their conclusion somewhat more strongly than they did—the DOD and PPI price series are quite different. Although they find one similar pair, namely, the DOD index for military construction and the PPI for construction, as they note, the DOD index is much more comprehensive, since the latter measures only the price of construction materials. Thus, these data provide no evidence that the DOD and PPI prices are the same for comparable categories.

Other categories of market goods they consider are three types of fuel, four types of citrus fruits, men's apparel and men's footwear, and hot rolled carbon plate. Only for one of these categories—that for men's footwear—do the two indexes show a nearly identical change over the 28 quarters for which the data are given (1972-I to 1978-IV), and even for that category one cannot say the indexes are similar, since some of the movements within that period are considerably different.

Prior to discussing sources of differences in the DOD and PPI indexes for specific categories, the authors note that the DOD measurement of prices as the average of many transactions over a quarter, and the measurement of prices for many categories of the PPI on the basis of prices on a single day of each month, provide a general source of discrepancies. Similarly, sources of discrepancies they note with respect to specific categories—for example, the exclusive use of spot prices in particular markets versus an average of types of transactions (spot and contract) in many geographic areas for the period of interest—are general issues in price measurement. Presumably, they have concluded that these sources of differences are important only for those categories where they are specifically noted, but a more unified framework for discussing sources of differences would help the assessment.

Other types of discrepancies noted by the authors arise from special aspects of DOD purchasing; an example of this is the requirement that DOD make certain purchases from noncompetitive suppliers, for example, the purchase of combat boots produced at federal prisons. An attempt to assess the quantitative importance of this factor would be useful.[2]

The final source of discrepancies they discuss from use of different weights for the two indexes. The authors cite an unpublished study by Allan Searle which found that substitution of PPI for DOD weights had an appreciable downward effect on the DOD indexes for clothing. Such a comparison would be useful here for other categories.

Notes

1. For a detailed discussion of problems in price measurement see, e.g., Triplett (1975).

2. If a large portion of expenditures on combat boots is in fact a subsidy to federal prisons, then that component might more appropriately be included elsewhere in the accounts. In any case, it is not clear that this should result in consistently higher price increases than faced for privately produced boots, even though the price level may be higher.

References

Commerce. U.S. Department of Commerce. 1979. *Price changes of defense purchases of the United States*. Washington, D.C.: Government Printing Office.

Fisher, Franklin M., and Shell, Karl. 1972. *The economic theory of price indexes*. New York: Academic Press.

Jack E. Triplett, 1975. The measurement of inflation: a survey of research on the accuracy of price indexes. In Paul H. Earl, ed., *Analysis of inflation*. Lexington, Mass.: Lexington Books.

4 Energy Efficiency, User-Cost Change, and the Measurement of Durable Goods Prices

Robert J. Gordon

4.1 Introduction

4.1.1 User-Cost Changes and the Quality Change Debate

Energy price increases in the 1970s have induced producers to supply more energy-efficient automobiles, appliances, aircraft engines, and structures. Technological advances in response to higher labor costs have resulted in reduced maintenance requirements for many types of durable goods. Other changes in efficiency, particularly those associated with environmental legislation, have had an adverse effect on user cost. Users value the savings in energy consumption and repair costs that new, more efficient models make possible, just as they would pay to avoid a shift to less efficient models. Yet the literature on price measurement has concentrated on the dimensional or performance characteristics of goods and contains little explicit discussion of the procedures by which price changes should be measured when new models embody changes in operating costs.

In price measurement the proper treatment of changes in energy efficiency and other aspects of user cost is related to the more general problem of adjusting for quality change. Data on the real output of consumer and capital goods, on real capital input, and on productivity at

Robert J. Gordon is with the Department of Economics, Northwestern University, and with the National Bureau of Economic Research.

This is a revised version of a paper presented at the Conference on Research in Income and Wealth, May 3, 1979, in Washington, D.C. This research is supported by the National Science Foundation and is part of the NBER's research on productivity. Any opinions expressed are those of the author and not those of the National Bureau of Economic Research. I am grateful to Gerald Goldstein, Zvi Griliches, Robert Hall, Dale Jorgenson, Sherwin Rosen, and especially Jack Triplett for helpful discussion, and to Ross Newman for research assistance.

both the aggregate and industry level require accurate price deflators that are adjusted for changes in quality.[1] Just as a price increase due solely to larger size or improved performance should not be allowed to raise the aggregate price index, but rather should be subject to a quality adjustment, so a price increase due solely to an engineering change that improves fuel economy should be subject to a similar quality adjustment rather than being treated as an increase in the aggregate price level.

Quality adjustments for changes in energy efficiency and other changes in user cost raise an important conceptual issue already familiar from the debate on quality changes in dimensional or performance characteristics of goods: should the criterion for quality adjustment be *production cost* or *user value*? Under the production (or resource) cost criterion, goods are considered of equal quality if they cost the same to produce. A difference in price between two models of a product would be adjusted for any difference in quality by subtracting from the price of the more costly model the amount by which its production cost exceeds that of the cheaper model. Under the user-value criterion, goods are considered of equal quality if they provide the same value to the user. A difference in price between two models would be subject to a quality adjustment based on the relative value of the two models to users, without regard to differences in the production cost of the two models.

In many cases the production-cost and user-value criteria lead to the same result. A competitive market leads to the production of "quality," for example, dimensional or performance characteristics, up to the point at which the real marginal cost of producing each characteristic is equal to the present value of its marginal product. A quality change resulting from a shift in the marginal value product of a characteristic, due to a change in product price or in the quantity of other inputs, takes place up to the point where the higher marginal value product is balanced by a higher production cost. In such cases quality adjustments based on the production-cost and user-value criteria are identical, and either method yields the same price deflator.

No new problems are posed for price measurement when there are changes in energy efficiency or other elements of user cost that take the form of proportional changes in production cost and in the present value of marginal product *net of operating costs*. A change in electricity prices, for example, tends to induce firms to produce more energy-efficient refrigerators, up to the point where the added production cost of insulation and other energy-saving devices is balanced by the present value of energy savings to users. The adjustment of a price difference between old model *A* and a more efficient model *B* can be handled by comparing production cost, and this difference in cost represents the difference in user value as well.

In such cases the normal "specification pricing" procedure of the U.S. Bureau of Labor Statistics (BLS) can handle changes in operating efficiency easily and routinely. If refrigerator model *A* is replaced by model *B*, which consumes less electricity but is otherwise identical, and if the manufacturer states that the entire price difference between the two models is due to the higher production cost of the better efficiency characteristics of model *B*, then the BLS would correctly record an absence of price change. What, then, justifies an entire paper devoted to the subject of the treatment of user-cost changes in price measurement?

4.1.2 Nonproportional Changes in Cost and Value

Numerous examples of quality change occur in which production cost does not change in proportion to user value, thus creating a difference between measures of quality change based on the production-cost and user-value criteria. In the past such quality changes have been misleadingly labeled "costless" but in fact are better termed "nonproportional." As seen below, the best way to characterize a nonproportional quality change is as a downward shift in the supply curve of user-desired characteristics. Examples of such shifts include the increased calculation ability of electronic computers of given size and resource content, the superior performance of the jet aircraft engine compared to the propeller engine it replaced, improvements in the picture quality of color TV sets without increases in cost, and improved fuel economy of automobile engines of given size and performance characteristics. These examples of nonproportional quality changes suggest that improvements in performance characteristics rarely occur without simultaneously involving changes in operating cost. The computer, jet aircraft, home appliance, and automobile industries all achieved savings in energy and maintenance requirements at the same time that performance innovations occurred.

The central issue in the quality change debate is the proper treatment of nonproportional changes in the construction of official price deflators. The "production-cost criterion" was originally set out by Edward Denison: "If the cost of two types of capital goods were the same (or would have been the same were both newly produced) in the year in whose prices the measures are expressed, they are considered to embody the same amount of capital regardless of differences in their ability to contribute to production" (1957, p. 222). The U.S. Department of Commerce has adopted the Denison production-cost criterion for purposes of deflating output.[2] Thus, if there is an innovation in the computer industry that doubles the calculation capacity of a computer without changing its production cost, the Denison criterion would treat both computers as the same quantity of investment and capital.

The contrasting position has been that user value should be the criterion for quality adjustment in those situations where quality change occurs but production cost and user value do not change in proportion.[3] Proponents of the user-value criterion often point to the computer industry as an important example in which use of the production-cost criterion leads to an understatement of increases in quality, in real investment, and in real GNP, together with an overstatement of increases in the aggregate price level.[4]

The distinction between the two criteria, however, is misleading. If the unit of measurement in the computer example were changed from "one computer" to "one calculation," then the production-cost criterion would correctly capture the reduction in cost per calculation and would lead to the same answer as the user value criterion. Recently, Triplett (see Chap. 5 this volume), building on the earlier work of Fisher and Shell (1972), has set forth a new analysis of quality change in which the units of measurement are a good's characteristics, for example, "calculations." He concludes that the production-cost criterion is correct for the construction of an output price index, while the user-value criterion is correct for the construction of an input price index. The effect of his analysis for the computer example is to yield a price index that accurately captures the reduction in the price of a calculation achieved by technical innovation and which thus satisfies those who have previously criticized the production-cost criterion for missing such reductions in price. The exposition in this paper, based on Triplett's analysis, shows that in many practical applications there is no longer any need to distinguish between the production-cost and user-value criteria of quality measurement.[5]

4.1.3   Plan of the Paper

A preliminary conceptual section sets the subsequent theory in the context of recent debates in the area of quality measurement. Among the topics treated are the meaning of the production-cost and user-value criteria, the distinction between input and output indexes that is central to the work of Fisher and Shell (1972) and Triplett (this volume), the conditions necessary for the prices of individual goods to be adjusted for changes in user cost, and the implications of the approach for productivity at the aggregate and industry level.

The theoretical analysis of operating cost changes involves a simple model in which producers' durable equipment varies along two dimensions, a composite performance characteristic, and a composite operating cost characteristic. Firms design each vintage of equipment to have a level of operating efficiency that is optimal, given the expected prices of operating inputs. Changes in specifications can respond to both changes in technology and changes in the expected prices of energy and other inputs and can lead to proportional or nonproportional changes in cost and user value. The model is used to analyze problems of extracting information on "true" price changes from observed changes in the price of a unit of equipment when changes in performance and operating efficiency characteristics occur.

The model can be applied not only to the measurement of price changes for new models but also to the analysis of changes in the prices of used models. Changes in operating characteristics, and in the prices of operating inputs, can alter both the prices and the service lifetimes of used assets. As a result the relative price of used and new assets may change, an effect that must be taken into account in any attempt that uses price data on used assets as a proxy for the unobservable transactions prices of new goods.

The ideas in the theoretical section are applied to the detailed practical problems involved in measuring the prices of an important type of producers' durable equipment—commercial aircraft. An application of the theoretical index formula yields a new deflator for the commercial aircraft industry that is radically different from the present official deflator. Although the new index mirrors the 6.2% annual rate of increase in the official index between 1971 and 1978, during the period 1957–71 its annual rate of increase is *minus 7.5%* annually, as opposed to the official increase of *plus 2.6%* per year. Among the implications of the new index is that as now measured productivity growth in the aircraft industry has been understated, and total factor productivity growth in the airline industry has been overstated.

4.2 Central Conceptual Issues

4.2.1 Input and Output Price Index Concepts

Triplett (this volume) has made Fisher and Shell's (1972) distinction between input and output price indexes the centerpiece of his analysis of quality change. Measures of real capital used as a productive input should be calculated using an input price index, according to Triplett, and measures of the output of the capital-goods producing industry should be calculated using an output price index. The following exposition, based on Triplett's analysis and concepts, examines the input and output price concepts in the case of technical innovations like those in the computer industry.

We begin by assuming that output (y) is produced by a vector of input characteristics (x). Since the primary focus of this paper is on the measurement of capital input and of the output of capital goods, henceforth we ignore labor input. One may think of y as ton-miles per truck per year and of x as including horsepower and truck size, or of y as the calculation services provided by a computer and x as including its memory size and ability to perform multiplications per unit of time. The flow of output that can be produced by a single unit of the durable good containing the vector of performance characteristics x can be expressed in a conventional production function:

$$(1) \qquad y = y(x), \qquad y_x > 0, y_{xx} < 0,$$

where y_x represents the partial derivative of y with respect to x.

The producers' durable good is manufactured under competitive supply conditions, according to a cost function that exhibits constant returns in the quantity of goods produced, and diminishing returns in the number of embodied units of the performance characteristic:[6]

$$(2) \qquad V(x) = Cc(x), \qquad c_x > 0, c_{xx} > 0.$$

Adopting the convention that lower-case letters represent "real" variables and upper-case letters "nominal" variables, we use c to represent the real unit cost function, C to represent shifts in the cost of producing a given product due to changing profit margins and/or input prices, and V to stand for the total value of each unit produced.

For any given level of technology, say that obtaining at time t, more inputs are required to produce more output. The input demand function depends on output and on the prices of inputs:

$$(3) \qquad x_t = x(y_t, C_t).$$

When the input demand function from (3) is substituted into the cost function of the supplying industry (2), it is seen that there is an indirect dependence of the cost of the good on the output produced by its user:

$$(4) \qquad V(x_t) = V(y_t, C_t) = C_t c[x(y_t, C_t)].$$

The criterion of comparison upon which the input price index (P_t^x) is based is that prices are compared holding constant output at a given level, say y^*. The optimal set of input characteristics (x^*) is defined by the demand functions for the characteristics at the given output level (y^*) and the differing input prices:

$$(5) \qquad x_t^* = x(y^*, C_t) \qquad \text{and} \qquad x_0^* = x(y^*, C_0).$$

The input price index can now be compared as the ratio of the cost (V) of obtaining the optimum (minimum-cost) combinations of the vector of input characteristics sufficient to produce output level y^* in the reference and comparison-period input price regimes. Thus the input price index is simply the ratio of (4) for the two price regimes, evaluated at the constant output level y^*:

$$(6) \qquad P_t^x = \frac{V(x_t^*)}{V(x_0^*)} = \frac{C_t c[x(y^*, C_t)]}{C_0 c[x(y^*, C_0)]}.$$

Because a change in input prices (C) between regimes can cause substitution in the quantities of the various input characteristics, the input price index allows for such substitution.

In this discussion the inputs into the production function are the individual characteristics of goods, the vector x, so that a quality change involves a change in the quantity of one or more productive characteristics, which in turn must change the level of output. Since any such quality change would thus violate the criterion of constant output (y^*) on which the input price index is based, price measures must be adjusted "for changes in input characteristics that result in changed output (or reduced cost to the user), and the correct quality adjustment is exactly equal to the cost change or the value of the output change that they induce. In the literature, this is known as the user-value rule" (Triplett, this volume, p. 286).

In contrast to the input price index, the output price index uses a standard that compares prices by holding constant the economy's endowment of productive factors and its production technology. Now we write the output symbol (y) as representing a vector of output characteristics. Triplett defines the output price index P_t^y as the ratio of the revenue (R) obtained from the optimum (maximum-revenue) combination of output characteristics in the reference and comparison-period output price regimes, holding constant both input quantities (x^*) and production functions [$y^* = y(x^*)$]:

$$(7) \qquad P_t^y = \frac{R(y_t^*, P_t)}{R(y_0^*, P_0)} .$$

Note that the numerator and denominator of the output price ratio differ both in the price regime and in the quantities of output characteristics (y_t^*) that are optimal, given the fixed input quantities (x^*) and the fixed production functions that establish the various output combinations that can be produced from those inputs.

A quality change now implies an increase in one or more output characteristics.[7] If we assume that the resources devoted to increasing quality are obtained by decreasing the output of some other good, in order to remain on the same production possibility frontier the output price index must be adjusted for the resource cost of the added output characteristics. "The [quality] adjustment required is equal to the value of the resources required to move the set of output characteristics included in the index back to the same production possibility curve. This is precisely the resource cost quality measurement rule that has been argued in the literature" (Triplett, this volume, p. 299).

4.2.2 Measuring the Input Price Index
When Quality Change is Nonproportional

Nonproportional technical innovations raise the performance of a good by increasing its built-in quantity of characteristics (x) relative to the resources used by the supplying industry. Thus such innovations take the form of a downward shift in the real cost of producing a given quantity of characteristics, say computer calculations.

The idea of nonproportional quality change can be brought into the measurement of the input price index by introducing a shift term λ_t into the cost function (4):

(8) $$V(y_t,C_t,\lambda_t) = C_t c[x(y_t,C_t),\lambda_t].$$

It is important to note that there is no shift in the using firm's production function (1), since a single calculation still produces the same amount of output in the using industry. Thus the units of characteristics to be defined as x must be those which directly enter the using firm's production function, for example, a computer's "calculations per second" and not its dimensions.

In this framework the total change in input cost consists of four terms:

(9) $$dV = dC(c + C_t c_x x_C) + C_t(c_x x_y dy + c_\lambda d\lambda).$$

These terms represent, respectively, the direct and indirect substitution effect of changing prices of the inputs to the supplying industry, the effect of changing input requirements due to changing output $(x_y dy)$, and the effect of technical change in shifting the real cost function $(c_\lambda d\lambda)$. Since the input price index (P_t^x) is the ratio of (8) evaluated for the comparison period to (8) evaluated for the reference period—holding the output level constant at y^*—the *change* in P_t^x can be written as the total change in cost minus the contribution to cost of the change in output:

(10) $$\frac{dP^x}{P^x} = \frac{dV - C_t c_x x_y dy}{V(y^*,C_0,\lambda_0)} = \frac{dC(c + C_t c_x x_C) + C_t c_\lambda d\lambda}{V(y^*,C_0,\lambda_0)}.$$

Here the middle expression indicates that the change in price would be measured by adjusting the observed change in cost of a new model for the change in its quantity of characteristics $(x_y dy)$ multiplied by the marginal cost of producing characteristics $(C_t c_x)$. The right-hand expression shows that the price change can be caused either by changes in input prices or profit margins in the supplying industry (dC) or by a technical shift $(d\lambda)$. Because the middle expression is used in actual measurement, the technical shift itself $(d\lambda)$ does not have to be observed directly.

Figure 4.1 illustrates the measurement of changes in the input price index in the presence of nonproportional quality change. The two upward sloping lines plot the unit cost function (eq.[8]) for two different values of the technical shift parameter λ. Initially, output level y^* is produced at an input unit cost of V_0 at point A. The technological shift represented by the higher value of λ improves quality by raising the quantity of input characteristics relative to their cost. This raises the demand for characteristics and the level of output, depicted by y_1 in the diagram. The unit cost

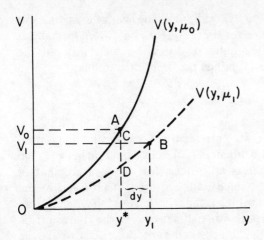

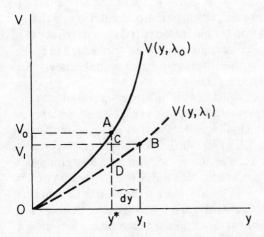

Fig. 4.1   Effects on input cost and output of a technological shift that raises the quantity of input characteristics relative to their cost.

of the durable good (V_1) could be either higher or lower than in the initial equation (V_0).

According to equation (10), the change in the input price index is equal to the change in unit cost (minus line segment AC) minus an adjustment factor equal to the change in output (CB) times the marginal cost (CD/CB) of building extra input characteristics capable of producing the extra output along a new supply schedule. Thus the change in the input price index is $-AC - CD = -AD$, that is, the vertical downward shift in the supply schedule itself. Note that the change in the real input quantity is measured by the change in output times the marginal cost of producing extra output under the new supply conditions. The change in an index of the real quantity of input characteristics (dQ^x) can be written formally as the proportional change in the number of units of capital (du/u), plus the change in cost per unit (dV/V), minus the input price index:

$$(11) \qquad \frac{dQ^x}{Q^x} = \frac{du}{u} + \frac{dV}{V} - \frac{dP^x}{P^x} = \frac{du}{u} + \frac{C_t c_x x_y dy}{V(y^*, C_0, \lambda_0)}.$$

Because it is the marginal cost of producing characteristics that is used to make the actual quality adjustment in (10), the distinction between the "user-value" and "production-cost" criteria for the measurement of quality change is misleading, since both are used in (10) and in the corresponding figure 4.1. User value is the criterion used to define x, that is, the choice of calculations rather than dimensions as the characteristic desired by the user. And production cost is the criterion used to make the actual quality adjustment. The earlier literature (as exemplified by the Denison quote in Section 4.1.2, e.g.) did involve a meaningful distinction between the two criteria, because the production-cost criterion was being applied to units of goods (u) rather than user-desired characteristics (x). Now, however, with the quality measurement procedure stated in terms of characteristics, we have a hybrid criterion in which both the user-value and production-cost criteria are integral parts.

For the purpose of quality adjustment in practice several alternative methods of estimating the marginal cost (c_x) are available. For instance, if an auto manufacturer were to make automatic transmission standard at no increase in price, and the BLS had information either on the price of automatic transmission when it was an option, or a manufacturer's estimate of the cost of producing an automatic transmission, then the present BLS pricing methodology would be adequate to measure the marginal cost. Often, when quality change involves continuous rather than discrete change, for example, a change in automobile acceleration and dimensions, or in computer performance, it is more convenient to use the hedonic regression technique to estimate the shadow price of a given characteristic, that is, its marginal cost. Clearly the proper technique to use in each case is independent of whether the nature of the quality change is "cost increasing" or "nonproportional."

4.2.2 Measuring the Output Price Index When Quality Change is Nonproportional

We now turn to the output price index and ask whether it gives a consistent treatment to an identical technological innovation. We imagine that the input price reduction depicted in figure 4.1 occurs because of a cost-saving technological innovation in the electronic computer industry. In this case, what happens to the output and price indexes for the value added of the computer industry, a component of real GNP? The nonproportional quality change can be introduced into the discussion of output price indexes by allowing the same shift term (λ) to enter the production function of the computer industry. A vector of output characteristics (y) is now produced in an amount that depends on the quantity of input characteristics (x), the relative prices of output characteristics (P), and the shift term (λ):

(12) $$y = y(x,P,\lambda), \qquad y_x>0, \ y_\lambda>0.$$

The output price index is now the ratio of revenue in two periods when output prices are allowed to change, holding constant the level of resources (inputs) and production technology:

(13) $$P_t^y = \frac{R(y_t^*,P_t)}{R(y_0^*,P_0)} = \frac{P_t y(x^*,P_t,\lambda^*)}{P_0 y(x^*,P_0,\lambda^*)} .$$

The total change in revenue between the reference and comparison periods is the total derivative of the revenue function:

(14) $$\frac{dR}{R} = \frac{dP(y + P_t y_P) + P_t(y_x dx + y_\lambda d\lambda)}{P_0 y(x^*,P_0,\lambda^*)} ,$$

where the terms represent, respectively, the direct and indirect substitution effects of changes in the output price, the effect on real output of increasing input usage, and the effect on real output of the technological shift itself.

The change in the output price index (13) consists of only two of the four terms in (14), since both input usage (x^*) and technology (λ^*) are being held constant:

(15) $$\frac{dP^y}{P^y} = \frac{dR - P_t(y_x dx + y_\lambda d\lambda)}{P_0 y(x^*,P_0,\lambda^*)} = \frac{dP(y + P_t y_P)}{P_0 y(x^*,P_0,\lambda^*)} .$$

The corresponding quantity index based on the output price index consists of the residual change in revenue:

(16) $$\frac{dQ^y}{Q^y} = \frac{P_t(y_x dx + y_\lambda d\lambda)}{P_0 y(x^*,P_0,\lambda^*)} .$$

What is the relationship between changes in the output price index and input price index defined by (10)? Figure 4.2 illustrates the calculation of changes in the output price index and quantity index when there is a technological change represented by a shift from λ_0 to λ_1. The increase in the output that can be produced by the initial resource endowment raises output directly by the term $y_\lambda d\lambda$ in equation (15), and indirectly by raising the marginal product of inputs and hence the demand for inputs (the term $y_x dx$). If the higher level of output is to be sold, the output price (P) must

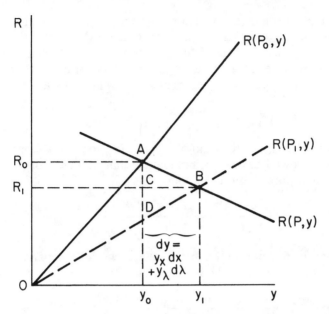

Fig. 4.2   Effects on revenue and output of a technological shift that raises the level of output relative to the quantity of input characteristics.

drop, as indicated along the appropriate industry demand curve. The downward sloping total revenue line in figure 4.2 is drawn on the assumption that demand is price inelastic. The upward sloping lines indicate the revenue that would be obtained from varying levels of output if the price level were fixed. Starting from an initial equilibrium at point A, the innovation-induced increase in output leads to a new equilibrium at point B, where the price level has dropped from P_0 to P_1, and total revenue has declined from R_0 to R_1. According to equation (15), the change in the output price index is measured by the change in revenue (minus the line segment AC) minus the new price level (CD/CB) times the change in output (CB), or the distance $-AD$.

Now the connection between figures 4.1 and 4.2 becomes evident. When we consider the output of a capital good, for example, an electronic computer, a technological shift causes a decrease in price measured by the vertical distance AD in figure 4.2. We note that this vertical downward shift AD also appears in figure 4.1 as the change in input prices as viewed by the user of the electronic computer. Once again, the input and output price index concepts are equivalent and would include in both real GNP and in real capital input technological shifts that raise the output capacity of capital goods relative to their production cost.

The model is equally applicable to "resource-using" or "cost-increasing" quality change. Imagine an upward shift in the demand for computers, without any change in technology. The previous equations are appropriate for measuring price and output change if we set the $d\lambda$ terms equal to zero. In figure 4.1, imagine an initial equilibrium at point D, where the lower supply curve meets an initial demand curve (not drawn). Then let the demand curve shift upward sufficiently to move the new equilibrium position to point B. The change in unit cost (dV) is exactly offset by the increase in the marginal cost of the additional characteristics, leaving the input price index as measuring shifts in the price of producing a given output; in this case there has been no such shift. The same conclusion applies to the output price index, which would be measured as unchanged, since the price of utilizing the initial level of resources has remained unchanged.

The major conclusion of this section has been that in principle both input price indexes and output price indexes treat quality change consistently, and the user-value and production-cost criteria lead to the same measures of prices and real output. This has always been recognized as true for "resource-using" quality change, where an increase in quality requires an increase in production cost. The novelty in this section is the demonstration that "nonproportional" quality change is also treated consistently by properly defined input and output indexes. Thus a technological change that raises the user value of a durable good relative to its production cost will be measured *in exactly the same way* in indexes of the real output of the industry producing the durable good and of the real capital input of the industry using the durable good.

4.3 A Model Incorporating Operating Costs

4.3.1 Energy Embodiment and Separability

Some recent research on the production technology of energy use, for example, Hudson and Jorgenson (1974), assumes that energy (e) enters the production function symmetrically with labor hours (h) and capital input (x):

$$(17) \qquad y = y(h,x,e), \qquad y_h > 0, \, y_x > 0, \, y_e > 0.$$

Thus changing relative prices, in particular the rising relative price of energy observed during the 1970s, can cause substitution both between energy and capital, and energy and labor. Because the price of labor influences the amount of labor used per unit of capital, there is no presumption in this framework that changes in energy efficiency call for adjustments in the prices of capital goods. Indeed, in his Comment on this paper Triplett prefers that changes in energy efficiency be reflected in measures of the user cost of capital (including interest, depreciation, energy, and labor usage), but not in price indexes needed to create estimates of the output and productivity of industries that produce capital goods.

Yet Triplett's position appears to prevent the consistent treatment of performance-increasing and energy-saving technological change in the measurement of prices, output, and productivity. The previous section shows why a technological shift in the performance of a capital good per unit of resources used in capital-goods-producing "Firm A" should be treated as an increase in real investment and real GNP. Now let us assume that another capital-goods-producing "Firm B" achieves a technological improvement in one of its products, yielding energy savings to users of equal value to the performance improvement achieved by Firm A. Should not the criteria for price measurement be designed to treat both types of technological change symmetrically?

In order to adjust the price of a capital good for changes in energy efficiency, it is necessary to assume that energy usage is "embodied" in capital goods and that the production function (17) can be rewritten in the separable form:

$$(18) \qquad y = y[h,k(x,e)],$$

where $k(x,e)$ is a subfunction with two inputs, performance characteristics (x) and energy (e), which produces capital input (k). Berndt and Wood (1979) describe the subfunction as follows:

> For example, consider the production of industrial process steam of given specified physical characteristics. In such a context utilized capital services (k) refers to the quantity of steam produced per unit of time using capital . . . and fuel inputs. This assumption of a separable utilized capital subfunction implies that the optimal e/x ratios . . . depend solely on (the prices of x and e and not on the other input prices) or the level of gross output y.[8]

Is this assumption of separability, which is essential to the discussion of price measurement in this paper, a reasonable one or, as Triplett claims, arbitrary and "unrealistic"? Three arguments can be presented to support the procedures proposed here:

1. Berndt and Wood (1979) have reexamined previous econometric studies in an attempt to reconcile disparate findings regarding the degree of substitution or complementarity between capital and energy. In these reconciliations "separability has played a prominent role" (p. 350), and their own empirical (1975) appears to support the separability assumption.

2. The study below makes the assumption not only that the production function is separable but that technology is "putty-clay," so that energy

usage is "designed in" when the capital good is built. In some industries the assumption that energy requirements are embodied in capital goods seems more reasonable than in others. The ability of a user to improve the energy consumption of an automobile, commercial airplane, electricity generating plant, or appliance is relatively minor compared to the latitude available to the manufacturer. Thus, a Cadillac owner might improve his gas mileage from 14 to 15 miles per gallon by careful driving habits, but to achieve 40 miles per gallon he would have to buy a Chevette or Honda.

3. Although users can alter energy consumption even when technology is putty-clay, for example, an automobile driver can save gasoline by careful avoidance of sudden starts, the techniques described below involve measuring an energy requirements function that holds constant the characteristics of users. In addition, performance characteristics are held constant, yielding a function translating energy into performance that fairly can be said to be under the control of the capital-goods manufacturer.

4.3.2 Adapting the Input Price Index to Incorporate Nonproportional Changes in Net Revenue

We now assume that the production of output (y) requires not only the acquisition of durable goods having productive input characteristics (x) but also involves a variable operating cost, the consumption of other inputs (e) times their price (S). In the present discussion e may be taken to represent the yearly consumption of energy of a capital good having performance characteristics x. The energy requirements function is taken as given by the equipment user, reflecting our assumption of a separable putty-clay technology:

$$(19) \qquad e = e(x,\sigma), \qquad e_x > 0, e_\sigma < 0,$$

where the parameter σ represents a technological shift factor that can alter the energy consumption of a given set of input characteristics.

The net revenue (N) of the durable good user consists of gross revenue less variable operating cost. Gross revenue is the output price times the production function (eq. [1] above) that allows for technical change, and operating cost is the price of the operating input (S) times the consumption of operating inputs (e):

$$(20) \qquad N = Py(x) - Se(x,\sigma).$$

An expression for real net revenue (n) can be obtained by dividing (20) by the output price:

$$(21) \qquad n = y(x) - se(x,\sigma),$$

where s is the real price of the operating input ($s = S/P$).

Recall that the input price index was previously defined as the ratio for two time periods of the nominal cost of inputs that are capable of producing a given level of output (y^*). A natural extension of this concept in the presence of variable operating costs is to hold constant between the two periods the level of real net revenue (n^*). This criterion reflects the assumption that users of durable goods do not care about the gross output produced but rather about the net revenue that the durable goods provide. Thus a user is assumed to be indifferent between 10 units of real net revenue obtained from a situation with 15 units of output and five units of real operating cost, and an alternative situation with 16 units of output and six units of real operating cost, holding constant his investment in capital goods.

The introduction of variable operating costs makes the demand for input characteristics depend on real net revenue (n), the vector of prices of input characteristics (C), the real price of operating inputs (s), and the technological shift parameter (σ):[9]

(22) $$x_t = x(n_t, C_t, s_t, \sigma_t), \qquad x_n > 0, x_s > 0, x_\sigma < 0.$$

Comparing the arguments here to the previous input demand function in equation (3) above, we note that real output has been replaced by real net revenue and that the two parameters of variable operating cost have been added (s and σ). The signs of the derivatives of (22) assume that the firm is operating in the region in which additional net revenue requires extra input to produce more gross output.[10] An increase in operating cost requires an increase in gross output (and hence capital input) to yield any fixed level of net revenue; hence the derivative is positive with respect to the relative price s and negative with respect to the technological parameter σ.

When the new input demand function in (22) is substituted into our input characteristic cost function that allows for technical change (equation 8 above), we obtain an expanded equation for the cost function:

(23) $$V(n_t, C_t, s_t, \sigma_t, \lambda_t) = C_t c[x(n_t, C_t, s_t, \sigma_t)\lambda_t].$$

Now the input price index is defined as the ratio of the cost function in the comparison period to that in the reference period of producing the same real net revenue, holding constant the relative price of operating inputs:

(24) $$P_t^x = \frac{V(n^*, C_t, s_0, \sigma_t, \lambda_t)}{V(n^*, C_0, s_0, \sigma_0, \lambda_0)}.$$

The decision to hold constant the relative price of operating inputs (s) in the numerator and denominator reflects the desire to limit changes in the input price index to factors internal to the firm manufacturing the durable good—its input prices and profit margin (C) and the level of technology built into the good (σ, λ). In this way changes in the relative price of an operating input like energy are not treated as changes in the price of capital input.

Now the change in the input price index can be written in two equivalent ways:

(25)
$$\frac{dP^x}{P^x} = \frac{dV - C_t c_x (x_n dn + x_s ds)}{V(n^*, C_0, s_0, \sigma_0, \lambda_0)}$$
$$= \frac{dC(c + C_t c_x x_C) + C_t (c_x x_\sigma d\sigma + c_\lambda d\lambda)}{V(n^*, C_0, s_0, \sigma_0, \lambda_0)}.$$

The extended model incorporating operating costs can be illustrated in figure 4.3, which repeats the axes of figure 4.1. The upward sloping schedule plots equation (23) and shows the increasing unit cost of input characteristics required to generate additional net revenue. The initial equilibrium position, where the quantity of output is chosen to make marginal net revenue equal to marginal cost, is shown at point A.

We consider first the proper treatment in price measurement of an improvement in quality that occurs when an equiproportionate increase in the prices P and S relative to C leads users to demand higher quality capital goods. Because the higher prices P and S shift the nominal

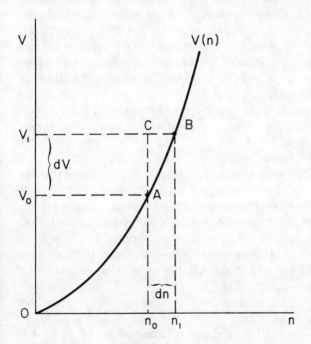

Fig. 4.3   Effects on input cost and net revenue of an equiproportionate shift in the nominal prices of output and energy.

marginal net revenue schedule upward, the equilibrium position shifts from A to B. If the manufacturer reports to the BLS that the entire addition to the price of the good from V_0 to V_1 is due to the higher cost (CA) of raising the specification of characteristics embodied in the good, the BLS would correctly conclude that there has been no price change. We note that the manufacturer's cost estimate does not represent simply the effect of higher x holding constant operating cost but rather the net extra cost of raising x while allowing energy consumption to increase along the $e(x)$ function. There is no danger that the substitution toward greater operating cost will be misinterpreted as a change in input price as long as the marginal cost (CA/CB) of the extra quantity of input characteristics is correctly measured.

Does the general formula (25) for the change in the input price index correctly conclude that there has been no price change? From the change in the cost of the durable good (CA) is to be subtracted the marginal cost (CA/CB) of the extra input characteristics required to raise real net revenue by the actual observed amount (CB). Thus the observed change in input cost (CA) minus the correction factor (CA) equals zero.

A second case, a reduction in the relative price of energy, is illustrated in figure 4.4. A decrease in the price of energy from S_0 to S_1, while the product price is held constant at P_0, shifts the unit cost schedule rightward, since a smaller nominal operating cost must be deducted from gross revenue for any given quantity of the input characteristic x, thus raising net revenue for any given value of V. The new equilibrium position is assumed to shift from point A to B. The input price index subtracts from the observed change in price (CA) the marginal cost (CD/CB) of the extra input characteristics required to raise real net revenue by the observed amount (CB) adjusted for the effect on input cost ($+AD$) of lower energy prices (ds) when real net revenue is constant. Once again, the observed change in input cost (CA) minus the correction factor ($-CD + AD$) equals zero.

As an example of this second case, we note that lower relative gasoline prices in the 1950s and 1960s induced firms and consumers to shift to larger automobiles that consumed more fuel.[11] But if an automobile with *given* horsepower had maintained its previous fuel consumption along a fixed $e(x)$ schedule, then no change would be imputed to the price of automobiles as a result of this substitution toward greater fuel consumption. (Wilcox [1978] has found, however, that during this period the fuel requirements function was not fixed.)

As a third example, let us consider a technological innovation that allows a given quantity of the input characteristic (x) to be used with a smaller consumption of fuel. To simplify the illustration in figure 4.4, it will be assumed that the shift takes the special form of reducing the marginal energy cost of a change in input quantity by the same amount as

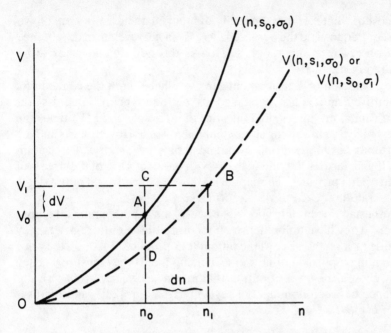

Fig. 4.4   Effects on input cost and net revenue of (*a*) a reduction in the relative price of energy, and (*b*) an innovation that improves fuel efficiency.

the decrease in the relative energy price examined in the previous two paragraphs:

$$(26) \qquad s_0 e(x,\sigma_1) = s_1 e(x,\sigma_0).$$

Now the lower schedule in figure 4.4 is relabeled to correspond to the new, more efficient consumption schedule in which σ_1 replaces σ_0.

In this third case, as in the first two cases, the equilibrium position moves from point A to point B. But now the input price index registers a decline in price instead of no change in price. From the change in the unit cost of the input characteristic ($dV = CA$) is subtracted the marginal cost (CD/CB) of the extra input characteristics required to raise real net revenue by the actual observed amount (CB). Thus the observed change in input cost (CA) minus the correction factor (CD) equals the change in the input price index ($-AD$).

4.3.3   Implementation of Operating Cost Adjustments

In each of the cases considered in the previous section, the observed change in unit cost of a durable good was adjusted for changes in net revenue caused by a shift in either an exogenous price or technological parameter. In each case the adjustment involved determining the marginal cost of whatever extra quantity of input characteristics would have been required to yield the observed increase in net revenue in the absence of the observed parameter shift. How is this adjustment factor to be measured in practice?

The discussion of measurement can usefully be set in the context of a competitive firm that uses capital goods to produce net revenue. Its user cost of capital multiplies the unit price of a durable good (V) times the interest rate r (representing some combination of borrowing costs and the opportunity cost of the firm's own funds), plus a geometric depreciation rate δ that measures the rate of decay with the asset's age of the stream of services that it provides. The capital market is assumed to set only a single interest rate that each firm takes as given.[12]

Firms using the durable good are price takers in both input and output markets. They have no influence on the price of the durable assets they purchase (V), on the price of the output they produce (P), or on the price of operating inputs (S) or cost of ownership ($r+\delta$) they must pay. They simply choose the level of output that maximizes yearly profit (π), the difference between nominal net revenue (from eq. [20]), and the user cost of capital:

$$(27) \qquad \pi = N - (r+\delta)V = Py(x) - Se(x,\sigma) - (r+\delta)V(x).$$

The only choice variable in the simplified structure of (27) is the quantity of input characteristics (x). If all producers and users of the durable asset are identical, then there will be a single model produced that embodies enough of the durable input characteristic to equate its real marginal cost of production to the present value of its real marginal net revenue:

$$(28) \qquad v_x(x) = \frac{y_x(x) - se_x(x,\sigma)}{r+\delta} = \frac{n_x(x,s,\sigma)}{r+\delta},$$

where $v_x(x) = V_x(x)/P$. The fact that the market usually provides numerous varieties containing different quantities of input characteristics has been explained by Rosen (1974) as resulting from the different tastes of consumers and technologies of producers.[13]

Figure 4.5 illustrates the equilibrium described in equation (28), with the real unit cost of durable goods on the vertical axis and real net revenue on the horizontal. As in figures 4.3 and 4.4, the purchase of additional input characteristics raises both unit cost (v) and net revenue (n), but the response of net revenue exhibits diminishing returns, both because of diminishing returns in the production function relating output to input characteristics, and also because of the increasing marginal cost of producing input characteristics. When the technical level of operating efficiency is represented by σ_0, the initial equilibrium occurs at point A, where the $v(n,\sigma)$ function is tangent to a straight line having the slope

$1/(r+\delta)$. The $v()$ function also depends on C/P and s, but these parameters are held constant in the present discussion of adjusting capital input prices for changes in operating efficiency, $d\sigma$.

If the level of operating efficiency were to shift to the improved level represented by σ_1, the firm would move to a new equilibrium position at point B, where the new $v(n,\sigma)$ function again has the slope $1/(r+\delta)$.[14] The change in the input price index, as in figure 4.4, is the observed change in unit cost (dv = line segment CA) minus an adjustment factor equal to the observed change in net revenue (dn = CB) times the marginal cost of producing input characteristics capable of providing that amount of net revenue, the slope CD/CB. Although points A and B can be observed, and thus dv and dn can be measured, point D cannot be observed directly. How can the slope CD/CB be calculated in practice in order to compute the quality change adjustment factor AD?

As figure 4.5 illustrates, the problem of estimating point D arises because of the curvature of the $v(n,\sigma)$ function. If the function were a straight line, then the unobservable point D would coincide with point D', which lies along a ray from the origin to point B having the slope

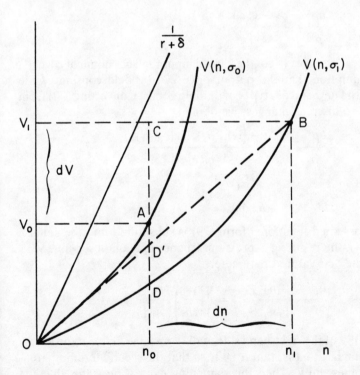

Fig. 4.5   The calculation of a quality adjustment when there is an innovation that improves fuel efficiency.

v_1/n_1. But, as long as there are *either* (a) diminishing returns in producing net revenue in response to an increase in the quantity of input characteristics or (b) an increasing marginal cost of producing input characteristics, then the curvature of the function will always make point D' lie above point D, and will make the segment AD' an underestimate of the required quality adjustment, segment AD.

Since the exact form of the function is unobservable, and because data are unlikely to be available to estimate it in many cases, the estimation of the quality adjustment factor must inevitably be based on some assumption about the function. Consider, for instance, the particularly simple relationship:

$$(29) \qquad v = \beta n^{\alpha},$$

where the curvature of the function depends on the parameter α. Technological changes that alter the position of the function are represented by shifts in the β parameter.

To use this function in the estimation of changes in input price, we first rewrite the basic formula (25) for a comparison in which the price of operating inputs (ds) is held constant:

$$(30) \qquad \frac{dp^x}{p^x} = \frac{dv - v_n dn}{v_0},$$

where the real unit cost (v) of the capital input replaces nominal cost (V) on the assumption that the output price can be held constant while comparing the new and old types of durable goods. Converting (30) from continuous to discrete changes, we obtain:

$$(31) \qquad \frac{\Delta p^x}{p^x} = \frac{\Delta v - [v(n_1,\sigma_1) - v(n_0,\sigma_1)]}{v(n_0,\sigma_0)}$$

$$= \frac{v(n_0,\sigma_1)}{v(n_0,\sigma_0)} - 1.$$

When the assumed functional form (29) is substituted into the general formula (34), the resulting expression depends only on observable variables and the "curvature" parameter:

$$(32) \qquad \frac{\Delta p^x}{p^x} = \frac{\beta_1 n_0^{\alpha}}{\beta_0 n_0^{\alpha}} - 1 = \left(\frac{v_1 n_0}{v_0 n_1}\right)\left(\frac{n_0}{n_1}\right)^{\alpha-1} - 1.$$

To make sense of the right-hand side of (32), imagine first that the $v(n,\sigma)$ function is linear, that is, that $\alpha = 1$, so that the second term in parentheses becomes unity. Then the remaining expression states that the "real" price change will be zero if both unit cost and net revenue grow in proportion in the shift to the new model, $(v_1/v_0) = (n_1/n_0)$. This is the case of "resource-using" or "cost-increasing" quality change. A nonproportional quality change, as illustrated in figure 4.5, would raise net revenue relative to cost and would result in an estimated change in the "real" input price index that is less than the observed change in price of models that remain identical.

When the $v(n,\sigma)$ function is nonlinear, then $\alpha > 1$, and the second term in parentheses in (32) becomes a fraction less than unity, corresponding in figure 4.5 to the fact that the unobservable point D lies below point D'. There seems to be no alternative in the estimation of equation (32) to making an arbitrary assumption about the value of the α parameter, or to presenting results for several alternative assumptions regarding the curvature of the $v(n,\sigma)$ function.

It is important to note that (32) is to be used to calculate a quality adjustment when comparing two different models, while holding constant output prices and the prices of operating inputs. Since this means in practice that the net revenue performance of two models must be compared in a particular year when both are in operation, equation (32) must implicitly be holding constant any factors that change the cost of manufacturing a given model in the given year of comparison, that is, changes in profit margins and/or the prices of inputs into the manufacturing process. Thus for practical measurement, equation (32), which computes the price change involved in the shift from one model to another, must be combined with an index of changes in the cost of producing identical models. Changes in the *nominal* input price index, then, are equal to changes in the *real* input price index plus changes in the cost of producing identical models:

$$(33) \qquad \frac{\Delta P^x}{P^x} = \frac{\Delta p^x}{p^x} + \frac{\Delta C[C_t c_x(x^*)]}{C_0 c(x^*)} .$$

Thus, if there is a 10% annual increase in the price of identical models, and all quality change is resource using as in figure 4.3, the quality change adjustment in equation (32) will be zero, and the nominal input-cost index in (33) will be recorded to increase at a 10% annual rate. But if the real quality change adjustment were minus 5%, then the increase in the nominal input-cost index would be reduced to a 5% annual rate.

4.4   A Case Study of Innovations in the Commercial Aircraft Industry

4.4.1   General Procedures

Most empirical work in the quality change literature in the past two decades has involved the estimation of hedonic regression equations in which the price (unit cost) of durable goods is the dependent variable.

More recently the appearance of new econometric studies has become less frequent, while the list of critical interpretations and survey papers has been growing.[15] In none of this literature, however, is there any significant discussion of the treatment in price measurement of changes in operating efficiency.

This oversight is easily understood in the context of our present simplified model of the production and operation of durable goods. At any given level of technology (σ constant), operating cost and particularly energy consumption tends to be a function of the quantity of input characteristics (x) embodied in each durable good. Any given cross-section hedonic regression of price on the quantity of input characteristics can provide no useful information about the effect on price of changes in energy efficiency, if the fuel consumption and input quantities are collinear, and if shifts in the level of fuel efficiency take place on all models at the same time.

There is another and perhaps more fundamental reason why the traditional hedonic regression approach cannot identify the value of changes in fuel economy, even if shifts in the level of fuel efficiency do not take place simultaneously on all models. As we shall see in the aircraft examples below, the net revenue advantage of new, more fuel-efficient models has not been fully reflected in a higher price, but rather the small price differentials set by firms have transferred the benefits of the efficiency advantage to the airlines and ultimately to their customers in the form of lower prices and lower load factors. Thus the dependent price variable in the hedonic regression does not exhibit sufficient variation to allow the analyst to capture the full value to users of improvements in fuel economy.

The aircraft example in this section is provided to suggest practical methods of implementing the rather general and abstract measurement framework outlined earlier in the paper. The basic formula for quality adjustment, equation (32), requires the comparison of the observed change in the price of a new model with the extra net revenue that the new model provides relative to the old model, holding constant the prices of output and operating inputs. Because data on changes in net revenue are required, ideal testing grounds for the methodology are regulated industries in which the government requires the publication of detailed information on the operating costs of given pieces of capital equipment.

The case study of airlines presented below can be duplicated for other regulated industries, particularly for the generating plants used by electric utilities. Other types of capital goods, for example, automobiles, raise different problems of estimation, because no data are available on the output of automobile services to consumers, and thus the level of net revenue cannot be calculated. The conclusion to the aircraft case study suggests means of dealing with the problems of quality adjustment in other industries.

4.4.2   Index of Sale Prices of Identical Models

The commercial aircraft industry has all the qualifications to be a perfect case study of our methodology. The major customers of the U.S. commercial aircraft industry are the U.S. airlines, which have been subject to government regulation throughout the postwar period and have been required to make available to the public incredibly detailed information on traffic by route as well as operating costs by airplane type and station location. Further, the airline production function clearly meets the separability requirement discussed above; the predominant determinant of fuel consumption per airplane seat-mile is the basic design of the manufacturer, and the pilot has only minor latitude to alter fuel consumption by varying speed and shutting down engines while taxiing.

Finally, the dramatic nature of the transition from piston airplanes to jet aircraft makes the aircraft example an interesting one. This innovation simultaneously increased gross revenue by raising aircraft size and speed, while reducing operating costs per seat-mile. In fact, any estimate of the value to users of the transition to jet aircraft will inevitably be too conservative if it concentrates solely on the net revenue of the airlines and omits the value to users of the time savings made possible by increased speed and the comfort value of reduced vibration. Yet this paper eschews these subjective areas in the belief that a careful treatment of objective revenue and cost data is sufficient to establish the presence of previously unmeasured quality change.

The existing national income accounts deflator for the aircraft category of purchases of producers' durable equipment is compiled by the U.S. Civil Aeronautics Board (CAB), Bureau of Operating Rights.[16] Since airlines are required to report regularly the historic cost for each individual aircraft in their fleet, and since these aircraft are identified on CAB form 41 by their month of acquisition and exact type (e.g., Boeing 707-331-B), the CAB has been able to construct an aircraft price index by measuring the year-to-year change in the unit price for each type of equipment delivered in *both of two adjacent years*. Because only identical pieces of equipment are compared in adjacent years, the index ignores any "true" price change involved in the transition from one aircraft type to another. As an example, the substantial price reduction involved in the switch by Douglas in 1958–59 from the manufacture of the DC-7 to the DC-8 is completely ignored, and the price index for the years of transition is based only on price changes for planes that were manufactured in both of the adjacent years. Thus the CAB index corresponds to the dC/C term in equation (33). Because the CAB methodology ignores technical change, it is not surprising that from 1956 to 1977 the aircraft deflator rose 97%, little different from the 117% increase of the aggregate GNP deflator over the same period.

The methodology proposed above adjusts changes in prices of identical models by comparing changes in price per unit across model changes with changes in the net revenue provided. Unit prices of commercial aircraft are obtained from the same source as the official deflator, CAB form 41.[17] Because only a sample of prices has been collected for the period 1946–78, rather than all of the information available at the CAB, we first display as the lower solid line in figure 4.6 an index constructed from our sample of price data using the CAB methodology. Because different airlines paid different prices for the same aircraft, our index compares *only identical plane types purchased by the same airline in successive years.* For the years 1957–77 our solid-line index tracks the CAB index (dashed line) extremely well, with respective annual rates of increase of 3.41% and 3.55%. Before 1957 our index exhibits a slower rate of increase than

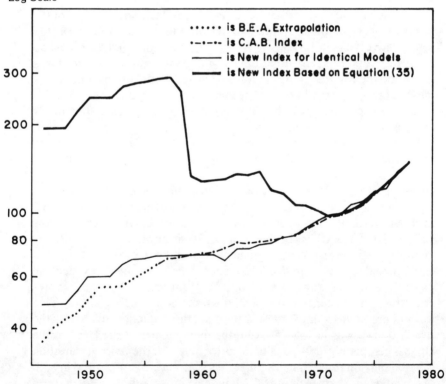

Fig. 4.6   The new quality-adjusted price index for commercial aircraft compared with a new index for identical models and with the BEA/CAB index.

the official deflator, which is extrapolated by the Bureau of Economic Analysis (BEA) for the earlier period when the CAB index is unavailable, by using a collection of producer price indexes that are unrelated to aircraft manufacture.[18] Thus our index indicates that during the interval 1946–57 aircraft prices increased less than the prices of the products used by the BEA in its proxy index, with annual rates of increase of 3.55% and 5.81%, respectively.

4.4.3 Quality Adjustments Based on Net Revenue Data

The technique of price measurement proposed in this paper adjusts price differences between models of a given product for changes in net revenue yielded by new models. Holding constant the prices of unchanged models, if a 10% increase in the price of model B compared to model A is accompanied by a 10% increase in net revenue, no quality adjustment is required to an index of the prices of identical models. But a disproportionate increase in net revenue made possible by embodied improvements in technology is valued by users and should be subject to a quality adjustment.

Table 4.1 presents the basic data required to compute the net revenue yielded by the most important types of commercial aircraft manufactured during the postwar period. Twelve comparisons appear in the table, involving 15 different aircraft models, including long-range, medium-range, and short-range models. In size the aircraft range from the small, two-engine piston short-range Convair 440, with 44 seats, to the large wide-bodied long-range turbofan Boeing 747, with 317 seats and capable of providing 28 times the annual capacity. In chronological time the aircraft models span the entire period 1946–78, beginning with the staple of early postwar air travel, the Douglas DC-6, and continuing through the planes that have carried the vast majority of U.S. air travelers in the late 1970s—the Boeing 747, Douglas DC-10, Boeing 727-200 and 727-100, and the Douglas DC-9-30. The major types of aircraft that are excluded (to limit the time devoted to the analysis) include planes that are virtual duplicates of those analyzed here, and a few planes that had short production runs or have been used mainly by local-service carriers.[19]

Table 4.1 is divided into three sections, according to the range of the various plane models, to correspond with a central fact of aircraft operating economics—both revenue and cost per seat-mile are extremely sensitive to the average "stage length," or "length of hop." A very short flight mainly consists of expensive take-off and landing operations, with a slow average speed, whereas a long flight amortizes the take-off and landing over a multihour flight segment at cruising speed. Thus every comparison in table 4.1 represents an attempt to compare the revenue and operating costs of planes flying the same stage length, in order to hold constant this crucial operating variable.

Our basic unit of measurement—the characteristic x in the above theoretical discussion—is an aircraft's ability to produce "available seat-miles per unit of time." Three basic figures are estimated in table 4.1 for the two planes in each comparison—total annual available seat-miles (asm), revenue per seat-mile, and cost per seat-mile. To control for the varying routes and operating practices of the airlines using each plane, annual utilization (col. 2) is held constant for each pair of planes, and speed is held constant when both planes in a comparison are jets. The number of seats, of course, is allowed to vary, since this is a major determinant of the differing productivity of the various plane types. The product of columns 2, 3, and 4, is annual available seat-miles (col. 10).

The fifth column displays the average stage length used for the calculation of revenue and operating costs. In the comparisons designated by the superscript "b," the actual recorded stage length of the second-listed ("newer") plane is chosen, and published cost curves are used to adjust the operating costs of the first-listed plane. For the comparisons designated by the superscript "e," arbitrary stage lengths of 250, 500, or 750 miles are employed to allow the use of the careful comparative study of Straszheim (1969), which provides a detailed cost breakdown of several major plane types for these standard stage lengths. In all comparisons the revenue figures refer to the particular year and stage length selected, with column 6 recording gross revenue per revenue passenger-mile, and column 7 recording revenue per available seat-mile after deducting from revenue the "overhead" costs of aircraft and traffic service, sales, reservations, advertising, administrative, and depreciation of nonflight equipment.

The measurement of revenue for a particular stage length and year in column 6 must be handled with extreme care. Published fares overstate the true revenue received by the airline, because of various categories of discounts that are available. Further, each aircraft, stage length, and year differs in the fraction of first-class and coach traffic carried. The method of revenue estimation employed in the construction of table 4.1 takes as its point of departure a yield curve of 1971 constructed by Douglas and Miller (1974, p. 90) that is adjusted for the incidence of discount fares. Then the revenue yield for earlier years is based on changes in observed average first-class and coach yields, adjusted for changes in the slope of the yield curve (over time the price of short-haul flights has increased substantially relative to long-haul flights). The mix of first-class and coach fares is available for each plane separately from CAB records.

The aircraft operating cost figures in column 8 exclude all capital costs, since our basic formula calls for the calculation of net revenue available to "cover" capital costs. The major categories of operating cost included are flight crew wages, fuel, insurance, and aircraft maintenance expenses. The operating cost estimates marked with the superscript "b" are based on the actual recorded experience of the U.S. domestic trunk airlines, with the costs of the first-listed plane type adjusted to correspond to the stage length of the second-listed plane type (thus the costs of the second-listed plane type are those actually recorded in CAB records). The operating cost estimates marked with the superscript "e" are based on Straszheim's comparisons, in some cases adjusted for wage changes between Straszheim's year of study (1969) and the comparison year.

Finally, adjusted revenue minus operating cost provides an estimate of net revenue per available seat-mile (col. 9), and this figure times annual seat-miles provides the basic computation of annual net revenue, needed for the comparison in equation (32) with the price of each plane type. We note that table 4.1 makes each pairwise comparison for a single year, thus holding constant output prices and the prices of operating inputs, particularly fuel and the wages of flight crews and maintenance labor. The plane that appears to have provided the highest level of net revenue per available seat mile is the short-range Douglas DC-9-30, while the highest absolute level of net revenue is provided by the largest plane, the Boeing 747.

Table 4.2 combines these net revenue estimates with data on the sales price of the various plane types to allow computation of the quality adjustments using equation (31) developed above. The prices are the same as those used in the development of the price index for identical models displayed as the lower solid line in figure 4.6. In most cases the "old" and "new" models being compared were not actually constructed simultaneously, requiring the adjustment of the "old price" for changes in the price of identical models between the year of its disappearance and the first sales year of the new model. In this way the sales prices of the two planes in each comparison are computed for the same year, thus allowing the price of output and operating inputs to be held constant.

One indication of the enormous profitability of the jet planes, compared to the piston planes they replaced, is given in column 5, which shows the ratio of net revenue in the comparison year to the replacement price of the plane in the same year. Because most airlines depreciated their piston planes over short seven- or eight-year intervals, it is apparent that the DC-7B and the Convair 400 barely covered depreciation expense, much less any interest cost or allowance for profit. On the other hand, some of the jets appear to have been extremely profitable, especially the "stretched" long-range DC-8-61 and short-range DC-9-30.

An interesting pattern in column 5 is the deteriorating profitability of a given model over its lifetime. For instance, the n/v ratio for the DC-8-61 declined from as much as .475 in 1967 (line 4) to .238 in 1972 (line 1). Similar declines occurred for the Boeing 727-100 (from .225 in 1963 to .173 in 1968), the Lockheed Electra L-188 (from .388 in 1959 to .243 in 1963), and DC-9-10 (from .340 in 1965 to .314 in 1967). This pattern makes sense if new models are continually introduced and allow the reduction of average operating costs and fares, while the costs of operating any given model are driven up by rising wages.

As discussed above, these estimates of the quality adjustment factor require an assumption to be made regarding the curvature of the function linking the price of the aircraft to their capability of earning net revenue, holding technology constant. There appears to be no direct way of estimating this function by examining the cross-section of planes built at any given time, because the planes built in the long-range, medium-range, and short-run categories are really separate products that defy comparisons. Further, at any given time, typically only the most advanced plane in each category is constructed. In lieu of any direct evidence on the curvature of the $v(n, \sigma)$ function, the curvature parameter has been assigned a value of 1.2 in table 4.2, implying diminishing returns in the provision of net revenue from increases in aircraft size (the assumed elasticity of net revenue to increases in cost is $1/1.2 = .833$). The resulting correction factor for curvature is listed in column 8; if the assumption of diminishing returns is incorrect, then the real price reductions in column (9) would be smaller. On the other hand, if the "true" function were to have a greater degree of curvature, then the real price reductions would be correspondingly greater.

Ironically the first comparison between the "stretched" DC-8-61, manufactured during 1966–69 and in continued use today, indicates that the introduction of the controversial wide-bodied DC-10-10 represented a "quality deterioration," in the sense that the price of the new model increased substantially more than the net revenue it was capable of providing. Thus the quality adjustment formula indicates a "real" price increase of 10.8%. All of the other comparisons indicate a quality improvement in the transition from the old to the new model, requiring the downward adjustment in the inflation rate recorded by the CAB index recording the change in prices of identical models.

It is not surprising that the largest indicated quality adjustments in column 9 are for two piston planes, the DC-7B and Convair 440. A considerably smaller adjustment is indicated for the transition from the medium-range DC-6B to the turboprop Lockheed Electra (L-188). It is well-known that the DC-7 series was a particularly inefficient airplane, representing the ultimate level of resources that could be usefully employed, given the obsolete piston-engine technology. The DC-7 may well have been incapable of making a profit at the time of the introduction of jets in 1959, only six years after the first commercial flight of the DC-7 in 1953; this interpretation is consistent with the precipitous decline in the prices of used long-range aircraft during the period 1958–62.

Among the other transitions between models documented in table 4.2, we note that the medium-range piston DC-6B, although not as inefficient relative to subsequent aircraft as the DC-7 and Convair 440, nevertheless was much less efficient than the "transition" turboprop Lockheed Electra. Further, the Boeing 727-100 represented very little further technological improvement over the Lockheed Electra, at least from the point of view of the airline operators; thus the subsequent disappearance of the Electras must at least partially reflect the favorable verdict of passengers regarding the speed and comfort of the Boeing 727.

We note that the transition from the first-generation to second-generation jets has resulted in efficiency improvements that in some cases are almost as important as the earlier transition from the pistons to turboprops and first-generation jets. Particularly important was the "stretching" of the DC-8, DC-9, and Boeing 727, yielding roughly a doubling of net revenue at only 10%–25% additional resource cost. In contrast, the shift to the wide-bodied DC-10 and 747 does not appear to have represented a major breakthrough in operating efficiency, and this fact is reflected below in the failure of our aggregate quality adjustment for aircraft to exhibit a major decline in the final 1970–71 transition period.

4.4.4   A New Deflator for Commercial Aircraft

The changes in "real" price in column 9 of table 4.2 can be used to create adjustment factors for each aircraft included in the comparisons. Because the current national income accounts deflator uses 1972 as its base year, the aircraft produced in that year are treated as having adjustment factors of 1.00. These planes include the long-range DC-10-10, the Boeing 747, the "stretched" Boeing 727-200, and the "stretched" DC-9-30. Then earlier planes are attributed quality relatives based on the change in "real" price in column 9 of table 4.2 between them and their successors.

How should these "quality relatives" for individual planes be combined into a "real" price-change index to be combined (as in eq. [33]) with the existing index of price change for identical models? First, prices and numbers of units sold were obtained for every important type of plane produced by U.S. commercial aircraft manufacturers and sold to U.S. airlines (both domestic and international) during 1946–78.[20] Then a method had to be devised for weighting together the changes in the "real" price index for individual planes when a transition was made from an old model to a newer model. Neither the conventional Paasche nor Laspeyres methods could be used to weight the relatives, since there were no years when all of the planes in a given group (long-, medium-, or short-range) were manufactured simultaneously. Instead, a variant on the Divisia index method was employed. Changes in quality relatives from one plane to a succeeding model were not weighted by sales in the transition year, because often sales of a discontinued model in its last year, or sales of a new model in its first year, were too small to properly represent the importance of the particular plane. Instead, the weights for planes involved in the transitions were based on their nominal sales during time intervals spanning periods when a particular group of planes was manufactured simultaneously. As an example, in the long-range group the transition in 1969–71 between the DC-8-61, and Boeing 707-100 and 707-300, on the one hand, and the Douglas DC-10-10 and Boeing 747, on the other hand, was handled by weighting changes in quality relatives between the individual old and new models by sales of each of the three old models during the entire 1966–69 period when they were all manufactured simultaneously. The resulting average change in the quality relative was phased in partially in 1970 (when the B747 was first delivered) and partially in 1971 (when the DC-10 was first delivered), with the weight on each year in proportion to the relative sales of the two new models in the 1970–75 interval.

The resulting indexes of changes in the quality relatives for the three major groups of planes were in turn weighted together to form an aggregate index of these changes, using as weights the nominal sales of each group in the three years surrounding the change.[21] These methods of weighting help to smooth out the final index and protect it from spurious changes due simply to the fluctuating nominal sales of different types of planes. Any index based on weighting the *levels* of the quality relatives by current year sales, as opposed to weighting *changes* in the quality relatives by sales over an interval, tends to give the appearance of marked year-to-year fluctuations in quality that in fact did not occur.

Table 4.3 and figure 4.6 illustrate the final index that results from these calculations. In table 4.3 the two sources for the current official national income accounts deflator for aircraft are shown in columns 1 and 2, and our new index for identical models purchased by identical airlines is displayed in column 3. The aggregate index of the weighted average of changes in the quality relatives is added together with the changes in column 3 for 1946–57 and 1977–78 and column 1 for 1957–77, as in equation (33) above. When the resulting sum of previously unmeasured quality change (dp^x/p^x) and the price change of identical models (dC/C) is added together to create the nominal input price-change index (dP^x/P^x), we obtain the index displayed in column 4. The timing of the newly measured quality change is apparent in column 5, which displays the ratio of the new index based on equation (33) to the existing CAB index from column 1.

As might have been expected, the most dramatic drop in the average adjustment factor in column 5 occurred in 1957–60, as a result of the replacement of the piston DC-6 and DC-7 series by the turboprop Lockheed Electra and pure jet Boeing 707 and 720, and the Douglas DC-8. Then the average adjustment factor remains essentially constant until

1966, when the first of the short-range DC-9-10 aircraft was phased in. Further rapid reductions occur in 1967–69, when the "stretched" second-generation jets replaced their earlier counterparts. Only a relatively small reduction in the adjustment factor is recorded in 1969–71, when the transition to the wide-bodied DC-10 and Boeing 747 occurred.

4.4.5   Possible Biases in the New Index: Evidence from the Used Aircraft Market

The new index in column 4 of table 4.3 is radically different from the official deflator. We naturally are led to ask, Which should we believe? The official deflator, based on the prices of identical models, excludes any comparison between successive models that are not identical. Implicitly this procedure involves treating successive models as differing in quality in exact proportion to their prices (adjusted for price changes in identical models). Thus if Douglas discontinued producing the $1.6 million DC-7 in 1958 and began producing the $4.4 million DC-8 in 1959, and other identical planes sold in both years remained unchanged in price, then the official deflator treats one DC-8 as equal to 4.4/1.6 (or 2.75) DC-7s. In contrast, our index imputes a 76% reduction in price to the transition, based on the observation that the new plane yielded 7.89 times as much net revenue and on an assumption about the nonlinearity of the technology relating net revenue to price.

To choose between the indexes, we are aided by the ample data available on the prices of used aircraft. If users considered a new 1959 DC-8 to be identical to 2.75 1958 DC-7s, we should see something like that ratio between the price of the two planes on the used aircraft market. On the other hand, if our new approach is more appropriate, we should find that a DC-8 was valued at an amount equal to 10 or 11 DC-7s. The first year in which both planes were sold simultaneously on the used market was 1966, and the observed price ratio was not just 10:1 but rather 22:1.[22] In the same source the price spread between the Lockheed Electra and Douglas DC-6 is not the 1.7:1 dictated by actual prices, or the 3.5:1 indicated by our quality adjustment, but rather 7.8:1.

Scattered evidence is also available to indicate that users concurred in our evaluation of the poor operating efficiency of the first-generation jets relative to the second-generation jets. For instance, in 1971 Eastern was willing to sell a fleet of 15 Boeing 720s for $2.1 million each in order to buy the same number of Boeing 727-200 models for about $6.5 million each (note the comparison in table 4.2, line 8). At the same time Eastern was able to sell its DC-8-61 aircraft at about 90% of the purchase price, while being forced to sell Lockheed Electras at 30% of the purchase price and Convair 440 aircraft at less than 10% of the purchase price.[23]

Quite recently a reasonably comprehensive report has compared prices of used aircraft in 1977. In table 4.4 are listed the ratios of used price to the new price in the most recent comparison year as well as our "quality relatives" derived from column 9 of table 4.2. Several interesting features stand out in table 4.4. First, we note that the top-listed plane in each category has a used/new relative of about 1.38. In the case of the DC-10, where the new price refers to 1972, this used/new ratio corresponds closely to the 37% increase in the official deflator between 1972 and 1977 (table 4.3 col. 1), indicating that used and new planes are regarded as perfect substitutes. For the other top-listed planes, the new prices refer to 1968 and 1967; since the national income accounts deflator increased by about 60% between 1968 and 1977, the used market indicates that the used versions of the Boeing 727-200 and Douglas DC-9-30 were not regarded in 1977 as perfect substitutions for new planes.

There is no reason why the ratios in the two columns of table 4.4 should correspond exactly. The year of the used price quotations is later than the year of the comparisons of successive models in table 4.2; the fact that the used market undervalues the older planes in comparison to our quality relatives may simply indicate that the older planes become progressively less profitable over time. A plane that the market overvalues in relation to our comparison is the DC-9-10; the source to table 4.4 indicates that this model is relatively scarce, due to the expansion of the local-service airlines. The DC-8-61 seems to be valued by the used market as much less efficient than the DC-10-10, in contrast to our conclusion. This verdict of the market appears to stem from the fact that, according to the source for table 4.4, this model has been affected adversely by U.S. government antinoise regulations, being "one of the most difficult aircraft to hush."

Passenger comfort is another factor that may explain why the used-aircraft market tends to establish greater differentials between old and new models than our comparison. This paper explicitly avoids any attempt to attribute dollar values to the value of consumer comfort or time. Nevertheless, one reason that the new wide-bodied jets may hold their value relatively well is the greater degree of comfort they offer. The seating configurations for the DC-10-10 and Boeing 747 used in table 4.1, column 4, allow for wider seats than for the "narrow-bodied" jets. Subsequent to the date of our comparison, most U.S. airlines have added an extra row of seats to all of their wide-bodied aircraft, thus reducing seat width to the narrow-bodied standard.[24] And, of course, the greater speed and comfort of jet aircraft induced a shift of passengers in the 1958–60 transition era that inevitably had to depress the used market for piston aircraft, independent of their operating cost disadvantage.

The used-aircraft market seems to provide no evidence that our comparisons exaggerate the true quality difference among old and new models and, in fact, indicates that our comparisons may understate these differences. If we review our comparison techniques to ask whether there is any consistent tendency that might understate the differences among old and new models, our attention is drawn to the amazingly high ratios of net revenue to aircraft price arrayed in table 4.2, column 5. Imagine that the real interest rate is 3%, and assume that aircraft are depreciated over 10 years at a 10% straight-line rate (many airlines use lives of 14–18 years). Then the cost of capital would be 13%, and yet the net revenue percentages for some of the newer models in table 4.2 range as high as 50%. It is possible that the resources used in tables 4.1 and 4.2 may systematically overstate revenue or understate costs, leading to exaggerated estimates of net revenue. If this tendency were uniform, all net revenue figures would be squeezed and the older planes would be pushed closer to break-even status, thus increasing the relative net-revenue advantage of the newer models. One systematic source of bias in our estimates is imparted by our assumption that future prices and costs are assumed to be the same as in the present. This conflicts with the observed tendency of net revenue to decline over the life of a plane, as operating costs rise relative to revenue yield. A slightly different conceptual framework in which the input price index held constant discounted *expected* net revenue (over the life of the plane), rather than actual first-year net revenue, would yield narrower margins for all planes and thus increase the advantage in table 4.2 of the more profitable models.

Another important source of conservatism in our estimates is the decision to use the same utilization rates for the old and new models (see source notes to table 4.1, col. 2). The actual utilization rates for piston aircraft were uniformly lower than for jets, allowing them to earn even less net revenue than indicated in table 4.1. Similarly, revenue yields on jets were higher than on propeller aircraft during the 1959–63 period due to the imposition of a "jet surcharge" on fares, while table 4.1 conservatively assumes that the propeller models had the same revenue yield as the jets that replaced them.

4.5   Conclusion

4.5.1   Potential for Application to Other Products

My own previous research and that of others suggests that there is a considerable potential for applying the techniques developed in this paper, together with other related methods, to the construction of new price deflators for types of equipment other than commercial aircraft. Another regulated industry, the generation of electricity, creates many of the same opportunities for improved measurement as in the case of airlines, because of the detailed operating data available. A preliminary analysis (Gordon 1974) indicates that the manufacturers of generating equipment achieved improvements in operating cost during the 1947–70 period that were extremely large relative to the value of the equipment, although there was a marked deceleration in this form of technological innovation after 1962. Just as in the aircraft case, the new deflator declined markedly during the 1947–70 period, unlike the official deflator, which in the case of electric generating equipment increased by a factor of 2.5.

Another appealing field of application is the whole range of consumer durables, including appliances and automobiles. Just as the operating costs of commercial aircraft were reduced by innovations that lowered fuel consumption and real maintenance input per unit of output, so consumer appliance manufacturers have evolved new models with lower energy and maintenance requirements than their predecessors. Color television sets require less electricity and have drastically lower repair frequencies than previously. Refrigerators and air conditioners use less energy, while air conditioners have become lighter and easier to install per unit of cooling capacity.[25]

Econometricians have devoted more attention to quality changes in automobiles than in any other single product. At least two studies are now available that measure the extent of technical improvement in the level of automobile fuel consumption over time. Long ago Fisher, Griliches, and Kaysen (1962, p. 446) created an index of the fuel usage of a constant-quality 1949 automobile and found a 12.8% improvement between 1949 and 1961. Using a different methodology to hold constant the quality attributes of automobiles, Wilcox (1978) has found an improvement similar to that of Fisher, Griliches, and Kaysen for their 1949–61 period (16.2%) and a further 12.5% improvement during the 1961–68 interval. Subsequently there was a deterioration in fuel economy that Wilcox relates to federal environmental legislation.

How can the value of the savings in operating cost in the appliance and automobile examples be converted into adjustments to the official price indexes for the same goods? Since no net revenue data are available, a different approach is required. In the above analysis we asked, "How much was the change in the price of the capital good needed to yield the same net revenue?" Instead we could ask, "How much would the price of the capital good have to be reduced to yield the same saving as the present value of the observed operating cost saving involved in the shift between the old and new model?" Wilcox's paper on automobiles estimates that improved fuel efficiency during the 1949–68 period was equivalent to a 10% reduction in the price of new automobiles, enough to eliminate about one-third of the observed inflation in new automobile prices over that interval.

4.5.2 Implications for the Measurement of Output and Productivity

Since real output for an individual commodity is measured as a residual by dividing nominal product by the appropriate price index, any conclusions reached above regarding the prices of durable goods have their counterpart in symmetric conclusions regarding the real output of durable goods as well as the productivity of those industries. The new deflator developed for the aircraft industry in table 4.3, column 4, can be applied to the official national income accounts figure on nominal purchases of aircraft as producers' durable equipment to yield a new real output series. In contrast to a 1957–72 annual growth rate of the official real aircraft output series of 6.2% the new output series grows at an annual rate of 16.9%. Productivity growth in the aircraft industry would also be increased at a corresponding rate. And, while labor productivity in the airline industry would not be altered, any index of the growth of total factor productivity in the airline industry would be much slower with a capital input series derived from the new deflator than with the existing official deflator. This shift of total factor productivity improvement from the airline industry to the aircraft industry makes sense, since it was the aircraft industry that invested the research and development resources to obtain the technological advances that made more modern aircraft possible (all these statements treat aircraft engine and fuselage production as occurring in a single industry).

Since this paper contains only a single detailed case study, it is impossible to determine whether aggregate official figures on real investment or real GNP are subject to minor or major revisions. The aircraft industry is so small that acceptance of our new deflator would raise the 1957–72 growth rate of real producers' durable equipment purchases from 4.52% only to 4.63% per annum. Any major impact on real investment data, not to mention real GNP data, would require a finding that corrections for nonproportional quality change apply to a broad range of industries. Thus a conclusion regarding the importance of potential revisions must await a more comprehensive study.[26]

While we are not yet in a position to assess the aggregate quantitative significance of the new measurement techniques proposed in this paper, nevertheless it is apparent from the aircraft example that the potential for revision in the official deflators for durable goods may be considerably greater than from the first round in the 1960s of econometric studies using the hedonic regression technique. Because improvements in operating efficiency by definition occur for durable goods, but not nondurable goods or services, a more comprehensive study would presumably yield the conclusion that the price of durable goods relative to other goods has declined in comparison to the relative prices registered in the national accounts.

Critics may protest that the process of correcting for changes in operating efficiency is inevitably so subjective that the resulting deflators have a wide margin of error. The detailed analysis of the airline case does indeed confirm that the estimation requires numerous steps, any one of which might be wrong, and also requires an arbitrary assumption about the shape of the function linking aircraft net revenue to capital cost. In contrast to our finding that the new 1972-base deflator in 1957 is about four times the official deflator, another investigator might find a ratio of three or six. Yet it would be unwise to reject the new index as subjective while clinging rigidly to the existing deflator, because the latter is based on the equally subjective evaluation that successive models of aircraft *differ in quality in exact proportion to observed differences in price.* Among the many pieces of evidence that deny the validity of this assumption is the observed behavior of the prices of used aircraft. In fact, the existing national income accounts are riddled with subjective decisions, including the continuing adherence to the procedure of setting permanently at unity the price index for producer purchases of electronic computers.

Finally, it must be recognized that any attempt to correct durable goods prices for changes in operating efficiency requires acceptance of the production separability assumption outlined at the beginning of Section 4.3. It must be assumed that improvements in fuel efficiency are achieved by manufacturers of the durable good and not by their users. Yet *some* assumptions are required to perform any kind of measurement work, and the most crucial assumptions employed in this paper can be validated by various pieces of outside evidence. Berndt and Wood (1975) provide evidence to support the separability assumption. The notion that users care about operating efficiency seems to be validated by the behavior of prices in the used aircraft market, not to mention the response of the prices of various types of used automobile models to changes in the price of gasoline. Similarly, the verdict that electronic computer prices should be based on prices per unit of computer service, and not on the production price per computer, is validated by the rush of users to shift to new-model computers with higher performance/price ratios. It may now be appropriate for critics to drop the accusation that new techniques of measurement are inherently subjective and to admit that the limited scope of quality adjustments in the present official deflators for durable goods conflicts with ample evidence that real-world users place a positive value on improvements in performance and operating efficiency.

Table 4.1   Basic Revenue and Operating Cost Data for U.S. Aircraft Efficiency Analysis

Comparison and Year	(1) Plane Types	(2) Rev. Hr/Yr	(3) Speed (mph)	(4) Seats	(5) Stage Length (miles)	(6) Gross Rev./rpm	(7) Rev. after Over-head/asm	(8) Aircraft Operating Cost/asm	(9) Cols. 7–8	(10) Annual asm's	(11) Annual Net Revenue ($million)
					Long Range						
1. 1972	DC-8-61	3073	463	175.0	942[a]	.0682	.0176	.0093[a]	.0083	249	2.067
	DC-10-10	2836[b]	483[b]	224.6	1067	.0682	.0176	.0082	.0094	320	3.008
2. 1972	B707-300B	3457	485	143.0	1429[a]	.0601	.0169	.0106[a]	.0063	240	1.512
	B747-100	3146[b]	507[b]	317.1	1962	.0601	.0169	.0087	.0082	532	4.362
3. 1967	B707-100B	3599	489	124.6	1166[a]	.0546	.0159	.0094[a]	.0065	219	1.424
	DC-8-61	3990[b]	485[b]	195.5	1223	.0546	.0159	.0070	.0089	344	3.062
4. 1967	DC-8-50	3836	479	130.7	873[a]	.0546	.0164	.0086[a]	.0078	240	1.872
	DC-8-61	3990[b]	485[b]	195.5	1223	.0546	.0164	.0070	.0094	359	3.375
5. 1959	DC-7B	c	248[d]	79.1[c]	750[e]	.0590	.0207	.0172[e]	.0035	65	0.228
	DC-8-50	3325[c]	410[d]	120.8[c]	750[e]	.0590	.0207	.0098[e]	.0109	165	1.799
6. 1959	DC-7B	c	248[d]	79.1[c]	750[e]	.0590	.0207	.0172[e]	.0035	60	0.210
	B707-100B	3084[c]	410[d]	121.9[c]	750[e]	.0590	.0207	.0098[e]	.0109	154	1.679
					Medium Range						
7. 1971	B727-100	2537	433	96.2	556[a]	.0797	.0242	.0149[a]	.0093	106	0.986
	B727-200	2610[b]	429[b]	124.3	518	.0797	.0242	.0110	.0132	137	1.808
8. 1971	B720	2576	451	116.6	847[a]	.0797	.0242	.0169[a]	.0073	135	0.986
	B727-200	2610[b]	429[b]	124.3	518	.0797	.0242	.0110	.0132	144	1.901
9. 1963	L-188	2409[c]	290[d]	75.1	500[e]	.0718	.0218	.0134[e]	.0084	52	0.437
	B727-100	c	376[d]	96.2	500[e]	.0718	.0218	.0117[e]	.0101	87	0.878
10. 1959	DC-6B	c	216[d]	65.5[c]	500[e]	.0708	.0248	.0176[e]	.0073	34	0.248
	L-188	2409[c]	290[d]	75.1[c]	500[e]	.0708	.0248	.0121[e]	.0127	52	0.660

Table 4.1 (continued)

Comparison and Year	(1) Plane Types	(2) Rev. Hr/Yr	(3) Speed (mph)	(4) Seats	(5) Stage Length (miles)	(6) Gross Rev./ rpm	(7) Rev. after Over-head/ asm	(8) Aircraft Operating Cost/ asm	(9) Cols. 7–8	(10) Annual asm's	(11) Annual Net Revenue ($million)
					Short Range						
11. 1967	DC-9-10	2621	378	66.6	280[a]	.0831	.0290	.0157[a]	.0173	66	0.878
	DC-9-30	2047[b]	348[b]	97.4	257	.0831	.0290	.0117	.0173	96	1.660
12. 1965	CV-440	[c]	165[d]	43.7	250[e]	.0848	.0296	.0242[e]	.0048	19	0.091
	DC-9-10	2621[c]	375[d]	66.6	250[e]	.0848	.0296	.0155[e]	.0141	65	0.917

Source by col.:

(2) Revenue hours per year. From United States Civil Aeronautics Board, *Aircraft Operating Cost and Performance Report* for the year in question (U.S. Federal Aviation Agency for 1963 and prior years). No figures are shown for piston planes, which are allocated the same utilization as the jet plane used in each comparison.

(3) Speed. All comparisons except those marked with superscript "d" are from the same sources as col. (2). Those marked with superscript "d" are from Straszheim (1969, p. 76).

(4) Seats. All comparisons are from the same sources as col. (2). For those marked with superscript "c," figures from the 1963 FAA document were used for 1959 as well.

(5) Stage length. All comparisons except those marked with superscript "e" are from the same sources as col. (2). For those marked with superscript "e," operating cost comparisons are taken from Straszheim (1969, p. 86) for the stage lengths indicated.

(6) Fare data are based on a yield curve adjusted for discounts displayed in Douglas and Miller (1974, p. 90). For earlier years, e.g., 1967, the 1971 data are multiplied by the following three ratios that, when multiplied together, adjust for the changing role of discounts and the gradually changing tilt of the yield curve: (a) the ratio of the 1967 to the 1971 published fare for the stage length in question, from the *Official Airline Guide*; (b) the ratio of the 1971 to the 1967 published coach fare for the 740-mile stage length; (c) the ratio of the 1967 coach yield to the 1971 coach yield, from the *CAB Handbook of Airline Statistics* (1973). First-class fare data are calculated by the same procedure independently and are weighted together with coach data using the ratio of first-class to coach-class revenue passenger miles for each year, from the *Handbook of Airline Statistics*.

(7) Gross revenue data are multiplied by two ratios to provide figures on net revenue attributable to a given aircraft per available seat mile: (*a*) load factor for the given plane in the given year, from the same sources used for col. (2); (*b*) the ratio of direct cost to total cost, taken as a percentage (57.2) of the direct cost categories (flying operations, maintenance, depreciation, and capital costs) to total costs (also including aircraft and traffic servicing, passenger service, promotion and sales, general administrative, and depreciation of nonflight equipment), as given for the year ending June 30, 1971, in Douglas and Miller (1974, table 2-1, p. 8).

(8) Except for comparisons designated by the superscript "e," cost figures (including flying operations and maintenance but excluding depreciation) were taken from the source of col. (2). Comparisons designated by superscript "e" were taken from Straszheim (1969, pp. 249–51), where the figures shown from 1965 were adjusted to the year shown by multiplying crew wages and maintenance expense by the ratio between the earlier year and 1965 of the BLS economy-wide nonagricultural average hourly earnings index.

(9) Col. (7) minus col. (8).

(10) Cols. (2) times (3) times (4) (expressed in millions of asm's per plane-year).

(11) Cols. (9) times (10).

Note: asm = available seat mile.

[a]Cost per asm was calculated using the stage length of the other plane in the comparison, adjusting the stage length shown for this plane by the cost curves illustrated in Straszheim (1969, p. 86).

[b]Annual asm's (col. 10) were calculated by using figures in cols. (2) and (3) for the other plane in the comparison.

[c]Seat totals used for 1950 are those listed for the particular plane in the USFAA volume for 1963.

[d]Speeds shown for the relevant stage length in Straszheim (1969, p. 76).

[e]Costs per asm adjusted from 1965 figures listed in Straszheim (1969, pp. 249–51) using the BLS average hourly earnings index for the nonfarm private economy.

Table 4.2 Comparisons of Purchase Price and Net Revenue for U.S. Aircraft Efficiency Analysis

Comparison and Year	(1) Plane Types	(2) Original Price (Year)	(3) Price in Comp. Year	(4) Net Rev. in Comp. Year	(5) n_t/v_t	(6) v_{1t}/v_{0t}	(7) n_{1t}/n_{0t}	(8) $\left(\dfrac{n_0}{n_1}\right).2$	(9) $\Delta p^x/p^x$ $=(6)\times(8)$ $\div(7)$ -1
				Long Range					
1. 1972	DC-8-61	7.7 (1969)	8.7	2.067	.238	1.736	1.455	.928	.108
	DC-10-10		15.1	3.008	.199				
2. 1972	B707-300B	6.7 (1968)	7.5	1.512	.202	2.627	2.885	.809	−.263
	B747-100		19.7	4.363	.221				
3. 1967	B707-100B	5.7 (1967)	5.7	1.424	.249	1.245	2.150	.858	−.503
	DC-8-61		7.1	3.062	.431				
4. 1967	DC-8-50	5.4 (1966)	5.6	1.872	.334	1.268	1.803	.889	−.375
	DC-8-61		7.1	3.375	.475				
5. 1959	DC-7B	1.6 (1958)	1.6	0.228	.143	2.750	7.890	.662	−.769
	DC-8-50		4.4	1.799	.409				
6. 1959	DC-7B	1.6 (1958)	1.6	0.210	.131	2.875	7.995	.660	−.762
	B707-100B		4.6	1.679	.365				

Medium Range

		(2)	(3)	(4)	(5)	(6)	(7)	(8)	(9)
7. 1968	B727-100	4.6 (1968)	4.6	0.794	.173	1.130	1.832	.886	− .453
	B727-200		5.2	1.455	.280				
8. 1968	B720	3.7 (1961)	4.4	0.794	.180	1.182	1.927	.877	− .462
	B727-200		5.2	1.530	.294				
9. 1963	L-188	1.7 (1959)	1.8	0.437	.243	2.167	2.009	.870	− .062
	B727-100		3.9	0.878	.225				
10. 1959	DC-6B	1.1 (1958)	1.1	0.248	.225	1.545	2.661	.822	− .523
	L-188		1.7	0.660	.388				

Short Range

		(2)	(3)	(4)	(5)	(6)	(7)	(8)	(9)
11. 1967	DC-9-10	2.7 (1966)	2.8	0.878	.314	1.107	1.891	.880	− .485
	DC-9-30		3.1	1.660	.535				
12. 1965	CV-440	0.6 (1957)	.65	0.091	.140	4.154	10.077	.630	− .740
	DC-9-10		2.7	0.917	.340				

Source by col.:
(2) USCAB form 41; 1967 and earlier observations from schedule B–43 dated December 31, 1967.
(3) Price in col. (2) for the first plane listed is multiplied by the change between the year shown in col. (2) and the year of the comparison of the CAB price index shown in table 4.3, col. (1). The price for the second-listed plane in each comparison is obtained for the comparison year from the same source as is listed in col. (2).
(4) Table 4.1, col. (11).
(5) Col. (4) divided by col. (3).
(6) The ratio of price in col. (3) for the second-listed plane to the price in col. (3) for the first-listed plane.
(7) The ratio of the net revenue listed in col. (4) for the second-listed plane to the net revenue listed in col. (4) for the first-listed plane.
(8) The inverse of col. (7), raised to the .2 power.
(9) Cols. (6) times (8) minus 1.0.

Table 4.3   **Alternative Price Indexes**
for Commercial Aircraft, 1946–1978
(1972 = 100)

Year	(1) CAB Index	(2) BEA Extrapolation	(3) New Index for Identical Models	(4) New Index Based on Eq. (33)	(5) Cols. (4) ÷ (1)
1946		36.8	48.0	196.3	
1947		41.9	48.0	196.3	
1948		44.7	48.0	196.3	
1949		46.5	54.4	222.8	
1950		49.0	60.9	249.3	
1951		55.9	60.9	249.3	
1952		55.6	60.9	249.3	
1953		56.8	66.5	272.5	
1954		57.5	68.3	279.8	
1955		59.8	69.0	282.6	
1956		65.2	70.1	287.2	
1957	68.5		70.4	288.1	4.206
1958	69.6		70.4	259.3	3.726
1959	72.1		70.4	133.0	1.845
1960	72.3		70.4	128.1	1.772
1961	73.2		70.4	128.6	1.757
1962	75.5		68.8	132.6	1.756
1963	78.7		75.6	136.9	1.740
1964	77.1		75.6	134.2	1.740
1965	78.7		77.8	137.1	1.740
1966	80.0		78.6	119.9	1.499
1967	83.0		81.0	116.4	1.402
1968	85.6		84.2	106.0	1.238
1969	88.7		88.7	105.4	1.188
1970	94.0		94.0	103.4	1.110
1971	98.1		98.9	98.1	1.000
1972	100.0		100.0	100.0	1.000
1973	103.6		106.0	103.6	1.000
1974	108.5		109.0	108.5	1.000
1975	118.4		119.5	118.4	1.000
1976	129.3		122.1	129.3	1.000
1977	136.9		137.7	136.9	1.000
1978			151.2	150.3	

Source by col.:
(1) and (2) CAB (1977).
(3) and (4) See table 4.2 and text explanation.

Table 4.4　　　　**Comparison of Used/New Price Ratios
and Quality Relatives for Commercial Aircraft (1977)**

Aircraft	(1) Used/New	(2) Quality Relative
Long Range		
DC–10–10	1.39	1.00
Boeing 747–100	1.19	1.00
DC–8–61	.67	1.11
Boeing 707–300B	.51	.74
Boeing 707–100B	.35	.55
DC–8–50	.31	.69
Medium Range		
Boeing 727–200	1.38	1.00
Boeing 727–100	.65	.54
Boeing 720B	.27	.54
Lockheed L–188	.23	.51
Short Range		
DC–9–30	1.37	1.00
DC–9–10	.82	.52
Convair 440	.08	.13

Source by col.:
(1) The used price is from Sweetman (1977). The new price is the second price shown for each aircraft in col. (3) of table 4.2.
(2) Based on table 4.2, col. (9).

Notes

1. For a general review of the central issues involved in the measurement of real output for productivity analysis, see the Panel to Review Productivity Statistics (1979, chap. 5).

2. The Denison criterion is also addressed in the debate between Denison (1969; 1972) and Jorgenson and Griliches (1967, 1972).

3. See Gordon (1971a, 1974).

4. This criticism was first made in Gordon (1971b).

5. In some applications involving departures from free competition, e.g., smog control devices, the two criteria do yield different measures. This paper is entirely concerned with examples in which choices of quality characteristics are made freely by business firms.

6. The assumption of costs that are constant in quantities, but increasing in quality characteristics, has been adopted by most previous papers in this literature, including Parks (1974) and Rosen (1974).

7. The vector of output characteristics (y) might be imagined to consist of m-1 homogeneous goods, plus an "mth" good having n separate characteristics: $y = (y_1, y_2, \ldots, y_{m-1}, y_{m1}, y_{m2}, \ldots, y_{mn})$. Now quality change involves an increase in one of the characteristics of the "mth" good. If resources and technology are fixed, this would in turn require a reduction in the output of one of the m-1 other goods.

8. Berndt and Wood (1979, p. 344), with the notation of the present paper substituted for that of the authors.

9. In what follows expected future values of the exogenous parameters are implicitly assumed to remain equal to their current values.

10. If the firm maximizes profit, which consists of net revenue less the user cost of its capital stock of durable input characteristics, it must be operating on the upward sloping segment of the net revenue function. This is evident in fig. 4.5 below.

11. During the two-decade period 1953–72, the nominal price of gasoline in the Consumer Price Index (CPI) increased 34% compared to 56% for the all-items CPI, representing a reduction in the relative price of 14.4%.

12. The depreciation rate should depend both on the built-in durability characteristics of the good and the user-chosen intensity of repair and maintenance services. In the simple version of the model considered here, with only a single composite operating cost characteristic, the depreciation rate is assumed to be fixed.

13. For some qualifications, see Muellbauer (1974).

14. Imagine that point B lies along an extension of the ray OA. Then the new level of net revenue per dollar of capital $(V_1 B / O V_1)$ would be the same as before $(V_0 A / O V_0)$. Since the percentage user cost per dollar of capital $(r + \delta)$ is constant, the rate of return on capital would remain constant.

15. Among the most important are Griliches's (1971) notes on technical problems in the hedonic literature, and the debate between Gordon (1971a, 1974) and Triplett (1976) on the extent of a significant quality bias in existing official price indexes.

16. This description is based on the United States Civil Aeronautics Board (1977). This document was kindly provided to me by Don Eldridge of the Bureau of Economic Analysis.

17. To minimize the burden of copying the required data, prices for all planes during 1968–78 were based on form 41 dated December 31, 1978, and during 1946–67 were based on schedule B-43 dated December 31, 1977. Data for the following sample of airlines were collected: American, Braniff, Delta, Eastern, TWA, United. Price quotations were obtained for 802 separate aircraft from the 1978 form, for 767 aircraft from the 1967 sheet.

18. Prior to 1957 the official deflator is based on a weighted average of the Producer Price Index component indexes for diesel engines, fabricated metal products, metalworking machinery, and electrical machinery. None of these indexes contains any components manufactured by the aircraft industry.

19. More specifically, the excluded Lockheed L-1011 duplicates the Douglas DC-10; the Convair 880 and 990 were high-cost jets that had short production runs and were phased out by their main users by the end of the 1960s; the short-range piston Martin 404 mirrors the performance of the Convair 440; and the Lockheed "Constellation" series (749, 1049, 1649) duplicates the Douglas DC-6, DC-6B, and DC-7 series.

20. Major sources are Avmark (1976, and earlier issues) and Douglas Aircraft annual reports.

21. If a change between models occurred in a group, say long-range aircraft, between 1969 and 1970, this change was weighted together with the changes recorded for the two other groups (medium- and short-range) using the nominal sales in the respective groups in 1969, 1970, and 1971.

22. The source is Aircraft Exchange and Services, Inc., (1966, p. 1). The average price quotation on the two DC-8-30s listed is $4,000,000, and of the nine DC-7s listed $183,000. Of course the DC-7s were somewhat older, being manufactured between 1953 and 1959, but this age difference cannot account for the price spread.

23. These price quotations are all from Watkins (1971).

24. In 1979 the average seat width on United's DC-8 aircraft was 16.89 inches and on its 747 and DC-10 aircraft 17.00 inches, from United brochure "Great Seats in the Friendly Skies."

25. Some crude adjustments to the prices of consumer appliances for savings in operating costs are contained in Gordon (1974, chap. 6).

26. This study is underway. The draft monograph (Gordon 1974) is under revision to update the figures, to incorporate the measurement techniques discussed in this paper, as well as other improvements suggested by reviewers and critics.

References

Aircraft Exchange and Services, Inc. *Market Report.* 1966, no. 145 (April 11).

Avmark Inc. in cooperation with Lockheed-Georgia Co. 1976. *Commercial aircraft fleets.* 3d ed. Lolo, Mont.

Berndt, Ernst R., and Wood, David O. 1975. Technology, prices, and the derived demand for energy. *Review of Economics and Statistics* 56 (August): 259–68.

———. 1979. Engineering and econometric interpretations of energy-capital complementarity. *American Economic Review* 69 (June): 342–54.

Denison, Edward F. 1957. Theoretical aspects of quality change, capital consumption, and net capital formation. In *Problems of capital formation.* NBER Conference on Research in Income and Wealth. Studies in Income and Wealth, vol. 19. Princeton: Princeton University Press for National Bureau of Economic Research.

———. 1969. Some major issues in productivity analysis: an examination of estimates by Jorgenson and Griliches. *Survey of Current Business* 49 (May, pt. II): 1–27.

———. 1972. Final comments. *Survey of Current Business* 52 (May, pt. II): 95–115.

Douglas George W., and Miller James C. III. 1974. *Economic regulation of domestic air transport.* Washington: Brookings Institution.

Douglas Aircraft Company, Inc. *Annual report.* Fiscal years 1950–66. Santa Monica, Calif.: Douglas Aircraft.

Fisher, Franklin M.; Griliches, Zvi; and Kaysen, Carl. 1962. The costs of automobile model changes since 1949. *Journal of Political Economy* 70 (October): 433–51.

Fisher, Franklin M., and Shell, Karl. 1972. *The economic theory of price indices.* New York: Academic Press.

Gordon, Robert J. 1971a. Measurement bias in price indexes for capital goods. *Review of Income and Wealth* 17: 121–74.

———. 1971b. A rare event. *Survey of Current Business* 51 (July, pt. II): 83–86.

———. 1974. The measurement of durable goods prices. Draft of monograph, National Bureau of Economic Research.

Griliches, Zvi. 1971. Introduction: hedonic price indexes revisited. In Zvi Griliches, ed., *Price indexes and quality change*, pp. 3–15. Cambridge, Mass.: Harvard University Press.

Hudson, E. A. and Jorgenson, D. W. 1974. U.S. energy policy and economic growth, 1975–2000. *Bell Journal of Economics and Management Science* 5: 461–514.

Jorgenson, Dale W., and Griliches, Zvi. 1967. The explanation of productivity change. *Review of Economic Studies* 34 (July): 249–83.

———. 1972. Issues in growth accounting: a reply to Edward F. Denison. *Survey of Current Business* 52 (May, pt. II): 65–94.

Muellbauer, John. 1974. Household production theory, quality, and the "hedonic technique." *American Economic Review* 64 (December): 977–94.

Panel to Review Productivity Statistics. 1979. *The measurement and interpretation of productivity.* Committee on National Statistics, National Research Council. Washington, D.C.: National Academy of Sciences.

Parks, Richard W. 1974. The demand and supply of durable goods and durability. *American Economic Review* 64 (March): 37–55.

Rosen, Sherwin. 1974. Hedonic prices and implicit markets: product differentiation in pure competition. *Journal of Political Economy* 82 (January/February): 34–49.

Straszheim, Mahlon R. 1969. *The international airline industry.* Washington, D.C.: Brookings Institution, 1969.

Sweetman, Bill. 1977. Airliner prices guide: *Flight International* 111 (March 12): 645–47.

U.S. Civil Aeronautics Board. 1973. *Handbook of airline statistics.* Washington, D.C.: Civil Aeronautics Board.

U.S. Civil Aeronautics Board, Bureau of Operating Rights. 1977. A price index for air frames and engines, 1957–76. Unpublished report (May 5).

U.S. Civil Aeronautics Board. *Aircraft operating cost and performance report.* Various issues.

U.S. Federal Aviation Agency. *Direct operating costs and other perform-ance characteristics of transport aircraft in airline service.* Various issues.

Watkins, Harold D. 1971. Eastern successful in used aircraft sales. *Aviation Week and Space Technology* (January 25), pp. 28–29.

Wilcox, James A. Automobile gasoline mileage and the costs of environmental regulations. Unpublished paper, University of California, Berkeley, 1978.

Comment   Jack E. Triplett

In the section dealing with Input and Output Price Index Concepts, Gordon suggests that we have reached substantial agreement on the major issue: quality change should be accounted for by user value in input price measures, but by a resource-cost rule for output price indexes. Yet, in subsequent sections exploring what he refers to as "nonproportional quality change," he presents an alternative that would be employed for *both* input and output price measures. Actually, it corresponds closely to one method currently used by the Bureau of Labor Statistics (BLS)—the use of manufacturers' cost data to make quality adjustments for some kinds of durable goods.

In this comment, I first describe briefly the BLS use of cost data for making quality adjustments and the rationale that has been used to justify it. The other sections address aspects of Gordon's paper.

What Does the BLS Do and Why Does It Do It?

It is well known that the BLS uses manufacturers' cost data to adjust prices of some goods for quality changes. This is documented for the Producer Price Index (PPI) in the Early and Sinclair paper in this volume. New cars are also handled this way in the Consumer Price Index (CPI), as are federal safety standards for a few other products.

Jack E. Triplett is assistant commissioner for research and evaluation, Bureau of Labor Statistics.

It is important to emphasize that use of manufacturers' cost data is not the only method for handling quality change in the indexes and is not necessarily even the preferred way of treating quality change. If equilibrium selling prices of new and old varieties were available in the same situation or time, one could link the index over from old to new varieties; in this case, the price ratio between the two becomes the implicit quality adjustment. If equilibrium price data are not available (and as Early and Sinclair note, they seldom are) an appropriate alternative for *input* price indexes would be measures of user value for the two varieties, again taken for the same situation. Gordon and I, as well as official BLS policy, all agree on this.

Still considering input price indexes, what is done if neither equilibrium price relatives nor user-value information is available? In practice, a quality change may be handled in one of several ways.

1. When there are no data available for making an *explicit* quality adjustment (the majority of cases), one of two options is employed.

a) Where quality change is deemed "small" (according to procedures adopted on a product-by-product basis) it is neglected.[1] This leads to the so-called direct price comparison, which means that all of the observed price change will be recorded as pure price change, with no allowance for quality change. The usual presumption is that quality changes are on balance improvements; if so, direct comparison imparts an upward bias to the indexes.

b) On the other hand, if the BLS finds that the quality change is greater than the cut-off value and so therefore cannot be ignored, this leads to one of two forms of "linking" procedure. The procedure used in the PPI takes the entire price differential between the new and old varieties as the measure of quality change.[2] Obviously, when all of the observed price differential is counted as quality change, the BLS misses any price change that may have accompanied the introduction of a changed item. The error could in principle go in either direction. If price changes are more likely to be made when new models are introduced, during an inflationary period the PPI linking procedure would tend to produce a downward error in the indexes; this downward error will occur regardless of whether quality changes are improvements or deteriorations. This reasoning depends on the presumption that producers try to "mask" price increases by coupling them with new model introductions, which may not be true even in inflationary times, and is even less likely when prices are falling.[3]

2. In some cases, the BLS obtains the cost of the quality change from the manufacturer who provides the price data to the BLS and uses cost as an explicit quality adjustment. The actual process involves two steps.

a) The first is a rule or criterion for judging whether or not a particular change in specifications reported by the manufacturer is or is not to be accepted as a quality change for the purposes of the index. The criterion used depends explicitly on whether the BLS index is interpreted as an input price index or as an output price index. In practice, both CPI and PPI indexes have been treated as if they were input price indexes; for input price indexes the quality criterion is user value.

As an example of the operation of the quality criterion, several years ago an auto manufacturer submitted as quality improvements a change from conventional to digital clock faces and a redesigned speedometer which did not register extremely high speeds. Both were disallowed because the BLS commodity specialist judged that neither change represented increased transportation value to the user of the automobile.[4]

b) If it is determined that a specification change does represent increased or decreased value to the user, the second step is to *estimate* that value. Using resource-cost data to estimate user value rests on the principle that in equilibrium the marginal cost of any change will approximate its incremental value to the user. Where manufacturers' cost data are used as quality adjustments in a BLS index that is interpreted as an input price index, they are explicitly regarded as an approximation to the user-value data that are considered theoretically appropriate for the index.

Thus, in using manufacturers' cost data the BLS distinguishes between the quality *criterion* and the quality adjustment *estimator*. The criterion for measuring quality change in a BLS input price index is always user value—the correct theoretical quality adjustment method for input price measures (see Sec. 5.3 of my paper in this volume). The estimator, on the other hand, is sometimes manufacturing cost because that may be the only information obtainable, and because cost should have an equilibrium relationship to the theoretical quality criterion of user value.

Any estimator may contain error, relative to the correct measurement. It happens that this particular estimator has some unique problems. One manifestation is the occasional manufacturer's report of increased quality at reduced cost, an obvious case where the estimator is in error (though one should not conclude that error is absent just because cost and user-value information move in the same direction). Second, "downsizing" and other complex changes in automobiles in recent years have caused the cost-based procedure to break down at times, so that some new automobile models have been handled in both CPI and PPI by imputation to quality adjusted price movements of cars which were less drastically changed.

The preceding has concerned input price measures. Output price measures have only recently become operational. In the output price index case, the correct quality criterion would be resource cost. Manufacturers' cost data do measure that.[5] However, for this case a resource-cost rule must also be applied as a decision rule for judging whether a particular product change is a quality change. One would not employ a user-value criterion to judge whether a particular specification change should be accepted as quality change for an output price index. Thus, there is no reason for using a "mixed" quality adjustment rule for output price measures.

Hedonic techniques are an alternative method for adjusting for quality change. A full discussion of the merits and disadvantages of hedonic methods is beyond the scope of the present note (on this, see Griliches 1971). No BLS index currently incorporates hedonic quality adjustments, despite extensive internal BLS research on hedonic methods over the last decade or so. That research suggests that they are probably best suited for products where conventional specification pricing is unworkable (computers, e.g., or aircraft [see Archibald and Reece 1977, 1979]), or to solve particular pricing problems (housing prices being an example [see Gillingham 1975]), or as a check on the validity of conventional procedures (Triplett and McDonald 1977; and the Early-Sinclair article in the present volume). It is well established that hedonic methods may break down for the same reasons that conventional methods fail, with automobiles a major case in point (Triplett 1969; Ohta and Griliches 1976).

Gordon's Alternative Method

In his section on nonproportional quality change, Gordon says that "the distinction between the 'user-value' and 'production-cost' criteria for the measurement of quality change is misleading, since both are used. . . . User value is the criterion used to define . . . the characteristic desired by the user. And production cost is the criterion used to make the actual quality adjustment" (p. 214). This proposal matches almost exactly what the BLS actually does with cost-based data in input price indexes—a user-value rule for defining quality change, with resource-cost data used as an estimator. Gordon's proposal appears in conflict with the results of my paper, and with the BLS rationale for what it is doing, but does not really amount to that.[6]

To clarify the matter, consider the first two equations from my paper in this volume (Chap. 5):

(1) $$G = G(C, K_G, L)$$

(2) $$C = C(K_C, L)$$

The objective is to compute an input price index for, say, computers, or for computer services (C)—that is, a measure of the price paid for computers by the using industry (which I named "gadgets"). As an input price index, the computer index is one component of an index for the right-hand side of equation (1). An output price index for computers is a price index for the left-hand side of equation (2).

In my paper, the analytical technique for handling quality change in input price index numbers involves respecification of the right-hand side of equation (1), so that the input price index is defined in terms of input characteristics of computers rather than in terms of the good "computers." For output price indexes, the left-hand side of equation (2) is similarly respecified so that the "computer" variable is replaced by measures of computer output characteristics.

Essentially, respecification from goods space to characteristics space serves to transform the discussion from an argument over how to treat the computer "box" (the form the quality change literature has taken in the past) to an analysis of the properties of computers that are important in its own production function and in the production functions for using industries. However, even in characteristics space there remain two theories—input and output price indexes have separate theoretical justifications and require separate, and different, theoretical treatments of quality change (see Secs. 5.3 and 5.4 of my paper). It is a misunderstanding of the theoretical result to suppose that shifting the unit of analysis from "boxes" to the characteristics of boxes yields a single method of quality adjustment, applicable to both input and output price indexes.

Consider the input case. Any input cost index (whether in goods space or characteristics space) depends only on the using industry's technology and the costs of acquiring inputs. To implement the theoretical quality adjustment method for input price indexes discussed in Section 5.3.3 of my paper, one would collect the following information from the gadget producer: (1) the list of computer characteristics important to gadget production; (2) the production function for transforming computer characteristics and other inputs into gadgets; and (3) the costs or prices paid for all inputs, including computer characteristics.

Believing that the second and third pieces of information are probably not available from the buyer of computer services, Gordon instead proposes to collect data from the seller. This can be justified by the same rationale that motivates the BLS introduction of production-cost data into the PPI and CPI—in equilibrium the marginal manufacturing cost of a computer characteristic will approximate its incremental value when used in the production of gadgets. This, then, is the basis for Gordon's equation (4)—which was obtained by substituting the input demand functions from the using industry (here gadgets) "into the cost function of the supplying industry" (Gordon, this volume, p. 210). The same rationale underlies his input price index (computed as the ratio of two valuations of eq. [4]), and the "shift-term" analysis that culminates in an input price index for computer service characteristics that is "measured by adjusting the observed change in cost of a new model for the change in its quantity of characteristics $(x_y dy)$ multiplied by the marginal cost of producing characteristics $(C_t c_x)$" (Gordon, this volume, p. 212).

The pure theory of an input cost index contains nothing on the technology of the supplying industry. Gordon's use of production cost data in an input price index is best interpreted as an empirical approximation to what is wanted in theory, exactly the rationale that motivates the BLS empirical procedures.

To be sure, a cost-reducing innovation in the computer-producing industry may be expected to reduce the cost of computations performed in the gadget industry. And an economist wants not simply to measure prices but also to analyze them. It is clearly true that a shift in the suppling industry, or an increase in demand from the using industry, will change the market prices for computers measured in computation units. But such shifts should not appear in the price index formula because that would tend to factor them out of the price measure. One wants to be sure that cost reduction in the computer-producing industry does show up as a measured reduction in the costs of computations performed in the gadget industry.

In conclusion, it is not true that the theory specifies a single treatment for quality change in both input and output price indexes. What Gordon's argument says is that under certain conditions the two theoretical quality adjustments will give similar estimates, and for this case one can use either adjustment and obtain the same result.

The "Resource-using" and "Nonproportional" Dichotomy of Quality Change

I have reservations about taxonomies of quality change. Most have not been very enlightening, primarily because they have often been constructed around examples that contained only part of the economic information needed to evaluate the cases being classified.

A "nonproportional" quality change is defined by Gordon as one "in which production cost does not change in proportion to user value" (p. 207), or as a situation where there is "a downward shift in the supply curve of user-desired characteristics" (p. 207). These two definitions can be inconsistent.

On the "supply shift" definition, a quality change from A to either B or C in figure 5.3 of my paper involves a shift in the supply schedule (F_1 to F_2), and so is classified as "nonproportional." This is similar to points A and B in Gordon's figure 4.1. On the other hand, a quality change such as B to C in my figure 5.3 implies an unshifted supply function; this change is classified as "resource using," or "proportional."

However, neither my figure 5.3 nor Gordon's figure 4.1 contains information about user value. Accordingly, one does not know whether a downward shift in the factor requirements function, F, or in Gordon's unit cost function, V, does or does not create a situation where user-value and resource-cost rules diverge. One can read from my figure 5.3 two alternative resource-cost quality adjustments, ∂L_1 and ∂L_2 (on Gordon's fig. 4.1, the latter one is equivalent to the vertical distance on the V-axis corresponding to the movement from points D to B). But the user-value measure cannot be obtained from resource-cost information, and there is therefore no way of knowing whether the user-value change corresponds to either ∂L_1 or ∂L_2.

Similarly, one cannot determine whether user-value and resource-cost rules agree solely from knowledge that the supply curve did not shift. The movement from point B to point C in my figure 5.3 might have been caused by a shift in the using industry's production function that raised the demand for characteristics. Thus, an unshifted supply curve could be consistent with deviation between resource-cost and user-value rules, creating inconsistency in Gordon's alternative definitions of "nonproportional" quality change.

What we do know is that in equilibrium the incremental value to the user of a quality change equals the increment to the cost of producing the additional characteristics. Thus, for small changes around the point of equilibrium, and on the assumption of a competitive world where functions are smooth and where government or other nonmarket forces do not intervene, one would get approximately the same values from resource-cost and user-value measures.

Shifting functions, whether on the demand or supply side, represent one case where the two quality change criteria can yield different answers. Characterizing quality change by whether the supply curve has or has not shifted may be useful for some purposes. But it is not necessarily the same thing as a situation where user-value and resource-cost quality adjustment rules diverge. Identifying the latter situation requires information on both the cost schedule for the supplying industry and the using industry's production function.

Handling Fuel-Efficiency Changes in Price Indexes

There is no question that fuel efficiency changes should be reflected in some way in a measure of the using industry's input costs, or in a measure of the consumer's consumption costs. It is not true, however, that the fuel-efficiency effect must necessarily enter into the measurement in the form of an adjustment to the price of the durable good whose fuel efficiency changed.[7] In fact, the theory of index numbers suggests just the opposite—that the theoretically appropriate method for incorporating fuel efficiency changes into the index normally involves an adjustment other than to the price of the durable good whose fuel efficiency changed.

Suppose the manufacturer of a durable good introduces a fuel-saving innovation. That is, the new product provides the same service as the old but requires less fuel to do it.

First consider the theoretical input cost index that encompasses all of the inputs used by a particular firm or industry (eqq. 4 and 4a from my paper in this volume). Recall that this index measures the change in cost between two collections of inputs—one set of inputs represents the minimum-cost method of producing a particular output level in the initial period, the other is the minimum-cost input set in the comparison period that can produce the same output level.

If a fuel-efficiency improvement occurs in the second period, then the cost of the collection of inputs necessary to produce a given output level will fall by the decrease in expenditure on fuel (net of any price increase charged for the new durable good). That is, an improvement in, say, aircraft fuel economy will be picked up in the airline industry's input cost index in the form of a decrease in quantities of fuel. No additional adjustment to the price of aircraft is necessary. The reason lies in the nature of the theoretical input cost index: the theoretical index permits quantities to adjust to find a minimum-cost combination, and the cost saving from an improvement in fuel efficiency occurs precisely from an adjustment in quantity of fuel required for a fixed amount of output. Therefore, in the total input cost index, adjusting the price of airplanes for fuel savings would double-count the effect of increased fuel efficiency, for that saving already shows up in decreased quantities of fuel purchased by airlines.

However, a measure of the total cost of all the airline's inputs is not the only relevant price index. For some purposes, it may be appropriate to ask how prices of some components of the full set of inputs are moving. One may want a price index only for the airplanes used by airlines, or a price index for producer durable equipment used as inputs to the airline industry. Pollak (1975) referred to indexes encompassing less than the full set of inputs as "subindexes."

If the objective is to produce a subindex (such as a price index for airplanes), then one must deal with the question, What subindex is justifiable in theory? Pollak (1975) distinguishes several kinds of subindexes, but the kind most relevant to the present discussion depends for its justification on the theory of separability, as applied to production functions.[8] It is convenient to approach the subindex question by reference to Gordon's treatment.

Gordon writes the production function (his eq. [18], p. 218):

$$y = y[h, k(x,e)],$$

where inputs h and e are labor and energy, respectively, and x is defined to be "performance characteristics" (which also implies that x is to be interpreted as a vector). As the notation makes clear, Gordon is discussing an *input* price index (a price index for x) and not output price indexes (which would refer to the price of y). Thus, what is wanted is a subindex of the full input-cost index for the y-industry's inputs.

Gordon cites Berndt and Wood (1975) to confirm that capital and energy may be treated as an aggregate, separable from labor, as he has written the equation. Realism, however, is not the difficulty with Gordon's use of equation (18).

The theory of separability states that the assumption made in equation (18) permits constructing a consistent index of *wages*, without worrying about capital or energy, or an index of some aggregate of capital and energy, without requiring data on labor. But equation (18) does not permit forming an index of capital goods prices, independent of energy—which is, of course, what Gordon proposes to do. For that, one would have to be able to write the vector of x's separable from e—that is, to maintain that marginal rates of substitution between aircraft characteristics (such as between speed and fuel economy) were independent of fuel usage. That is not a plausible specification at all. Gordon seems to have misunderstood what separability theory says about forming subindexes.[9]

Instead, the assumption embodied in Gordon's equation (18), and justified by Berndt and Wood's empirical work, specifies that the theoretically appropriate subindex is an index for airplanes combined with fuel. An input subindex for airplanes alone is not theoretically justifiable. Treating fuel-efficiency changes in the airplane-fuel subindex gives a result similar to the one for the overall input cost index: because the input cost subindex is defined on airplanes combined with fuel, the effect of fuel efficiency improvement is again completely accounted for by the reduction in fuel quantities. No airplane price adjustment is called for.

Thus, neither the overall input cost index nor the subindex implied by Gordon's equation (18) calls for a quality adjustment to *aircraft* prices for increases in fuel efficiency. The reason is that economic input cost indexes (whether the full index or the subindex) are ratios of *costs*; the change in cost caused by increased fuel efficiency enters the cost calculation directly in the form of reduced expenditure on fuel. No additional quality adjustment to the price of the durable good is necessary.[10] Fuel-efficiency changes pose index number problems only when the objective is to compute fixed-weight approximations to input cost indexes, such as by use of Laspeyres or Paasche formulas. For these cases, fuel is entered with a fixed weight, and no quantity adjustments occur.

Consider this problem within the context of the Consumer Price Index. The BLS now prices a durable good (cars) and also other inputs (gasoline, repairs, etc.) necessary to use the car. Because the CPI is a Laspeyres index, there are fixed expenditure weights that apply to all of these things.

Suppose manufacturers introduced more fuel-efficient cars without reducing their size or performance characteristics. Any higher price changed for a more fuel-efficient automobile is offset by a decrease in the quantities of purchased fuel.

The problem the index maker faces is that the fixed-weight index does not permit adjustment of any quantities. This realistic problem is the one that concerns Gordon. It is important to understand, however, that the theory provides no guidance. The theory of index numbers is a theory of the exact or theoretical index, and in that index fuel-efficiency adjustments to durable goods prices are not required. The problem arises in the fixed-weight index precisely because of the condition (fixed weights) by which the Laspeyres or Paasche formula differs from the true index of input costs.

One could make the argument that in the fixed-weight framework adjusting the price of the durable good for increased fuel efficiency is at least going in the right direction and is better than no adjustment at all. I would not be unsympathetic to an argument along that line.

I would strongly prefer, however, a different approach to the problem. It has long been established that a consumption measure should pertain to the services of durable goods and not to the quantities of durables purchased. In that context, the BLS would be pricing the cost per mile of a constant quality automotive service (constant quality being defined in terms of comfort, carrying capacity, and other use characteristics). If the BLS were to price the services of durable goods, then fuel efficiency changes would appear, appropriately, as simple changes in the cost of the service. In that context, they would not present themselves in the form of a "quality problem" at all (see Triplett 1971b). One may rationalize Gordon's empirical work on fuel efficiency as an approximation to this alternative approach. The rationalization, however, is quite different from the one that appears in his paper.

In summary, the theory of index numbers provides scant support for fuel-efficiency adjustments to the prices of durable goods, for the reason that the theoretical input price indexes (including the input cost index discussed in my paper in this volume as well as the cost-of-living index concept) already admit into the measurement adjustments in fuel quantities occasioned by increases in the fuel efficiency of durable goods. In fixed-weight indexes, quantity adjustments do not enter into the measurement. Consequently, anything done in the fixed-weight context amounts to an ad hoc procedure, quite outside index number theory, justifiable on the hope that the adjustment will go in the right direction, and is of approximately the right magnitude. That does not necessarily condemn the empirical work; measurement can sometimes be done without tight theoretical support. But the theoretical rationale for such work is not the one Gordon gives and, so far as I can determine, does not really exist.

Conclusion

These comments have been concerned exclusively with the theoretical sections of Gordon's paper, and the paper is primarily an empirical one. Because the empirical work does not stand or fall on the particular formulations used in the theoretical section, my comments are not to be interpreted as strictures on the empirical work, which can stand on its own, and should be studied and absorbed by anyone interested in the empirical side of the quality measurement question.

I am more concerned about the interpretation to be given to empirical work of this kind than I am with the numbers actually produced. To observe that most empirical work on quality change and on hedonic methods has proceeded with little or no reference to the theory of index numbers is no new insight. But it is also true that a good part of the theorizing on this subject served up to the empirical workers has been beside the point, or worse. We are a long way, as Gordon notes, from having a good empirical grasp of the magnitude of the quality problems in our economic measurements. But unless we have a better grasp of what we want to measure—that is, of the theory and the economic concepts— we will not be able to tell whether empirical work has improved the measurement.

Notes

1. The procedures imply a rule or criterion exists for specifying which product changes are to be accepted as quality changes. The criterion for this case is the same as the one stated in 2(*a*), below.

2. In comparable situations, the CPI uses a different linking procedure that implicitly imputes to the good whose quality changed the price movement of similar goods whose quality did not change. As with the PPI procedure, one expects CPI linking to impart a downward bias when prices are rising, but this presumption has not been tested empirically.

3. A more extended discussion is in Triplett (1971*a*). Empirical attempts to evaluate the PPI linking procedure are Triplett and McDonald (1977) and Early and Sinclair (in this volume). A survey of studies on quality error in price measures is contained in Triplett (1975).

4. That such judgments may sometimes be arbitrary is an unavoidable flaw with the procedure, but judgment always plays a role in the construction of price measures. The cost-based quality measures are not unique on that score.

The complexity of the role of the automobile in modern society has required some controversial interpretations of the user-value criterion. For example, in 1971 Commissioner Geoffrey Moore, responding to the recommendations of a U.S. Government Inter- agency Committee, decided that legally mandated changes (smog devices, safety equip- ment, fuel economy standards and the like) would be treated as quality changes in all BLS indexes on the grounds that Congress had made a political judgment that the value of these changes was worth their cost. The price index treatment of some of these items remains controversial, with arguments marshaled on either side, but that issue cannot be explored fully here.

5. This does not say that they always conform precisely to the theoretical resource-cost rule. For a variety of reasons the data reported may be imperfect (see Triplett 1971*a*).

6. Conversations with Prof. Gordon have been valuable in resolving points discussed in this section.

7. This question was first raised by Fisher and Shell (1972).

8. Blackorby and Russell (1978) subsequently argued that indirect separability or separa- bility of the cost function is the appropriate starting point for constructing input price

indexes. To preserve the notation of Gordon's paper, we merely note that fact, without incorporating it.

9. On p. 242, Gordon identifies the separability assumption as having something to do with whether "improvements in fuel efficiency are achieved by manufacturers of the durable good and not by their users." Separability of a using industry's production function is simply a way of depicting technology in the using industry; it does not depend on the supplying industry's cost or production function, nor does it depend on the sector in which fuel efficiency changes originate.

10. An additional effect may occur in the input cost index for changes in usage of other inputs that may be complements or substitutes with fuel. Also, we have not explicitly considered whether increased fuel efficiency of the durable good was a response to rising fuel prices, which would of course also be included in the input cost index.

References

Archibald, Robert B., and Reece, William S. 1977. The impact of the energy crisis on the demand for fuel efficiency: the case of general aviation. *Transportation Research* 2:161–65.

———. 1979. Partial subindexes of input prices: the case of computer services. *Southern Economic Journal* 46:528–40.

Berndt, Ernest R., and Wood, David O. 1975. Technology, prices, and the derived demand for energy. *Review of Economics and Statistics* (August), pp. 259–68.

Blackorby, Charles, and Russell, R. Robert. 1978. Indices and subindices of the cost of living and the standard of living. *International Economic Review* (February): 229–40.

Fisher, Franklin M., and Shell, Karl. 1972. *The economic theory of price indices.* New York: Academic Press.

Gillingham, Robert F. 1975. Place-to-place rent comparisons using hedonic quality adjustment techniques. *Annals of Economic and Social Measurement* 4 (January): 153–73.

Griliches, Zvi, ed. 1971. *Price indexes and quality change.* Cambridge, Mass.: Harvard University Press.

Ohta, Makoto, and Griliches, Zvi. 1976. Automobile prices revisited: extensions of the hedonic hypothesis. In Nestor E. Terleckyj, ed., *Household production and consumption*, pp. 325–90. NBER Conference on Research in Income and Wealth. Studies in Income and Wealth, vol. 40. New York: Columbia University Press.

Pollak, Robert A. 1975. Subindexes of the cost of living. *International Economic Review* 16 (February): 135–50.

Triplett, Jack E. 1969. Automobiles and hedonic quality measurement. *Journal of Political Economy* 77 (May/June): 408–17.

———. 1971a. Quality bias in price indexes and new methods of quality measurement. In Zvi Griliches, ed., *Price indexes and quality change*, chap. 6. Cambridge, Mass.: Harvard University Press.

———. 1971b. The theory of hedonic quality measurement and its use in price indexes. BLS Staff Paper no. 6. Washington, D.C.: U.S. Department of Labor, Bureau of Labor Statistics.

————. 1975. The measurement of inflation: a survey of research on the accuracy of price indexes. In Paul H. Earl, ed., *Analysis of Inflation*, chap. 2. Lexington, Mass.: Lexington Books.

Triplett, Jack E., and McDonald, Richard J. 1977. Assessing the quality error in output measures: the case of refrigerators. *Review of Income and Wealth* 23 (June): 137–56.

Reply

Triplett's constructive set of comments helps to clarify the relation of my new work on energy—efficiency adjustments to the traditional literature on index numbers. Our sole remaining disagreement concerns his doubt that energy-efficiency adjustments to the prices of durable goods are useful or appropriate in input indexes. But for my area of concern, the measurement of net investment in the national income and product accounts, changes in the service price of durable goods must be decomposed to determine the portion attributable to the manufacturer of the durable goods. This is achieved by my proposed quality adjustment procedure, which leads to a price index for durables that moves in proportion to Triplett's service price when the price of fuel is held constant.

Criteria versus Estimators for Quality Change

The first half of Triplett's comment provides a correct interpretation of my framework for quality adjustments. The approach that I advocate for input cost measurement is not the pure theoretical concept that Triplett develops in his paper. As Triplett states, the pure concept would require for its implementation a set of data collected only from *purchasers* of durable goods, including details on their production functions for every product and on the prices paid for all inputs. I reject the pure concept on grounds of practicality. The collection of price data from buyers has proven feasible only in selected pilot projects (esp. Stigler and Kindahl 1970). Since the sellers' side of the market for most manufactured goods is so much more concentrated than the buyers' side, virtually all efforts to measure prices by both official agencies and outside investigators have involved the collection of data from the seller. This leads to my hybrid concept for input cost measurement. Here the quality *criterion* is user value (e.g., the characteristic valued by the computer user is its calculations rather than dimensions of the computer box); the *estimator* used to adjust computer price indexes for differences in characteristics across models is based on the seller's marginal cost. Because this distinction between the criterion and the estimator is identical to that used by the Bureau of Labor Statistics, my criticism of their price indexes does not involve a theoretical dispute but rather concentrates on sins of omission (e.g., the failure of BLS to develop a price index for computers or commercial aircraft), and on detailed procedures (e.g., the BLS decision in 1970 to treat electronic calculators as a new product rather than as a price reduction for existing desk calculators). In fact my strongest criticisms are directed not at the BLS but at the Bureau of Economic Analysis.

It is the BEA that has chosen to deflate electronic computers by a price index (always equal to 1.0) that ignores the rapidly declining price of computer calculations, and to deflate commercial aircraft by an index that ignores the improvement represented by the invention of the jet engine.

Energy Efficiency Adjustments

The main criticism in Triplett's comment concerns my proposal to adjust the price indexes of durable goods for nonproportional quality changes taking the form of improvements in energy efficiency. In preference to my approach, Triplett prefers that the input service price of durable goods be measured, for example, the flow price per unit of time of the costs of capital, fuel, and maintenance ("The BLS would be pricing the cost per mile of a constant quality automotive service"). In this comment I make a two-step argument that, first, my proposed quality adjustments lead to durable goods price indexes that move in proportion to Triplett's service price when the costs of other inputs (fuel, maintenance labor) are held constant, and, second, that these other input costs must be held constant in performing quality adjustments if our national income accounts are to make any sense.

In the case of a "proportional" quality change taking the form of an improvement in energy efficiency, neither the service price nor my durable goods price index would register any change. Consider a situation in which a change in relative prices leads a refrigerator producer to add the quality characteristic "energy efficiency" up to the point where its marginal cost equals its value in energy saving to the consumer. There will be no change in the service price of the new-model refrigerator compared to that of an old model in the new energy price regime, since the reduction in the annual value of energy consumption will offset the increase in the annual depreciation and interest cost of the higher quality refrigerator. In exactly the same way, my own procedure would find that there had been an increase in net revenue measured at constant fuel prices that was proportional to the higher unit price of the equipment, and consequently no quality adjustment would be called for.

Now consider a "nonproportional" innovation that cut annual expenditures on energy by $20, while increasing the annual capital cost of a refrigerator by only $10. Triplett's service price of refrigerators would register a decline, as would my price index for refrigerators based on a finding that net revenue had increased by more than equipment cost.[1] Either measure of price would be adequate for a study of the demand for refrigerators in a period of constant energy prices and would be far preferable to an index that failed to register any decline in price. In the case of commercial aircraft, the subject of the empirical study in my paper, a demand study for the 1950s and 1960s (a period of roughly constant fuel prices), would be highly misleading if it used the official BEA price index.

Despite the equivalence of the service price concept and my quality adjusted price index in this example, for general purposes the two concepts are not equivalent in periods like the 1970s when fuel prices have changed. The second part of my argument is that, while the service price measure must be used in demand studies to reflect the adverse impact of rising fuel prices on the demand for aircraft, the national income and product accounts must be based on a quality adjusted price index that holds the costs of fuel and maintenance labor constant. Since our basic measures of net national product and aggregate productivity include net investment as a major component, price indexes used for deflation in the national accounts should incorporate a quality adjustment procedure that decomposes changes in the service prices of durable goods into a portion "caused" by the manufacturer and a remaining portion (including changing fuel prices) that occurs after the equipment is acquired by the user. If we are only interested in an input index like the CPI, a comprehensive service price concept would be sufficient. But for the measurement of net investment in the national accounts, changes in service prices must be split between manufacturers and users.

Why is it important to measure changes in energy efficiency achieved by the manufacturer? Consider a hypothetical nonproportional innovation that doubled aircraft speed with no increase in aircraft price. This would represent a decline in the price of aircraft seat-miles per unit of time, an increase in the real capital represented by the new-model aircraft, and thus an increase in net investment and net national product. Let us imagine instead that the same research expenditures in the aircraft industry were invested in lower fuel usage rather than in faster speed, and let us assume that a hypothetical energy-saving innovation yielded precisely the same increase in airline net revenue as a doubling of aircraft speed, with no increase in aircraft price. The service price of aircraft (including capital cost and fuel expense) measured per seat-mile would fall by the same amount in either case, and a price index for aircraft services that held constant the price of fuel would fall in proportion. My justification for energy-efficiency adjustments is that changes in service price that occur with fixed input prices should be credited to the manufacturer of the equipment, reflecting the observation that major nonproportional shifts in both performance and energy efficiency tend to be "embodied" in capital goods by their manufacturers rather than achieved by their users. When fuel prices are held constant, a service price criterion and my net revenue criterion lead to the same quality adjustment, because they are two different methods of measuring the same thing.

My quality adjustment procedure is essential not only to capture the higher level of net investment and the higher level of aggregate productivity resulting from energy-saving innovations, but also to allocate correctly the credit for the innovations to the industry achieving them—the airframe and aircraft engine industries in my example rather than the airline industry. The importance of a correct allocation is obvious for those who are attempting to trace the current U.S. productivity slowdown to changes in capital and R&D input in particular industries (Griliches 1980). Such studies will be hopeless failures if they credit the achievements of the research-intensive aircraft industry to the airline industry, which does no research at all!

Note

1. Consider the following division of annual operating revenue: (*a*) annual labor cost, (*b*) annual fuel cost, (*c*) annual capital cost (interest plus depreciation), (*d*) annual profit. Triplett's service price includes *b* plus *c*. A nonproportional improvement in energy efficiency by definition reduces *b* more than it raises *c*, thus reducing the service price. My "net revenue" is *c* plus *d*. A nonproportional improvement in energy efficiency by my definition raises net revenue (*c* plus *d*) by more than capital cost (*c*) when calculated at fixed prices of output, labor, and fuel. Thus both criteria give the same answer; the reduction in service price parallels the decline in the equipment price index that results from my method.

References

Griliches, Zvi. 1980. R & D and the productivity slowdown. *American Economic Review* 70 (May): 343–48.

Stigler, George, and Kindahl, James K. 1970. *The behavior of industrial prices*. New York: Columbia University Press for National Bureau of Economic Research.

5 Concepts of Quality in Input and Output Price Measures: A Resolution of the User-Value Resource-Cost Debate

Jack E. Triplett

5.1 Introduction

The appropriate treatment of quality change is a very old issue in the analysis of productivity, the measurement of capital, and in many other areas of economic measurement.

Many economists have advocated a "user-value" criterion. Under this concept, a new computer which does more calculations would be taken as a higher quality machine (provided this aspect of performance is valuable to the computer user). Price indexes would be adjusted for the value to the user of the performance difference, regardless of what it cost to produce the new computer. Because the performance difference has been removed from the price measure, it shows up in quantity measures. Despite the wide acceptance of the user-value criterion (based on my own informal poll), to my knowledge no explicit theoretical justification has ever appeared.

The alternative "production-cost" criterion is associated with Edward Denison[1] and accepted in the national accounts. This concept requires that quality differences among various computer models be evaluated using data on the resource cost of building computers, regardless of their relative performance in use.

Jack E. Triplett is assistant commissioner for research and evaluation, Bureau of Labor Statistics.

Erwin Diewert, Edward Denison, Robert Gillingham, Dale Jorgenson, and Robert Pollak commented on an earlier draft of this paper, which was read at the Summer 1979 meetings of the Econometric Society in Montreal. Their helpful contributions are greatly appreciated, as are valuable conversations with colleagues B. K. Atrostic and Richard J. McDonald. The paper also benefited substantially from seminar presentations at the University of Michigan, Michigan State University, University of Oregon, University of Wisconsin, University of Washington, and Washington University. Views expressed are not intended as official policy statements of the Bureau of Labor Statistics.

One might suppose the conceptual issue to be of small practical importance. In equilibrium the two methods should yield similar numbers; and whether at equilibrium or not, most practical quality adjustment proposals make use of market price information (hedonic methods and traditional "linking" methods share this property). Prices reflect, obviously, both value and cost, rendering a distinction between them inoperative.

Yet counterexamples abound. Griliches (1964) and Jaszi (1964) discussed an example (birth-control pills) for which resource cost and user-value treatment of a technical change gave different measures. More recently, a controversy over the appropriate price index treatment of legally mandated smog control and safety devices again showed that the conceptual treatment of quality change has a perceptible impact on economic measurements, and that resolving the conceptual and theoretical issues has clear practical importance. Such examples provide the motivation for the present paper.

The approach followed combines theoretical specifications that have been developed for input price indexes (among which are closely related theories of the "true cost-of-living index" and the "true input cost index") and for output price indexes (sometimes known as "true output deflators") with previous work of the author (Triplett 1971b, 1973, 1976). The latter argues that "quality," in economics, can best be understood by shifting the analysis from goods space to characteristics space, along lines proposed by Lancaster (1971). The results show that the Denison–Bureau of Economic Analysis production-cost criterion is correct if what is wanted is a measure of the output of capital goods (as the numerator, e.g., in a productivity measure for a machinery-producing industry). However, the user-value criterion is correct if one wants to construct an input measure—for example, a measure of capital services for incorporation into a production function.

The plan of the paper provides separate treatments for input and output price indexes. The distinction between the two is made in the first section, along with some discussion that sets the stage. Section 5.3 sets out the input price index case, with output price indexes discussed in Section 5.4. Each of these two central sections is organized along parallel lines—a first subsection which sets out the basic theory of input and output price indexes (these sections could be skipped by readers who are familiar with the technical index number literature), followed by a second section which explains the concept of characteristics (done separately for input and output price indexes because the characteristics concepts differ according to their use). Subsections 5.3.3 and 5.4.3 contain the core of the paper—the statements of input and output price index theory in characteristics space and the demonstration that theory leads to two different treatments of quality change. Section 5.5 concerns two arguments the protagonists of alternative approaches have made against each other's positions; the characteristics-space price index theory developed in this paper shows that both are false, thus illustrating its utility for clearing up many of the murky disputes that have so long dominated the literature on quality change. The final Section 5.6 contains an overall perspective on the paper and its conclusions.

5.2 Some Preliminary Observations

The distinction between input and output price indexes has been present in the price index literature for some time, at least implicitly, but Fisher and Shell (1972) were the first to work out the relationship between them.[2] It will be useful to discuss the setting in which the distinction is important.

Consider a simple two-sector model. Suppose a production function for "gadgets," in which computers, gadget-making machinery, and labor are inputs, and another production function for computers, which uses as inputs computer-making machinery and labor:

$$(1) \qquad G = G(C, K_G, L),$$

$$(2) \qquad C = C(K_C, L).$$

An output price index for computers is a price index for the output of the computer industry—that is, a price index for the left-hand side of equation (2). One might want an output price index for use in calculating measures of output and productivity for the computer industry, or in the computation of the national accounts.

An output price index for the computer industry presupposes that there are different kinds of computers (otherwise, there would be no aggregation problems in computing the industry's output price, and therefore no need for index numbers). Clearly, the interesting case occurs at the level of aggregation where one must deal with aggregation over products *and* with quality variations within a single "product." The former is a standard index number problem; the latter is the concern of the present study.

When computers figure in an input price index, it is a price index for the inputs to the gadget industry—in other words, a price index for the right-hand side of equation (1) where computers are one of three components in the input-price index. One might also wish to calculate a price index for computers used in the gadget industry. For example, the computer price index might be wanted for purposes of estimating the production function for gadgets. This would be a "subindex" (the term originates with Pollak [1975]) of the full input-price index. Another subindex would involve measures of wages. The theory of subindexes is relevant for many problems that arise in treating quality change.

In principle there are all kinds of economic differences between input and output price measures. The example involves a capital good—as does much of the quality change literature. The production function use really concerns the flow of capital services; an output measure is, of course, a flow of capital *goods*.[3] However, the distinction between a durable good and the flow of services is not central to the quality measurement issues the present paper addresses. And either case—output of goods or input of services—will probably be measured either directly or indirectly by deflating a value aggregate by a price index.[4]

Thus, in the actual computation of either an output measure or an input measure of capital goods, the point at issue comes down to the choice of the appropriate price index to deflate value data. This is, in fact, the issue on which the quality measurement debate has focused.

One point deserves emphasis. One frequently encounters in the literature some functional notation for the "production" of, say, computer services—that is, a measure of computer services is written as the "output" of a process in which the stock of computers, or the characteristics of the stock of computers, is taken as the "input." Whatever value such notation has for some purposes, this is not the meaning of inputs and outputs as used in the present study.

As a matter of practical computation, input and output price indexes for a commodity, industry, or sector may involve numerous other distinctions. Even at relatively detailed levels, a price index is still an aggregation, and even if the prices were all measured in the same way, the weights for input and output price indexes for a similarly named commodity would make them different measurements. A price index for the output of steel mills has weights that differ from those of an input price index for steel used in the auto industry. This paper's concern for input and output price measures is, however, limited to theoretical implications and to the quality measurement question. We pursue no other issues (see Early 1978).

5.3 A Theory of Quality Adjustment for Input Price Indexes

An input price index has many applications. For a firm or industry using a "KLEM" production process (capital, labor, energy, and materials), an input price index measures the price change of these four productive factors. The Bureau of Labor Statistics (BLS) Employment Cost Index is a form of input price index, in this case an index for only the labor portion of total inputs (in Pollak's [1975] term, it is a "sub-index" of the full input price index). Another example is the Consumer Price Index (CPI), which is an input price index for consumption.

Very little has been published on input price indexes for production. However, the theory can be developed by analogy to the theory of the cost-of-living index, on which the literature is voluminous (see Pollak 1971; Fisher and Shell 1972; Samuelson and Swamy 1974).

Section 5.3.1 states the theory of production input price indexes, drawing on the cost-of-living index literature. The standard theory applies to goods (or services), on the implicit assumption that they are homogeneous and the quality problem does not exist. In Section 5.3.2 quality change is defined as variation in the quantities of characteristics embodied in heterogeneous goods. Section 5.3.3 combines the first two sections, extending the theory of input price indexes from goods space into characteristics space; this extension proves the result that quality change in an input index must be handled by a measure of user value.

Readers who are familiar with theoretical index number literature may wish to turn directly to Section 5.3.2.

5.3.1 Input Price Indexes for Goods

The consumption price index literature distinguishes a cost-of-living index (sometimes termed a "true cost-of-living index") from the conventional fixed-weight price index formulas normally used by statistical agencies (the Laspeyres or Paasche formulas). We follow this practice, and define an "input cost index"[5] as a measure which answers the question: What is the cost change, between two periods, of collections of inputs sufficient to produce some specified output level? In the following, we speak of this as the "theoretical" or the "economic" input price index, in distinction to fixed-weight formulas.

The rationale for the input cost index definition is analogous to the one for the cost-of-living index. We begin with a production function,

$$(3) \qquad Z = f(X_1, \ldots, X_j, \ldots, X_n),$$

where the X's are identified as quantities of market-purchased inputs (i.e., as goods). We ignore possible complications by assuming there is only a single output, or if there are multiple outputs that they may be aggregated into a suitable scalar measure. The theory does not require profit maximization (or any particular market structure on the output side) but does assume that the firm minimizes production cost.

Let Z^* be some output level relevant to the comparison, and designate the reference period as time 0. There is a cost-minimizing set of inputs $(X^*_{10}, \ldots, X^*_{j0}, \ldots, X^*_{n0})$, or, more compactly, $[X^*_0]$, for the reference period's set of input prices $(P_{10}, \ldots, P_{j0}, \ldots, P_{n0})$, which we write alternatively as $[P_0]$. The cost, C^*_0, of acquiring the optimal set of inputs can be determined from the cost function that is dual to the production function, f, but can also simply be added up:

$$C^*_0 = \sum_{i=1}^{n} X^*_{i0} P_{i0}.$$

We now consider some comparison period, t, with input prices $(P_{1t}, \ldots, P_{jt}, \ldots, P_{nt})$. For the same output level, Z^*, the production problem may again be solved for the cost-minimizing set of inputs, $[X_t^*]$. Wherever substitution is possible among factors, $[X_0^*]$ is not the same as $[X_t^*]$, unless relative factor prices are the same in $[P_0]$ and $[P_t]$. The cost of the set of inputs which minimizes the cost of producing Z^* in period t is C_t^*, and the input cost index is:

$$(4) \qquad I = \frac{C_t^*}{C_0^*} = \frac{\Sigma X_{it}^* P_{it}}{\Sigma X_{i0}^* P_{i0}} .$$

In words, the index is the ratio of the minimum cost of acquiring inputs sufficient for producing output Z^* in the comparison period (t) to the minimum cost of producing the same output in the reference period (0).

The input cost index can be thought of as pricing two sets of inputs which lie on the same production isoquant, with each set corresponding to the cost-minimizing point for one of the two periods. The isoquant for which the index comparison is made (output level Z^*) may correspond to the actual output of the reference period (Z_0 in fig. 5.1), or of the comparison period (Z_t), or to some other output.[6]

Consider the input cost index with Z^* defined to be the actual output of the reference period (Z_0). Designate this form of input cost index as I_L, or as the "Laspeyres-perspective" input cost index (because it takes the perspective of the initial period as the basis for the comparison). For this input cost index, point A of figure 5.1 provides the denominator and point B the numerator of equation (4).

For actual computation, $[X_0^*]$, or point A's inputs, are obtainable from survey data, Census of Manufactures, and other sources, and C_0^*, the denominator of equation (4), is reference period actual costs. Determining $[X_t^*]$, and therefore C_t^*, however, requires knowledge of the production function—point B in figure 5.1 is not observed directly but must be estimated.

For this reason, one normally approximates the theoretical input cost index I_L by some traditional fixed-weight formula, such as the Laspeyres index (dropping the i subscripts):

$$(5) \qquad L = \frac{\Sigma P_t X_0^*}{\Sigma P_0 X_0^*} .$$

The only difference between L and I_L (i.e., between eqq. [4] and [5]) lies in the quantities in the numerator—($[X_t^*]$ in I_L, as opposed to $[X_0^*]$ in the L index). Note that neither index I_L nor L uses the *actual* inputs purchased in period t (in figure 5.1, period t's actual inputs are those corresponding to point C). The reason, of course, is that the index computation requires Z^* to be held constant in order to obtain a price measure; for various reasons, actual output and therefore actual inputs may change.

It is well known that the Laspeyres fixed-weight index provides an upper bound on the Laspeyres-perspective input cost index (the theoretical input cost index based on the reference period Z_0). This also implies that the Laspeyres index is an upward-biased measure of the true index, with the extent of the bias depending on the amount of substitution that takes place in response to changes in relative factor prices.[7] The mathematical proof of this proposition is identical to that provided by Pollak (1971) for the consumption case and need not be repeated here. However, for heuristic reasons, it is worth relating the result to the diagram of figure 5.1.

We have already noted that the Laspeyres-perspective input cost index of equation (4) compares the cost of point A's inputs at $[P_0]$ prices with point B's inputs at $[P_t]$ prices. Moreover, the actual cost (in prices $[P_0]$) of point A's inputs provides the denominator of both the input cost index I_L, and of L, its fixed-weight approximation.

Using the Laspeyres formula to obtain a measure of the change in the cost of inputs involves pricing point A at the new set of relative prices $[P_t]$, giving $\Sigma P_t X_0$, the numerator of L. The dashed line passing through point A shows combinations of inputs that could be acquired for the same cost as $\Sigma P_t X_0$ (i.e., the same cost in period t as input bundle A evaluated at period t's prices). However, Z_0 could be produced more cheaply in period t by substituting from point A to point B, an input substitution which would realize a cost saving shown by the distance between the parallel lines passing through A and through B. This cost saving is equal to the "substitution bias" in the fixed-weight Laspeyres index.

An alternative fixed-weight price index frequently employed is Paasche's formula, which is based on reference-period output level ($Z^* = Z_t$) and input quantities:

(6) $$P = \frac{\Sigma P_t X_t^*}{\Sigma P_0 X_t^*}.$$

The national accounts imply this price index formula.

Corresponding to the Paasche fixed-weight index is an input cost index which uses the isoquant and input quantities of period t (the comparison period) rather than of period 0. We designate this input cost index as I_P, or the "Paasche-perspective input cost index." It is computed by comparing points C and D from figure 5.1. That is, I_P can be computed from equation (4) by specifying that Z^*—and therefore $[X_t^*]$ and $[X_0^*]$—be defined in terms of the isoquant which actually obtains in period t.

Thus, there are two economic indexes of input costs. They have orientations analogous to the differing orientations of Laspeyres and Paasche fixed-weight indexes: The I_L input cost index (in common with the Laspeyres formula) computes the change between periods 0 and t

from the perspective of the actual situation in period 0. The I_P index, on the other hand, derives from the perspective of the actual situation in period t, which likewise forms the basis for the weights for the Paasche fixed-weight formula.[8]

Except for special cases, these two input cost indexes will have different values, since they look at the change from different perspectives. This is the "index number problem" in its purest form.

A standard index number result is that the fixed-weight Paasche index *understates* the "Paasche-perspective" input cost index. In other words, in the Paasche index case the substitution bias in index P causes it to understate the true cost change, as measured by I_P. Index P provides an approximation to—and lower bound on—the true index, I_P. This relation is analogous to the upper-bound property of the L-index, relative to the I_L input cost index.

The relationships among the two true, or economic, indexes and their two fixed-weight bounds invalidate the widespread notion that the economic index must lie between values computed from Paasche and Laspeyres formulas. Liviatan and Patinkin (1961) give a particularly clear statement of the correct relation. The same relationships imply as well that the full difference between the fixed-weight Paasche and Laspeyres indexes cannot be taken as a measure of substitution bias or biases in fixed-weight indexes—some of the difference between L and P may be accounted for by the difference between I_L and I_P.

Comment. The approach to input cost indexes followed in this section amounts to a direct analogy to the cost-of-living index concept. Hence, the economic theory on which it is erected consists solely of the firm's cost-minimizing behavior, and ignores the fact that changes in input prices may cause the competitive firm to alter its output level as well as its factor proportions. Whether output effects should or should not be ignored in constructing an economic measurement depends, it seems to me, solely on the nature of the questions the economic measurement is supposed to answer. It does not necessarily depend, or certainly does not solely depend, on the nature of the maximization problem that the firm faces. These issues are too complex to be explored here; but comment is required because alternative approaches have been followed (see n. 18, and "Comment," p. 292). Note also that the theory is static and therefore abstracts from technical change. Fisher and Shell (1972) explore index number theory in the presence of taste and technical change.

Summary and Conclusions to Section 5.3.1

The section has discussed two input cost indexes and two associated fixed-weight price index formulas. It is conventional to think of these as the (two) theoretical indexes on the one hand and two practical indexes on the other hand. The content of the conventional theory of index numbers distinguishes a crucial property of these two sets of index numbers: it emphasizes that the input cost indexes take account of, as the fixed-weight indexes cannot, the effect of factor substitution in response to relative price change.

The purposes of the present paper, however, require emphasis on another property of input cost indexes: for either input cost index, I_L or I_P, output must be held constant in order to obtain the measure of price change. This is very important for the remainder of this paper. In the following, we refer to this property as the constant-output *criterion* for an input price measure.

The notion that the theoretical input price measure requires a constant-output criterion suggests an alternative interpretation of the role of fixed weights in conventional Paasche and Laspeyres index numbers. Textbooks usually explain that the quantity weights are held constant in a fixed-weight price index in order to decompose a value aggregate into price and quantity terms. The economic reason for fixed weights is quite different. Holding the quantities of inputs fixed is one way of holding output fixed, and it is output constancy that is required for an input price measurement. The bias introduced into fixed-weight indexes by substitution stems from the fact that they only hold output approximately fixed; the deviation from the constant-output criterion that both Paasche and Laspeyres indexes permit is the substitution bias of the fixed-weight index.

Thus, *constant output is the guiding rule for constructing any input price measure*, whether one of the true economic indexes, or one of the approximations. The concept of the index "criterion" plays a major role in this paper. We return to it in Section 5.3.3.

5.3.2   Modeling Quality Change: Input Characteristics

Conventional index number theory implicitly assumes that quality variation does not exist—it applies to a world of homogeneous goods. I incorporate quality change into the theory of index numbers by making use of the following proposition: when we use the term "quality" in economics, we are really making a kind of shorthand reference to the *quantities* in a vector of "characteristics." Under this way of looking at it, "quality change" is intrinsically quantifiable. It can be measured or evaluated in terms of quantities of characteristics—units that resemble in essential ways the goods whose quantities enter into conventional economic measurement.

Over the past decade or so, the term "characteristics" has been used in economics in a variety of ways. Moreover, in the present paper, we distinguish "input characteristics" from "output characteristics." For these reasons, some definitions and assumptions are required:

a) "Characteristics" are properties or attributes of goods. A house, for example, has characteristics such as floor space, number of bathrooms, or whatever is relevant. A machine's characteristics may include lifting or hauling capacities, cutting speeds, core size, and so forth. Labor services may also be described in terms of characteristics: standard human capital analysis distinguishes education and experience as productive characteristics of labor, and strength, dexterity, and other elements are frequently cited in the labor literature.

b) As the examples imply, characteristics are defined to be a lower level of aggregation than goods. That is, goods are aggregates of characteristics, not the other way around.

c) We assume that quantities of characteristics are the true inputs into the production function, and not quantities of goods or any other quantity obtained by reaggregating characteristics in some manner. This is primarily a simplifying assumption, intended to rule out a number of alternatives that have appeared in the literature but which are not especially relevant for present purposes and would greatly complicate the exposition of the basic theory. For example, much of the empirical literature is written as if labor, once disaggregated into human capital elements, must be reaggregated into some "labor aggregate," with the labor-aggregator function entering the production function. In this paper, we assume that labor characteristics enter the production function directly, without the necessity for any intervening "aggregator function." Another example concerns services of capital goods. For some purposes, investigators have combined a truck, let us say, with its associated labor and fuel inputs to produce a measure of "trucking services." That is, they have assumed a "production function for trucking services" (with trucks, labor, and fuel as inputs), and used the output of this secondary "production function" as the input into the primary production function. Parallels with the household production literature on the consumption side are obvious.

In the present paper, we dispense with all intervening aggregator functions. The basic reason is that these subproduction aggregator notions, even where relevant, unduly obscure and confuse the exposition, without adding much of consequence (though other reasons could also be cited).[9]

d) *Input* characteristics are defined by the following process. For a multifactor production function having at least one factor which is nonhomogeneous, consider substituting one example of this nonhomogeneous factor for another example of the same factor. That is, if the factor is labor, substitute Ms. B for Mr. A; if it is a machine, substitute the XYZ Co's model 200 for the ABC Co's model 55.

The substitute differs in quality from the original if there is a change in output when the substitution occurs, or if the substitution affects other factor usage in such a way that there would be a change in the value of the dual cost function if the substitute and the original were available at the same price. Another way of putting it is to say that quality variation in an input exists if substitution of different varieties or examples of this input creates variations in output or cost that are not explained by the factors included in the production or cost function. *A quantity is an input characteristic if it reduces that unexplained variation.* Years of education is a labor input characteristic if its use in the production or cost function accounts for all or part of the unexplained variation associated with the substitution of Ms. B for Mr. A; cutting speed is a machine input characteristic if its use in the production or cost function accounts for all or part of the unexplained variation associated with the substitution of the XYZ 200 for the ABC 55.

This definition of an input characteristic amounts to saying that something is an input only if it makes a contribution to production. A formal definition is warranted largely because the quality change literature has been filled with various taxonomies, and in order to make more clear the distinction between input characteristics and output characteristics (see Section 5.4.2).

e) We assume that only the quantities of characteristics matter, and not how they are embodied in goods. This means that a two-ton truck is assumed to provide equivalent hauling capacity to two one-ton trucks. This has sometimes been referred to as "linear" characteristics; "additive characteristics" is a more suitable term. The assumption is a very restrictive one.

The assumption is made primarily for the sake of simplicity. Obviously, even if two tons of hauling capacity makes an equivalent contribution to output whether in one vehicle or two, the number of vehicles used may imply variation in the labor input (one driver instead of two). But this is a complication to the basic characteristics theory rather than (as has sometimes been thought) an objection. Elsewhere (Triplett 1973) I have referred to it as the "package-size" problem, as it arises also in the consumption case. A recent paper by Trajtenberg (1979) has reopened this issue.

f) To avoid misinterpretation, a few disavowals must be listed. First, nothing in the present paper implies any linearity assumptions on the production function or on any other function or relationship. One could write a lengthy treatise attempting to straighten out what critics of different parts of the characteristics literature have put under the "linearity" rubric. This is not the place to deal with these matters; I have discussed some of them elsewhere (1980).

Second, nothing in the paper has anything directly to do with the form of hedonic functions or with their interpretation. In particular, the distinction between input characteristics and output characteristics has nothing whatever to do with the function Ohta-Griliches (1976) posited to exist between what they described as "engineering characteristics," such as "memory size", on one hand, and "performance characteristics," such as "computational capacity," on the other. Any engineering relation between "engineering" and "performance" characteristics, if it exists, is not one that is relevant for the theory of price indexes. The distinction arose from alternative empirical specifications for the variables in hedonic functions. This paper is not concerned with the empiricist tradition of hedonic studies.

Neither does the paper relate to the common technique of forming "hedonic price indexes" from the ratio of two period's regressions, as is so often done. One *might* use hedonic functions to help identify the characteristics that are wanted for input and output price indexes and, perhaps, to measure their costs as well (I say "perhaps" because of the problems of applying and using hedonic results, problems that will not be explored here [see Triplett 1971a; and Pollak 1979]). But how this has been done in the past, or how it should be done, is outside the scope of this paper.

5.3.3 Quality Change and Input Price
Indexes for Characteristics

This section combines results of Sections 5.3.1 and 5.3.2 in order to examine the treatment of quality change in input price indexes. The method involves translating the "goods-space" index number theory of Section 5.3.1 into the notion of "characteristics space" developed in Section 5.3.2.[10]

Four results from Section 5.3.1 are required for this section:

1. An input cost index prices a collection of inputs in two periods that represent minimum-cost points on the same production isoquant.

2. For any comparison, a number of different input cost indexes can be computed, depending on which isoquant is used for the comparison; indexes based on isoquants appropriate to reference and comparison periods were designated, respectively, as "Laspeyres-perspective" (I_L) and "Paasche-perspective" (I_P) input cost indexes.

3. The usual fixed-weight Laspeyres and Paasche index formulas may be viewed as approximations to the true economic indexes, I_L and I_P. The Laspeyres index provides an upper bound to I_L, whereas the Paasche index is a lower bound to I_P.

4. Whether the economic index or the fixed-weight index is used, computing an input cost index requires that output be held constant over the span of the comparison; this condition was referred to as the "constant-output criterion" for the input cost index.

Carrying through the input cost index number analysis in characteristics space requires that characteristics—not the units in which market transactions are carried out—enter the production function. For certain advantages in the exposition (and no loss in generality), assume that only one input (the jth input) in the production function of equation (3) is nonhomogeneous and that this input has m characteristics. For a capital good (properly speaking, the services of a capital good; we use the terms synonymously), these characteristics may be thought of as cutting speeds, storage capacities, and so forth, as described in Section 5.3.2.

Substituting the m characteristics $(\chi_{j1}, \ldots, \chi_{jm})$ embodied in the nonhomogeneous good X_j for the good itself, we can rewrite (3) as

$$(3a) \qquad Z = g(X_1, \ldots, \chi_{j1}, \chi_{j2}, \ldots, \chi_{jm}, \ldots, X_n),$$

so that the production function contains not n but $n + m - 1$ inputs (including the m characteristics of input j). Suppose input j, in equation (3), is a truck. In (3a), the input that enters the production function is no longer thought of as a quantity of trucks; rather, if characteristic $j2$, say, is a capacity measure, hauling capacity is the input. The firm chooses the number of units of truck capacity (as well as other truck characteristics, such as fuel economy, etc., and other labor, material, and capital inputs) that are optimal for its production process and output level.[11]

The Input Cost Index in Characteristics Space

The characteristics input cost index starts from the production function, g, from equation (3a). The index theory proceeds along similar lines to the formulation for the goods-space input cost index developed in Section 5.3.1.

We adopt the convention that a homogeneous input is itself a characteristic whose cost is equal to the market price, so that all $n + m - 1$ inputs in equation (3a) can be thought of as characteristics. With this convention, let $[\chi_0^*]$ designate the minimum-cost set of inputs, at time 0, sufficient to produce output level Z. The cost of acquiring this set of inputs can be written as:

$$(7) \qquad C_0^* = C(\chi_0^*).$$

The "characteristics production cost" function, C, is interpreted as the minimum cost of producing output level Z^*, where the inputs to the production function are input characteristics rather than conventional goods.

The characteristics space cost function may be considerably more complicated than is the case of the analogous relation in the goods index section (the denominator of eq. [4]). In goods space, the input cost for any desired level of output can be determined from knowledge of the production function, f, and the prices of input goods (i.e., from the cost function that in conventional production theory is dual to the production function, f). The input characteristics case is more complicated because in general the costs of acquiring characteristics are not simple parameters (as are prices in the goods-space case), but are themselves determined by functional relations involving the market prices of input goods and the quantities of characteristics they contain. Because the purpose of this paper requires only the most general formulation of the notion of a characteristics input cost index, we will not extend the discussion to explore the complexities that arise in a more exact formulation (on this, see Pollak 1979).

The characteristics input cost index is defined analogously to the goods input cost index of Section 5.3.1: it is the ratio of the minimum-cost combination of inputs (characteristics) sufficient to produce output level Z^* in the reference and comparison period price regimes. Thus, it is the ratio of two values of equation (7)—the denominator embodies the cost regime of period 0, the numerator reflects period t's costs. This can be thought of as a modification of equation (4) to incorporate the characteristics production cost function of equation (7):

$$(4a) \qquad I = \frac{C_t^*}{C_0^*} = \frac{C(\chi_t^*)}{C(\chi_0^*)} .$$

The notation emphasizes that the cost function, C, is to be evaluated for a constant output level, Z^*, and for price or cost regimes corresponding to periods 0 and t.

In terms of index theory itself, the characteristics input-cost index has form, derivation, and properties similar to the conventional input-cost index for goods. In effect, the basic theory is identical—we merely adjust our thinking to let characteristics such as carrying capacities, cutting speeds, and so forth, play the roles conventionally assigned to "goods."

In particular, differences in characteristics quantities $[\chi_0^*]$ and $[\chi_t^*]$ arise from the same source as analogous effects in the goods index: changes in relative costs of acquiring inputs (characteristics) may lead the firm to substitute among inputs (characteristics). For example, changes in wages and in the price of fuel may lead to change in the optimal quantity of truck-carrying capacity in production function (3a). The characteristics input cost index would allow for such shifts, pricing a set of minimum-cost inputs that would produce constant output for the new structure of relative characteristics costs.

As with the goods input cost index, the characteristics input cost index can be based on the isoquant prevailing in the initial or reference period, the one for the comparison period, or some other one. If Z^* equals the reference period output level, Z_0, the characteristics input cost index is designated the "Laspeyres-perspective" index. The comparison period output level (Z_t) gives a "Paasche-perspective" index. In the goods index section, these alternative input cost indexes were referred to as the I_L and I_P indexes.

Quality Variation in the Characteristics
Input Cost Index

In the ordinary meaning of the term, two varieties of a nonhomogeneous good may be thought to differ in quality whenever they are not exactly identical. The task of this section is to show that the only differences which matter in an input cost index are differences in input characteristics—that is, that only the user-value implications of goods need to be accounted for in the input cost index.

Suppose the I_L version of the input-cost index is to be computed and the nonhomogeneous input in equation (3a) is a machine. The denominator of the I_L index is the cost of the reference period's vector of inputs $[x_0^*]$. This vector implies a particular machine or combination of machines.

The theoretical input cost index of equation (4a) permits shifts in characteristics quantities in response to changing relative costs of acquiring characteristics. Accordingly, if the cost-minimizing characteristics in the numerator of equation (4a) differ from those in the denominator, this implies either a shift to some other machine, a shift in the mix of machines employed, or both.

This relation can be illustrated by supposing that the nonhomogeneous input of equation (3a) has two characteristics and that the relations between the two can be portrayed in figure 5.1. That is, the axes of figure 5.1 are interpreted as referring to two characteristics, χ_a and χ_b, instead of to two goods, and the solid and dashed isocost lines represent the relative costs of acquiring the two characteristics.[12] Under this interpretation, point A designates the bundle of characteristics embodied in machine A, and point B the characteristics of machine B. As figure 5.1 shows, a shift in relative characteristics costs (in the figure drawn as straight lines) induces a switch from one machine to the other.

An input cost index compares, as Section 5.3.1 shows, precisely such points as A and B. Thus, the characteristics input cost index need not be computed on identical varieties of nonhomogenous goods. Generally, an index which includes nonhomogeneous goods will encompass changes from one variety to another. In the everyday meaning of the term, this is a "quality change," and indeed machines A and B embody differing quantities of input characteristics. But in the context of the input cost index, the two machines are of equivalent quality. They both produce the same output level, and if introduced into equation (3a) they both have the same implications for the cost of the *other* inputs included in the production function. Thus, for the theory of input cost indexes, we say that machine A and machine B are of equivalent quality.[13]

Notice, however, that machines A and B do not necessarily sell for the same price in either period 0 or period t, and in both periods the using firm clearly chooses one over the other (a different one in each period). This is worth additional comment, in view of the fact that most of the quality change literature takes price equivalence in some period, or some "equally likely to be chosen" condition, as a definition of equal quality.

An intuitive rationale for the production-function definition of the present paper can be obtained by following through the analogy between the theory of the firm's choice of inputs when those inputs are assumed to be homogeneous goods and its choice of inputs when they are characteristics. Whether the theory relates to goods or to characteristics, there are a great many different bundles of inputs that are equally satisfactory in terms of their output productivity—all those bundles on a given isoquant. In both cases, only one of these equivalent bundles is actually chosen— the cost-minimizing one. In the characteristics case, this says that there may be many different machines that are equivalent in the production function; but the firm chooses the one (or combination) that provides the minimum-cost bundle of input characteristics.

In the conventional view, equal quality is inferred from identical selling prices for two goods. This amounts to a quality definition that takes all machines that lie on the same isocost line (in characteristics space) to be of equal quality. The characteristics-space analysis followed here shows that definition to be inconsistent with the nature of the input cost index. Equal quality is determined from equivalence of alternative machines in the production function that is the basis for the input cost index and not from equality in prices.[14]

Thus, substitution effects in the characteristics input cost index lead to changes in the varieties of nonhomogenous goods included in the index. This takes place because characteristics are obtained packaged in bundles; in order to change characteristics proportions, the purchaser must choose a different variety of good, or a different mix of varieties.

Quality "Adjustments" in the Input Cost Index

The preceding section has shown that a new machine whose characteristics imply that the firm has remained on the same production isoquant is treated in the input cost index as equivalent in quality to the old one. If, on the other hand, a new machine has characteristics inconsistent with remaining on the same production isoquant, some quality adjustment is called for in the measurement.

Suppose in period t a machine corresponding to point C of figure 5.1 is observed, and machine A (whose characteristics were included in $[\chi_0^*]$) is unavailable for inclusion in the index. Machine A's "unavailability" may simply acknowledge that it is not actually in use in the particular using firm or industry for which the input price index is being constructed, or that for some reason the agency or investigator compiling the index does not have access to data on machine A in time period t. It does not necessarily mean that it has disappeared from the face of the earth.[15]

We describe the quality difference between machines A and C by the vector of differences in their characteristics, or $\widetilde{\Delta}\chi$.[16] The question to be answered takes the form: How should $\widetilde{\Delta}\chi$ be dealt with in the input cost index of equation (4a)?

It is clear that the change in characteristics quantities implies a shift in output (in fig. 5.1, from Z_0 to Z_t). Thus, introduction of machine C in the production function g violates the constant-output criterion on which the input cost index is constructed. Beyond this, $\widetilde{\Delta}\chi$ may have implications in g that cannot be depicted in the two dimensions of figure 5.1—for example, a shift to trucks with greater load-carrying capability may imply a reduction of direct labor and increased use of fuel. Adjustments in other factor usage may indirectly violate the constant-output criterion.

The input cost index therefore must be adjusted for the quality change in order to maintain its constant-output criterion. Maintaining the con-

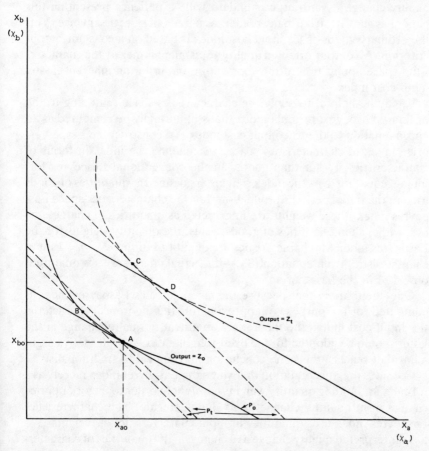

Fig. 5.1   Production isoquants in goods and characteristics spaces (basis for computing input price indexes and quality adjustments).

stant-output criterion implies that the appropriate adjustment is one exactly *equivalent to the output implications of* $\widetilde{\Delta}\chi$. That is, the appropriate compensation for the difference between machines A and C is equal to the difference in output between isoquants Z_0 and Z_t. The correct quality adjusted index is one that can be interpreted as the change in cost of a collection of inputs just sufficient to produce output level Z_0.

We have thus reached the conclusion that in a measure of input prices the adjustment for quality change must be output oriented. Adjustments are to be made only for changes in input characteristics that result in changed output (or reduced cost to the user), and the correct quality adjustment is exactly equal to the cost change or the value of the output change that they induce. In the literature, this is known as the user-value rule.

The conclusion that an input cost price measure requires evaluating quality change by an output standard will (experience presenting this paper has shown) strike many readers as paradoxical, at first glance. Yet, the ordinary goods-space input cost index is based on a constant-output criterion. An output-oriented quality adjustment is merely the characteristics-space application of the constant-output criterion inherent in any input cost index.

It may be helpful to apply the characteristics-space reasoning to the ordinary Laspeyres-formula index that will normally be computed as an approximation to the true input cost index. To construct the Laspeyres-price index in characteristics space, we redefine the index in terms of characteristics, rather than goods. In the conventional Laspeyres formula—equation (5)—the index weights are defined as quantities of goods used in the initial period's production. For the characteristics-space Laspeyres index, these weights are interpreted as quantities of characteristics, rather than quantities of goods. Thus, the quantity weights for the Laspeyres index for characteristics are quantities of the $n + m - 1$ input characteristics from equation (3a)—the actual characteristics quantities observed in the base period.

One could argue that because the characteristics Laspeyres index is computed for the purpose of approximating the theoretical characteristics input cost index, the theoretical treatment of quality change in the latter should be adopted for the fixed-weight index. An alternative argument that reaches the same conclusion may appeal to traditionalists.

Consider the interpretation that views the Laspeyres index merely as a formula for holding quantity weights constant in order to factor out price change from quantity change in a value aggregate. The characteristics Laspeyres index uses quantities of input characteristics as weights. We have interpreted quality change as a change in the quantities of characteristics. Thus, when quality change occurs, the quantity weights in the Laspeyres formula would no longer be held constant.

Making a quality adjustment to the Laspeyres index, therefore, may be interpreted as restoring the index quantity weights to their reference-period values. It has sometimes been said that there is no rationale for making quality adjustments within the Laspeyres framework. However, in the disaggregation approach to quality change the act of seeking a quality adjustment for the Laspeyres index has exactly the same significance and interpretation as holding constant the weights in the index formula—so long as weights are defined appropriately as characteristics quantities.

So far, discussion of quality change has been conducted within the framework of the Laspeyres-perspective characteristics input cost index. A similar line of reasoning holds for the Paasche-perspective index. For the I_P index it is, of course, isoquant Z_t that provides the constant-output criterion; accordingly, the quality adjustment appropriate to the I_P index is one that adjusts the reference period observation to assure that the I_P input cost index measures two combinations of inputs lying on the Z_t isoquant. This argument is a straightforward translation of the reasoning that has gone before.

Note that the existence of I_L and I_P versions of the characteristics input cost index implies that there are two possible quality adjustments for an input cost index. Both are based on a user-value rule, but one (the I_P index) takes the current user value as relevant, the other (the I_L index) is based on the initial period's user valuation. Obviously those two quality adjustments might not give the same answer, but this is nothing more than the old index number problem in a new and intriguing form.

Summary

The appropriate quality adjustment for an input cost index is one based on user value. The input cost index is derived from the cost of bundles of inputs that lie on the same production isoquant. Taking contribution to output as the quality adjustment for the input cost index assures that the inputs in both numerator and denominator of the index do correspond to points on the same production isoquant.

5.4   A Theory of Quality Adjustment for Output Price Indexes

The format of this section parallels the one followed in the section on input price indexes. We first sketch briefly the content of the theory of output price indexes applied to goods, then consider the concept of output characteristics. Section 5.4.3 extends the price index theory from goods space into characteristics space, from which the results on quality change emerge. Readers familiar with the theory of "goods" output price indexes may wish to skip directly to Section 5.4.2.

5.4.1   Output Price Indexes for Goods

The theory of output price indexes has been discussed from an economy-wide perspective by Moorsteen (1961), Fisher and Shell (1972), Samuelson and Swamy (1974), and others. The approach requires motivation. One method is to ask what properties we wish an output quantity measure to have, and to design an output price measure that is consistent with the quantity measure.

The relationship between an economy's fixed stock of resources and its output possibilities is represented by the standard textbook production possibility frontier diagram. Suppose that in the initial period the economy is at point A, as shown in figure 5.2, that in the subsequent period the

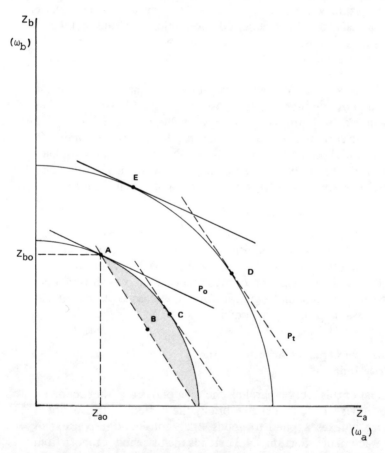

Fig. 5.2   Production possibility curves in goods and characteristics spaces (basis for computing output price indexes and quality adjustments).

economy grows, shifting to a higher production possibility frontier, and (because of changes in relative prices) moves to point D.

A natural method for measuring the output change from A to D is to allow for a movement along one production possibility curve, such as. from A to C, and to take the distance between the curves at this point (CD) as a measure of the change in output. Of course, there are many such points: one could also move along the higher production possibility curve from D to E, and take the distance EA as the output measure. Unless the production possibility curves are radial displacements of each other, these two measures of output change may not agree. As we shall show, these alternative output measures correspond to the traditional Paasche-Laspeyres "index number problem."

We may wish to compute a price measure that is compatible with CD as the output quantity measure. Alternatively, we may wish to produce the output measure by deflation; if so, the correct output price index will produce CD as the measure of output.[17] Compatibility with CD as a measure of output requires the price index to treat two collections of outputs lying on the same production possibility curve (such as A and C) as equivalent. The theoretical output price index does just that: it compares the value of output collection A in period 0 prices with output collection C in period t's prices. This theoretical measure has usually been termed the "true output price deflator" in the price index number literature.

It is easy to show that the Laspeyres fixed-weight price index relates to the initial situation (point A) and that it *understates* the price change associated with remaining on a constant production possibility curve. Hence, when the Laspeyres index is used as a deflator it will produce an overestimate of the real output change CD. A geometric proof follows.

The economy depicted in figure 5.2 produces two outputs, Z_a and Z_b. For the price set $[P_0]$ (indicated by the slope of the line so labeled), the economy will produce at point A, with outputs Z_{b0} and Z_{a0}, which we label as the output set $[Z_0]$. The quantity $\Sigma P_{i0} Z_{i0}$ ($i = a, b$) is the value of output for the reference period, which is also the denominator of the Laspeyres-formula price index (eq. [5], from the section on input price indexes).

Let the slopes of the dashed lines in figure 5.2 represent relative prices prevailing in the new, or comparison, period (period t). The dashed line passing through point A (the reference period's output) corresponds to the quantity $\Sigma P_t Z_0$, that is, to the numerator of the Laspeyres-price index formula (eq. [5]). This quantity is interpreted as the reference period's outputs $[Z_0]$, valued at the comparison period's prices, $[P_t]$.

Any point on the dashed line passing through A (such as point B) represents an output combination whose value is equal to that of A. With resources sufficient to produce point A, however, the economy could attain a collection of outputs having higher value than those on the AB line. Any output in the shaded area of figure 5.2 would have greater value than the value of A's outputs. The output combination with highest value, at period t prices, is point C.

From the standpoint of resource use or opportunity cost point C is equivalent to point A, because they can both be produced from the same resource availability. The fact that the numerator of the Laspeyres index prices a collection of outputs with a value which lies below a portion of the production possibility frontier suggests a bias in the Laspeyres index. This bias is indicated by the distance between the line tangent to point C and the parallel line passing through point A (i.e., the distance BC). The output change BC is the "substitution" bias in the fixed-weight Laspeyres price index when it is used as an approximation to the theoretical, or "true," output price measure.

Note that the Laspeyres index is downward biased when used as an output price measure, though it is upward biased when used as an approximation to an input price index. The downward bias in the output deflator creates an exactly equal error of opposite sign in the output quantity measure. Using the Laspeyres price index as a deflator gives BD as the output measure, which is larger than CD (the correct measure) by BC, the substitution bias in the fixed-weight index.

Thus, an appropriate output-price index is one that compares the value of output bundles A, valued at prices $[P_0]$, and C, valued at prices $[P_t]$. This index is the economic or theoretical output-price index and is computed from equation (10), below. It is termed the "Laspeyres-perspective" output price index.

The implicit output price deflators emerging from the computation of the national accounts are Paasche-formula price indexes. The Paasche-price index can also be derived from figure 5.2.

Point D represents the actual output combination in period t. Parallel to the "Laspeyres-perspective" output price index is the "Paasche-perspective" index which compares the ratio of the values of outputs D and E (which lie on the same production possibility curve); deflation by this index gives EA as the true measure of output quantity change. By an analogous line of reasoning to that presented above for the Laspeyres case, it can be shown that the fixed-weight Paasche price index, which prices output collection D in both periods, gives an upward-biased measure of price change, compared to the value of the economic output price index based on points D and E of figure 5.2. Consequently, a measure of output produced through deflation by a Paasche price index will understate the true change in output. Note that the fixed-weight Paasche-formula index is upward biased because of substitution, when it is used as an output price index; when used as an input price index the substitution bias goes in the opposite direction (see Section 5.3.1).

A more formal statement of the ideas so far presented intuitively follows. Suppose there are n input quantities, $X_i (i = 1, \ldots, n)$, which are available in strictly fixed amounts $(X_i = X_i^*)$. The production transformation relation between the n inputs and the economy's m outputs is given by

(8) $$T(Z_j, X_i^*) = 0$$

where $j = 1, \ldots, m$, and $i = 1, \ldots, n$.

We assume that inputs are not specialized, so that different combinations of outputs can be produced from them, and consider only those quantities of outputs that will completely exhaust the set of fixed available input quantities, $[X^*]$. The set of such output combinations $(Z: X = X^*)$ defines the production possibility curve; for compactness, outputs lying on the production possibility curve will be designated as $[Z^*]$.

The revenue function

(9) $$R = R(Z^*, P)$$

indicates the revenue obtained from the set of outputs produced, given a set of output prices, $[P]$. The optimal set of outputs is determined by maximizing (9), with input quantities and output prices specified at levels appropriate to the comparison. For prices P_0, for input quantities $X^* = X_0$, and assuming a competitive structure, $Z^* = Z_0$ (optimal outputs at time 0 equal actual outputs). Thus, maximum revenue is $\Sigma Z_{j0} P_{j0}$, the actual value of output in the reference period. This is point A in figure 5.2.

We now pose the question, What output combination would have been forthcoming had prices been $[P_t]$, all else remaining as before—that is, with input quantities $X^* = X_0$, and unchanged transformation function T (which together imply an unshifted production possibility frontier). Maximizing the revenue function of equation (9) with reference-period inputs and prices $[P_t]$ yields a new set of revenue-maximizing quantities, which we designate $[Z_t^*]$. These, of course, are not the quantities actually produced in period t, as both resource availability and technology may have changed between the two periods (i.e., we are interested in determining point C on figure 5.2, not point D).

The output price index J can be found as the ratio of

(10) $$J = \frac{R_t}{R_0} = \frac{\Sigma Z_t^* P_t}{\Sigma Z_0^* P_0},$$

where it is understood that both halves of the ratio are computed using equations (8) and (9). When input quantities are fixed for both computations at the original resource endowment (i.e., $X^* = X_0$), the result is the

Laspeyres-perspective output price index, which compares points A and C in figure 5.2. This index is designated J_L.

There are (at least) two interesting output price indexes. The J_L index takes the perspective of the initial situation, answering the question: What is the (maximum) value ratio, between reference and comparison periods, of collections of outputs that can be produced using the reference period's resource endowment? This Laspeyres-perspective output price index, J_L, is analogous to the I_L input-cost index of Section 5.3.1.

A Paasche-perspective theoretical output price index can also be defined. We refer to this as J_P. The J_P index takes the comparison-period resource endowment as relevant, so that actual levels of inputs in time t are specified ($X^* = X_t$), and the production relations (eq. [8]) are those prevailing at time t. It is therefore computed from equation (10) by letting Z^* in equation (9) be determined by the level of inputs available in time t, or X_t. For the J_P economic output price index, the ordinary fixed-weight Paasche price index is an approximation and *upper*bound (see Fisher and Shell 1972, Essay II).[18]

Comment. There is an interesting anomaly in the price index literature between the treatment of output price indexes, on the one hand, and input cost indexes and cost-of-living indexes, on the other. The theory of output indexes arose out of the need for international comparisons, and therefore its exposition has always proceeded from an economywide perspective rather than from that of an individual (multiproduct) firm. It is reasonable (though not strictly realistic) to specify that the economy has a fixed quantity of productive inputs; but a price index formulation based on the production possibility curve poses problems in applications where it seems inappropriate to assume fixed resource availability. An individual firm or a competitive industry faces, for example, not fixed amounts of inputs but rather fixed input prices. Fisher and Shell (1979) have worked on generalizing the traditional output price index theory to fit other situations.[19] This work is not developed far enough to be incorporated into this paper.

However, even if a more general theory can be worked out, it does not follow that the traditional approach is necessarily rendered obsolete. In some situations, it will still be meaningful to ask: How would the resources actually used in the reference period (or in the comparison period) have been allocated among the various outputs had relative output prices been different from those experienced at the time?

Summary and Conclusions to Section 5.4.1

This section has developed two theoretical output price indexes (J_L and J_P) and discussed the relation between these two indexes and the Laspeyres and Paasche (L and P) fixed-weight formulas. As in the input price index case, the economic indexes take account of substitution caused by changes in relative prices, as the fixed-weight indexes do not. However, the signs of substitution biases in L and P used as output price indexes are reversed, compared to the input price index case presented in Section 5.3.1.

All output price indexes hold constant the collection of productive inputs employed. We refer to this as the "constant-input" *criterion* for an output price measure. The theory of output price measures is thus symmetric with that of input price indexes, for the latter (as shown in Section 5.3.1) have a constant-output criterion.

When used as an output price index, the usual fixed-weight index (L or P) may be thought of as holding inputs constant through the device of holding base-period outputs constant. The superiority of the theoretical output price index arises from the fact that it holds inputs constant directly: it specifies a constant production possibility curve, and permits output combinations to shift along that curve rather than restricting the comparison to a single point on the production possibility curve. Again, this result is parallel to the input cost index, where the L and P indexes were thought of holding output constant by using fixed weights for inputs.

5.4.2 Modeling Quality Change:
The Concept of Output Characteristics

As was true for the input cost index, I incorporate quality change into output price indexes by transforming the theory into characteristics space. The present section serves to define the concept of "output characteristics" required for the theoretical work in Section 5.4.3.

The term "characteristics," when used in economics, has become strongly identified with *input* characteristics. The well-known work of Lancaster (1971), for example, argued that disaggregation of consumer goods into characteristics gave a better explanation of consumer behavior because characteristics, rather than goods, were the true inputs into the utility function. We noted in Section 5.3.2 that a similar interpretation could be given to the human capital literature—years of education, of experience, and of training can be treated as labor characteristics on the specification that these, rather than the number of labor hours, are the true inputs into the production function.

It does not seem to have been recognized that a similar disaggregation can be applied to output. Any production function (such as eq. [3]) relates a set of inputs to output (usually written as a scalar quantity). If output is not a homogeneous good, it may be useful in understanding production to disaggregate output into characteristics, treating the production process as creating a set of jointly produced outputs (the characteristics). One relevant theoretical precedent for this is Dano (1966).

The distinction between input characteristics and output characteristics requires elaboration. A variable is an input characteristic if it acts as an input in a production or utility function. Put another way, one selects input characteristics empirically according to whether they provide something that is wanted or is valued in use.

An output characteristic is different. In this case what matters is the producing industry's production function, not that of the using industry. Referring to the two-sector model of equations (1) and (2), an input characteristic of computers is something that contributes to the production of gadgets; an output characteristic of computers, on the other hand, is something that requires productive activity in the computer industry.

One can overload the distinction between input and output characteristics. Normally, an output is not produced unless someone wants it, so in most cases an output characteristic will also be an input characteristic. But that does not invalidate the conceptual distinction between them; and there are exceptions—sometimes things get produced that are not wanted by users.

The idea of an output characteristic can be defined by a process symmetric to the one used for input characteristics in Section 5.3.2.

a) The production of a nonhomogeneous good is considered as the *joint output of* a set of characteristics. That is, instead of defining output as quantities of goods, such as trucks or boxes of soap, we break these goods down into outputs of characteristics, such as "load-carrying capacity," "number of ounces in the box," and so forth.

In principle, treating an output as the joint production of a set of characteristics amounts to assuming a production process not materially different from other and better known joint production examples (such as beef and hides)—except that we assume that characteristics can be produced in variable proportions, at least over some ranges. As in the beef-hide case, there may be limits on the proportions in which characteristics can be produced—there may be some characteristic which from the technological view must be present in every output bundle. So even though we treat characteristics as if they were separate outputs, there may well be technical reasons why they are bundled together in the first place.

b) As in the input case, output characteristics are a finer level of aggregation than are goods, and goods, of course, are the units in which market transactions take place.

c) To define an output characteristic, suppose output is computers. Suppose further that the substitution of a model 490 computer for a model 390 causes changes in input usage (in the production function of eq. [2]) that are not explained by the count of numbers of machines produced. *Something is an output characteristic if it accounts for, or partly accounts for, the unexplained variation in resource usage occasioned by changes in the varieties of nonhomogeneous goods produced.*

This definition of an output characteristic says, in effect, that an output is something that uses resources. Indeed, that is the reason why the theory of production is concerned with the transformation of inputs into outputs. An output is not an output because someone wants it; being useful or desired is the definition of an input (compare the definition of an output characteristic with the input characteristic definition in Sec. 5.3.2).

d) We assume that only the quantity of characteristics matters in the production function and not how the output of characteristics is packaged into the output of goods. This assumption implies there are no "packaging size" economies or diseconomies associated with building larger quantities of characteristics into a single variety of an output good (an equivalent assumption was made on the input side in Sec. 5.3.2). It also rules out production complementarities between the "quality" of output goods (the amounts of characteristics they contain) and the quality of the inputs. Making more comfortable and longer wearing shoes is assumed to require more leather and more shoemaking labor, not different kinds of materials or more highly skilled shoemakers. The assumption is wholly a simplifying one, though it does eliminate interesting, relevant, and realistic cases.

5.4.3 Characteristics Output Price Indexes and the Treatment of Quality Change

This section proceeds in parallel with Section 5.3.3 to extend the "goods space" or conventional output price index theory to incorporate the idea of output characteristics. I first summarize results from Section 5.4.1 that are required for this section.

1. The theoretical output price index is constructed from the values of collections of outputs in two periods that represent maximum revenue points on the same production possibility frontier.

2. For any comparison, a number of output price indexes can be computed, depending on which production possibility frontier is used for the comparison; indexes based on production possibility frontiers appropriate to reference and comparison periods are designated, respectively, as "Laspeyres-perspective" and "Paasche-perspective" output price indexes (J_L and J_P).

3. The usual fixed-weight Laspeyres and Paasche index formulas (L and P) may be viewed as approximations to the true economic indexes. The Laspeyres index provides a lower bound to J_L, whereas the Paasche index is an upper bound to J_P (i.e., $L \leq J_L$ and $P \geq J_P$).

4. The bounding conditions in (3) are a reversal of the bounds for input cost indexes (as noted in Sec. 5.3.1, $L \geq I_L$ and $P \leq I_P$).

5. Computing an output price index, whether the theoretical index or the fixed-weight approximation, requires that resource use be held constant over the comparison in order to eliminate from the price measure shifts in the production possibility curve—the only unambiguous measure

of output change; this condition is referred to as the constant-input "criterion" for the output price index.

6. The output index criterion stated in (5) is a symmetric reversal of the criterion for the input cost index; the input cost index required a constant-output criterion (Sec. 5.3.1).

It remains to use the concept of output characteristics from Section 5.4.2 to extend the basic price index theory from goods space to characteristics space.

Assuming, for simplicity, that only one of the economy's outputs (eqq. 8 and 9, above) is nonhomogeneous, we treat that output as the joint output of a set of output characteristics. We can, without loss of generality, specify that the first good is the nonhomogeneous one, with r characteristics. Adopting the convention that a homogeneous good is itself a characteristic, the production transformation equation (8) is rewritten as

$$(8a) \qquad T(\omega_{11}, \ldots, \omega_{1r}, \omega_2, \ldots, \omega_m; X_i) = 0,$$

where $i = 1, \ldots, n$. This says that if the good "boxes of soap," for example, has output characteristics "size of box," a measure of "washing power per ounce," and some sort of packaging convenience element, then the economy's outputs are the quantities of these characteristics it produces and not the quantity "number of boxes of soap." Once these substitutions have been made, equation (8a) relates $m + r - 1$ attainable output characteristics (each ω) to the quantities of the available n inputs. Note that the definition of an "output characteristic" presented in Section 5.4.2 is implied by the construction of the production transformation function in characteristics space.[20]

A Characteristics-Space Index for Output Prices

The transformation of the goods output price index of Section 5.4.1 into an equivalent price measure in characteristics space is parallel to the development of the characteristics input cost index in the subsection "The Input-Cost Index in Characteristics Space" under Section 5.3.3.

Considering the output characteristics in the production transformation function (8a), a characteristics revenue function can be defined by modifying equation (9) to incorporate output characteristics. That is, the set of output characteristics is substituted for the nonhomogeneous output, Z_1. This function is written:

$$(9a) \qquad R = R(\omega^*, P).$$

The nature of the characteristics concept makes equation (9a) a complex one, because it must depict the maximum revenue obtainable from various combinations of characteristics. A similar difficulty has already been encountered in the discussion of the characteristics input-cost index and need not, therefore, be discussed a second time.

Any theoretical output price index is formed out of ratios of maximum revenues obtainable, under two price regimes, for collections of outputs located on the same production possibility curve.[21] What we will term the "theoretical characteristics output price index"[22] is formed by taking ratios of equation (9a) under two output price regimes, or

$$(10a) \qquad J = \frac{R_t}{R_0} = \frac{R(\omega^*, P_t)}{R(\omega^*, P_0)} .$$

In words, the characteristics-space output price index amounts to pricing points from the same production possibility curve, with the two points corresponding to optimal output mixes under two different price regimes; the major difference from the output price index for goods is that the production possibility curve and the revenue function are both defined on characteristics of goods rather than on the goods themselves.

To understand the interpretation of the output price index in the characteristics context, it may intuitively be helpful to examine the conventional Laspeyres-index formula, where (output) quantities provide the weighting structure.

To construct the Laspeyres output price index in characteristics space, the index is redefined in terms of characteristics rather than goods. The index weights in the conventional Laspeyres price index formula—equation (5)—are then reinterpreted to be quantities of characteristics rather than quantities of goods. Reverting to our soap example, there is an output weight for base-period production of "number of ounces," for the measure of "washing power," and for the "packaging convenience" element.

Several points need to be emphasized. First, as in the characteristics input cost index, the characteristics output price index has a form, derivation, and properties similar to the output price index for goods.

Second, in common with the goods output price index, the characteristics output price index must be computed for a given production possibility curve.[23] This means that the characteristics output price index is computed by holding the input dosage constant, because changes in quantities of productive inputs (as well as changes in the technology) mean a shift in the production possibility curve.

Third, as with the goods index, there may be more than one characteristics output price index. In effect, figure 5.2 still applies. We wish to decompose the change between outputs A and D into a change in output and a change in price, and there are (at least) two perspectives—that of A and that of D. The argument leads to Laspeyres-perspective (J_L) and Paasche-perspective (J_P) indexes and is the same as the one presented in

Section 5.4.1 for the goods output price index. The resulting two indexes, J_L and J_P, have as counterparts the I_L and I_P characteristics input cost indexes of the subsection on "The Input Cost Index in Characteristics Space" under Section 5.3.3 (pp. 281–82 above).

Quality Variation and Quality Adjustments
in Output Price Indexes

Much of the present paper involves a series of parallelisms between the output price index and input price index cases; crucial results are often reversed in the two cases. Both the parallelisms and the reversals are straightforward consequences of the relations between inputs and outputs in the theory of production. As the patterns have become familiar by now, the exposition of the characteristics output price index case can be shortened by noting that it amounts to a translation of the parallel discussion of the characteristics input cost index (in the second and third subsections under Sec. 5.3.3, pp. 283–87), but with the results transformed according to the framework of output price index theory.

As was true of the characteristics input cost index, the characteristics output price index may include a different machine in the numerator and denominator of the measure. The theoretical index always incorporates shifts (in this case in the output of characteristics) that occur in response to relative price changes. Therefore, if the relative revenue a seller receives from two characteristics changes, the producer has an incentive to change the proportions of those characteristics embodied in the machine it sells. In the ordinary view of things, this will take the form of a new "model"; if the "price" of speed has risen in relative terms and that of fuel economy has fallen, the new model may have more speed relative to its fuel economy. However, if the two machines correspond to revenue-maximizing sets of characteristics in comparison and reference periods, respectively, they are included in the numerator and denominator of the theoretical output price index. The reader is referred to the subsection "Quality Variation in the Characteristics Input Cost Index" under Section 5.3.3 for a comparable result for the input cost index case.

One could use figure 5.2 to illustrate the theoretical characteristics output price index by supposing that the axes of the figure correspond to characteristics ω (rather than to goods Z), with the production possibility curve and revenue lines similarly reinterpreted. Then points such as A and C are interpreted as two machines having different combinations of characteristics, but which can be produced with the same resources used in the reference period. Points such as A and D, on the other hand, represent machines using different quantities of resources. The reader is cautioned that this use of the figure is heuristic.

Thus, a constant-quality output price index can be thought of as an index based on two sets of characteristics (two machines) that lie on the same production possibility curve but correspond to maximum revenue points under two price regimes (the comparison and the reference periods).

If there is a change in output characteristics which, taken together, implies movement to a different production possibility curve (comparison of points such as C and D in fig. 5.2), some "quality adjustment" is called for in order to restore the constant-input criterion for an output price index. The adjustment required is equal to the value of the resources required to move the set of output characteristics included in the index back to the same production possibility curve. This is precisely the resource cost quality measurement rule that has been argued in the literature.

Note that, as in the input cost index case, there are two possible adjustments and that they correspond to the J_L and J_P forms of the output price index. One can adjust the new machine to correspond to a set of characteristics that could have been produced with the initial period's resource stocks and technology; this gives C-D in figure 5.2 as the appropriate quality adjustment, with the price index based on comparison of points A and C. Because this adjustment corresponds to the J_L form of the output price index in characteristics space, one could look at it as a "Laspeyres-perspective" quality adjustment. The appropriate quality adjustment for the J_P index, on the other hand, involves points E and A. This quality adjustment yields an output price index based on period t's resource utilization and technology, that is, a price index computed from comparison of points D and E.[24]

It may be useful, heuristically, to go through the quality adjustment process in terms of the familiar Laspeyres index. The traditional interpretation refers to this index as a formula for holding quantity weights constant in order to factor out price from quantity change in a value aggregate. Note the similarity of the following to a comparable line of reasoning in Section 5.3.3.

In the characteristics Laspeyres output price index, output characteristics quantities are the weights. Quality change is interpreted as a change in the quantity of characteristics embodied in a good, which means the quality change amounts to a change in the (output) weights in the characteristics Laspeyres index. Making a quality adjustment to the "goods" Laspeyres index can be interpreted as an adjustment which holds constant the weights in the "characteristics" Laspeyres output price index. Because in the output characteristics case, characteristics are resource using (on the argument pursued in Sec. 5.4.2), the adjustment to the Laspeyres output price index is, as in the case of the theoretical index, referenced by resource use.

Summary

In output price indexes (the fixed-weight forms as well as the theoretical ones based on production possibility curves), the quality adjustment required is equal to the resource usage of the characteristics that changed. Only with a resource-cost adjustment does the index price a set of outputs that can be produced with the resources available in the reference period (for the characteristics-space form of index J_L). Alternatively, only a resource-cost quality adjustment assures that the J_P form of the output price index prices a collection of outputs that could have been produced with comparison-period resources. This resource-cost adjustment is precisely the production-cost criterion for quality measurement advocated for price measures by such economists as Denison (1975) and Jaszi (1971).[25]

5.5 Using Characteristics-Space Theory to Resolve Quality Change Issues

Imbedding the analysis of quality change in the theory of index numbers proves a powerful tool for clearing up confusions found in the quality change literature. Two examples are addressed in this section.

5.5.1 "Costless" Quality Change

Adherents to the user-value view have often presumed that the resource cost method could not *in principle* deal with quality changes that increase performance but are cheaper to produce—the so-called costless quality change argument. This presumption, for example, underlies much of the discussion of output measures in the report of the Panel to Review Productivity Statistics (1979), and determines the report's conclusion that use of a resource-cost quality adjustment rule for output-price indexes is "not adequate for dealing with changes in quality that do not result from changes in cost" (the report cites improvements in computers as an example; see p. 8).

The discussion of costless quality change in the Panel's report (as elsewhere) was marred by confusion over what the resource-cost criterion really said and by considerable ambiguity about what was meant by the term "costless." We address the latter point first.

For simplicity (in order to permit the diagrammatic presentation of fig. 5.3), suppose computers have only one output characteristic (call it "computations") and are made from only one input (labor). Figure 5.3 graphs what is known in the production literature as a "factor requirements function," showing the minimum input requirements for, in this case, computers of different capacities. As figure 5.3 is drawn, in the initial period (requirements function F_1) minimum labor requirements per unit of computational capacity occur for computer size C_0; so we

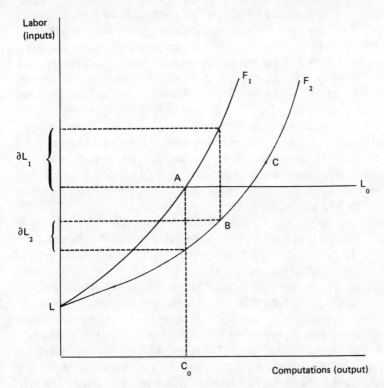

Fig. 5.3   Factor requirements function for the output characteristic "computations."

assume that in the initial period available computers cluster around size C_0.

If increments to computer capacity were really "costless" in the initial period, the factor requirements function would be horizontal beyond some point (such as the line LAL_0 in fig. 5.3). If this is what was meant by "costless" quality change, then the argument has a certain validity: a resource cost method would treat all computers lying on the horizontal segment of LAL_0 as equivalent and would indeed make no quality adjustments for expansions in computer capacity in this range.

However, it is doubtful that a horizontal factor-requirements schedule was the basis for the "costless" quality change discussion. Little of value is truly costless, and to my knowledge, functions such as LAL_0 have never been encountered empirically.

If not "costless" in this sense, how does one rationalize the frequent observation of technical improvements that cost less than what went before? For this empirical observation lies at the root of the "costless" discussion, and computers are a favorite example.

A better characterization of what its proponents must have meant by "costless" is to suppose a shift of the factor requirements function (corresponding to cost-reducing technical advances in producing computers), as in F_2 in figure 5.3. With minimum average labor requirements per computational unit now occurring at B, we may observe computer size B in the second period. Compared with machine A (produced only in the initial period), machine B in the second period requires fewer labor inputs to produce (thus it costs less), yet yields more computations. As a practical matter, if there are scale economies, or only a small number of computer varieties are marketed, something like this example may well show up in a comparison of different years' data. Without fully specifying it, parties to the costless quality change debate undoubtedly had comparison of points like A and B in mind.

There is no sense, however, in which the movement from A to B invalidates a resource-cost quality adjustment, despite frequent contrary assertions. In fact, there are *two* possible resource-cost adjustments. From the perspective of the initial period, function F_1 gives ∂L_1 as the real resource cost of the quality change. Alternatively, one could use F_2, giving ∂L_2 as the basis for making a quality adjustment.

Thus, the charge that a resource-cost criterion could not deal with "costless" quality change involved basic confusion between a shift in a schedule and a movement along it. The schedules involved are in characteristics space rather than goods space, and the insight which resolves the debate emerges from an explicit characteristics-space analysis. The resolution of the costless quality change issue is one example of the usefulness and power of the characteristics space analysis.

One or two additional points can be made about the computer example. Note that as drawn $\partial L_2 < \partial L_1$, which seems realistic: the incremental cost of "computations" is lower today than in the past. For this example, F_1 provides the appropriate adjustment for the "Laspeyres-perspective" output price index, J_L, of Section 5.4.3, F_2 is relevant for the sister J_P index. Thus, choice between the two is the classic index number problem.

The GNP deflators are Paasche-formula indexes (current period weights), making F_2 the relevant basis for adjustment. This implies a smaller quality adjustment (and a greater price increase) than if F_1 were used. Any empirical work using data from F_1 (or, alternatively, the average of F_1 and F_2) tends to overstate the quality correction to be applied to a Paasche-formula output price index. Empirical work on quality change in the deflators has ignored this distinction.

Although examples of "costless" quality change have nothing whatever to do with the feasibility or conceptual appropriateness of user-value and resource-cost alternatives for making quality adjustments, there is, to be sure, a practical problem facing index makers. Usually, neither requirements function is known. If any information is available at all, it may consist only of cost data for two points, such as A and B, or A and C, that lie on different functions. That is, there may be data on the cost of the old machine under the old technology and the cost of the new machine under the new technology, but no data at all on the cost of both under comparable technologies.

In this case, nothing can be done under the resource-cost criterion, for the necessary information is not available. Obviously, direct comparison of labor inputs for A and B adjusts the index in the wrong direction, whether by user-value or resource-cost criteria. And even though resource cost for A and C would go in the right direction, using this information as a quality adjustment also contains an error, for *either* quality adjustment criterion. However, this very serious practical difficulty has nothing whatever to do with the conceptual one of determining the theoretically appropriate basis for making the adjustment.

5.5.2   The Elimination of Productivity Change Objection

An objection frequently raised against the user-value criterion was cited in the report of the Panel to Review Productivity Statistics (1979, p. 13): "If capital is measured in terms of its output-producing capacity, the output capital ratio becomes an uninteresting statistic, since it will tend to show no change."

It is hard to see what is going on in this quotation if one remains in goods space.[26] However, moving into characteristics space makes it easy to show the Panel's statement to be wrong; it involves (as did the costless quality change matter) confusing a shift in a function with movements along it.

Consider the production function defined in equation (3a) from Section 5.3.3. In that case, inputs were defined as characteristics. Productivity change in a characteristics world is defined in the same way as it is in goods space—productivity change is a shift in the production function, in this case a shift in equation (3a). In the characteristics input cost index, quality change was defined by that same production function: changes in quantities of input characteristics embodied in input goods were counted as quality change. This means that a user-value measure of quality change represents a movement from one isoquant to another *along* the production function (3a).

Valuing quality change as movements along the using industry's production function (as the user-value criterion does) in no way precludes a production function shift—no more so than a production function shift is precluded by measuring inputs in any other way. Accordingly, productivity change (a production function shift) is not tautologically eliminated by employment of a user-value quality adjustment rule.

As with the "costless" issue discussed above, the element of validity in the "unchanged productivity" proposition arises when one has observations on but two points. If we only know inputs and outputs for two periods, *and do not know the production function*, then of course there is no way of partitioning the change between the contributions of increased characteristics (movement along a production function) and a shift in a production function. Attributing all the output change to input change would clearly eliminate measured productivity change. But that is not what the user-value criterion is about.

This section serves to show the power of characteristics-space analysis in resolving issues that have plagued the quality measurement literature for years. The technique will work profitably on other examples as well, but that can be done elsewhere.

5.6 Summary and Conclusions

The appropriate theoretical treatment of quality change has been an issue in economic measurement for years. There have long been two schools of thought.

The "user-value" approach looks at the output implications of quality change in some productive input; a machine is higher quality if it has higher productivity when used in producing something else. On the "resource-cost" view, the cost of making a machine is the proper basis for making quality adjustments, not the productivity of using machines to produce other goods.

The present paper resolves this old debate by noting (1) that there are two different uses of the data (input measures and output measures), (2) that it is well established in the index number literature that inputs and outputs imply different theoretical price index treatments, and (3) by showing that the difference in theoretical treatments carries over into the issue of adjusting for quality change.

Rather satisfying is the result that the two sides to the quality adjustment debate are both right, each for the purpose it (implicitly) had in mind—the "user-value" and "resource-cost" positions correspond to correct theoretical treatments of quality change for input-price indexes and output-price indexes, respectively. This "you are both right" resolution extends to prominent researchers on the subject as well as to positions taken by the major statistical agencies (the Bureau of Economic Analysis having taken, historically, the correct theoretical position for output measures, while the Bureau of Labor Statistics has historically taken different theoretical positions for input uses and for output uses of data—both, it turns out, correct for the uses specified).

The method of this paper is to extend the basic theories of input and output price indexes from goods space to characteristics space. That is, the usual theory (and the usual index computations) involve prices and quantities of goods; the extension redefines the variables of interest to be the costs and quantities of the *characteristics* of goods (and of labor services). The rationale for redefinition is the specification that "quality change" involves changes or rearrangements of the quantities of characteristics embodied in goods. Thus, rather than treating "quality change" as an ad hoc procedure outside the basic theory of index numbers (as has often been true in the past), the paper extends index number theory into the dimension in which empirical investigation has taken place.

The finding that there are two correct methods for making quality adjustments, not just one, fits in with other results for input and output price indexes. Much of the content of the theory of input cost indexes and output price indexes is parallel, except the results are, for the most part, essentially reversed. The "reversal" phenomenon is intuitively appealing, once it is understood that the perspectives of the two economic measurements are from opposite ends of the production process. The mirror-image view of production one gets from altering perspective from the input side to the output side is fundamental to the process of production itself.

The results of this paper preserve in characteristics space index number results that are well established for goods space. A "characteristics" *input* price index requires holding *output* constant, just as does a "goods" input price index; and a "characteristics" *output* price index, following in sequence the "goods" output price index, requires that the *resources* going into the productive process be held constant. These two conditions (constant output for input price indexes, constant inputs for output price indexes) were referred to in the body of the paper as index "criteria."

The conclusion that input price indexes require a user-value quality adjustment is a consequence of the requirement that input price indexes be based on a constant-output criterion. The result that output price indexes must use a resource-cost quality adjustment method flows from the fact that output price indexes are based on a constant-input criterion.

Having established that the theory requires different procedures for input and for output price measures, how much difference does the theory make for practical measurement? My answer is: For most cases, probably not a lot, but more for lack of data to implement the theoretical methods than for lack of relevance of the theory.

One would expect that in equilibrium the marginal cost of producing a quality change must approximate the incremental value of it to the user—otherwise a reallocation of resources would take place. Thus, real differences in the magnitude of the quality adjustments one gets from user-value and resource-cost adjustments presumably reflect shifts in functions, interference with competitive allocation, or wrong data. That does not mean, contrary to assertions made by some participants in the quality measurement debate, that working out the theoretical properties and appropriateness of the two quality adjustment systems is irrelevant.

There are two reasons for theoretical discussion of user-value and resource-cost adjustments. First, previous discussion of these issues has been so confused that it is worth trying to straighten it out.[27] Had it been realized that input measures and output measures call for different treatments of quality change, the past course of debate on this issue would have been far different. One might even have seen better decisions in statistical measurements. For this purpose, the index number theory contained in this paper is in no sense vitiated if empirically the numbers would come out about the same, provided quality change amounted to small movements around equilibrium points, curves were smooth, and we had all of the information necessary to make the theoretically correct adjustments in both input and output indexes.

Second, much of the data on quality change, taken at its face value, suggests that the world is not so neat as the theoretical model we have in our heads. It is of considerable importance to straighten out what the right model is in order to understand whether we are getting the wrong data, or whether the data that come to us are simply reflecting discontinuities, shifts, and other unfortunate attributes of the real world.

Ultimately, limitations on implementing the theory come from lack of data. Full implementation of the theoretical results requires, at minimum, estimation of production functions on characteristics for both supplying and using industries. What we have are, at most, fragmentary information about the outcomes. The practical reality is that in most actual situations there is not enough information to implement even one theoretically appropriate measure. We simply do not have the luxury of computing both measures and deciding on theoretical grounds which to choose. Nevertheless, it is still important to understand what should be done with the data if we were ever to get them.

Notes

1. The statement by Denison (1957) is still well worth reading and remains consistent with his later writings on the subject, incorporating as they do issues which have developed over the past two decades. See, e.g., his debate with Dale Jorgenson and Zvi Griliches (Denison 1972), and his article on pollution control and safety regulation expenditures (1979). The Bureau of Economic Analysis position is similar. See, for example, Jaszi's 1964 debate with Griliches.

2. They were also the first to deal with quality change in the context of input and output price indexes (see n. 25 below).

3. In a recent survey, Usher (1980) identified five uses for capital measures. Two of the five—"an argument in an investment function" and "use in the national accounts"—are those considered in this paper. An extension of the analysis in this paper to consideration of other uses for capital measures could lead to different concepts for quality measurement, so it should not be inferred that the alternatives considered here comprise all those that are

relevant in other contexts. See Christensen and Jorgenson (1973) for a development of measurement concepts of capital for different purposes.

4. This is not an innocuous step. It is well established in the economic theory of index numbers that deflation by the theoretically appropriate price index will not always produce the theoretically appropriate quantity index (see Pollak 1971).

5. The term "input cost index" has unfortunately also been used in a different way—an index of input prices computed *in lieu of* a measure of the price of output (wage rates and materials prices, e.g., as a proxy for a price index for new houses). That has nothing to do with the measure discussed in the present paper.

6. There could be many input cost indexes, for the isoquant one might like to use for comparisons is not limited to those corresponding to actual outputs in reference or comparison periods. E.g., one might compare input price change between 1979 and 1980 in terms of 1972 production levels (1972 being the last Census of Manufactures). This point is made for the consumption case in Pollak (1971).

7. For an empirical estimate of the size of the bias in a fixed-weight index relative to a true input price index (of consumption), see Braithwait (1980).

8. An analogous set of cost-of-living indexes exists for consumption measures; see Pollak (1971). The two alternative versions of the cost-of-living index correspond to the alternative decompositions of income and substitution effects in the standard theory of consumption.

9. In some forms, these aggregator functions are very restrictive assumptions, which, moreover, have mainly computational convenience (such as reducing the number of coefficients to be estimated in a multifactor production function) to recommend them. Others are simply not relevant for present purposes. I would interpret, e.g., a "production function for trucking services" as having something to do with subindexes (see Pollak 1975, or Blackorby and Russell 1978). One never needs to form subindexes in order to compute the aggregate index, and the latter is the primary concern of the present paper.

10. Klevmarken (1977) and Pollak (1979) have also discussed input price indexes defined in characteristics space. Both were concerned with the cost-of-living index (see also Diewert 1980). The approach in this section follows a similar methodology but was conceived independently. To my knowledge, the first suggestion that the analysis of quality change in index numbers would take the form of redefining the price index in characteristics space appears in Triplett (1971*b*).

11. The reader is reminded of simplifying assumption (*d*) in Section 5.2.2.

12. The example could be justified technically if it were possible to form a subindex on just the two characteristics, but the two-dimensional representation on figure 5.1 is intended to be heuristic. The full set of inputs in eq. (3a) yields a multidimensional production surface rather than an isoquant, but the argument is similar.

13. Production function equivalence, or equivalence with respect to other inputs in the cost function, was the quality definition introduced in Section 5.3.2. That definition was derived from and motivated by the characteristics input cost index analysis of the present section.

14. For small quality changes around point *A*, two machines whose characteristics lie on the same production isoquant will also have approximately the same selling price. Thus, the conventional view can be supported for small changes in the neighborhood of equilibrium.

15. Much of the quality literature is written as if the problem is to figure out what the price of a new (or old) machine would have been had it in fact been available. A change in the number and types of machines available would cause changes in relative prices of the varieties that were available, so one cannot use data on the varieties that were in fact available to infer anything about the price schedules that might exist under some other conditions. It seems better to avoid general equilibrium problems by assuming that the task of quality adjustment involves only the more limited problem of estimating the price of a variety that was offered on the market somewhere, but whose price was not collected by the

agency that was responsible for producing the indexes. I owe this distinction to Robert Gillingham.

16. In effect, this amounts to assuming that the new machine embodies simply a rearrangement or "repackaging" of characteristics previously available (the "repackaging" term stems from Fisher and Shell [1972]). If the new machine has a truly new characteristic, not available anywhere before, the method of analysis breaks down. If the characteristic is truly new, we are facing the intractable new product problem. A standard proposal for dealing with new products in the goods index literature is to use the demand reservation price (the lowest price at which none will be demanded) for periods in which the product does not exist. One could apply the same solution to truly new characteristics. Fortunately, it seems reasonable to assert that most new products do not involve characteristics that have never before existed. Burstein (1961) gives a persuasive argument that innovation in delivery and distribution methods is far more pervasive than provision of truly new characteristics (Burstein observed that television was just a new method for distributing ball games and vaudeville shows).

17. Note the caveat on forming quantity measures by deflation in n. 4.

18. Of course, these two are not the only possible relevant indexes since for some purposes some other basis for evaluation may be appropriate (a comparison of 1929 and 1969 prices using 1950 resources and production technology). See also n. 6.

19. An earlier attempt is an article by Archibald (1977) who follows a different course from the rest of the literature. Starting from the observation that the firm's goal is profit maximization, rather than optimization with respect to outputs and inputs themselves, Archibald constructs what he calls a "price index for profit"—defined as the ratio of the profit function under two price regimes. The usefulness of this "price index for profit" is not readily apparent, partly for reasons Archibald himself notes, as well as other considerations (it cannot be defined when profits are zero or negative, for instance). Nevertheless, Archibald derives the output price index as a "subindex" (Pollak 1975) of the price index for profit.

The notion of deriving a useful index (the output price index) as a component of a concept which itself may not be useful is not a very appealing procedure. Moreover, one can question the appropriateness of basing the theory on the firm's profit function. It is indisputable that the competitive firm maximizes profit and does not maximize revenue for its own sake. But the appropriate way to set up price index theory is determined by the questions one wants the index to address, and not necessarily by the nature of the optimization problem the economic unit is trying to solve. In any event, Archibald's output index section, standing on its own, largely duplicates Fisher and Shell (1972).

20. In Section 5.4.2 an "output characteristic" was defined as an attribute of a good that was *resource using* (as distinguished from an input characteristic, an attribute valued by the user). Eq. (8a) determines a production possibility curve in characteristics space; the information contained in a production possibility curve concerns output combinations that can be produced from a stock of inputs. Thus, if there existed a characteristic which was not resource using, increasing or decreasing its quantity would have no implications for the other outputs that can be produced. Accordingly, a characteristic which uses no resources has no role in eq. (8a), even if it were desired by users (color is perhaps an example).

21. But see the "Comment" on p. 292, above.

22. Terminology is made difficult by the extra complication of eq. (9a) over eq. (9): The revenue received from sale of a good is simply its price, but the values of characteristics are in general not fixed quantities (as we normally think of prices) but are themselves variables, which may depend on the quantities of characteristics embodied in output goods. Thus, it might have been more precise to speak of an "output value index" instead of an output price index (in parallel with the input cost index terminology of Section 5.3). This terminology was rejected as cumbersome, as it lacks precedent in either the theoretical or pragmatic index number literature. As already noted, Fisher and Shell (1972) use the terminology "true output deflator."

23. Again reference is made to the caveat expressed in the "Comment" on p. 292.

24. This distinction between reference-period and comparison-period resource-cost quality adjustments is elaborated upon in Sec. 5.5 below.

25. Fisher and Shell (1972) provide the only other theoretical discussion of quality change in the explicit context of input price indexes and output price indexes. Fisher-Shell's analytic method for incorporating quality change into price index theory is different from my own. They consider kinds of quality change that can be represented as a parameter shifting (as the case may require) a production, utility or transformation function defined on goods. Moving the analysis into characteristics space, as I do, may be considered a more explicit representation of one form of Fisher-Shell "parametrizable" quality change, a technique which is more powerful in the sense that it can be brought to bear on specific problems, yielding more explicit index number results than they were able to extract. The cost of so doing, it must be admitted, is the move into the intrinsically difficult characteristics-space notion, with all the problems that involves. Whichever method is advantageous for a particular case, the results of both agree. Speaking of quality change in output price indexes, Fisher-Shell write (1972, p. 106): "If more steel, labor, and other inputs are embodied in new cars than in old ones, then the production of a given number of cars represents a bigger output when new cars are involved than when old ones are. Moreover, this is true regardless of how consumers view the change." Thus, an output index requires a resource-cost quality adjustment rule.

26. Indeed, Fisher and Shell (1972), working in goods space, find quality and technical change indistinguishable.

27. One could note in this regard that the Panel to Review Productivity Statistics endorsed, though not without qualification, a user-value quality adjustment rule in its chapter on output, but a resource-cost criterion in its chapter on capital inputs—just the opposite from the theoretically correct output and input price index adjustments.

References

Archibald, Robert B. 1977. On the theory of industrial price measurement: output price indexes. *Annals of Economic and Social Measurement* 6 (Winter): 57–72.

Blackorby, Charles, and Russell, R. Robert. 1978. Indices and subindices of the cost of living and the standard of living. *International Economic Review* 19 (February): 229–40.

Braithwait, Steven D. 1980. The substitution bias of the Laspeyres price index: an analysis using estimated cost-of-living indexes. *American Economic Review* 70 (March): 64–77.

Burstein, M. L. 1961. Measurement of quality changes in consumer durables. *Manchester School of Economic and Social Studies* 29 (September): 267–79.

Christensen, Laurits R., and Jorgenson, Dale W. 1973. Measuring economic performance in the private sector. In Milton Moss, ed., *Measurement of economic and social performance*. NBER Conference on Research in Income and Wealth. Studies in Income and Wealth, vol. 38. New York: National Bureau of Economic Research.

Dano, Sven. 1966. *Industrial production models*. New York: Springer-Verlag, Inc.

Denison, Edward. 1957. Theoretical aspects of quality change, capital consumption, and net capital formation. In *Problems of capital formation: concepts, measurement and controlling factors*, pp. 215–26. NBER Conference on Research in Income and Wealth. Studies in Income and Wealth, vol. 19. Princeton, N.J.: Princeton University Press.

———. 1972. Some major issues in productivity analysis: an examination of estimates by Jorgenson and Griliches. *Survey of Current Business* 52 (May, pt. II): 37–63.

———. 1979. Pollution abatement programs: estimates of their effect upon output per unit of input, 1975–78. *Survey of Current Business* 59 (August, pt. I): 58–63.

Diewert, W. E. 1980. Aggregation problems in the measurement of capital. In Dan Usher, ed., *The measurement of capital*, pp. 433–528. NBER Conference on Research in Income and Wealth. Studies in Income and Wealth, vol. 45. Chicago: University of Chicago Press.

Early, John. 1978. Improving the measurement of producer price change. *Monthly Labor Review* 101 (April): 7–15.

Fisher, Franklin M., and Shell, Karl. 1972. *The economic theory of price indices*. New York: Academic Press.

Griliches, Zvi. 1964. Notes on the measurement of price and quality change. In *Models of income determination*, pp. 381–404 and 414–18. NBER Conference on Research in Income and Wealth. Studies in Income and Wealth, vol. 28. Princeton, N.J.: Princeton University Press.

Jaszi, George. 1964. Comment. In *Models of income determination*, pp. 404–9. NBER Conference on Research in Income and Wealth. Studies in Income and Wealth, vol. 28. Princeton, N.J.: Princeton University Press.

———. 1971. An economic accountant's ledger. *Survey of Current Business* 51 (July): 183–227.

Klevmarken, Anders N. 1977. A note on new goods and quality change in the cost of living index in view of Lancaster's model of consumer behavior. *Econometrica* 45: 163–73.

Lancaster, Kelvin. 1971. *Consumer demand: a new approach*. Columbia Studies in Economics 5. New York: Columbia University Press.

Liviatan, Nissan, and Patinkin, Don. 1961. On the economic theory of price indexes. *Economic Development and Cultural Change* 9 (April): 502–36.

Moorsteen, Richard H. 1961. On measuring productive potential and relative efficiency. *Quarterly Journal of Economics* 75 (August): 451–67.

Ohta, Makoto, and Griliches, Zvi. 1976. Automobile prices revisited: extensions of the hedonic hypothesis. In Nestor E. Terleckyj, ed., *Household production and consumption*, pp. 325–90. NBER Conference on Research in Income and Wealth. Studies in Income and Wealth, vol. 40. New York: Columbia University Press.

Panel to Review Productivity Statistics. 1979. *Measurement and interpretation of productivity*. Washington, D.C.: National Academy of Sciences.

Pollak, Robert A. 1971. The theory of the cost of living index. Bureau of Labor Statistics, U.S. Department of Labor, BLS Working Paper no. 11.

————. February 1975. Subindexes of the cost of living. *International Economic Review* (February): 135–50.

————. 1979. The treatment of quality in the cost of living index. University of Pennsylvania, Center for Analytic Research in Economics and the Social Sciences, CARESS Working Paper no. 79-03.

Samuelson, Paul A., and Swamy, S. 1974. Invariant economic index numbers and canonical duality: survey and synthesis. *American Economic Review* 64 (September): 566–93.

Trajtenberg, Manuel 1979. Quality is all very well but two fiddles don't make a Stradivarius. Falk Institute discussion paper.

Triplett, Jack E. 1971*a*. Quality bias in price indexes and new methods of quality measurement. In Zvi Griliches, ed., *Price indexes and quality change*, chap. 6. Cambridge, Mass.: Harvard University Press.

————. 1971*b*. *The theory of hedonic quality measurement and its use in price indexes*. BLS Staff Paper no. 6. Washington, D.C.: Department of Labor, Bureau of Labor Statistics.

————. 1973. Review of *Consumer demand: a new approach*, by Kelvin Lancaster. *Journal of Economic Literature* 10 (March): 77–81.

————. 1976. Consumer demand and characteristics of consumption goods. In Nestor E. Terleckyj, ed., *Household production and consumption*, pp. 305–24. NBER Conference on Research in Income and Wealth. Studies in Income and Wealth, vol. 40. New York: Columbia University Press.

————. 1980. Producer and consumer constraints in characteristics space. Paper presented at the annual meetings of the American Economic Association at Denver (September).

Usher, Dan. 1980. Introduction. In Dan Usher, ed., *The measurement of capital*. NBER Conference on Research in Income and Wealth. Studies in Income and Wealth, vol. 45. Chicago: University of Chicago Press.

6   Round Table of GNP Users

The round table session on the national accounts, chaired by Stanley J. Sigel, was designed to elicit views from prominent users of the accounts. Each of the panelists submitted in advance a very short written statement, all of which are reproduced here. A discussion then followed, first among the panelists and then by members of the audience. Only some of the comments from the audience appear in the volume.

Statements

Introductory Statement
Edward F. Denison

Murray Foss asked me to remain on this panel of users of the national income and product accounts even though I have moved from the Brookings Institution to the fount of the estimates. I agreed to participate, but I shall speak in my previous capacity as an outsider who uses NIPA data in economic analysis.

Because my chief concern has been studying long-term economic growth, my main interest has been in the annual series that the Bureau of Economic Analysis (BEA) publishes each July rather than with current, more summarized, quarterly and monthly estimates. The interests of

Edward F. Denison is with The Brookings Institution.
Written statements by Edward F. Denison, Otto Eckstein, Alan Greenspan, Lawrence Klein, Arthur M. Okun. Eckstein was unable to be present but submitted a statement. Discussion participants: among panelists—Edward F. Denison, Alan Greenspan, Lawrence Klein; from the floor—V. Lewis Bassie, Robert Eisner, Saul Hymans.

users in my category tend to be overlooked. At one stage of the Creamer Committee deliberations, it was even suggested that what were called the July "revisions" be skipped in alternate years. People seem to forget that most of the data that analysts like me require is first published in the July *Survey of Current Business*. The initial charge to the Creamer Committee overemphasized the timing and accuracy of the earliest quarterly estimates, but fortunately the report ended up with recommendations that were well balanced as among quarterly, annual, and benchmark data.

I have used NIPA data in four growth-accounting studies, scattered from 1961 to the present. Perhaps the most visible improvement in data for this use has been in the measurement of fixed capital. The improvement helped both my measure of ouput—the national income—and measures of capital input. In 1961, BEA's current dollar national income series was not usable without adjustment because business incomes were based on the depreciation charged on tax returns or calculated by BEA with original cost valuation. BEA had no series then for constant-dollar national income or for the capital stock. I therefore had to turn to outside sources for estimates of economic depreciation in current and constant prices, and of the capital stock. By my second study, around 1965, BEA's capital stock project was providing data for depreciation and capital stock in current and constant dollars that were consistent with the NIPAs. BEA was not itself using these data to measure national income, but it was easy for the user to do so. The situation was formally unchanged at the time of my third study, about 1971, but the capital stock estimates had been improved. One procedural change, introduction of the Winfrey S-3 distribution of retirements, significantly bettered the gross stock series. By my latest study, around 1978, economic depreciation had been incorporated into the NIPAs. National income in current and constant prices can now be taken directly from the NIPAs. The capital stock data had also been further improved. I suspect that they are now about as good as they can be made until new data sources, such as surveys of service lives, are developed.

Isolation of a separate housing sector in the latest NIPA revision was another change helpful in analyzing capital's role in growth. Since my second study, I have measured the contribution of residential capital to growth of output directly by finding out how much output the NIPA estimates include for the services of housing. Formerly, this required tracking through several BEA worksheets. With the new format, it can be done easily from published data.

Of the many other changes in the NIPAs over the same time span, most were improvements that provided more information or more reliable information. However, in statistics all is not onward and upward. Agencies upon which BEA relies for data have suffered from falling response rates to voluntary surveys. Tabulations of corporate tax returns were shifted from complete count to sampling, and then the sampling ratios were reduced. New complexities in the tax laws have also introduced new problems.

Analysts of long-term growth and structural change have been needlessly plagued by incessant tinkering with the Standard Industrial Classification (SIC). So have the agencies that collect data or, like BEA, process them. No one would complain if all changes made had truly been required by real developments in the economy—although even then one might have expected comparability to be maintained at the most detailed level feasible, whether that is industry divisions, two-digit industries, or whatever. But I have been convinced for 35 years that the reasons for *most* changes in the SIC have ranged from marginal to frivolous, and that their effect is wholly mischievous from the standpoint of economic analysis. Assemble 10 people to develop a SIC for an industry division and they will come up with one classification. Assemble any other 10 people and they will propose a different classification. Reassemble either group a few years later and they will arrive at a third classification. The practice of reviewing the SIC periodically assures periodic changes having nothing to do with changes in the economy. Each new version of the SIC hampers time series analysis, the principal analytical tool open to economists. In addition, it requires agencies collecting data to spend large sums to reclassify respondents, money that could better be devoted to data improvement.

BEA has devoted much effort over the years to adjusting data by industry to obtain time series covering long periods. In the last NIPA Supplement, BEA managed to get by with two classifications, one covering 1929–47, the other 1948–74. (Within these periods the series obviously would have been more accurate if the basic data had been collected in accordance with a stable classification.) Now the 1972 SIC has made it impossible to continue the 1948–74 classification. Data now are on a new classification, with estimates starting only in 1973 so that time series against which to appraise current developments are available for only a very few years. Nor is this the end. The *Statistical Reporter* informs its readers of plans for still another round of SIC revisions. Why users of economic statistics do not rebel is beyond my understanding.

Let me conclude by affirming my impression, based on use of NIPA data in growth accounting, that BEA was doing an excellent job within the limits of the possible. But much remains to be done.

The NIPA Accounts: A User's View
Otto Eckstein

The national income and product accounts are the central statistical construct of the U.S. economy. While there are other important statisti-

Otto Eckstein is chairman of Data Resources, Inc., and Paul M. Warburg Professor of Economics at Harvard University.

cal systems such as the indexes of production, flow-of-funds accounts, and the input-output tables, most short- and long-run economic analyses use NIPA as the organizing framework. The United States is blessed that she possesses an elaborate and thoughtful system of accounts and that imagination and high intelligence continue to be applied to its development.

NIPA has many purposes: to gauge economic performance, compare economic welfare over time and across countries, measure the mix of resource use between the private and public sectors and between consumption and investment, and to identify the functional distribution of income and of the tax burden. Inevitably, these purposes clash and the accounts must be a compromise.

As the builder and user of a large econometric model, my needs are narrow, and I would like to see a particular emphasis in the accounts hardly likely to be shared by everyone. Since it is the purpose of this panel to identify the desires of a small sample of users, let me plead my case.

The National Income and Product Accounts as Information

To the econometrician forecaster, all time series, whether in NIPA or elsewhere, are simply information, grist for establishing historical relations that have predictive value in the future: it is information content which matters. Is the series based on reliable reporting systems in the economic units? Is it intrinsic to their operations? Is the underlying information audited by accountants to assure compliance with an accepted and recognizable body of reporting principles? Is it a survey, filled out because the respondent is under a legal obligation or cannot say no to an interviewer? Is the series an imputation, constructed by statisticians to fill a gap in coverage, designed for conceptual completeness or as a "correction" for some immeasurable effect?

There have always been some major series in the accounts which had little information content. The inventory valuation adjustment is a primitive calculation, fortunately with a known recipe, which can only bear a loose relationship to the concept it seeks to measure. The rent imputed on owned dwellings also has an ancient history. But in recent years the "conceptual" series have been proliferating, and there is steady pressure to add more of them. For example, the capital consumption adjustment to approximate replacement cost accounting has loosened considerably the relationship between the circular flow of income and observable information. When the SEC required the accounting profession to develop corresponding concepts to be included in the exhibits of annual reports of public companies, the initial experience was poor, and financial analysts feel that the initial figures that are being produced are of little value.

There is much interest in correcting the GNP for environmental factors, which could lead to a further injection of unmeasured series that would identify, at least as a first approximation, the magnitudes of such effects. But I would urge BEA to adopt as one of its main guiding principles that it include nothing in the national income and product accounts which cannot be measured.

The Role of Estimation

Even within the more traditional areas of the accounts, I would urge BEA to do less estimating and more measuring. The areas that are information intensive provide much of the variation of the data. Many areas of the accounts have a weak information base and consequently are estimated to move rather gently. As a result, the volatile components of the GNP are diluted and the information content dissipated in a picture of the economy which is smoother and more regular than the reality.

At times, I have been tempted to build an econometric model out of the primary data that feed into the national income and product accounts, to link retail sales to payroll employment, plant and equipment to publicly reported returns, sales surveys, and capital costs, and measures of markets and output derived from industrial data. But even with its limitations, the NIPA data set adds so much through its logic, consistency, and data interpretation that it is still preferable to use it as the organizing principle of the analysis.

In summary, then, let me engage in some special pleading for information content rather than conceptual or theoretical neatness, and for the adoption of the principle that the NIPAs shall add nothing which cannot be measured. But win or lose, the econometric models will continue to stand on the firm foundation of the accounts as they are produced by BEA, and we will do well to work toward the same kind of solidity in the models as we find in the base on which they stand.

Weekly GNP
Alan Greenspan

I should like to use my opening remarks to recount a particular episode in which the GNP accounts, both in concept and in detail, became a critical issue in the formulation and, eventually, the implementation of economic policy.

In the fall of 1974, as you may recall, the bottom seemed to be dropping out of the economy. New orders were slipping, production began to fall rapidly, and unemployment started to increase in discontinuous jumps. That the economy was heading into a recession (if it were not, in fact, already in one) didn't require much debate. The key question for economic policy at the time was whether we were looking at an inventory recession, which meant a sharp but temporary erosion in production and

Alan Greenspan is with Townsend-Greenspan & Co., Inc., New York.

employment, or a far more dangerous, final demand-oriented weakening in the economy.

As 1974 drew to a close, retail sales and home building were soft, and much of what we consider final demand was slipping, as was inventory investment. By Christmas 1974, the question of whether we were facing a sharp, but temporary, decline, or whether something far more profound was confronting us, was an up front issue for the president. An answer had to be formulated as quickly as feasible. The types of economic policy initiatives that one should employ depended on the answer. For a short-term inventory recession, the optimum policy was to do as little as possible and let the natural forces of the economy bring the recession to a halt. If it looked as though the bottom were falling out of final demand, much more drastic policy options would have to be confronted.

We don't have, as you well know, even a monthly GNP series, but I submit that, starting in December 1974, we had what amounted to a weekly GNP. It may not have passed the rigid statistical standards of the BEA, but it was more than adequate—in fact quite instrumental—in answering the question of whether we had an inventory recession, or a final demand recession, or both.

While the Department of Commerce has since abandoned its presumably poor weekly retail sales series, it nonetheless did yeoman service during that period in indicating that personal consumption expenditures was not undergoing a downward plunge. Trade sources coupled with the latest data on building permits, and housing starts outlined the residential sector on a weekly basis. The plant and equipment survey and some monthly machinery shipment data were a crude proxy for producer's durable equipment.

From the insured unemployment system we were able to get a rough indicator of aggregate work hours, which with a guess at output per workhour yielded total real GNP.

Putting all of these unquestionably "exact" statistics together indicated something which we knew for a fact only much later; that the rate of inventory liquidation, that is, the gap between GNP and final demand, was exceptionally large by historic standards and was unlikely to get wider in the period immediately ahead. Therefore, if final demand continued to stabilize, as apparently it was doing in the early weeks of 1975, the recession's low point was close at hand and a marked recovery from it was a statistical necessity. It soon became clear from the insured unemployment data and several qualitative indicators that the worst was over.

At that point we could conclude that the administration's rather moderate tax-cut proposal was adequate, and further expansionary measures would, in the long run, turn out to be counterproductive. Short-term emergency GNP monitoring was no longer necessary, and the short history of the weekly GNP came to a creditable end.

What I believe this episode demonstrates is that, while our underlying GNP data system is less than perfect, it nonetheless sets a structure for understanding what is happening in the economy at any particular point in time, which considerably facilitates our capacity to make current evaluations and short-term forecasts. Without the existence of third-quarter 1974 detailed data and some rough cuts of the fourth quarter, the weekly GNP system would not have been possible for the weeks immediately preceding, and following, Christmas of 1974.

NIPA Statistics: A User's View
Lawrence Klein

I am going to approach this problem from the point of view of a model builder. We would say, "Count your blessings." We are pleased with the numbers, but there is no point in telling this group how great they are.

I prepared a kind of wish list or Christmas list of things we would like to have that follows these remarks. It is very much like trying to find out what present to get for the person who has everything.

There are three kinds of issues in this list that I would like to focus on. One set of issues deals with a more complete reconciliation and integrated publication of national income and product accounts, input-output accounts, and the flow-of-funds accounts. For that purpose I have sketched out a set of boxes (fig. 6.1). This is very important in the kind of model building we do in the Wharton group, particularly for medium- to long-term modeling. We actually do integrate an input-output system of intermediate flows, which is the center square, and a rectangular flap at one side, which is the GNP, delineated in columns with the deliveries from each of the producing sectors to that final demand category. And then the rectangular flap at the bottom is the value added or the national income by sector. Each column of that array would give intermediate and value added inputs in terms of product originating, and each row would give intermediate and final delivery output adding up to gross output in terms of delivery. We make use of this very intensively and particularly in terms of the things that were discussed at the previous session dealing with the vast changes in oil prices, the vast changes in exchange rates associated with the floating rate system, and other kinds of relative price adjustments in the economy. We find there is a need for making a very close monitoring of the shifting of the production process through time. The initial goal, of course, is to have such an integrated system of technical and expenditure and income accounts on an infrequent basis, maybe once or twice a decade. But we would really like to see this on an annual basis. In fact, we are in the position of trying to interpolate such

Lawrence Klein is professor of economics, University of Pennsylvania.

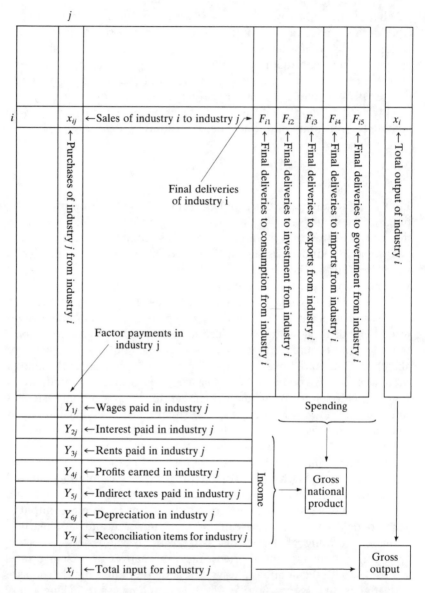

Fig. 6.1   Relationship between interindustry transactions, final demand, and factor payments.

annual estimates, in large measure using economic theory, trying to estimate, by some surrogates of elasticities of substitution, the way in which the input-output table would move through time and also the way in which the industrial composition of the GNP or the value added would move through time. I find that very important in trying to introduce the concept of more supply side modeling into our system. I think that our models are terribly deficient in this respect, and this is one of the central things that we must push for.

In a similar way, with these kinds of diagrams or accounting statistics for things like national balance sheets and the NIPA statements, one would want an integration between the flow-of-funds accounts and the national income accounts. I take the view that we would know as much as we want to know about the economic functioning of our system if we could put those three accounts (NIPA, input-output, flow of funds) together, and, indeed, if one were building up an accounting system for a large-scale enterprise we would want a sources-and-uses statement, an income statement, an operating statement (physical operations), and a balance sheet. Then we would know as much as is needed to be known about the financial and physical operations of that enterprise. We would like to do the same for the nation. I think that this has high priority and is, perhaps, one instance where other countries are ahead of us in terms of more frequent updating of input-output tables with better integration of these accounts. I think we should move very much in that direction.

One of the items on my wish list, of course, is more frequent publication of the national income accounts. That really follows directly on what Alan Greenspan had to say about weekly and monthly GNP. Being a big user of the personal income by months, then the wish list says, Couldn't we have a broader or more comprehensive set of measures at more frequent intervals?

In a vein similar to the integration of the input-output, flow of funds, and the national income accounts would be regional integration of accounts. That would be an essential item in the concept of trying to model the nation or the country by the summation of regional models, which is a challenging exercise that I and some of my associates are engaged in at the moment. In order to complete that we are lacking two fundamental sources of information. (1) Interregional trade on the same kind of basis as we have for international trade. This is naturally a thorny problem, a messy problem, a lack-of-data problem, but it does seem to be one that has high priority. (2) The other issue is the allocation of corporate profits by region. I feel those two things are the two biggest stumbling blocks to putting together a consistent set of regional accounts that add up to the national accounts. Now what do we do? In fact, in our approach to regional modeling, we finesse the problem by building systems that don't make use of the interregional flows or that don't make use of the regional allocations of corporate profits. But, to use the econometric lingo, we derive reduced forms and use all other kinds of techniques to avoid the issue, although we don't face up to the issue. That certainly would be an area for which we need much better accounting information and a direction in which the national income accounting activities ought to move.

A great deal of model building activity that I am engaged in at the moment deals with international model building for the world, as a whole, treating America as a component of a world system. In that respect, the most serious issue is developing appropriate price data for valuing exports and imports. Naturally, I am aware and appreciate the attempts to move from overall unit value indexes for exports and imports to genuine price indexes. But I find that an appropriate kind of modeling at the detailed level requires looking at types of exports and imports, in particular, by Standard International Trade Classification (SITC) categories. That may be somewhat arbitrary, but it is a very convenient one and the one that has widest international usage at the moment. For that, many surrogates are used. Foreign wholesale prices properly marked up for duty and exchange rate are used as our estimates of price indexes of American imports. Quotations on world markets for basic commodities are used in order to find some of our import prices by SITC category. Of course, whenever we are engaged in model building we always want a long history of these. We want to recover the last 20 or 30 years. This may be overcome to the extent that in the last year or two one finds a shift to proper indexes by the Bureau of Labor Statistics. But then the individual researcher is forced to extend the series back in order to establish the basic relationships. It seems to me that a genuine set of price indexes for imports and exports by fairly refined classes is needed. I think that this country should follow the German practice of publishing these indexes in detail. Now we are forced to use a large number of surrogates in order to deal with that kind of issue.

Finally, I would like to close this talk about the wish list to argue that we are living in a more interdependent, international world. It seems to me that it would be more useful if thinking in this country could be shifted to analysis of the GDP instead of the GNP, so as to be more in line with international comparisons. Not that we don't publish it, but that it's not our central focus of interest, and I think it ought to be. It ought to be so in an era where oil earnings on the international market are so vast that it makes a big difference on occasion.

At the same time, we should try to become more uniform in our breaking down of government spending into a current account and capital account, because in studying fiscal and other kinds of policies across countries it is quite important to separate out public spending in those two categories.

Year by year, benchmark by benchmark, the NIPA accounts improve both from the viewpoint of the general user and the professional. My comments have focused on what I perceive to be the needs of the econometrician, who will never be completely satisfied despite the steady progress that is being made.

Standard issues of concern:

1. Statistical discrepancies—their size, their instability, their allocation.

2. Valuation adjustments—depreciation and inventory change.

3. Measurement of capital stock.

4. Government spending—separation into current and capital account, especially to study more carefully government capital formation and output originating in the public sector.

5. More complete reconciliation and integrated publication of national income and product accounts (NIPA), input-output accounts (I-O), and flow-of-funds accounts (F/F).

6. More frequent compilation of I-O accounts.

7. More frequent publication of main aggregates in NIPA accounts—monthly and weekly data for deeper monitoring of business conditions.

8. Reconsideration of estimation of *potential* output.

9. Further analysis of net economic welfare (NEW)—elaborating the approach of Tobin and Nordhaus.

The BEA should be congratulated for paying more attention to systematic reporting of revision changes and estimated amounts for the preliminary releases. Continued expansion of information relating to errors in the data is a splendid activity.

International aspects: the world *is* becoming more interdependent, and the international economic position of the United States should be more carefully reported. Relevant issues for the NIPA accounts, in this respect, are:

1. Our basic measure of gross output should be GDP instead of GNP—in accordance with the growing importance of international investment income for the United States and conformity with practice in other countries.

2. Preparation and use of genuine price indexes of imports and exports by SITC classes—to replace unit values.

3. Speeding up of reporting of international data on current account and balance-of-payments account.

4. Preparation of quick updates of fully balanced matrices of world trade/payments—including both merchandise and invisibles.

5. Publication of comparative NIPA data for main trading partners, for the world as a whole, and for indexes of exchange rates.

The National Accounts in an Inflationary World
Arthur M. Okun

I will focus my remarks on a few issues about the national accounts that stem particularly from our era of chronic inflation.

The late Arthur M. Okun was a senior fellow at The Brookings Institution.

Output Measurement

In principle, there are two basic strategies of estimating output: (1) direct measurement of physical volume, and (2) indirect inference from applying a deflator to a dollar volume of sales. The latter, deflation technique, is used for most of the components of real GNP, although the former is applied in important areas like home building, mobile homes, automobiles, and the gross government product. And I believe that reflects sound judgment. Most groups of products are too heterogeneous and too poorly defined to permit reliable direct measurement of output. On the other hand, it is clear why the good data on units provided by automobile manufacturers give us a sterner basis for measurement of real automobile consumption than could be derived by applying a deflator to retail sales data that necessarily combine sales of new cars with those of used cars and parts. I suspect that, in a fair number of areas, a case could be made for either volume measurement or deflation.

I want to stress that the more variable and volatile changes in prices are, the more attractive physical volume estimation becomes relative to deflation. The deflation of flows rests heavily on the assumption that our price indexes are good measures of actual transactions made during the relevant period. If the P that is measured by price indexes does not match the unobserved but "true" P in the transactions that are reflected in PQ flow data, then deflation will introduce errors in the measured growth of output that are equal proportionately and opposite in sign to the errors in the price index. In the quarterly relationship between percentage changes in real product and percentage changes in price, any errors in the price indexes will tend to bias the observed price elasticity of demand toward -1. The quarterly data since 1972 show changes in real food consumption are reduced by .69 percentage point for each one percentage point increase in the food deflator during the quarter. Since all the evidence I know suggests that the price elasticity of demand for food is far less than .7 in absolute value, I offer this as a bit of circumstantial evidence of deflation bias. I would urge that similar (and indeed more sophisticated) checks be made on all components of GNP to identify suspected areas of deflation bias. I would also urge a major effort to develop direct estimates of physical volume in "fringe areas," initially for use as a cross check to deflation rather than to supplant it.

Income Adjustments

Inflation raises serious conceptual and analytical issues about the measurement of income and income shares. Our national accounts show two kinds of income adjustments for inflation—the inventory valuation adjustment, and the capital consumption adjustment. A number of other adjustments have been suggested, but I believe they are analytical—not accounting—adjustments and hence cannot usefully be incorporated in the national accounting system. I favor the two adjustments that are being made, but I want to urge that the capital consumption adjustment should be presented differently. First, the two distinct parts of that adjustment should always be shown in the process of aggregation. One part corrects capital consumption allowances a la IRS to consistent accounting at historical cost. Because economic lives of assets, as estimated by the Department of Commerce, are longer than the lives used in tax returns, that correction lowers capital consumption allowances. The other part is the inflation adjustment, moving from historical cost to current replacement cost. Because of inflation, that correction necessarily adds to the uncorrected figure. These are entirely different animals and should be shown separately whenever the overall adjustment is shown.

Second and more important, the inflation adjustment applies to corporate-profits and corporate-interest-paid combined—not to profits alone, as now shown. When physical capital is debt financed, the expectation of inflation is reflected in the interest payments, and the "real" risk of deviations of inflation from that expectation is borne by the bondholder. Allocating the inflation adjustment between the property income of shareholders (called profits) and the property income of bondholders (called interest) is an intriguing analytical issue that our national accountants should leave to academic researchers. But the tables in the national accounts now appear to make an allocation—100% to profit, 0% to interest. That possibly misleading presentation can be remedied. The tables should show the sum of corporate profits and net interest originating in corporations and *that sum* (not any of its parts) should incorporate the inflation component of the capital consumption adjustment.

As a further example of an analytical problem that is not an accounting problem, I turn to the inventory valuation adjustment. The IVA is sizable because many corporations do not take advantage of the permission under the tax laws to use last in first out (LIFO) accounting. The national accounts, on the other hand, apply the equivalent of LIFO accounting to the entire country; I believe that is the correct decision. Yet, I also believe that the attachment to first in first out (FIFO) accounting by firms is well-founded—not, as some have suggested, as an effort to fool the shareholders about their profitability but as a correct scoring system given their pricing practices. If all firms priced all current sales on a LIFO-cost basis, their quarterly uncorrected before-tax profits should be up $1 for each $1 increase in the absolute value of the IVA; that is, IVA-corrected profits before tax would be uncorrelated with IVA. In fact, I can report that statistically that coefficient is less than one-half. Firms are not collecting their inventory capital gains from their customers; rather the FIFO accounting firms are to a significant extent setting their prices on a

FIFO basis—marking up actual historical costs rather than replacement costs. And, if we had the time, I would be glad to argue that that pricing strategy is thoroughly consistent with rationality and optimization.

The fact is that a slowdown or speedup of cost inflation is passed through by firms into final prices only with a lag. The national accounts reflect that one way, and the pricing and accounting systems of much of business reflect it differently. And both are right for their purposes. If this seems perplexing, it is only one of many confusions introduced by an era of inflation.

Discussion

Among Panelists

SIGEL: Let's try to get the speakers to react to some of the issues that have been raised. Some of the speakers offered shopping lists of what the accounts should be doing given the kinds of short-run economic policies that were being considered and the kinds of economic analysis being made. Two speakers did not, and I wonder if they would care to.

GREENSPAN: I have always believed that one of the critical areas for economic analysis that can be improved upon is the inventory system. As you know, we rely almost wholly on owned book-value data, but that system has several faults. The critical issue, especially in a period of inflation, is to get as refined an estimate as we can on real inventory change. We have a substantial amount of physical volume data on inventories which I believe can be appropriately embodied into an inventory estimate system. While that obviously raises many technical questions of where you displace the owned-inventory data system with physical volume parts, it nonetheless, in my judgment, will probably significantly improve the physical volume estimating of one of the most important statistics in the GNP accounts for the short term.

There are obviously major problems with LIFO and FIFO estimation and the price indexes. Frankly, I am surprised that the data look as good as they do considering their essential weaknesses. Another subject I have always thought we should really look at, and which I have discussed with George Jaszi and others, concerns inventory in transit. We do not capture this inventory in our accounting system. When a good is shipped out of an establishment, it moves from "inventory" to

Discussion participants: Edward F. Denison (The Brookings Institution); Alan Greenspan (Townsend-Greenspan & Co., Inc.); Lawrence Klein (University of Pennsylvania); Stanley J. Sigel, moderator (Federal Reserve Board).

"accounts receivable" and it stays there until it arrives into the book-keeping system of the receiver, when you get a credit to "inventory" and a debit to "accounts payable." There is always a net receivables in our system. In large part this reflects inventory in transit, the total of which we know is always a positive number. As a consequence, since there is a long-term uptrend in our economy, it must also follow that the expected value for in-transit inventory investment is positive, on average. It strikes me therefore that we have a bias in our statistical discrepancy account reflecting this gap in the data. I am not sure how large it is, but since we know its bias—since its expected value is positive—it strikes me that even a rough estimate is better than none.

I have a very long shopping list, but I guess I will stop there because that's the one for which I think the most advance can be made at this time.

DENISON: Mostly, I will pass on grounds of conflict of interest, but there is one small thing that will set me off completely from everyone else. The basic data now begin with 1929, which really is fine, but it would be much better if one could just go back a little bit farther. One really can't use 1929 without knowing what the years immediately preceding were like, so one has to look at them too. I think it would be possible and useful to go back to about 1926 with much the same sort of data as are used in 1929–39. I do not say BEA is going to do it, or even that it should have a high priority. But at some point, it really would be very useful. A lot has been done on those years, and I don't think it would be an enormous job to complete a set of estimates. A few years for the period immediately preceding the depression would be better than one.

SIGEL: One other issue that was raised by some of the speakers touched on the problems that the rapid rate of inflation might create for the use of the accounts for certain kinds of analysis. Is the usefulness of the accounts and the ways they are used affected by rapid rates of inflation as opposed to moderate rates?

GREENSPAN: I would just like to raise an issue which really has not been discussed here, namely, the extent to which real GNP changes are a function of the arbitrary choice of the base we employ for pricing. We will get a significant revision by moving the base of the price index from 1967 to 1972, or from 1972 to 1977. It is fairly obvious when you try to employ various bases that you will get different views of history. The problem of pricing becomes a terribly critical issue in a period such as this. The most important advances we can make at this stage, as Art Okun correctly points out, is to see whether we can create alternate systems in a physical volume sense. I don't know whether Art has looked at the unit food consumption series that the Department of Agriculture employs, which theoretically tries to go directly to a physical volume basis. I have not checked it recently against the deflated series, but I suspect we will find a lot of problems there, largely because of indexing and deflation problems. There is no doubt that Art raises the critical question at this point, namely, that the usefulness of the GNP accounts will now require far greater concentration on deflation than they had either in the very early years of formulation or more specifically, in the years when the major expansion in the accounts occurred, that is, during periods in which inflation really wasn't all that important. Whether you chose an index which was 102.1 or 102.2 really didn't make that much difference. Now the problem is whether prices are rising at an 8% or 9% rate. That does make a difference.

KLEIN: There is an issue about the base, but I don't think it is an inflation issue. I think it is a relative price issue. If one looks at the U.K. accounts, one sees that the new figures in 1975 prices give an entirely different story about very short-run growth of that economy compared with the older one, which was based on pre-1973 prices. When you have an economy that is producing a lot of oil and you give it a very high weight in the present statistics with a very high price, then it gives an entirely different picture on growth. That is an old index number problem. I don't think that is particularly an inflation problem.

GREENSPAN: But isn't it, in the sense that the dispersion of prices is a function of change in level?

KLEIN: Yes. However, I have in mind that the old arguments between American and Soviet statisticians about the use of 1926 rubles all during the thirties involved a question of heavy production of goods that had gone up in value a fair amount. It wasn't an overall inflation issue. We are now getting that with oil. However, there are one or two interesting little things about the inflation situation. Art mentioned the IVA and the depreciation adjustments. I can well appreciate from an intuitive point of view the fact that the IVA should be very sensitive to short-run inflation. I think it is less obvious that the depreciation or capital consumption adjustment should move significantly when you have spurts of inflation. If you think that a principal reason for wanting the capital consumption adjustment as being one in which you want to get a replacement value of capital assets, you must bear in mind that you've got a big slow-moving stock and a period in the distant future when you want to replace that stock. Under these circumstances I feel that the depreciation adjustment ought to be very smooth and not jump around with short-run bursts of inflation so much, although it is not completely insensitive to that particular issue.

Another problem that I find troublesome with the inflation situation is in dealing with the statistical discrepancy. When the 15-day estimate comes out every quarter, I have the problem of deciding what the profit figure was, and that is the problem of deciding where the statistical discrepancy is going to be. The statistical discrepancy by all tests that have been made in the past is not a random series; maybe it would be good if it were but it is not a random series by tests of randomness. It seems to make violent moves from quarter to quarter. It can swing quite easily by $5 billion at an annual rate in one quarter. Somehow that just doesn't sit right with me. If it did depart from a random series then one would expect very high serial correlation. There isn't. Serial correlation is moderate but not high. The statistical discrepancy is closely enough associated with rather sensitive issues about profits in a period when there are very high prices, so that it seems to me that it is much too erratic a series to satisfy the user.

DENISON: We have a productivity disaster, according to the data for the last five years. I have given quite a lot of thought to what might be responsible for it. One suggestion is that something is wrong with the data. But I don't know of anything that's likely to have gone wrong with the current dollar data, other than perhaps things associated with the measurement of inventory change, which itself depends on the price data. So if there is something wrong with the output data—the labor and other data may also have errors—then it probably would be underdeflation. But I really haven't thought of anything that would tell me exactly why a high rate of inflation would make changes over a period extending for a few years less reliable.

Even for quarterly changes, it is not clear that high rates of inflation would make the consumption data worse, since BLS collects price data directly from retail stores. Inflation clearly causes some problems for GNP components for which there are both contract prices and delivery prices or for which there are special timing problems, or for which there is reporting of list prices that differ from actual prices. But these cases don't account for a whole lot of total output. And the things that are likely to be wrong with them seem to relate more to short-term ups and downs than to changes over, say, three or four or five years. I have not concluded that inflation necessarily makes the data worse nor, if it does, in which direction it would be likely to bias real output series. I am not aware of evidence that it really makes estimates worse over any sustained time period.

From Floor

BASSIE: I would like to make a plea here regarding the mention of monthly GNP data. Thirty years ago I constructed a monthly GNP series and carried it out for several years into the mid-1950s. It wasn't much good. I decided then that it wasn't worth doing because it was too erratic. The monthly estimate depends so much on highly variable

Participants from floor include V. Lewis Bassie (University of Illinois, Urbana), Robert Eisner (Northwestern University), Saul H. Hymans (University of Michigan).

items, namely, what was then the net foreign investment and the inventory change. The monthly series misbehaved in various ways. I decided it wasn't worth the time and effort, so after a while I dropped it.

Now I would like to comment also on integrating the accounts. The more integration we do, the more we have to build boxes with rather crude estimates. Adding these to good data creates problems. It is like some proposals to add more imputations to the gross national product. The more we do of this sort of thing the cloudier the whole process of interpretation becomes. I would like therefore to put in a plea for keeping clean data as clean as possible and not messing them up. The same thing happens in the business of reconciliation. I don't like reconciliation much, because it means that you make modifications in the things you are reconciling. You make modifications in the direction of "improving" the estimate. Those improvements don't give us a really better basis for analyzing the economy. Very often they are distortions of the kind we should best avoid.

EISNER: I would just like to pick up quickly on three related matters—on the capital consumption adjustment, on inflation, and on the use of flow-of-funds balance sheets. If we make a capital consumption adjustment for inflation it is important to recognize not only increased cost in terms of capital being used up but increased value of existing capital. As we look at inflation we try to note what is happening, for example, to interest rates. Another way of looking at inflation is to note that there is a very substantial capital gain on the part of all those who have fixed money obligations, and a capital loss for those who have fixed money assets.

If we are interested in distribution of income, interested in investment, interested in implications of asset holdings and net worth positions for consumption, it is very important to take into account what is happening, for example, to the real asset position of homeowners. This may leave them both able to consume more and, looking prospectively at what happens to their real assets in home ownership, to buy more homes.

A lot of the focus on the alleged high cost of investment or the alleged shortage of capital may get a different perspective if we have data handy which will show us the true cost of capital. We will then recognize the capital gains that businesses get when obligations to pay nominal interest and principal lose real value as interest and discount rates, along with inflation, rise above those anticipated, and as they therefore realize capital gains due to declines in the real value of their liabilities. Indeed, any reconstruction of accounts to adjust for distorting effects of inflation may leave us worse off than with no adjustment if it does not include full and proper accounting for capital gains and losses.

HYMANS: I would like to make three quick comments mostly about data reliability: Every time I am at a meeting like this and somebody starts saying "monthly GNP" I start to get the willies. The Grimm-Hirsch paper discussed this morning dealt with revisions that are quite different from what we would be dealing with in the case of monthly GNP. Hirsch and Grimm dealt with revised data that resulted from a benchmark revision. There is also the problem, about which one can draw no inferences from the kind of paper we heard this morning, about what happens if one could improve those first estimates of GNP that are published 18 days after the end of the quarter. Those are very noisy data, as we know. The authors indicated a couple of reasons why. And that gives quite a different story about how much better one would be able to do in short-term forecasting with better GNP data, in that sense, not in the sense of benchmark revision of already revised data. So that is a quite different problem.

We heard some talk yesterday and again today by Lawrence Klein about regional modeling and yesterday about sectoring. Let's mention regional modeling. We run and maintain a model of the economy of the State of Michigan. For reasons that Larry mentioned, that model has to be built on state personal income statistics rather than product statistics. In terms of regional modeling we don't have any kind of product data. That would be very useful in addition to the interregional trade. It would be nice to have product data. What we do have—the state personal income data—is atrocious. First of all, the data come out with a four-month lag, which is an inconvenience for many users. Second, they come out with very substantial revisions, year by year. The whole series of state personal income data come out late, are very inaccurate, and cause enormous problems in regional or state modeling.

In terms of sectoring—a number of us—including myself, have had experience building industry models. There we have to deal with data like industry shipments data. Those are also atrocious data. And that—the published industry shipment data—I am convinced does not have to be as bad as it really is. I have been building a model for the furniture industry. The National Association of Furniture Manufacturers, just as an example, surveys its members every month to get shipments data from the members, which they put together into an aggregate shipment series. It turns out that this comparatively small sample of shipments data is extremely accurate by standards of the *revised* industry shipments data which the government comes up with a year later. The government shipments data that come out month by month and which can be put together into quarterly shipments bears very little resemblance to what the government will publish as the within-the-year shipments movements one year later when the numbers are revised. But the industry association can put together month by month an aggregate shipments series that comes very close to what the government data will say a year later. We should be able to do better, it seems to me, in state personal income data and in industry shipments data or in industry new orders and so on than we are doing now. I think it is a far higher priority to try to improve the quarterly first-shot GNP numbers than to worry about monthly numbers.

7   The Impact of the 1976 NIPA Benchmark Revision on the Structure and Predictive Accuracy of the BEA Quarterly Econometric Model

Bruce T. Grimm and Albert A. Hirsch

7.1   Introduction

This study investigates the effects of the January 1976 benchmark revision of the national income and product accounts (NIPAs) on both the structure of a working quarterly econometric model—that is, on its estimated parameters and, where changes are warranted, on its specification—and on the accuracy of model predictions. The published revision included definitional and classificational revisions of historical data as well as statistical revisions from 1959-I through 1975-III. For purposes of the present study, however, the definitional and classificational revisions have been removed from the published data, because only the statistical component of the revision is of interest. The econometric model used is the Bureau of Economic Analysis (BEA) quarterly model as it existed just prior to the revision.[1]

The main purposes of the study are: (1) to evaluate the robustness of a model's structure and reduced form with respect to the most extensive kind of revision of NIPA data, and (2) to determine whether earlier availability of the revised (and presumably more accurate) data would have resulted in improved predictive performance. Improved predictions could come about either because the "better" data result in a better model (i.e., with more nearly correct parameter estimates and possibly some better specifications), or because more accurately estimated initial conditions improve the model's predictive capacity (or both).

Bruce T. Grimm and Albert A. Hirsch are with the Bureau of Economic Analysis.

The authors are greatly indebted to the staff of the National Income and Wealth Division of BEA—in particular to John Gorman—for providing unpublished data that made this study possible, to Mark Rees for developing the needed computer software and managing the extensive data processing underlying the study, and to Carolyn Kennedy for computational and clerical assistance. They also wish to thank Saul Hymans for providing helpful comments on the preliminary draft of the paper.

The first major part of this paper (Sec. 7.2) concerns the impact of the revised data on the model structure. First, the extent of changes in estimated structural parameters when the pre-benchmark NIPAs replaced by the series containing the statistical component of the benchmark revision are examined. For this purpose, the last pre-benchmark version of the model had to be reestimated, using the same sample period as before, with the statistically revised data. Also examined is the equation respecification called for by excessive deterioration of previous forms when these were estimated with the revised data. Finally, a comparison is made of values of key multipliers in the original model, the model with reestimated parameters but without respecified equations, and the reestimated model with selected respecifications. The multipliers provide comparative measures of the overall sensitivity of the model structure to the benchmark revision.

Section 7.3 examines the comparative predictive accuracy of the three models—as determined from ex-post simulations—using unrevised data for initial conditions and exogenous variables for one model and revised data for all three models. With the four sets of error statistics, it is possible to assess the separate contributions of changes in initial conditions and exogenous variables, changes in estimated model parameters (for the original equation specifications), and changes in specification. In addition to measures of predictive accuracy, the comparative degrees of bias and efficiency in predictions are also examined.[2]

This study differs from earlier investigations of the effects of data revisions on econometric models (Denton and Kuiper 1965; Cole 1969; Denton and Oksanen 1972) in several respects: (1) except for Cole, these studies dealt only with revisions of preliminary data for the most recent observations not benchmark revisions; (2) only extremely simple models constructed on an ad hoc basis for purposes of the study (Denton and Kuiper) or single equations (Cole) were analyzed;[3] and (3) the impact of revisions on specification was not considered. Thus, the present study complements earlier investigations by analyzing the impact of a benchmark revision on a full-scale econometric model which was being used in regular forecasting and policy applications at the time of revision.

The present study does, however, share with earlier studies the shortcoming that it is (necessarily) confined to examining simulation with known values of exogenous variables and nonjudgmental constant adjustments, thus excluding direct tests of the effects of data revision on actual (ex-ante) forecasting performance. Such tests are precluded because we cannot construct, in an objective manner, judgmental projections of exogenous variables and revised constant adjustments (compared with those used in original ex-ante forecasts) purely on the basis of data revisions and consequent model changes.

7.1.1   Main Structural Features of the Econometric Model

The version of the BEA quarterly used in this study contains 148 structural equations of which 80 are stochastic equations. It has a typical post-Keynesian structure with many nonlinear equation forms.

The model has equations—all specified in real terms—for personal consumption expenditures (12 components), residential and nonresidential fixed investment, inventory investment (two components), and imports (two components). The basic output variable in the model is private domestic nonfarm GNP except housing (XNF); this output variable is not disaggregated further. A single equation relates XNF (and corresponding potential output) to employment. Average weekly hours are determined by a similar function. Labor force is determined by two participation rate equations. Unemployment is determined residually from labor force and employment.

The average money wage for the sector defined by XNF is determined by a variant of the Phillips-curve relationship. A single equation determines the implicit price deflator for XNF as a variable markup on "standard" unit labor cost. Implicit deflators for most GNP final demand components are determined primarily by empirical relationships of component deflators to the XNF deflator. Other equations determine nonwage personal income components, corporate profits, and the main components reconciling GNP and national income. A unique feature of the model is the method of income-product reconciliation: the statistical discrepancy is initially solved as a residual in the income-product identity. If the trial solution value exceeds preset limits on the absolute values of the level and first difference in the discrepancy, the initial value is replaced by the binding limit value, and the excess is allocated among income components.[4]

Completing the model are equations for manufacturers' new orders and shipments, federal and state and local receipts and federal net interest payments, state unemployment benefits, and a monetary sector. Broadly speaking, the monetary sector represents the LM component of an IS-LM construct, while the rest of the model may be considered an elaborate IS structure.[5]

7.2   Model Reestimation: Methodology and Impact on Model Characteristics

Three versions of the BEA quarterly model were needed in order to conduct the analyses contained in this paper. The first, model A, is the version that existed just before the benchmark revision, which included the originally estimated parameters (hereafter abbreviated as "parameters"), except for needed transformations to conform to the shift from 1958-base deflators to 1972-base deflators in the benchmark revision; the latter transformations are made for purposes of comparison with models B and C. In the second, model B, which uses the specifications and sample periods of model A, all parameters have been reestimated using post-benchmark data. The third, model C, contains respecified equations where indicated by deterioration of estimated parameters from model A to model B.

7.2.1 Data Preparation

In order to estimate models B and C, it was first necessary to recreate the data available at the time of the benchmark revision, that is, without subsequent further revisions. For NIPA variables, it was necessary to purge the new published NIPA series of the definitional and classificational revisions (hereafter abbreviated as "definitional" revisions), leaving only the statistical component of the revision.[6] Data for non-NIPA variables are those that existed just before the benchmark revision; they are left unrevised in models B and C in order that we may study the effect of the NIPA revision alone.

Fifty-seven NIPA series, including 30 current-dollar series, 19 constant-dollar series, four deflators, and four other NIPA series (e.g., the personal saving rate), had to be revised. For 1958 through 1974, the records of definitional revisions for seven current-dollar series were available only on an annual basis.[7] Quarterly values for the definitional revisions for these series were calculated using BEA's MCVIM interpolating program.[8] In addition, the definitional revisions for four constant-dollar series were available only on annual basis.[9] Quarterly interpolations of these series were obtained using the corresponding (quarterly) current-dollar series. For most of the definitional revisions, only annual values were available before 1958; for these, most of which moved smoothly on an annual basis, quarterly values were interpolated judgmentally.

No attempt was made to adjust GNP component price deflators at the model's level of disaggregation for changes in composition resulting from definitional revisions. The resulting adjustments would have been small and the calculations necessary to produce them prohibitively time consuming. (While the other revisions could be calculated using the model's data handling system, the calculation of deflators is done by the National Income and Wealth Division [NIWD] at the most detailed level of information available for GNP components; this is at least one order of fineness greater than is either published or carried in the model's data system.) However, the aggregate deflator was adjusted for compositional changes.

Although 1974 is the last year used in estimating the model's equations and for which definitional revisions were available from the NIWD, estimates of the revisions for 1975–77 were needed for the experiments described in Section 7.3. These estimates were calculated with the aid of NIWD personnel. In general, the estimates were made by linking movements of the revisions to existing detailed NIPA information. For a few series, it was necessary to extrapolate from past trends.

7.2.2   Adjustments for Conversion of the Deflator Base

The NIPA benchmark revision converted deflators from a 1958 base to a 1972 base. As a result, in order to make model A comparable with models B and C, some parameters in model A's equations—specifically in equations that include constant-dollar variables, relative prices, or levels of deflators—had to be recalculated to take into account this base change. These changes were made by assuming that the 1958-base deflator is equal to the 1972-base deflator times a scalar—a simplifying assumption at the level of aggregation of deflators used in the model. The scalar used is the ratio of the 1958-base deflator to the 1972-base deflator in 1975-II. For the ith component's deflator in the tth time period, the assumption may be written as

$$(1) \qquad P_i^{58}(t) = \left(\frac{P_i^{58}(752)}{P_i^{72}(752)} \right) P_i^{72}(t).$$

For linear equations with constant-dollar dependent variables, all coefficients are changed. For example,

$$(2) \qquad \frac{Y\$(t)}{P_Y^{58}(t)} = a_0 + a_1 X(t)$$

can be transformed to

$$(3) \qquad \frac{Y\$(t)}{P_Y^{72}(t)} = \left(\frac{P_Y^{58}(752)}{P_Y^{72}(752)} \right) \left(a_0 + a_1 X(t) \right).$$

For linear equations with constant-dollar explanatory variables, only the coefficients of those variables are changed. For example,

$$(4) \qquad Y(t) = a_0 + a_1 \left(\frac{X\$(t)}{P_X^{58}(t)} \right)$$

can be transformed to

$$(5) \qquad Y(t) = a_0 + a_1 \left(\frac{P_X^{72}(752)}{P_X^{58}(752)} \right) \left(\frac{X\$(t)}{P_X^{72}(t)} \right).$$

Linear equations with relative price terms have only the coefficients of these terms changed. For example,

(6) $$Y(t) = a_0 + a_1 \left(\frac{P_i^{58}(t)}{P_j^{58}(t)} \right)$$

can be transformed to

(7) $$Y(t) = a_0 + a_1 \left(\frac{P_i^{58}(752)}{P_i^{72}(752)} \right) \left(\frac{P_j^{72}(752)}{P_j^{58}(752)} \right) \left(\frac{P_i^{72}(t)}{P_j^{72}(t)} \right).$$

For log-linear equations with constant-dollar dependent variables, only the constant term is changed. For example,

(8) $$\log \left(\frac{Y\$(t)}{P_Y^{58}(t)} \right) = a_0 + a_1 \log X(t)$$

can be transformed to

(9) $$\log \left(\frac{Y\$(t)}{P_Y^{72}(t)} \right) = \log \left(\frac{P_Y^{58}(752)}{P_Y^{72}(752)} \right) + a_0 + a_1 \log X(t).$$

For log-linear equations with constant-dollar explanatory variables, only the constant term is changed. For example,

(10) $$\log Y(t) = a_0 + a_1 \log \left(\frac{X\$(t)}{P^{58}(t)} \right)$$

can be transformed to

(11) $$\log Y(t) = a_0 + a_1 \log \left(\frac{P_X^{72}(752)}{P_X^{58}(752)} \right)$$
$$+ a_1 \log \left(\frac{X\$(t)}{P^{72}(t)} \right).$$

In a similar manner, relative price terms in log-linear equations require only changes in the constant term. Combinations of the above examples within the same equation lead to multiple adjustments. No other types of nonlinear equations in the model have terms that required adjustment.

7.2.3   Estimation of Model B

The parameters of model B were estimated using the revised data.[10] The method of estimation was the same as used to estimate the base model—ordinary least squares with Cochrane-Orcutt corrections for serial correlation where needed. The time periods used for estimating the equations were the same as those used in estimating model A. The sample periods in model A were distributed as shown below.[11]

Sample Period	Number of Equations
1955-I to 1972-IV	8
1955-I to 1973-III	7
1955-I to 1973-IV	35
1955-I to 1974-IV	21
Other	9

Table 7.1 shows, in the form of a frequency distribution, the extent of changes in the structural parameters from model A to model B.[12] There are, excluding constant terms, 180 structural parameters in the 64 reestimated equations. Of these, 93 parameters increased in absolute size, 84 decreased, and three changed sign. There is a surprisingly large range of changes in parameter sizes: 25 parameters increased more than 50%, and, correspondingly, 26 parameters decreased more than 33.3%. Conversely, 39 parameters increased less than 10%, and, correspondingly, 20 parameters decreased less than 9.2%.

Table 7.1 also shows the distribution of changes in autocorrelation coefficients. Thirty-seven equations had serial correlation corrections in model A. All of these equations also had significant autocorrelation coefficients in model B. Of these, 15 had lower and 22 had higher values. In addition, seven equations had newly significant serial correlation coefficients. Counting these new corrections as increases, the hypothesis of no change in mean serial correlation correction in the 64 equations reestimated may be rejected at the 95% level of confidence (using the sign test).

Finally, table 7.1 summarizes the changes in the goodness of fit of the equations as measured by their standard errors of estimate. (Wherever a dependent variable is affected by the shift in the deflator base, the corresponding standard error in model A was adjusted accordingly.) There is no particular tendency in the goodness of fit: 34 equations had increases in standard errors, and 30 had decreases. Somewhat disturbingly, five equations showed increases of more than 100%; however, the importance of most of these increases is mitigated by the fact that the standard errors remained small relative to the variance of the dependent variables.

While it is interesting to examine the degree of change in individual structural parameters and associated regression statistics, this does not suffice for evaluating changes in the response characteristics of the model as a system. Specifically, the relatively frequent occurrence of large changes in individual parameters may give an exaggerated impression of the degree of change in the model's responsiveness to exogenous shocks and even of that of particular model sectors. For example, within equations there may be large offsetting changes in coefficients of variables that are not merely collinear in the statistical sense but that move jointly in response to a given exogenous shock. When offsetting changes occur between the coefficients of an explanatory variable and a lagged dependent variable, there will be large differences in initial responses, followed by diminishing differences over time (i.e., the "final form" of the equation is more stable than the structural form). As another example, there may be large offsetting changes among equations in the coefficients of common explanatory variables, for example, income coefficients in equations for consumption components. Finally, for variables that have comparatively little impact on the system, large changes in associated parameters may not matter much.

It is possible to illustrate the relationship between changes in individual parameters and system responses by focusing on the parameter changes in a specific sector. Table 7.2 shows how the benchmark revision affected the parameters for real disposable personal income and relative price in each of the equations in the consumption sector. The "direct" changes are those in the coefficients of the (current and lagged) explanatory variables. The "total" changes combine the direct changes with the changes in the indirect effects that are transmitted over the long run through lagged dependent variables where these are present.

The direct changes in the income parameters are relatively large, with four increases and six decreases. In the nondurables and services equations with lagged dependent variables, however, the total changes are smaller in all cases. This probably reflects primarily collinearity between income and the lagged consumption variable, which results in offsetting changes in parameters. To some (unknown) extent, it may be that the revised data correctly imply a shorter lag structure. The largest negative change—in the income parameter for other durables—is due to collinearity. Income has a correlation of .995 with a wealth measure, whose coefficient increases substantially.

The overall effect of the various changes in income parameters can be evaluated by calculating the marginal propensity to consume (MPC) for each model. Model A has a one-quarter MPC of .36 and a long-run MPC of .61. Model B has modestly higher MPCs: The one-quarter value is .40, and the long-run value is .66.[13] These relatively moderate changes in the aggregate MPCs, in contrast to the large relative changes for many of the consumption components, of course reflect offsetting changes.

The relative price coefficients show generally larger percentage changes than do the income coefficients. Again, there is a wide range in the extent of change, with four increases and three decreases in both direct effects and total effects. In contrast to the result for income, three of the four equations with lagged dependent variables show larger changes in the total effect than in the direct effect.

7.2.4   Estimation of Model C

Normally, when in the process of model reestimation previously used equation forms break down, substantial experimental research takes place before new forms are settled upon. Since it is in the nature of such experimentation that one cannot sort out respecifications made strictly in response to the breakdown of old equation forms from those made in response to new ideas that could have been applied previously, certain explicit and fairly restrictive rules for respecification had to be adopted consistent with the objective nature of this study.

Two criteria were adopted as indicating the need for respecification: (1) *t*-ratios below 1.0 for parameters whose *t*-ratios were 1.0 or higher in model A, and (2) changes in the sign of parameters. Using these criteria, it was necessary to respecify 10 equations. These were for new orders received by manufacturers, personal consumption expenditures (PCE) for durables, PCE for food, the consumer price index (CPI), average weekly hours, fixed nonresidential investment, the deflator for gross private nonfarm business GNP, the 90-day Treasury bill rate, thrift institution deposits, and rental income of persons. In each instance, one of three alternative rules was adopted for making specification changes: (1) drop the variable with the bad parameter, (2) drop a variable highly collinear with the variable with the bad parameter, or (3) adopt the revised specification used in the model that was estimated right after the benchmark revisions. The third alternative was a last resort because, when respecifications were adopted after the benchmark revision, they often resulted from considerable experimentation with alternative specifications.

Rule (1) was used in eight equations; rules (2) and (3) were used for one equation each.[14] The relatively small number of respecifications and the relatively minor changes in specification needed under the rules of this experiment suggest that the much more extensive respecification of the model following the benchmark revision (31 equations were respecified on the basis of regression tests with the new data) resulted largely from incorporating the very turbulent 1974–75 period into the sample rather than from the benchmark revision.

In the eight equations that were respecified according to the first rule, 15 out of 18 coefficients of remaining explanatory variables changed less than 5% in absolute value from model B to model C. The other three parameters whose values changed by more than 5% were relatively unimportant.

7.2.5   Comparative Multipliers in the Three Models

Examination of the effects of specific parameter changes on the implied overall marginal propensity to consume illustrates a partial summarization of the impact of data revision on model structure. A broader, more inclusive approach is to study key multipliers (i.e., reduced-form coefficients) which indicate the sensitivity of the model's response mechanism to the structural parameter changes that resulted from the revision. The multipliers automatically weight the parameter changes by their relative importance and measure the net impacts of offsetting parameter changes on variables of major interest.

Because of the nonlinearity of the model, the multipliers are variable, depending on the state of the economy and, to some extent, on the size of assumed changes in exogenous variables. Hence, multipliers are derived by simulation under specified conditions rather than by mathematical analysis. For purposes of comparing multipliers among models A, B, and C, any exogenous variables could have been chosen as instruments. As a matter of convenience, three policy instruments were chosen for the multiplier calculations: nonborrowed reserves of Federal Reserve System member banks; federal corporate profits taxes; and federal government purchases of goods and services other than compensation of government employees.[15] These instruments were selected for their differing ways of impacting on the system.

Multipliers were calculated for one through 20 quarters after the assumed change in the value of each instrument. A baseline solution for calculating the multipliers was obtained by forcing the model to track the actual course of the economy over the period 1970-I through 1974-IV. In the "disturbed" solution, the level of the policy instrument in question was increased by a constant $5 billion over its historical levels, and the model was re-solved. Differences between the disturbed and baseline solution values of the endogenous variables were then divided by 5 to yield normalized multipliers.[16]

For each of the three instruments, the corresponding multipliers in models B and C are very similar. This is not surprising given the limited changes in specification between model B and model C (most changes were simply the deletion of highly insignificant variables with small resulting changes in remaining parameters). Accordingly, in the following discussion, comparisons are generally made between model A on the one hand and the two reestimated models (models B and C) on the other.

Table 7.3 shows the multipliers for nonborrowed reserves. All three models agree that this instrument is strongly stimulative in terms of both current- and constant-dollar gross national product. The large multipliers reflect the fact that a $1 billion increase in nonborrowed reserves represents about a 3% increase in reserves in the period for which the multipliers were calculated. For the first four quarters, the current-dollar GNP multipliers are quite close for all three models. Thereafter, the differences widen and peak at about eight quarters and shrink slightly thereafter. Model C's multipliers are somewhat lower than model B's, which are in turn weaker than model A's. This pattern also holds generally for the components of GNP: the greatest relative differences in multipliers are in fixed nonresidential investment where early quarter multipliers are substantially lower than those of model A. Multipliers for personal income, corporate profits, and the federal surplus are similar among all three models up to eight quarters. Multipliers for non-NIPA variables are also similar among the models.

The most striking difference between model A on the one hand and models B and C on the other is in the price level responses. The GNP deflator multiplier, which begins to be noticeably large by the fourth quarter, is about twice as large in model B as in model A by the eighth quarter; the 2:1 ratio holds through the sixteenth quarter and then drops somewhat.

Several factors appear to account for the stronger price response. First, the revised data show a slightly slower trend rate of growth in labor productivity (.2 percentage points annually); this factor, interacting with the money wage rate in the "standard" unit labor cost term of the overall price equation, produces a stronger price impact for a given demand stimulus. Second, the unemployment rate has a larger effect in the wage rate equation. Finally, the demand terms in the general price equation yield a stronger price response. These factors more than offset the weakening effect of a somewhat lower coefficient on lagged prices in the wage rate equation.

The stronger price multipliers in models B and C become reflected (with a lag) in smaller constant-dollar GNP multipliers: higher prices result in weaker demand. By the twelfth quarter, the real GNP multiplier is 29% smaller in model B than in model A; this compares with a 5% lower current-dollar GNP multiplier.

Table 7.4 shows the multipliers for a $1 billion decrease in corporate profits taxes. As is typical for this policy instrument, the multipliers are relatively small in all cases. Models B and C have larger current-dollar GNP multipliers than model A. The spread in the multipliers, which is initially modest, builds up gradually over time and is still increasing, though slowly, at 20 quarters. Constant-dollar GNP multiplier differences mirror those for current-dollar GNP: although the reestimated models again have somewhat larger deflator multipliers, the values for these are quite small in all three models, and the difference is not large enough to produce smaller real GNP multipliers, as occurred in the case of nonborrowed reserves. Personal income and corporate profits multipliers are larger in models B and C, reflecting larger current-dollar GNP multipliers. Similarly, the federal surplus multipliers are less negative in models B and C, reflecting larger receipts due to larger increases in taxable income and corporate profits in these models. The unemployment rate and short- and long-term interest rate multipliers are very small for all three models.

Table 7.5 shows multipliers for an increase of $1 billion in federal purchases of goods and services other than compensation of government employees. The current-dollar GNP multipliers are generally similar for all models up to eight quarters. Thereafter, multipliers in models B and C are substantially larger than those in model A. These differences are spread throughout the components of GNP. The differences are due entirely to price multipliers: the potentially stronger final demand responses of models B and C are offset by the negative effects of higher prices. As a result, model A's real GNP multipliers are almost identical to those of models B and C. The comparative price multiplier patterns among models are similar to those for nonborrowed reserves (although the size of the multipliers is smaller because of the weaker stimulus). The real GNP multipliers peak at six to seven quarters and then decline. This reflects the diminishing real stimulus of government purchases as the price level for purchases rises, the demand weakening effects of higher prices in general, and negative accelerator feedbacks, which occur mainly through business fixed investment and inventory investment.

Differences among models in personal income and corporate profits multipliers again reflect those for current-dollar GNP. Federal deficit multipliers are similar for the first four quarters and are smaller in models B and C than in model A thereafter. The small differences in unemployment rate multipliers reflect the differences in constant-dollar GNP multipliers.

To summarize: changes in early quarter multipliers due to the parameter and specification changes that resulted from the benchmark revision are moderate in comparison with the rather large changes in many structural parameters. (This result is analogous to the comparison of changes in the overall marginal propensity to consume with changes in income parameters in the consumption component equations.) The increasing differences in multipliers after four to eight quarters are the result of a dynamic feeding forward of smaller differences in the earlier periods. In particular, the reestimated models produce, over longer periods, substantially larger price multipliers; for two of the three policy instruments investigated, this ultimately results in smaller real GNP multipliers. It should be noted, however, that differences for horizons beyond 12 quarters are of limited interest in a model whose focus is on short-run behavior.

7.3 Comparative Error Characteristics
7.3.1 Methodology

In order to test the effect of the benchmark revision on the predictive accuracy of the BEA quarterly model, ex-post simulations using models

A, B, and C were run. Ex-post simulations use historical data for the initial conditions (i.e., lagged values of model variables up to and including the base period) and for the exogenous variables in the simulation period.

Two sets of simulations were run with model A: (1) using pre-benchmark data for initial conditions and exogenous variables ("old ICEVs"), and (2) using revised post-benchmark data ("new ICEVs"). Models B and C were run only with new ICEVs. In all four cases, the latest revised values were used for variables against which predicted values were compared to determine prediction errors. Comparisons among the four sets of error statistics permit evaluation of both the overall effect of the benchmark revision on predictive accuracy and the contribution of the separate aspects of the adaptation of the model to the revision: (1) the substitution of new ICEVs for old ICEVs, (2) reestimation of the model, and (3) respecification of equations induced by the revision.

Twenty overlapping eight-quarter dynamic simulations were run with base periods from 1970-IV through 1975-III (thus covering the period 1971-I through 1977-III). The full set of simulations is divided into two subsets. The first subset (12 simulations) lies essentially within the period for which data are used to estimate the model (the sample period), and the second subset lies largely outside the sample period (the postsample period). The dividing line is between the simulations, whose base periods are 1973-III and 1973-IV, respectively.

Ideally, only postsample data should be used because, in principle, predictive tests should only be made against data that were not used to estimate the model (Christ 1976). Moreover, in the within-sample tests, there is a natural bias in favor of the reestimated models (B and C) because the revised data are used for error measurement. However, because of the paucity of postsample observations for each prediction horizon—a degrees-of-freedom problem that is aggravated by the fact that the simulations are overlapping, so that observed errors are not truly independent—within-sample statistics were derived and used to provide needed supplementary evidence; thus, statistics for the combined sets of simulations as well as for the subsets are analyzed.

The within-sample/postsample partitioning also groups the simulations into those dominated by the 1974–75 recession and early recovery (the postsample period) and those in which recession quarters carry relatively little weight. To a considerable degree, therefore, it serves to isolate the exceptionally poorly predicted 1974–75 period.

In each simulation, adjustments were made to (normalized) equation intercepts according to the following formula for the ith time horizon:

$$(12) \qquad \text{Adj}_i = \frac{1}{2}\hat{\rho}^i\left[(r_0 - \bar{r}_{-0:7}) + \hat{\rho}(r_{-1} - \bar{r}_{-0:7})\right] + \bar{r}_{-0:7},$$

where $\hat{\rho}$ is the estimated first-order autocorrelation coefficient and $\bar{r}_{-0:7}$ is the mean single-equation residual for the eight consecutive quarters ending in the base period. For equations in first difference form, the adjustment is simply $\bar{r}_{-0:7}$. This formula provides a mechanical adjustment rule intended to correct both for serial correlation and specification errors that tend to result in systematic underpredictions or overpredictions, especially beyond the sample period. (This formula long served as an adjustment rule in actual forecasts made with the BEA econometric model when alternative judgmentally derived adjustments did not override it.)[17]

Further Data Compilation

Further modifications and extensions of data (in comparison with those described in Part I) were needed for this portion of the study. First, while the NIPA data used to derive models B and C were (appropriately) those from the initial benchmark revision, the "actual" data that were used both as a basis for error measurement and as new ICEVs are the latest revised data, which incorporate successive July revisions of the NIPAs. These revisions modify the benchmark revised NIPAs as far back as 1973-I. These data again had to be adjusted to remove the definitional and classificational components of the benchmark revision. In this connection, definitional and classificational revisions, which were available only through 1974, had to be extrapolated through the period covered by the simulations; this was done as discussed in Section 7.1.

Second, for the simulation with model A using old ICEVs, implicit deflators and constant-dollar values had to be converted from a 1958 base to a 1972 base. The same conversion factors were used as were used for the formulas employed in converting the coefficients in model A.[18] Also, for these simulations, exogenous variables had to be projected beyond 1975-III—the last quarter for which pre-benchmark data were published. These were derived by linking the latest revised cumulative changes (adjusted, where necessary, for definitional revisions) from 1975-III to the pre-benchmark levels for that quarter.

Error Statistics

The basic error statistics compiled from the four sets of model simulations are the mean absolute error or, in cases of some trending variables, the mean absolute percent error. They are compiled separately for simulations one quarter ahead, two quarters ahead, . . . , eight quarters ahead. The formulas for the mean absolute error (MAE) and mean absolute percent error (MAPE) for the ith quarter ahead are, respectively,

$$\text{(13)} \qquad \text{MAE}_i = \frac{1}{n} \Sigma_j \left| P_i - A_i \right|, j = 1, \ldots, n;$$

and

$$(14) \qquad \mathrm{MAPE}_i = \frac{100}{n} \Sigma_j \left| \frac{P_i - A_i}{A_i} \right|, j = 1, \ldots, n;$$

where A is the actual value of the variable (defined, as noted above, by the latest revised data), P is the corresponding predicted value, and n is the number of simulations.

In the case of simulations with model A using old ICEVs, the predicted level of each variable analyzed is adjusted for the revision of the variable in the base period. This is done because of the bias in the pre-benchmark data in relation to the (presumably more accurate) revised data and because in the case of NIPA data we are usually interested in cumulative changes rather than in levels. (If base-period values in simulations are identical or are adjusted to be identical to actual values, then amount or percent errors for any horizon i are also the errors in the cumulative change to period i.) The adjustment formula for predicted values in the ith quarter ahead is

$$(15) \qquad P'_i = P_i + A^r_o - A^u_o$$

where $A^r_o - A^u_o$ is the difference between revised and unrevised values in the base period.

It might seem at first blush that the base-period adjustment of predicted values neutralizes the differences in measured predictive accuracy between simulations of model A using old and new ICEVs. This is, however, not necessarily so for two reasons: (1) the adjustments apply to output, not input variables (for instance, revisions in the initial levels of stocks affect the subsequent dynamic behavior of certain flow variables); (2) revisions in the trajectories of lagged variables up to the base period and of exogenous variables during the simulation period modify the dynamic behavior of output variables. (Because of the way in which unrevised exogenous variables are projected after 1975-III, there is no differences in their trajectories after 1975-III.)

Also examined, in addition to MAEs or MAPEs of variables in level form, are the MAEs of the quarterly percent changes (at annual rates) in real GNP and the GNP implicit price deflator. For these measures, no base-period adjustment is needed.

MAEs and MAPEs, rather than the frequently used root mean square errors (RMSEs), are examined here because the latter are penalized by extreme errors, thus giving a less clear picture of average performance. In addition, we show the mean error (indicating bias), the t-statistic for the mean error, and the Theil inequality coefficient which for errors of type P-A in the ith quarter is

$$(16) \qquad U_i = \sqrt{\frac{\Sigma(P_i - A_i)^2}{\Sigma(A_i - A_o)^2}}, \; j = 1, \ldots, n.$$

A U_i value of zero implies perfect predictions and a value of unity implies predictions that are, on the average, no better than a prediction of no (cumulative) change. An advantage of this statistic is that because it is a "pure" (i.e., dimensionless) number, it permits comparisons of predictive efficiency among different variables and over varying horizons.

The t-statistic, which purports to indicate the significance of bias, should be interpreted with great caution because of the nonindependence of observed errors for a given horizon: serial interdependence arises from the fact that the mean errors are compiled for overlapping forecasts and that in any given simulation prediction errors are strongly autocorrelated.

7.3.2 Results

Table 7.6 shows mean absolute errors, mean errors, t-tests of the mean error, and Theil coefficients for major NIPA aggregates and endogenous final demand components of real GNP, the GNP implicit price deflator, the unemployment rate, and representative short- and long-term interest rates. The data are grouped as within-sample, postsample, and combined in accordance with the partitioning of the simulation period described in the previous section.

The first column in each block of statistics (designated A^u) results from the simulations with model A using old ICEVs. The remaining three columns (denoted with the superscript r) are statistics from simulations with models A, B, and C using new ICEVs.

Before comparisons are made among results for the A^u, A^r, B^r, and C^r simulations, some generalizations can be made concerning the overall results. First, as is typical for dynamic simulations (and ex-ante forecasts), MAEs (or MAPEs) for level variables generally grow with the prediction horizon. The extent of deterioration is, however, better indicated by the Theil coefficient, which takes into account the greater difficulty of forecasting over long than over short horizons.[19] Second, MAEs and even MAPEs for trending variables in the postsample simulations are generally larger than corresponding MAEs and MAPEs in the within-sample simulations. This is to be expected, not only because it is a typical property but also because the postsample simulations are dominated by the period of the 1974–77 recession and recovery.[20] Third, prices are systematically and substantially underpredicted in all the simulations; this appears to reflect both inherent deficiencies in the price and wage equations in capturing the inflationary process and the lack of explicit (exogenous) treatment of the energy and other material prices, which exploded on a worldwide scale during the period under review. Finally, the Theil coefficients typically either steadily decrease with lengthening of the prediction horizon, or follow an inverted V pattern (i.e., at first rise and then fall).

For the real GNP simulations (table 7.6A, D, and L) the largest reduction in both MAEs (or MAPEs) and the Theil coefficients occurs from the A^r to the B^r simulations, that is, as a result of reestimation with the statistically revised data. This holds for the within-sample and post-sample simulations as well as for the combined simulations. Differences in prediction errors between the A^u and A^r simulations and between the B^r and C^r simulations are very small in the combined statistics. Indeed, differences in error statistics between the B^r and C^r simulations are generally very small—analogous to multiplier results in Part Section 7.2—and will, accordingly, not be discussed hereafter.

Looking more closely at the comparative results for within-sample and postsample simulations, however, one notes substantial differences. In the postsample subset, the A^r simulations yield somewhat more accurate predictions than the A^u simulations, while in the within-sample subset the reverse is true. More important, in the postsample simulations, the degree of improvement from the A^r to the B^r predictions increases dramatically with lengthening of the time horizon; in the within-sample simulations it does not. Two quarters ahead, for example, the B^r MAPE for the postsample real GNP predictions is 22% smaller than the A^r MAPE, but eight quarters ahead the B^r MAPE is 37% smaller. Bias is generally not significant at high confidence levels for the real GNP predictions.

In the within-sample and combined simulations, the greatest improvement in the price-level predictions (table 7.6B) occurs from the A^u to the A^r simulations; that is, revisions in the estimated initial conditions and exogenous variables improve the accuracy of the price level predictions more than do revisions in the parameters. Improvement diminishes sharply with the prediction horizon, however: in the combined set, the relative reduction in the MAPE between A^u and A^r simulations falls from 49% one quarter ahead to 23% eight quarters ahead.

In the postsample simulations, the pattern is quite different. Substantial reductions in the MAPE occur between the A^r and B^r simulations as well as between the A^u and A^r simulations. Indeed, the former dominate the latter with long prediction horizons; in the eighth quarter the relative reduction is 29%. Thus, there is a repetition of the comparative pattern of prediction errors observed for real GNP. Because prices are almost consistently underpredicted, the pattern of mean errors faithfully reflects that of the MAPE's.

The MAPEs for current-dollar GNP are sharply reduced proceeding from A^u to A^r to B^r simulations. In the A^u simulations, MAPEs for current-dollar GNP are almost always larger than MAPEs for corresponding constant-dollar GNP predictions; this reflects reinforcing (i.e., same-signed) errors in the deflators and real GNP predictions. In the A^r and B^r simulations, the MAPEs for current-dollar GNP are smaller than corresponding MAPEs for constant-dollar GNP, indicating offsetting price and real GNP errors. The reduction of prediction errors from the A^u to A^r to B^r simulations is most pronounced in the postsample subset. The relatively frequent occurrence of significant negative bias in the current-dollar GNP predictions reflects that found in the price level predictions.

Error statistics for major endogenous components of real GNP are shown in parts E through I of table 7.6. For the combined simulations, the tendency for the improvement in accuracy in predicting real GNP to occur mainly from the A^r to B^r simulations is most clearly mirrored in fixed nonresidential investment and, to a lesser extent, in inventory investment.

MAEs for personal consumption expenditures decrease markedly from the A^u to A^r to B^r simulations in the postsample subset—decreases are strongest in the early and late quarters; but for the within-sample simulations, MAEs are progressively larger for long horizons. The strong negative bias in the postsample A^u predictions largely disappears in the other postsample simulations.

For residential investment, the MAEs from the combined sets of simulations differ very little among the various model versions. Mirroring the error patterns for other variables, MAEs in the postsample subsets do diminish somewhat from the A^u to the B^r simulations for the longer horizons. The postsample prediction errors from the A^r, B^r, and C^r simulations have a significant positive bias.

MAEs for real imports show an anomalous substantial deterioration from the A^u to the A^r simulations—a pattern which is most pronounced for the within-sample subset. Such an anomaly in all likelihood reflects inadequacy in the specification of the imports function. There is slight further deterioration from the A^r to the B^r simulations; this tendency is again centered in the within-sample simulations. The within-sample simulations are strongly negative biased.

The comparative patterns of error statistics for personal income (pt. J, table 7.6) roughly mirror those for the GNP implicit deflator. Presumably this reflects the predictions of the average money wage rate, which is a major common element to the two variables. Specifically, there is again substantial reduction in MAPEs from the A^u to the A^r simulations, with relatively little further change to the B^r simulations, except for the longer horizons in the postsample simulations. Moreover, predictions are again uniformly negatively biased.

In the combined and within-sample simulations, predictions of corporate profits (pt. K, table 7.6) show the greatest relative improvement in the early quarters from the A^u to the B^r simulations. In the postsample simulations, there is sharp improvement from the A^r to the B^r simulations for longer horizons. Bias is generally not significant at high confidence levels.

In comparing MAEs for rates of growth of real GNP among simulations, the only persistent tendency one finds is a moderate improvement from the A^r to the B^r simulations. For the inflation rate (% change in the GNP implicit price deflator—pt. M, table 7.6), there is consistent improvement in predictions from the A^u to the B^r simulations, though MAEs for the A^r simulations are in some instances larger than for the A^u simulations. For both of these change variables, the greatest improvement from the A^u to the B^r simulations occurs in the postsample predictions for the longer horizons.

MAEs for the unemployment rate predictions show substantial improvement from the combined A^u to the A^r simulations. There is significant positive bias in the errors of the within-sample simulations; in the postsample simulations, bias is negligible except for the longest prediction horizons.

There is a slight deterioration in the MAEs for the Treasury bill rate and long-term bond yield from the A^u to the B^r simulations. In the postsample simulations, errors in the Treasury bill rate predictions generally show a significant positive bias.

To summarize: on the basis of the combined simulations, slight gains result on balance from substituting revised initial conditions and exogenous variables for the pre-benchmark data; however, such gains are far from consistent among the variables examined. There is, on the whole, clearer evidence of improved predictive accuracy from reestimation of the model than from replacing old with new ICEVs; the opposite is true, however, for the GNP implicit deflator. Generally, negligible differences in MAEs or MAPEs result when the respecified equations are inserted into the reestimated model.

For many variables there are marked differences in the comparative error statistics between the within-sample and postsample subsets of simulations. For instance, in some cases, where there is deterioration from the A^u to the A^r simulations in the within-sample subset, there is improvement in the postsample subset. More significantly, there is a persistent tendency for relatively large reductions in MAEs or MAPEs from the postsample A^u to B^r simulations for the longest horizons, compared with much smaller gains or even deterioration for the shorter horizons; this tendency is largely absent in the within-sample simulations.

Finally, there are relatively few instances where significant bias occurring in the predictions from the A^u simulations is reduced to nonsignificant levels in the A^r, B^r, or C^r simulations. Comparative efficiency of prediction among types of simulations, as measured by the Theil coefficient, generally reflects the comparative patterns of predictive accuracy as measured by the MAEs or MAPEs.

An obviously interesting question—not adequately handled by the error statistics—is whether adaptation of the model to the benchmark revision resulted in better tracking of the 1974–75 recession. When individual simulations used for the calculation of the postsample error statistics are studied, tracking is generally so poor that no meaningful comparisons among simulations result. One can only conclude that the overwhelming failure to capture the cyclical path is inherent in the model structure (and perhaps in the mechanical method of constant adjustments) and not in measurement error.

An important missing element in the model structure is the explicit treatment of energy prices. The emergence of the OPEC cartel's power was evidently an important contributing factor to the downturn.[21] Moreover, experimentation revealed that the use of the moving eight-quarter average residual as the basis for constant adjustment (see eq. [12]) also contributed substantially to the poor tracking. As a result, new simulations were run with price deflators made exogenous and automatic adjustments replaced by zero adjustments. Specifically, eight-quarter simulations with 1973-III and 1974-IV as the initial periods were tried, and the behavior of real GNP, inventory and investment, and final sales examined.

Although all of these simulations showed much better tracking—including the prediction of turning points—than those used for the error calculations, they fail to show unequivocal improvements in tracking due to the revision, either through replacement of ICEVs or reestimation. It was widely believed, for instance, that initial underestimation of inventory increases in 1973 contributed to failure to predict the 1974 downturn; yet the A^r simulation initiated in 1973-III substantially overpredicts inventory investment in 1974, while both the A^u and B^r paths are closer to the actual levels. Accuracy in tracking of final sales, however, yields a different relative ordering: the A^r simulation initiated in 1973-III does somewhat better than the A^u simulation, and the B^r simulation does most poorly. Similarly equivocal results obtain for the simulation initiated in 1974-IV.

7.4   Conclusions

The statistical component of the benchmark revision had only moderate effects on both the structure and the predictive accuracy of the BEA quarterly econometric model. Although many structural parameters underwent large relative changes upon reestimation with the revised data, the early quarter multipliers changed relatively little. The revision, on balance, moderately improved model predictive accuracy both as a result of better measures of initial conditions and exogenous variables and as a result of revised parameter estimates. These improvements, however, were not uniform across all variables examined or when comparing within-sample with postsample accuracy or for all time horizons. There is no clear evidence that the revision improved the model's tracking of the 1974–75 recession. Finally, within the rules adopted for this experiment, there were few equation specification changes necessitated by the revision; these changes, moreover, had very little effect either on the multipliers or on predictive accuracy.

Table 7.1   **Distribution of Parameter Revisions:**
Model B versus Model A

Percent Revision	Number of Coefficients Revised		
	Explanatory Variables	Serial Correlation Correction	Standard Error of Estimate
200 +	2	0	1
100 to 200	12	0	4
50 to 100	11	4	6
20 to 50	14	4	5
10 to 20	15	4	6
5 to 10	15	4	3
0 to 5	24	6	9
−0 to −4.8	15	12	6
−4.9 to −9.1	5	1	9
−9.2 to −16.7	13	1	3
−16.8 to −33.3	25	1	8
−33.4 to −50.0	13	0	4
−50.0 to 66.7	4	0	0
−66.7 to −100.0	9	0	0
Change in sign	3	n.a.	n.a.
Totals	180	37	64

Note: n.a. = not applicable.

Table 7.2   **Percent Changes in Absolute Value of**
Selected Parameters of Consumption Sector Equations

Dependent Variable	Real Disposable Income		Relative Prices	
	Direct	Total	Direct	Total
Automobiles	29.9	29.9	−45.9	−45.9
Auto parts, tires, and accessories	n.a.	n.a.	n.a.	n.a.
Furniture and equipment	−12.6	−12.6	n.a.	n.a.
Other durables	−80.3	−80.3	121.8	121.8
Clothing and shoes	−19.8	−19.8	−18.7	−18.7
Food	146.2	9.4	167.1	7.3
Gasoline and oil	−11.5	−2.5	32.9	46.4
Other nondurables	−16.6	−4.1	14.8	32.0
Housing	n.a.	n.a.	n.a.	n.a.
Household operations	42.7	4.3	n.a.	n.a.
Transportation	35.5	34.0	−39.9	−40.5
Other services	−28.4	4.2	n.a.	n.a.

Note: n.a. = not applicable.

Table 7.3   Multipliers for Nonborrowed Reserves: GNP Components and Related Measures
(Change, in $Billions, Unless Otherwise Noted, per $Billions of Increase in Nonborrowed Reserves)

					Quarters after Change						
	1	2	3	4	5	6	7	8	12	16	20
Gross national product:											
Model A	.35	1.06	1.82	2.48	3.12	3.74	4.27	4.74	5.88	6.78	7.73
Model B	.35	1.08	1.81	2.36	2.89	3.41	3.82	4.22	5.58	6.92	7.33
Model C	.33	1.02	1.72	2.23	2.69	3.15	3.52	3.88	5.10	6.52	7.15
Personal consumption expenditures:											
Model A	.21	.52	.86	1.19	1.65	1.99	2.23	2.48	3.20	3.68	4.38
Model B	.19	.48	.81	1.12	1.56	1.88	2.09	2.33	3.07	3.43	3.93
Model C	.16	.41	.71	.99	1.38	1.66	1.85	2.06	2.72	3.15	3.75
Fixed nonresidential investment:											
Model A	.03	.12	.27	.44	.63	.80	.96	1.09	1.37	1.46	1.64
Model B	.02	.07	.16	.29	.43	.57	.70	.83	1.26	1.67	1.78
Model C	.01	.06	.15	.27	.40	.52	.64	.75	1.12	1.50	1.66
Residential investment:											
Model A	.21	.57	.74	.74	.71	.76	.87	.96	1.22	1.86	2.24
Model B	.21	.58	.74	.74	.70	.75	.86	.94	1.09	1.82	2.20
Model C	.22	.59	.76	.75	.72	.76	.87	.96	1.20	1.84	2.24
Change in business inventories:											
Model A	-.10	-.12	.01	.20	.31	.41	.44	.45	.47	.24	.13
Model B	-.07	-.02	.15	.30	.36	.43	.42	.41	.49	.56	.18
Mobel C	-.06	-.02	.14	.28	.33	.39	.38	.37	.43	.52	.22
Imports of goods and services:											
Model A	.01	.03	.06	.09	.17	.23	.27	.32	.45	.56	.78
Model B	.01	.03	.06	.09	.17	.22	.25	.29	.43	.56	.77
Model C	-.00	.02	.04	.07	.14	.18	.21	.25	.37	.50	.72

Personal income:											
Model A	.14	.45	.82	1.16	1.50	1.82	2.10	2.37	3.14	3.91	4.86
Model B	.11	.40	.77	1.09	1.38	1.66	1.90	2.13	2.85	3.55	4.24
Model C	.10	.38	.73	1.03	1.29	1.54	1.75	1.96	2.61	3.33	4.09
Corporate profits (share):											
Model A	.18	.52	.84	1.09	1.34	1.58	1.80	1.98	2.33	2.35	2.29
Model B	.22	.61	.92	1.11	1.30	1.50	1.65	1.82	2.41	3.04	2.70
Model C	.20	.58	.89	1.05	1.21	1.39	1.53	1.68	2.21	2.88	2.67
Federal surplus or deficit (−):											
Model A	.12	.36	.62	.84	1.01	1.20	1.37	1.51	1.86	2.09	2.43
Model B	.13	.40	.65	.85	1.01	1.21	1.37	1.51	2.01	2.44	2.53
Model C	.12	.38	.62	.80	.95	1.11	1.26	1.39	1.83	2.29	2.47
GNP (billions of $1972):											
Model A	.38	1.10	1.83	2.38	2.94	3.44	3.87	4.25	4.76	4.56	4.41
Model B	.37	1.09	1.77	2.20	2.56	2.88	3.11	3.29	3.39	3.22	3.03
Model C	.35	1.04	1.68	2.08	2.39	2.66	2.86	3.01	3.10	3.10	3.05
Implicit price deflator, GNP (1972 = 100):											
Model A	.00	.01	.01	.02	.03	.04	.05	.05	.09	.14	.20
Model B	.00	.01	.02	.03	.04	.06	.07	.09	.18	.27	.31
Model C	.00	.01	.02	.03	.04	.05	.07	.08	.18	.28	.33
Unemployment rate (%):											
Model A	−.01	−.02	−.04	−.06	−.08	−.09	−.10	−.11	−.11	−.09	−.09
Model B	−.01	−.03	−.05	−.07	−.08	−.10	−.10	−.11	−.11	−.09	−.09
Model C	−.01	−.02	−.05	−.06	−.08	−.09	−.10	−.10	−.10	−.09	−.09
Treasury bill rate (%):											
Model A	−.56	−.53	−.49	−.46	−.40	−.37	−.36	−.34	−.31	−.35	−.36
Model B	−.58	−.54	−.50	−.47	−.41	−.39	−.38	−.36	−.34	−.37	−.38
Model C	−.60	−.55	−.52	−.48	−.42	−.40	−.39	−.37	−.35	−.39	−.39
Corporate bond rate (%):											
Model A	−.13	−.14	−.17	−.22	−.25	−.28	−.31	−.32	−.36	−.39	−.42
Model B	−.14	−.14	−.18	−.22	−.26	−.29	−.32	−.34	−.38	−.42	−.45
Model C	−.14	−.15	−.18	−.23	−.26	−.30	−.33	−.35	−.39	−.43	−.46

Table 7.4   Multipliers for Corporate Profits Taxes: GNP, GNP Components, and Related Measures (Change, in $Billions, Unless Otherwise Noted, per $Billions of Tax Reduction)

	Quarters after Change										
	1	2	3	4	5	6	7	8	12	16	20
Gross national product:											
Model A	.03	.06	.12	.20	.30	.41	.53	.64	.92	1.08	1.25
Model B	.03	.07	.15	.25	.39	.54	.70	.85	1.30	1.62	1.83
Model C	.03	.07	.15	.25	.39	.55	.71	.86	1.32	1.64	1.85
Personal consumption expenditures:											
Model A	.03	.04	.07	.09	.13	.17	.21	.26	.39	.52	.68
Model B	.02	.03	.06	.09	.14	.19	.25	.31	.53	.71	.89
Model C	.02	.03	.06	.09	.14	.20	.26	.32	.54	.72	.90
Fixed nonresidential investment:											
Model A	.01	.03	.08	.13	.19	.25	.32	.36	.48	.57	.65
Model B	.01	.04	.10	.17	.25	.33	.43	.50	.72	.90	1.07
Model C	.01	.04	.10	.17	.25	.33	.43	.51	.72	.90	1.08
Residential investment:											
Model A	-.00	-.00	-.01	-.00	-.00	.00	.01	.01	.02	.01	.01
Model B	-.00	-.00	-.00	-.00	-.00	.00	.01	.01	.03	.02	.00
Model C	-.00	-.00	-.00	-.00	.00	.00	.01	.01	.03	.02	.01
Change in business inventories:											
Model A	-.01	-.00	-.00	.00	.01	.02	.04	.06	.10	.08	.06
Model B	-.00	.00	.00	.01	.02	.05	.06	.08	.12	.14	.08
Model C	-.00	.00	.00	.01	.02	.05	.06	.08	.12	.14	.08
Imports of goods and services:											
Model A	.01	.01	.01	.02	.02	.03	.04	.05	.07	.10	.15
Model B	.00	.01	.01	.02	.03	.03	.04	.06	.10	.14	.21
Model C	.00	.01	.01	.02	.03	.03	.05	.06	.10	.14	.21

Personal income:											
Model A	.08	.10	.15	.19	.26	.33	.40	.47	.69	.88	1.09
Model B	.06	.09	.14	.19	.28	.36	.46	.55	.88	1.14	1.38
Model C	.06	.09	.14	.20	.28	.37	.46	.56	.88	1.15	1.39
Corporate profits (share):											
Model A	.01	.03	.05	.09	.14	.19	.24	.29	.40	.42	.41
Model B	.02	.04	.08	.13	.20	.27	.34	.40	.56	.67	.66
Model C	.02	.04	.08	.13	.20	.27	.34	.41	.58	.68	.66
Federal surplus or deficit (−):											
Model A	−.99	−.96	−.95	−.87	−.92	−.90	−.90	−.86	−1.03	−1.11	−1.08
Model B	−.99	−.94	−.93	−.83	−.87	−.82	−.81	−.74	−.86	−.88	−.75
Model C	−.99	−.94	−.93	−.82	−.86	−.82	−.81	−.74	−.85	−.87	−.74
GNP (billions of $1972):											
Model A	.04	.07	.12	.20	.29	.39	.50	.60	.80	.81	.80
Model B	.03	.07	.15	.24	.37	.50	.63	.74	.98	1.01	.99
Model C	.03	.08	.15	.25	.37	.50	.64	.75	.99	1.02	1.00
Implicit Price deflator (1972 = 100):											
Model A	.00	.00	.00	.00	.00	.00	.00	.01	.01	.02	.02
Model B	.00	.00	.00	.00	.01	.01	.01	.01	.03	.04	.05
Model C	.00	.00	.00	.00	.01	.01	.01	.01	.03	.04	.06
Unemployment rate (%):											
Model A	−.00	−.00	−.00	−.00	−.01	−.01	−.01	−.02	−.02	−.02	−.02
Model B	−.00	−.00	−.00	−.01	−.01	−.01	−.02	−.02	−.03	−.03	−.03
Model C	−.00	−.00	−.01	−.01	−.01	−.02	−.02	−.02	−.03	−.03	−.03
Treasury bill rate (%):											
Model A	.00	.00	.00	.00	.01	.01	.01	.01	.01	.01	.02
Model B	.00	.00	.01	.01	.01	.01	.01	.01	.02	.02	.02
Model C	.00	.00	.00	.00	.01	.01	.01	.01	.02	.02	.02
Corporate bond rate (%):											
Model A	.00	.00	.00	.00	.00	.00	.01	.01	.01	.01	.02
Model B	.00	.00	.00	.01	.00	.00	.01	.01	.01	.02	.02
Model C	.00	.00	.00	.01	.00	.00	.01	.01	.01	.02	.02

Table 7.5 Multipliers for Federal Government Purchases: GNP, GNP Components, and Related Measures (Change, in $Billions, Unless Otherwise Noted, per $Billions Added Government Purchases)

	Quarters after Change										
	1	2	3	4	5	6	7	8	12	16	20
Gross national product:											
Model A	.87	1.40	1.82	2.08	2.28	2.39	2.41	2.39	1.96	1.80	1.93
Model B	.95	1.55	1.96	2.20	2.41	2.57	2.63	2.68	2.75	2.93	2.83
Model C	.95	1.55	1.96	2.21	2.41	2.57	2.63	2.69	2.76	2.92	2.82
Personal consumption expenditures:											
Model A	.13	.30	.47	.55	.67	.72	.75	.76	.69	.78	1.04
Model B	.13	.32	.53	.64	.80	.88	.94	1.00	1.12	1.27	1.47
Model C	.13	.32	.53	.64	.80	.88	.94	1.00	1.12	1.26	1.46
Fixed nonresidential investment:											
Model A	.03	.12	.22	.31	.37	.41	.43	.41	.22	.16	.13
Model B	.04	.12	.24	.34	.44	.51	.56	.58	.58	.67	.65
Model C	.04	.12	.24	.35	.44	.51	.56	.58	.58	.66	.65
Residential investment:											
Model A	.00	.00	.01	.01	.02	.03	.03	.03	.03	.01	.01
Model B	−.00	.00	.01	.02	.03	.04	.04	.04	.05	.01	−.01
Model C	−.00	−.00	.01	.02	.03	.04	.04	.04	.05	.02	−.01
Change in business inventories:											
Model A	−.28	.03	.20	.30	.33	.35	.33	.31	.15	−.01	−.06
Model B	−.20	.15	.28	.21	.28	.29	.24	.22	.17	.19	.01
Model C	−.20	.15	.27	.31	.28	.29	.24	.22	.17	.19	.00
Imports of goods and services:											
Model A	.02	.05	.08	.09	.11	.12	.13	.13	.12	.13	.18
Model B	.02	.05	.09	.11	.13	.14	.15	.16	.17	.22	.29
Model C	.02	.05	.09	.11	.13	.14	.15	.16	.17	.21	.29

Personal income:											
Model A	.32	.62	.83	.98	1.09	1.17	1.22	1.24	1.17	1.23	1.48
Model B	.32	.69	.95	1.14	1.27	1.38	1.45	1.50	1.58	1.72	1.88
Model C	.32	.69	.95	1.14	1.27	1.38	1.45	1.50	1.58	1.72	1.88
Corporate profits (share):											
Model A	.49	.67	.84	.94	1.01	1.04	1.01	.98	.69	.45	.27
Model B	.59	.73	.90	.94	.99	1.04	1.02	1.02	1.04	1.08	.79
Model C	.59	.79	.90	.94	1.00	1.04	1.03	1.04	1.05	1.07	.78
Federal surplus or deficit (−):											
Model A	−.67	−.50	−.36	−.27	−.23	−.20	−.20	−.22	−.37	−.44	−.42
Model B	−.64	−.44	−.31	−.22	−.17	−.11	−.09	−.08	−.05	−.02	−.07
Model C	−.64	−.44	−.31	−.22	−.17	−.11	−.09	−.07	−.05	−.02	−.08
GNP (billions of $1972):											
Model A	1.08	1.56	1.91	2.08	2.22	2.27	2.28	2.22	1.62	1.14	.98
Model B	1.13	1.66	1.98	2.11	2.17	2.17	2.14	2.05	1.50	1.10	.87
Model C	1.13	1.66	1.99	2.11	2.17	2.18	2.14	2.05	1.50	1.10	.86
Implicit deflator, GNP (1972=100):											
Model A	−.01	−.00	.01	.01	.02	.02	.02	.02	.03	.04	.06
Model B	−.00	−.00	.01	.02	.03	.04	.05	.06	.10	.14	.15
Model C	−.01	.00	.01	.02	.03	.04	.05	.06	.10	.14	.15
Unemployment rate (%):											
Model A	−.02	−.04	−.05	−.06	−.06	−.06	−.06	−.06	−.04	−.02	−.02
Model B	−.02	−.04	−.06	−.07	−.08	−.08	−.08	−.07	−.05	−.03	−.01
Model C	−.02	−.04	−.06	−.07	−.08	−.08	−.08	−.07	−.05	−.03	−.03
Treasury bill rate (%):											
Model A	.01	.01	.02	.03	.03	.03	.03	.03	.02	.02	.02
Model B	.01	.02	.02	.02	.03	.03	.03	.04	.03	.03	.04
Model C	.01	.01	.02	.02	.03	.03	.03	.04	.04	.04	.04
Corporate bond rate (%):											
Model A	.00	.00	.01	.01	.01	.01	.02	.02	.03	.03	.03
Model B	.00	.00	.01	.01	.01	.01	.02	.02	.03	.03	.04
Model C	.00	.00	.01	.01	.01	.01	.02	.02	.03	.04	.04

Table 7.6 Error Statistics

A. Gross National Product, Constant Dollars—Percent Errors

Quarters Ahead	Mean Absolute Percent Error				Mean Percent Error				t-(Mean Percent Error)				Theil U			
	A^u	A^r	B^r	C^r	A^u	A^r	B^r	C^r	A^u	A^r	B^r	C^r	A^u	A^r	B^r	C^r
							Within-Sample									
1	.44	.54	.40	.42	.07	−.08	−.00	−.03	.41	−.43	−.01	−.20	.39	.45	.34	.37
2	.79	.97	.74	.78	.15	−.20	−.20	−.24	.53	−.60	−.78	−.89	.37	.44	.34	.36
3	1.06	1.38	1.04	1.07	.13	−.28	−.43	−.47	.34	−.59	−1.23	−1.27	.36	.44	.34	.37
4	1.40	1.79	1.36	1.42	.07	−.31	−.63	−.67	.14	−.50	−1.41	−1.39	.36	.45	.35	.37
6	2.40	2.91	2.48	2.53	−.06	.21	−.50	−.51	−.07	.19	−.57	−.57	.45	.55	.45	.46
8	2.86	3.54	3.18	3.21	.64	1.16	.08	.11	.62	.90	.07	.10	.47	.59	.49	.50
							Postsample									
1	1.39	.98	.81	.85	−.53	.34	.28	.32	−.80	.78	.75	.86	1.20	.79	.68	.68
2	2.55	2.40	1.88	1.75	−.33	.81	.91	.84	−.31	.87	1.17	1.13	1.08	.97	.85	.81
3	3.51	3.29	2.52	2.43	−.42	1.05	1.32	1.19	−.28	.77	1.25	1.13	1.09	1.04	.86	.84
4	4.19	4.12	3.14	2.98	−.68	1.12	1.64	1.46	−.40	.68	1.37	1.20	1.05	1.03	.81	.80
6	4.96	4.62	3.03	3.17	−2.56	.25	1.42	1.19	−1.36	.13	1.17	.94	1.07	.94	.67	.68
8	5.03	4.26	2.69	2.75	−4.27	−1.14	.71	.48	−2.54	−.66	.65	.43	.91	.69	.44	.43
							Combined									
1	.82	.71	.56	.59	−.17	.09	.11	.11	−.61	.42	.65	.62	.84	.62	.52	.53
2	1.49	1.54	1.20	1.17	−.04	.21	.25	.19	−.09	.49	.69	.55	.76	.71	.61	.59
3	2.04	2.14	1.63	1.62	−.09	.25	.27	.19	−.14	.41	.54	.38	.74	.74	.61	.60
4	2.52	2.72	2.07	2.04	−.23	.26	.28	.18	−.32	.35	.47	.31	.70	.72	.57	.57
6	3.42	3.59	2.70	2.78	−1.06	.22	.27	.17	−1.14	.23	.37	.23	.69	.69	.52	.53
8	3.73	3.83	2.98	3.03	−1.32	.24	.33	.26	−1.26	.23	.43	.33	.66	.63	.47	.48

Note: Superscript denotes version of model and status of initial conditions and exogenous variables (u = unrevised, r = revised).

B. Implicit Price Deflator for GNP—Percent Errors

Quarters Ahead	Mean Absolute Percent Error				Mean Percent Error				t-(Mean Percent Error)				Theil U			
	A^u	A^r	B^r	C^r	A^u	A^r	B^r	C^r	A^u	A^r	B^r	C^r	A^u	A^r	B^r	C^r
								Within-Sample								
1	.59	.16	.17	.17	-.59	-.02	.05	.05	-7.76	-.28	.88	.87	.46	.13	.14	.14
2	.69	.20	.23	.24	-.69	-.05	.05	.04	-11.60	-.67	.54	.48	.26	.10	.10	.10
3	.71	.34	.38	.39	-.71	-.16	-.03	-.03	-9.13	-1.26	-.17	-.21	.18	.11	.12	.12
4	.87	.52	.57	.57	-.87	-.33	-.13	-.14	-6.15	-1.77	-.59	-.63	.17	.12	.13	.13
6	1.40	1.07	1.20	1.18	-1.40	-.98	-.59	-.61	-3.79	-2.41	-1.26	-1.29	.19	.17	.18	.18
8	2.88	1.98	1.95	1.92	-2.88	-1.95	-1.33	-1.34	-4.94	-3.11	-1.89	-1.92	.27	.22	.21	.20
								Postsample								
1	1.34	.89	.76	.76	-1.34	-.89	-.76	-.76	-6.17	-6.79	-6.30	-6.30	.65	.42	.36	.37
2	1.93	1.37	1.09	1.12	-1.93	-1.37	-1.09	-1.12	-16.88	-9.72	-8.80	-8.42	.45	.33	.26	.27
3	2.39	1.83	1.42	1.47	-2.39	-1.83	-1.42	-1.47	-15.34	-7.38	-5.14	-5.48	.39	.31	.26	.26
4	2.91	2.32	1.76	1.82	-2.91	-2.32	-1.76	-1.82	-10.94	-6.37	-4.19	-4.44	.38	.32	.27	.27
6	3.75	3.25	2.37	2.43	-3.75	-3.25	-2.37	-2.43	-8.73	-6.24	-3.83	-4.01	.38	.34	.28	.28
8	5.16	4.32	3.05	3.08	-5.16	-4.32	-3.05	-3.08	-10.23	-7.34	-4.22	-4.34	.42	.36	.28	.28
								Combined								
1	.89	.45	.40	.40	-.89	-.36	-.27	-.27	-7.06	-3.17	-2.56	-2.57	.59	.35	.30	.30
2	1.19	.67	.57	.59	-1.19	-.58	-.41	-.43	-7.92	-3.53	-2.82	-2.84	.39	.26	.22	.22
3	1.38	.94	.79	.82	-1.38	-.83	-.58	-.61	-6.79	-3.71	-2.78	-2.86	.32	.25	.21	.21
4	1.69	1.24	1.05	1.07	-1.69	-1.13	-.79	-.81	-6.39	-3.95	-2.82	-2.91	.30	.25	.21	.22
6	2.34	1.94	1.67	1.68	-2.34	-1.89	-1.31	-1.33	-6.15	-4.69	-3.13	-3.21	.29	.26	.23	.23
8	3.79	2.91	2.39	2.38	-3.79	-2.90	-2.02	-2.04	-8.06	-5.70	-3.77	-3.84	.33	.28	.24	.24

Table 7.6 (continued)

C. Gross National Product, Current Dollars—Percent Errors

Quarters Ahead	Mean Absolute Percent Error				Mean Percent Error				t-(Mean Percent Error)				Theil U			
	A^u	A^r	B^r	C^r	A^u	A^r	B^r	C^r	A^u	A^r	B^r	C^r	A^u	A^r	B^r	C^r
							Within-Sample									
1	.65	.53	.37	.44	−.52	−.10	.05	.02	−3.23	−.50	.31	.10	.28	.25	.20	.21
2	1.01	.97	.63	.69	−.55	−.25	−.15	−.20	−1.73	−.80	−.67	−.79	.24	.22	.16	.18
3	1.25	1.29	.81	.91	−.60	−.44	−.46	−.51	−1.49	−1.08	−1.64	−1.60	.21	.20	.15	.17
4	1.50	1.57	.94	1.05	−.85	−.65	−.78	−.82	−1.85	−1.34	−2.56	−2.28	.19	.19	.14	.16
6	1.95	2.12	1.57	1.60	−1.52	−.82	−1.13	−1.15	−2.73	−1.17	−2.43	−2.27	.18	.19	.14	.15
8	2.53	2.07	1.77	1.80	−2.34	−.90	−1.33	−1.31	−4.25	−1.30	−2.78	−2.54	.17	.14	.12	.13
							Postsample									
1	1.95	.74	.79	.75	−1.89	−.55	−.48	−.44	−2.35	−1.43	−1.36	−1.28	1.24	.51	.46	.44
2	2.65	1.80	1.62	1.47	−2.32	−.57	−.20	−.30	−2.13	−.73	−.29	−.45	.82	.48	.40	.39
3	3.49	2.56	1.90	2.02	−2.90	−.83	−.14	−.31	−2.17	−.76	−.16	−.38	.69	.46	.34	.34
4	4.00	3.02	2.04	2.06	−3.71	−1.26	−.18	−.41	−2.52	−.99	−.21	−.47	.62	.42	.26	.27
6	6.31	3.65	1.73	1.94	−6.31	−3.08	−1.04	−1.32	−4.40	−2.33	−1.54	−1.83	.57	.36	.16	.18
8	9.30	5.47	2.40	2.67	−9.30	−5.47	−2.40	−2.67	−7.92	−4.79	−4.23	−5.03	.56	.36	.16	.17
							Combined									
1	1.17	.61	.53	.56	−1.07	−.28	−.16	−.17	−2.98	−1.44	−.94	−.96	.76	.36	.31	.31
2	1.66	1.30	1.02	1.00	−1.25	−.38	−.17	−.24	−2.52	−1.07	−.57	−.81	.53	.34	.28	.27
3	2.15	1.80	1.25	1.36	−1.52	−.60	−.33	−.43	−2.44	−1.23	−.90	−1.16	.45	.32	.24	.24
4	2.50	2.15	1.38	1.45	−1.99	−.90	−.54	−.66	−2.83	−1.57	−1.42	−1.65	.41	.29	.19	.21
6	3.70	2.73	1.63	1.74	−3.44	−1.72	−1.09	−1.22	−4.11	−2.45	−2.90	−2.99	.38	.27	.15	.16
8	5.24	3.43	2.02	2.15	−5.13	−2.73	−1.76	−1.86	−5.34	−3.46	−4.67	−4.67	.38	.26	.14	.15

D. Gross National Product (Billions of $1972)

Quarters Ahead	Mean Absolute Percent Error				Mean Percent Error				t-(Mean Percent Error)				Theil U			
	A^u	A^r	B^r	C^r	A^u	A^r	B^r	C^r	A^u	A^r	B^r	C^r	A^u	A^r	B^r	C^r
							Within-Sample									
1	5.15	6.29	4.66	4.90	1.04	−.73	.15	−.17	.53	−.32	.09	−.09	.40	.46	.35	.38
2	9.33	11.52	8.76	9.19	2.08	−2.06	−2.15	−2.60	.62	−.52	−.72	−.82	.38	.44	.34	.36
3	12.74	16.50	12.32	12.74	1.92	−2.98	−4.91	−5.37	.41	−.53	−1.19	−1.21	.37	.44	.34	.37
4	16.79	21.42	16.19	16.92	1.14	−3.40	−7.36	−7.75	.19	−.46	−1.38	−1.35	.36	.45	.35	.37
6	28.54	34.74	29.64	30.19	−.85	2.28	−6.20	−6.28	−.08	.18	−.60	−.59	.44	.54	.44	.45
8	34.31	42.46	38.25	38.58	7.26	13.34	.40	.75	.58	.87	.03	.06	.46	.57	.48	.49
							Postsample									
1	16.71	11.76	9.76	10.16	−6.43	3.97	3.30	3.74	−.81	.76	.73	.84	1.22	.79	.69	.69
2	30.82	28.77	22.46	20.90	−4.54	9.29	10.52	9.75	−.35	.83	1.14	1.10	1.09	.96	.83	.79
3	42.68	39.55	30.16	28.98	−6.13	11.62	15.15	13.62	−.34	.83	1.14	1.10	1.09	1.03	.84	.82
4	51.26	49.86	37.71	35.74	−9.89	12.15	18.91	16.76	−.47	.62	1.32	1.15	1.06	1.01	.79	.78
6	62.27	57.22	37.14	38.89	−33.58	1.39	16.54	13.68	−1.43	.06	1.11	.89	1.07	.92	.64	.65
8	65.29	54.66	34.09	34.91	−56.02	−16.04	8.12	5.14	−2.56	−.72	.59	.37	.91	.69	.42	.42
							Combined									
1	9.77	8.48	6.70	7.00	−1.95	1.15	1.41	1.39	−.58	.47	.69	.67	.87	.63	.53	.54
2	17.93	18.42	14.24	13.87	−.57	2.48	2.92	2.34	−.10	.49	.69	.57	.77	.72	.60	.59
3	24.72	25.72	19.46	19.24	−1.30	2.86	3.12	2.22	−.17	.39	.53	.38	.75	.74	.60	.60
4	30.58	32.80	24.80	24.45	−3.27	2.82	3.15	2.06	−.36	.31	.45	.29	.72	.72	.56	.56
6	42.03	43.73	32.64	33.67	−13.94	1.92	2.90	1.71	−1.21	.16	.33	.19	.70	.69	.51	.52
8	46.70	47.34	36.59	37.11	−18.05	1.59	3.49	2.51	−1.36	.12	.37	.26	.67	.62	.46	.46

Table 7.6 (continued)

E. Personal Consumption Expenditures (Billions of $1972)

Quarters Ahead	Mean Absolute Percent Error				Mean Percent Error				t-(Mean Percent Error)				Theil U			
	A''	A'	B'	C'	A''	A'	B'	C'	A''	A'	B'	C'	A''	A'	B'	C'
							Within-Sample									
1	4.68	5.11	4.36	4.68	-2.15	-.73	-1.45	-1.88	-1.33	-.41	-.97	-1.21	.57	.58	.51	.54
2	6.68	7.17	6.61	6.90	-4.13	-2.49	-3.85	-4.28	-1.77	-.99	-1.80	-1.86	.47	.46	.43	.47
3	8.05	9.19	8.62	9.17	-3.20	-4.34	-6.59	-6.97	-1.12	-1.40	-2.47	-2.36	.38	.42	.42	.45
4	8.65	11.14	10.77	11.46	-5.54	-6.45	-9.91	-10.19	-1.84	-1.88	-3.36	-3.02	.34	.39	.41	.45
6	12.40	16.17	18.31	18.32	-7.26	-7.39	-13.74	-13.68	-1.82	-1.42	-2.94	-2.71	.33	.41	.45	.47
8	16.34	20.87	22.60	22.99	-6.48	-4.78	-14.92	-14.45	-1.33	-.72	-2.50	-2.29	.33	.42	.47	.48
							Postsample									
1	12.19	4.86	5.61	4.90	-11.30	-1.61	-1.86	-1.22	-3.44	-.62	-.67	-.46	1.62	.80	.86	.81
2	14.03	10.51	10.09	9.51	-13.37	-1.04	-1.62	-1.22	-2.62	-.22	-.37	-.29	1.17	.75	.73	.68
3	17.22	14.76	14.12	13.89	-12.88	-.99	-1.74	-1.63	-1.87	-.15	-.29	-.28	.96	.75	.69	.66
4	20.16	19.23	16.29	16.36	-15.14	-.87	-1.21	-1.51	-1.84	-.11	-.18	-.23	.87	.69	.59	.58
6	29.87	25.30	20.06	20.36	-26.24	-7.76	-6.98	-8.06	-2.50	-.74	-.85	-.99	.81	.61	.48	.48
8	39.60	25.49	19.88	20.35	-38.99	-16.00	-13.87	-15.56	-4.02	-1.62	-1.77	-2.02	.73	.48	.39	.40
							Combined									
1	7.69	5.01	4.86	4.77	-5.81	-1.08	-1.61	-1.62	-3.08	-.75	-1.17	-1.18	1.04	.66	.64	.64
2	9.62	8.51	8.00	7.94	-7.83	-1.91	-2.96	-3.05	-3.00	-.83	-1.39	-1.44	.78	.58	.55	.55
3	11.72	11.42	10.82	11.06	-7.07	-3.00	-4.65	-4.83	-2.13	-.95	-1.64	-1.68	.64	.56	.52	.53
4	13.25	14.37	12.98	13.42	-9.38	-4.22	-6.43	-6.71	-2.48	-1.13	-1.95	-1.98	.58	.51	.48	.50
6	19.38	19.82	19.01	19.14	-14.85	-7.54	-11.03	-11.43	-2.90	-1.49	-2.60	-2.63	.57	.50	.46	.47
8	25.64	22.71	21.51	21.93	-19.48	-9.27	-14.50	-14.89	-3.27	-1.66	-3.13	-3.13	.56	.45	.43	.44

F. Fixed Nonresidential Investment (Billions of $1972)

Quarters Ahead	Mean Absolute Percent Error				Mean Percent Error				t-(Mean Percent Error)				Theil U			
	A''	A'	B'	C'	A''	A'	B'	C'	A''	A'	B'	C'	A''	A'	B'	C'
Within-Sample																
1	2.87	1.59	1.44	1.42	2.47	−.36	−.24	−.25	3.68	−.66	−.49	−.52	1.11	.62	.54	.53
2	2.66	2.44	2.10	2.10	1.45	−.72	−.65	−.68	1.68	−.80	−.84	−.90	.58	.55	.47	.47
3	2.97	3.23	2.42	2.46	−1.08	−1.19	−1.37	−1.44	−1.10	−1.09	−1.74	−1.86	.44	.49	.37	.37
4	3.47	4.06	2.48	2.54	−.45	−1.60	−2.22	−2.32	−.37	−1.12	−3.08	−3.35	.40	.49	.32	.32
6	7.06	8.22	5.34	5.17	−.74	−.79	−2.69	−2.81	−.28	−.26	−1.42	−1.52	.58	.69	.46	.45
8	10.70	11.63	8.89	8.84	.76	1.65	−1.39	−1.47	.20	.39	−.44	−.48	.68	.76	.56	.55
Postsample																
1	4.55	2.68	2.26	2.28	4.09	1.52	1.14	1.15	3.16	1.44	1.31	1.30	1.39	.83	.67	.68
2	7.36	5.86	4.18	4.20	3.88	2.88	3.08	3.07	1.38	1.19	1.95	1.97	1.13	.95	.70	.69
3	11.01	10.03	6.72	6.70	1.99	4.10	5.92	5.87	.44	1.02	2.67	2.74	1.15	1.09	.79	.78
4	15.25	14.49	9.18	9.05	2.39	4.74	9.18	9.05	.39	.84	3.54	3.63	1.25	1.20	.88	.86
6	20.09	19.48	15.15	14.94	−1.93	3.76	15.15	14.94	−.24	.48	5.35	5.39	1.37	1.36	1.10	1.08
8	20.39	21.01	18.93	18.78	−7.72	−.03	18.93	18.78	−.95	−.00	6.22	6.43	1.52	1.48	1.37	1.35
Combined																
1	3.54	2.03	1.76	1.77	3.12	.39	.32	.31	4.72	.70	.68	.66	1.26	.74	.61	.61
2	4.54	3.81	2.93	2.94	2.42	.72	.84	.82	1.98	.63	.98	.95	.92	.79	.61	.60
3	6.19	5.95	4.14	4.16	.15	.92	1.55	1.48	.08	.52	1.22	1.19	.90	.87	.64	.63
4	8.18	8.23	5.16	5.14	.69	.93	2.34	2.23	.28	.38	1.39	1.35	.95	.93	.67	.66
6	12.27	12.73	9.26	9.08	−1.22	1.03	4.44	4.29	−.36	.29	1.75	1.71	.99	1.02	.79	.78
8	14.58	15.38	12.90	12.82	−2.63	.98	6.74	6.63	−.66	.24	2.13	2.12	1.01	1.03	.88	.87

Table 7.6 (continued)

G. Residential Investment (Billions of $1972)

Quarters Ahead	Mean Absolute Percent Error				Mean Percent Error				t-(Mean Percent Error)				Theil U			
	A''	A'	B'	C'	A''	A'	B'	C'	A''	A'	B'	C'	A''	A'	B'	C'
							Within-Sample									
1	1.55	1.49	1.23	1.24	−1.53	−.87	−.67	−.66	−4.22	−1.93	−1.66	−1.62	.71	.63	.54	.54
2	3.67	3.63	3.30	3.31	−2.14	−1.50	−1.16	−1.12	−2.09	−1.33	−1.07	−1.03	.74	.74	.70	.70
3	5.23	5.58	5.31	5.32	−1.79	−1.71	−1.22	−1.16	−1.11	−.98	−.71	−.67	.73	.78	.75	.76
4	6.51	6.81	6.73	6.76	−1.78	−1.50	−.84	−.78	−.86	−.68	−.38	−.35	.72	.76	.75	.75
6	8.67	8.99	9.12	9.13	.33	.38	1.30	1.36	.12	.13	.44	.46	.68	.71	.72	.72
8	10.12	10.68	11.03	11.02	3.20	3.37	4.46	4.52	1.00	.98	1.30	1.32	.68	.73	.75	.75
							Postsample									
1	1.34	2.90	2.63	2.60	.36	2.90	2.63	2.60	.63	6.00	5.31	5.32	.55	1.12	1.04	1.03
2	3.21	4.52	4.05	3.97	1.54	4.52	4.05	3.97	1.19	4.72	4.72	4.77	.73	1.01	.90	.88
3	4.94	5.56	4.92	4.83	2.82	5.56	4.92	4.83	1.50	3.71	3.56	3.56	.81	.97	.87	.86
4	5.94	6.59	5.86	5.75	2.99	6.18	5.49	5.40	1.27	3.06	2.89	2.88	.82	.97	.89	.87
6	7.04	6.97	6.45	6.35	1.97	5.46	4.93	4.83	.68	2.08	1.97	1.95	.77	.87	.81	.80
8	7.40	6.64	6.36	6.28	−1.43	1.90	1.70	1.61	−.47	.69	.65	.62	.64	.59	.57	.56
							Combined									
1	1.47	2.05	1.79	1.79	−.78	.64	.65	.65	−2.07	1.20	1.35	1.35	.65	.86	.79	.78
2	3.49	3.98	3.60	3.58	−.67	.91	.92	.91	−.76	.89	.99	.99	.74	.85	.78	.77
3	5.11	5.57	5.15	5.13	.05	1.20	1.24	1.23	.04	.83	.92	.93	.76	.85	.80	.80
4	6.28	6.72	6.38	6.35	.13	1.57	1.69	1.69	.08	.90	1.03	1.03	.75	.83	.79	.79
6	8.02	8.18	8.05	8.02	.98	2.41	2.75	2.75	.49	1.15	1.35	1.36	.71	.76	.74	.74
8	9.03	9.06	9.16	9.12	1.35	2.78	3.36	3.36	.59	1.22	1.47	1.48	.67	.69	.70	.70

H. Change in Business Inventories (Billions of $1972)

Quarters Ahead	Mean Absolute Percent Error				Mean Percent Error				t-(Mean Percent Error)				Theil U			
	A^u	A^r	B^r	C^r	A^u	A^r	B^r	C^r	A^u	A^r	B^r	C^r	A^u	A^r	B^r	C^r
								Within-Sample								
1	3.08	2.95	2.90	2.86	-1.88	-.30	.93	.98	-1.69	-.30	.97	1.04	.96	.77	.76	.75
2	3.45	2.97	2.37	2.38	.24	-.06	.68	.60	.21	-.06	.82	.73	.74	.65	.55	.53
3	3.99	3.00	2.76	2.88	2.61	.47	.22	.09	2.27	.44	.22	.09	.79	.61	.57	.58
4	5.21	4.47	3.48	3.66	3.37	1.04	.07	-.06	2.02	.65	.05	-.05	.93	.77	.62	.62
6	6.73	6.91	5.32	5.41	3.37	2.81	.84	.74	1.21	.91	.32	.29	.80	.86	.71	.70
8	8.30	8.42	6.91	7.01	6.33	5.79	3.60	3.55	2.12	1.72	1.16	1.14	.75	.80	.69	.69
								Postsample								
1	5.93	5.59	5.11	5.06	-.29	.98	1.24	1.17	-.09	.39	.58	.55	.64	.52	.45	.44
2	10.02	8.93	8.00	7.46	2.28	2.97	5.16	4.11	.54	.76	1.37	1.16	.71	.68	.70	.64
3	11.74	11.44	10.82	9.80	3.35	3.34	6.63	5.11	.64	.65	1.44	1.10	.79	.77	.76	.73
4	12.78	13.07	11.77	11.29	1.92	2.92	6.63	4.91	.34	.50	1.32	.93	.70	.73	.68	.68
6	10.94	10.54	7.99	9.59	-2.75	.71	5.05	3.36	-.63	.16	1.39	.75	.59	.60	.54	.61
8	10.30	8.03	4.99	5.35	-7.86	-4.60	.06	-1.28	-2.58	-1.42	.03	-.52	.63	.55	.36	.37
								Combined								
1	4.22	4.01	3.78	3.74	-1.25	.21	1.05	1.05	-.91	.18	1.06	1.08	.69	.56	.50	.50
2	6.08	5.35	4.62	4.41	1.05	1.15	2.47	2.00	.60	.70	1.54	1.34	.72	.67	.68	.63
3	7.09	6.38	5.98	5.65	2.91	1.61	2.78	2.10	1.36	.77	1.40	1.07	.79	.75	.74	.72
4	8.23	7.91	6.80	6.71	2.79	1.79	2.69	1.93	1.17	.73	1.23	.86	.73	.73	.68	.67
6	8.41	8.36	6.39	7.08	.92	1.97	2.52	1.79	.38	.77	1.17	.77	.67	.70	.61	.64
8	9.10	8.27	6.14	6.34	.65	1.63	2.18	1.62	.25	.62	1.05	.76	.70	.70	.57	.57

Table 7.6 (continued)

I. Imports (Billions of $1972)

Quarters Ahead	Mean Absolute Percent Error				Mean Percent Error				t-(Mean Percent Error)				Theil U			
	A^u	A^r	B^r	C^r	A^u	A^r	B^r	C^r	A^u	A^r	B^r	C^r	A^u	A^r	B^r	C^r
						Within-Sample										
1	2.04	1.98	1.94	2.00	−.90	−1.81	−1.85	−1.92	−1.38	−3.13	−3.20	−3.39	.60	.68	.69	.69
2	2.66	2.90	2.93	3.01	−1.83	−2.82	−2.93	−3.00	−2.38	−4.34	−4.60	−4.88	.65	.74	.75	.76
3	2.89	3.85	4.10	4.17	−1.74	−3.85	−4.10	−4.17	−2.00	−5.92	−6.54	−6.62	.65	.84	.88	.89
4	3.06	5.13	5.56	5.61	−2.24	−5.13	−5.56	−5.61	−2.44	−8.36	−9.33	−8.97	.59	.87	.92	.94
6	3.80	7.24	8.06	8.07	−3.80	−7.24	−8.06	−8.07	−5.04	−9.67	−10.46	−10.19	.53	.90	.99	1.00
8	4.96	8.92	9.51	9.46	−3.14	−7.31	−8.65	−8.60	−2.46	−4.20	−5.35	−5.32	.46	.81	.88	.88
						Postsample										
1	1.92	3.11	3.10	3.23	1.92	−.18	−.14	−.04	2.71	−.14	−.10	−.03	.66	.87	.86	.89
2	2.77	4.34	4.34	4.31	1.34	.05	.15	.19	1.08	.02	.08	.10	.49	.70	.70	.69
3	3.75	5.05	4.97	4.77	1.54	.38	.57	.55	.90	.17	.24	.24	.50	.64	.66	.64
4	4.06	5.14	5.01	4.80	1.28	.81	1.18	1.09	.71	.36	.51	.49	.43	.53	.55	.53
6	3.49	4.20	3.47	3.25	.45	.78	1.61	1.40	.31	.46	1.28	1.15	.28	.33	.27	.25
8	3.52	3.44	2.43	2.50	−2.93	−2.69	−1.29	−1.59	−2.37	−1.91	−1.22	−1.65	.30	.31	.21	.20
						Combined										
1	1.99	2.43	2.41	2.49	.23	−1.16	−1.17	−1.17	.40	−1.81	−1.82	−1.78	.63	.76	.76	.78
2	2.70	3.48	3.50	3.53	−.56	−1.67	−1.70	−1.73	−.75	−1.89	−1.91	−1.95	.56	.71	.72	.72
3	3.23	4.33	4.45	4.41	−.43	−2.16	−2.23	−2.28	−.47	−2.01	−2.02	−2.08	.55	.71	.73	.73
4	3.46	5.14	5.34	5.29	−.83	−2.76	−2.86	−2.93	−.86	−2.38	−2.35	−2.44	.49	.66	.69	.69
6	3.68	6.02	6.23	6.14	−2.10	−4.03	−4.19	−4.28	−2.45	−3.38	−3.29	−3.42	.39	.60	.64	.63
8	4.38	6.73	6.67	6.68	−3.06	−5.46	−5.71	−5.79	−3.43	−4.30	−4.31	−4.49	.38	.60	.63	.63

J. Personal Income—Percent Errors

Quarters Ahead	Mean Absolute Percent Error				Mean Percent Error				t-(Mean Percent Error)				Theil U			
	A^u	A'	B'	C'	A^u	A'	B'	C'	A^u	A'	B'	C'	A^u	A'	B'	C'
Within-Sample																
1	.44	.21	.26	.27	−.41	−.06	−.15	−.16	−3.23	−.80	−1.70	−1.73	.23	.10	.13	.14
2	.74	.42	.46	.51	−.70	−.25	−.39	−.42	−3.02	−1.76	−2.69	−2.62	.22	.11	.13	.14
3	.93	.56	.78	.80	−.92	−.49	−.77	−.80	−3.38	−2.92	−4.37	−3.98	.18	.11	.14	.15
4	1.48	.79	1.23	1.26	−1.48	−.79	−1.23	−1.26	−5.39	−4.75	−6.91	−5.98	.18	.10	.14	.15
6	2.21	1.35	1.96	1.98	−2.21	−1.16	−1.96	−1.98	−9.37	−4.00	−7.95	−7.65	.17	.11	.15	.16
8	3.15	1.53	2.64	2.63	−3.15	−1.38	−2.64	−2.63	−13.18	−4.26	−10.36	−10.34	.18	.10	.15	.15
Postsample																
1	1.99	.77	.83	.83	−1.99	−.45	−.56	−.55	−4.06	−1.48	−1.85	−1.81	1.02	.40	.42	.41
2	2.47	1.49	1.53	1.46	−2.45	−.50	−.61	−.66	−3.64	−.82	−1.05	−1.20	.66	.37	.36	.35
3	2.91	1.91	1.89	1.83	−2.90	−.71	−.77	−.86	−3.33	−.85	−1.05	−1.22	.55	.34	.31	.31
4	3.59	2.22	1.91	1.94	−3.59	−1.05	−.98	−1.09	−3.57	−1.07	−1.25	−1.43	.51	.32	.26	.26
6	5.57	2.85	2.30	2.40	−5.57	−2.65	−2.09	−2.23	−4.80	−2.29	−2.69	−2.95	.49	.31	.23	.23
8	8.25	4.81	3.58	3.72	−8.25	−4.81	−3.58	−3.72	−7.88	−4.52	−4.89	−5.27	.51	.32	.24	.24
Combined																
1	1.06	.43	.49	.49	−1.04	−.22	−.31	−.31	−3.87	−1.63	−2.31	−2.32	.64	.25	.27	.27
2	1.44	.85	.89	.89	−1.40	−.35	−.48	−.52	−3.97	−1.40	−2.00	−2.20	.44	.24	.24	.24
3	1.72	1.10	1.22	1.21	−1.71	−.58	−.77	−.82	−3.97	−1.73	−2.57	−2.79	.37	.23	.22	.22
4	2.32	1.37	1.50	1.53	−2.32	−.90	−1.13	−1.19	−4.82	−2.30	−3.54	−3.74	.34	.21	.20	.20
6	3.55	1.95	2.09	2.14	−3.55	−1.75	−2.01	−2.08	−5.92	−3.48	−6.07	−6.31	.33	.21	.18	.19
8	5.19	2.84	3.02	3.07	−5.19	−2.75	−3.02	−3.07	−7.28	−4.63	−8.98	−9.22	.34	.21	.19	.19

Table 7.6 (continued)

K. Corporate Profits and IVA—Percent Errors

Quarters Ahead	Mean Absolute Percent Error				Mean Percent Error				t-(Mean Percent Error)				Theil U			
	A^u	A^r	B^r	C^r	A^u	A^r	B^r	C^r	A^u	A^r	B^r	C^r	A^u	A^r	B^r	C^r
							Within-Sample									
1	6.09	4.46	3.61	3.93	2.44	-.07	1.98	1.79	1.17	-.04	1.36	1.16	1.48	1.08	1.05	1.09
2	9.78	7.26	5.69	6.17	6.24	.43	2.26	2.00	1.94	.16	1.14	.94	1.62	1.13	.91	.96
3	13.39	10.97	8.21	8.91	8.13	1.58	2.89	2.62	1.75	.41	1.10	.93	1.78	1.30	.93	.99
4	17.73	15.46	12.04	12.88	12.40	3.81	4.93	4.71	1.98	.72	1.31	1.19	1.89	1.41	1.04	1.08
6	25.36	23.17	19.26	20.26	20.39	9.36	11.32	11.28	2.64	1.24	1.94	1.86	1.92	1.57	1.32	1.35
8	24.92	22.23	20.97	22.13	19.52	10.68	14.95	15.16	2.66	1.47	2.35	2.26	1.67	1.42	1.39	1.45
							Postsample									
1	14.59	7.02	7.36	7.22	9.54	-4.29	-2.92	-2.71	1.77	-1.41	-.89	-.84	1.76	.94	.94	.92
2	20.28	14.08	10.18	10.81	9.27	-3.75	1.08	.08	1.15	-.66	.24	.02	1.39	.93	.73	.80
3	24.09	19.62	12.76	13.81	4.85	-4.39	2.54	1.14	.50	-.57	.46	.18	1.16	.93	.66	.73
4	23.72	21.40	12.35	14.02	-.55	-7.07	1.85	.24	-.06	-.88	.35	.04	.96	.84	.52	.60
6	18.08	18.00	8.19	10.84	-13.01	-15.49	-1.79	-3.45	-2.23	-3.09	-.48	-.73	.65	.66	.32	.42
8	21.73	20.56	7.29	8.87	-21.73	-20.56	-3.17	-4.75	-7.28	-8.39	-1.16	-1.51	.64	.60	.22	.26
							Combined									
1	9.49	5.48	5.11	5.25	5.28	-1.75	.02	-.01	2.08	-1.11	.01	-.01	1.68	.98	.97	.97
2	13.98	9.99	7.48	8.02	7.45	-1.24	1.79	1.23	2.05	-.46	.85	.53	1.45	.98	.77	.84
3	17.67	14.43	10.03	10.87	6.81	-.81	2.75	2.03	1.47	-.22	1.04	.70	1.32	1.02	.73	.80
4	20.13	17.84	12.16	13.34	7.22	-.55	3.70	2.92	1.33	-.12	1.23	.88	1.27	1.02	.70	.76
6	22.45	21.10	14.83	16.49	7.03	-.58	6.08	5.39	1.11	-.10	1.52	1.24	1.20	1.03	.78	.83
8	23.65	21.56	15.50	16.83	3.02	-1.82	7.70	7.20	.47	-.32	1.75	1.53	1.05	.91	.76	.80

L. Gross National Product, Constant Dollars—Percent Change (Annual Rate)

Quarters Ahead	Mean Absolute Percent Error				Mean Percent Error				t-(Mean Percent Error)				Theil U			
	A''	A'	B'	C'	A''	A'	B'	C'	A''	A'	B'	C'	A''	A'	B'	C'
							Within-Sample									
1	2.04	2.24	1.65	1.74	-.01	-.37	-.04	-.16	-.01	-.48	-.06	-.24	.41	.45	.34	.37
2	1.87	2.07	1.78	1.79	-.23	-.55	-.86	-.91	-.36	-.72	-1.27	-1.32	.40	.48	.45	.45
3	1.61	2.04	1.62	1.68	-.31	-.41	-1.01	-1.02	-.52	-.53	-1.64	-1.57	.37	.49	.43	.45
4	1.63	2.17	1.94	2.00	-.33	-.23	-.91	-.88	-.55	-.29	-1.30	-1.20	.38	.50	.46	.48
6	2.47	3.07	2.84	2.89	.98	1.47	.71	.77	.94	1.26	.62	.68	.63	.73	.67	.68
8	2.84	3.22	2.76	2.81	.83	1.51	.81	.88	.69	1.25	.71	.77	.67	.70	.63	.64
							Postsample									
1	3.23	3.91	3.24	3.38	.74	1.18	.99	1.14	.49	.67	.64	.76	.67	.79	.69	.68
2	4.60	5.86	5.46	5.29	.00	1.63	2.32	1.88	.00	.66	1.09	.86	.90	1.00	.90	.89
3	5.06	5.67	4.76	4.70	-.86	.62	1.40	1.13	-.37	.25	.70	.55	.91	.94	.79	.81
4	4.90	5.05	4.14	4.23	-1.40	.01	1.09	.88	-.63	.00	.58	.46	.88	.86	.74	.75
6	4.35	3.86	3.56	3.58	-4.28	-3.00	-1.55	-1.61	-2.99	-2.04	-1.08	-1.11	.90	.78	.65	.66
8	3.37	2.79	2.10	2.11	-3.32	-2.44	-1.06	-1.05	-2.79	-2.23	-1.00	-1.01	.83	.68	.54	.53
							Combined									
1	2.52	2.91	2.29	2.39	.29	.25	.37	.36	.40	.30	.53	.51	.53	.61	.51	.52
2	2.96	3.59	3.25	3.19	-.14	.32	.41	.21	-.14	.30	.42	.21	.70	.79	.72	.71
3	2.99	3.49	2.88	2.89	-.53	.00	-.05	-.16	-.55	.00	-.06	-.17	.71	.76	.64	.66
4	2.94	3.32	2.82	2.89	-.75	-.14	-.11	-.18	-.81	-.14	-.13	-.20	.68	.71	.62	.64
6	3.22	3.38	3.13	3.17	-1.12	-.32	-.20	-.18	-1.11	-.31	-.22	-.20	.76	.75	.66	.67
8	3.05	3.05	2.50	2.53	-.83	-.07	.06	.11	-.86	-.07	.08	.13	.73	.70	.60	.60

Table 7.6 (continued)

M. Implicit Price Deflator for GNP—Percent Change (Annual Rate)

Quarters Ahead	Mean Absolute Percent Error				Mean Percent Error				t-(Mean Percent Error)				Theil U			
	A''	A'	B'	C'	A''	A'	B'	C'	A''	A'	B'	C'	A''	A'	B'	C'
								Within-Sample								
1	.99	.65	.71	.71	.15	−.07	.20	.20	.40	−.29	.87	.87	.21	.13	.14	.14
2	1.00	.43	.48	.48	−.39	−.16	−.02	−.04	−1.07	−1.15	−.12	−.21	.21	.08	.09	.09
3	.95	.69	.85	.84	−.02	−.48	−.32	−.33	−.04	−1.42	−.82	−.84	.22	.18	.20	.20
4	1.35	.94	1.00	.99	−.70	−.76	−.50	−.51	−1.29	−1.87	−1.10	−1.12	.26	.21	.21	.21
6	2.50	1.81	1.81	1.79	−2.13	−1.71	−1.27	−1.28	−2.67	−2.50	−1.77	−1.78	.40	.33	.31	.31
8	4.01	2.29	2.10	2.09	−3.90	−2.29	−1.77	−1.77	−5.05	−3.44	−2.58	−2.59	.52	.36	.32	.32
								Postsample								
1	3.64	3.82	3.27	3.27	−2.93	−3.82	−3.27	−3.27	−2.99	−6.79	−6.35	−6.35	.41	.43	.37	.37
2	2.56	2.12	2.00	1.78	−2.56	−2.12	−1.48	−1.63	−3.71	−3.45	−2.02	−2.48	.34	.29	.26	.26
3	1.89	2.07	1.78	1.72	−1.86	−2.07	−1.46	−1.53	−2.39	−2.93	−1.85	−2.01	.33	.33	.30	.30
4	2.16	2.12	1.57	1.60	−2.16	−2.12	−1.53	−1.56	−2.64	−2.85	−1.89	−1.93	.40	.38	.35	.35
6	2.25	2.00	1.26	1.24	−2.25	−2.00	−1.26	−1.23	−6.23	−5.94	−3.47	−3.33	.44	.39	.28	.28
8	3.61	2.42	1.49	1.45	−3.61	−2.42	−1.49	−1.45	−15.56	−10.57	−4.92	−4.77	.66	.45	.30	.30
								Combined								
1	2.05	1.92	1.73	1.74	−1.08	−1.57	−1.19	−1.19	−1.95	−3.18	−2.59	−2.59	.35	.35	.31	.31
2	1.62	1.11	1.09	1.00	−1.26	−.95	−.60	−.67	−3.00	−2.84	−1.77	−2.07	.30	.23	.21	.21
3	1.33	1.24	1.22	1.20	−.76	−1.11	−.78	−.81	−1.69	−2.93	−1.93	−2.04	.28	.27	.26	.26
4	1.67	1.41	1.23	1.24	−1.28	−1.31	−.91	−.93	−2.69	−3.24	−2.14	−2.18	.33	.29	.28	.28
6	2.40	1.88	1.59	1.57	−2.18	−1.82	−1.27	−1.26	−4.43	−4.30	−2.83	−2.83	.41	.34	.31	.31
8	3.85	2.34	1.86	1.84	−3.78	−2.34	−1.66	−1.64	−8.14	−5.81	−3.93	−3.91	.55	.38	.32	.32

N. Unemployment Rate (Percent)

Quarters Ahead	Mean Absolute Percent Error				Mean Percent Error				t-(Mean Percent Error)				Theil U			
	A''	A'	B'	C'	A''	A'	B'	C'	A''	A'	B'	C'	A''	A'	B'	C'
Within-Sample																
1	.32	.20	.17	.18	.26	.13	.09	.10	2.67	2.11	1.69	1.75	2.60	1.53	1.31	1.36
2	.59	.36	.27	.28	.52	.28	.22	.24	3.24	2.89	2.51	2.62	2.44	1.40	1.23	1.27
3	.87	.56	.50	.52	.81	.48	.44	.46	4.54	3.95	4.13	4.16	2.46	1.52	1.38	1.43
4	1.17	.74	.70	.72	1.16	.69	.70	.71	6.74	5.51	7.26	7.19	2.38	1.48	1.41	1.45
6	1.70	1.05	1.09	1.09	1.51	.78	.92	.93	5.32	2.96	4.43	4.68	1.35	.89	.87	.87
8	1.86	1.25	1.28	1.28	1.48	.61	.95	.94	3.65	1.66	3.03	3.10	1.01	.68	.71	.70
Postsample																
1	.46	.53	.53	.53	.00	.07	.12	.11	.01	.29	.52	.50	.73	.78	.77	.77
2	1.08	1.14	1.20	1.16	.05	-.01	.09	.12	.10	-.03	.18	.26	.84	.89	.91	.87
3	1.40	1.46	1.47	1.42	.14	-.07	.08	.14	.23	-.12	.13	.22	.83	.86	.86	.83
4	1.61	1.68	1.65	1.58	.23	-.09	.07	.14	.35	-.13	.11	.21	.77	.80	.78	.77
6	1.78	1.75	1.51	1.56	.98	.48	.57	.65	1.41	.67	.93	1.04	.87	.82	.72	.73
8	2.18	1.69	1.50	1.58	2.12	1.47	1.43	1.52	3.43	2.25	2.65	2.82	1.24	1.05	.94	.96
Combined																
1	.37	.33	.32	.32	.16	.11	.10	.11	1.48	1.09	1.12	1.13	.94	.84	.81	.82
2	.79	.67	.64	.63	.33	.16	.17	.19	1.59	.82	.87	1.02	1.02	.93	.93	.90
3	1.08	.92	.89	.88	.54	.26	.30	.33	2.05	1.00	1.19	1.35	1.01	.91	.90	.88
4	1.35	1.11	1.08	1.07	.79	.38	.45	.48	2.68	1.31	1.64	1.80	1.00	.87	.84	.84
6	1.73	1.33	1.26	1.28	1.29	.66	.78	.82	4.05	2.07	2.91	3.06	1.04	.84	.77	.78
8	1.99	1.43	1.37	1.40	1.74	.95	1.14	1.17	5.04	2.77	4.03	4.17	1.11	.86	.82	.82

Table 7.6 (continued)

O. Three-Month Treasury Bill Rate (Percent)

Quarters Ahead	Mean Absolute Percent Error				Mean Percent Error				t-(Mean Percent Error)				Theil U			
	A''	A'	B'	C'	A''	A'	B'	C'	A''	A'	B'	C'	A''	A'	B'	C'
Within-Sample																
1	.56	.57	.60	.60	−.05	−.07	−.10	−.14	−.26	−.33	−.49	−.65	.71	.72	.76	.78
2	.63	.64	.67	.68	−.11	−.13	−.21	−.25	−.50	−.56	−.86	−1.05	.56	.58	.62	.63
3	.68	.71	.73	.73	−.13	−.14	−.27	−.32	−.52	−.54	−1.06	−1.24	.52	.53	.56	.58
4	.88	.90	.94	.95	−.01	−.01	−.19	−.23	−.02	−.02	−.56	−.68	.55	.56	.57	.58
6	1.03	1.07	1.11	1.16	.00	.06	−.20	−.23	.00	.14	−.53	−.60	.46	.48	.47	.49
8	1.04	1.06	1.09	1.17	−.08	.06	−.23	−.26	−.26	.19	−.69	−.72	.38	.40	.40	.43
Postsample																
1	.71	.71	.85	.91	.43	.43	.57	.62	1.27	1.34	1.61	1.68	1.26	1.21	1.38	1.46
2	.92	.93	.97	1.00	.62	.70	.88	.91	1.67	1.90	2.40	2.42	.89	.92	1.00	1.03
3	.96	.95	1.12	1.15	.76	.90	1.12	1.15	2.09	2.54	3.61	3.52	.83	.88	.94	.97
4	.87	.98	1.15	1.14	.65	.86	1.11	1.12	2.00	2.63	3.84	3.77	.69	.79	.87	.89
6	1.10	1.29	1.33	1.30	.33	.69	1.03	1.02	.77	1.46	2.35	2.35	.63	.75	.81	.81
8	1.27	1.45	1.41	1.43	.08	.56	1.00	1.00	.15	.99	2.01	1.97	.69	.81	.85	.86
Combined																
1	.62	.63	.70	.72	.14	.13	.16	.16	.76	.73	.82	.78	.92	.91	1.00	1.05
2	.74	.75	.79	.81	.18	.20	.23	.21	.86	.94	.97	.87	.71	.73	.79	.81
3	.79	.81	.89	.90	.23	.28	.29	.27	1.01	1.19	1.15	1.03	.65	.68	.72	.74
4	.88	.93	1.02	1.03	.26	.34	.33	.31	1.06	1.35	1.24	1.13	.60	.64	.67	.69
6	1.06	1.16	1.20	1.21	.13	.31	.29	.27	.48	1.04	.95	.86	.51	.56	.57	.59
8	1.13	1.22	1.22	1.27	−.02	.26	.26	.25	−.07	.87	.85	.77	.47	.53	.54	.56

P. Corporate Bonds Yield (Percent)

Quarters Ahead	Mean Absolute Percent Error				Mean Percent Error				t-(Mean Percent Error)				Theil U			
	A^u	A^r	B^r	C^r	A^u	A^r	B^r	C^r	A^u	A^r	B^r	C^r	A^u	A^r	B^r	C^r
							Within-Sample									
1	.18	.18	.19	.19	−.01	−.01	−.02	−.03	−.07	−.12	−.23	−.35	1.01	1.00	1.02	1.03
2	.17	.18	.19	.20	−.03	−.03	−.05	−.07	−.41	−.46	−.71	−.87	.86	.87	.91	.92
3	.18	.19	.21	.21	−.04	−.04	−.08	−.09	−.50	−.54	−1.00	−1.20	.65	.66	.70	.72
4	.23	.23	.26	.28	−.05	−.05	−.11	−.12	−.48	−.51	−1.06	−1.25	.52	.52	.55	.56
6	.26	.26	.32	.32	−.11	−.10	−.20	−.23	−1.04	−.94	−1.90	−2.14	.35	.35	.39	.41
8	.28	.30	.35	.36	−.12	−.08	−.24	−.27	−1.11	−.72	−2.06	−2.29	.31	.31	.36	.37
							Postsample									
1	.25	.25	.26	.27	.10	.10	.13	.15	.79	.77	.97	1.05	1.05	1.07	1.14	1.18
2	.38	.39	.39	.39	.10	.12	.16	.17	.53	.62	.82	.87	.83	.85	.90	.90
3	.42	.42	.43	.43	.10	.14	.20	.22	.47	.63	.89	.95	.77	.79	.85	.84
4	.49	.52	.54	.53	.12	.18	.27	.28	.50	.72	1.02	1.08	.84	.88	.97	.96
6	.62	.68	.69	.68	.15	.28	.44	.45	.51	.90	1.36	1.43	1.05	1.14	1.25	1.23
8	.68	.77	.83	.82	.08	.30	.54	.55	.26	.87	1.55	1.63	1.22	1.38	1.52	1.50
							Combined									
1	.20	.21	.21	.22	.04	.04	.04	.04	.56	.53	.61	.60	1.03	1.04	1.09	1.12
2	.26	.26	.27	.28	.02	.03	.03	.03	.25	.30	.35	.31	.84	.85	.90	.91
3	.28	.28	.30	.30	.02	.03	.04	.03	.20	.32	.34	.29	.74	.75	.81	.81
4	.33	.34	.37	.38	.02	.04	.05	.04	.18	.37	.37	.31	.70	.73	.79	.79
6	.40	.43	.47	.47	−.00	.05	.05	.04	−.03	.38	.35	.28	.62	.67	.73	.73
8	.44	.49	.54	.54	−.04	.07	.07	.06	−.29	.45	.41	.34	.57	.63	.70	.70

Notes

1. The model has since undergone substantial modification and enlargement. However, use of a pre-benchmark version of the model, rather than a more recent version containing structural improvements that derive from both improvements in knowledge or methodology and the benefit of additional hindsight, was necessary because it would be impossible to sort out the changes in specification that have occurred in response to data revisions—an element that is the subject of testing in this study.

2. The related question of how information concerning biases in preliminary relative to revised data can be used to improved predictive accuracy has been recently investigated by Howrey (1978).

3. Cole (1969) also evaluated ex ante business forecasts for the effects on accuracy of errors in unrevised data.

4. More precisely, equations for income components are adjusted by amounts such that on re-solving the model the excess discrepancy is eliminated.

5. Duggal, Klein, and McCarthy (1976) contains an explanation of this view as it pertains to the Wharton quarterly model.

6. A description of the definitional and classification revisions is found in Bureau of Economic Analysis (1976). This article also contains a summary table of the amounts of these revisions on an annual basis for several postwar years.

7. These series were interest paid by consumers to business, net interest paid by the federal government, net interest paid by state and local governments, corporate profits federal tax liability, corporate dividends, federal government transfer payments, and state and local government transfer payments.

8. For a description of this program and its theoretical basis, see McGeary (1977).

9. These series are personal consumption expenditures for automobiles, furniture and equipment, housing services, and other services.

10. Sixteen equations (included in the tabulation) had no NIPA series as either explanatory or dependent variables. The parameters of these equations were thus the same in all three models used in this study.

11. There are several reasons for the varying sample periods in the original model. The equations whose sample periods ended in 1972-IV had problems when the sample periods were extended. Equations whose sample periods extended through 1974-IV had been respecified and reestimated during the second half of 1975. The "other" equations had sample periods which began after 1955-I due to the unavailability of data in the early years.

12. The table is set up in terms of relative changes in the absolute values of parameters: e.g., a parameter which is estimated as -1.0 in model A and -1.1 in model B would be said to have increased 10%. Also, the table takes into account the fact that parameter increases are bounded by 0 and infinity, while decreases are bounded by 0 and minus 100%. The % decrease intervals were calculated by the formula

$$\left(\frac{1}{1+X} - 1 \right)_* 100,$$

where X is the corresponding increase interval boundary (expressed in decimal form). Hence, e.g., the interval 0 to -4.8% corresponds to the positive interval 0 to 5.0%.

13. Cole also found that sets of considerably different coefficients are associated with the same long-run marginal propensity to consume (Cole 1969, pp. 75–77).

14. In the PCE for other durables equation, the wealth variable was dropped rather than the income variable. In the thrift institution deposits equation, it was necessary to substitute the 90-day Treasury bill rate for the commercial bank time deposit rate and to constrain the coefficient of this rate to be equal but of opposite sign to the savings and loan association deposit rate.

15. A more complete discussion of the methodology underlying the calculation of multipliers is found in Hirsch (1977).

16. Changes of $5 billion rather than $1 billion were used because of the nonconstancy of multipliers referred to above and because such amounts are more representative of realistic changes.

17. It was also used in a previous comparative study of predictive accuracy (Hirsch, Grimm, and Narasimham 1976).

18. In order to avoid accounting inconsistencies, aggregate real magnitudes and price deflators were derived by adding (or weighting) components rather than by direct application of scalar conversion factors to the aggregate measures.

19. For an extended discussion of alternate measures of forecast deterioration, see McNees (1975).

20. It should be noted that even the simulations beginning after the 1975-I trough yielded poor predictions, in part because the use of the mechanical formula (eq. [12]) led to much more negative constant adjustments than would judgmental adjustments, because the latter would have given less weight to the anomalous residuals of the recession period.

21. Using the Data Resources Inc. quarterly model, Eckstein (1978) estimates that the "energy crisis" contributed 1.7 percentage points to 1974's inflation rate and 1.9 percentage points to 1975's unemployment rate.

References

Bureau of Economic Analysis. 1976. The national income and product accounts of the United States: revised estimates 1929–74. *Survey of Current Business* 56 (no. 1, pt. I): 1–38.

Christ, Carl F. 1976. Judging the performance of econometric models of U. S. economy. In Lawrence R. Klein and Edwin Burmeister, eds., *Econometric model performance: comparative simulation studies of the U. S. economy*. Philadelphia: University of Pennsylvania Press.

Cole, Rosanne. 1969. Data errors and forecasting accuracy. In Jacob Mincer, ed., *Economic forecasts and expectations: analyses of forecasting behavior and performance*. New York: National Bureau of Economic Research.

Denton, Frank T., and Kuiper, John. 1965. The effect of measurement error on parameter estimates and forecasts: a case study based on the Canadian preliminary accounts. *Review of Economics and Statistics* 47:198–200.

Denton, Frank T., and Oksanen, Ernest H. 1972. A multi-country analysis of the effects of data revisions on an econometric model. *Journal of the American Statistical Association* 67:286–91.

Duggal, Vijaya G.; Klein, Lawrence R.; and McCarthy, Michael D. 1976. The Wharton model mark III: a modern IS-LM construct. In Lawrence R. Klein and Edwin Burmeister, eds, *Econometric model performance: comparative simulation studies of the U.S. economy*, pp. 188–210. Philadelphia: University of Pennsylvania Press.

Eckstein, Otto. 1978. *The great recession*. Data Resources Series, vol. 3. Amsterdam: North Holland Publishing Co.

Hirsch, Albert A. 1977. Policy multipliers in the BEA quarterly econometric model. *Survey of Current Business* 57:60–71.

Hirsch, Albert A., Grimm, Bruce T.; and Narasimham, Gorti V. L. 1976. Some multiplier and error characteristics of the BEA quarterly model. In Lawrence R. Klein and Edwin Burmeister, eds., *Econometric model performance: comparative simulation studies of the U.S. economy*, pp. 232–47. University of Pennsylvania Press.

Howrey, E. Phillip. 1978. The use of preliminary data in econometric forecasting. *Review of Economics and Statistics* 60:193–200.

McGeary, Foster. 1977. Interpolation and distributions; estimation and extrapolation, and prediction; and seasonal adjustment: a new approach. Mimeographed. Washington, D.C.: Bureau of Economic Analysis.

McNees, Stephen K. 1975. An evaluation of economic forecasts. *New England Economic Review* (Federal Reserve Bank of Boston) (November/December).

Comment   Saul H. Hymans

Let me begin by laying out the situation being confronted by Grimm and Hirsch. They have (1) an estimated macroeconometric model, the respected BEA model of the U.S. Department of Commerce; (2) the data used to estimate the model; and (3) a massive revision of the data, including the original sample period and subsequent years.

What interesting questions can be asked? The authors suggest that the following questions are of principal interest:

1. Is the model robust to the data revision? That is,
    a) Do the new—and presumably better—data lead to large revisions in estimated parameters and/or in specification?
    b) Do the new—and presumably better—data lead to large revisions in the estimated dynamic properties of the model?
2. Do the new—and presumably better—data lead to better within-sample forecasts?
    a) Through improvement in estimation of initial conditions even without reestimating the model, or
    b) only if the model is reestimated?
3. Question 2 repeated for postsample forecasts.

These do indeed seem to be the right questions to ask; but the more one thinks about the questions, the harder they are to answer. The simplest question would seem to be: Do parameter values change much? But how

Saul H. Hymans is with the Department of Economics, University of Michigan.

do we interpret "much"? Are we looking for a statistically significant change? Do we even know how to test for statistical significance in the situation at hand? And suppose statistical significance does not coincide with substantive significance? Do we care if two estimated price elasticities of $-2\frac{1}{2}$ and -3 are different at a 5% significance level, or even a .5% level? How much do we care about individual coefficients when regressors are not orthogonal? Suppose the old data suggest the following estimated dynamic consumption function:

(1) $C = .5YD + .4C_{-1},$

where C is consumption and YD is disposable income. Consider two alternative possibilities for the effects of data revision:

(2) $C = .7YD + .4C_{-1},$

(3) $C = .7YD + .16C_{-1}.$

There is an obvious sense in which (2) looks closer to (1) than (3) does. But we know that (2) would be rejected by the old data set whereas (3) might not be; that is, the estimated covariance matrix of coefficients would tell us to expect the coefficients of YD and C_{-1} to move in opposite directions. And indeed equations (1) and (3) have identical steady-state versions. The long-run multiplier properties of a stable linear model would be invariant to equations (1) and (3).

All of this suggests that the authors were correct in resisting the temptation to focus great attention on the matter of individual parameter stability. Indeed, if some parameters *do* change, *model* stability in at least some useful senses fairly requires that quite a few parameters change.

Studying the robustness of the model's multiplier properties strikes me as a far more fruitful venture, and the results displayed in tables 6.3 and 6.5 of the paper are really quite fascinating. It appears that the big story in the model revision is that sometime during the second year following a perturbation the reestimated model (model B) begins to develop a much stronger price-level response than the original model (model A). In the experiment in which unborrowed reserves are increased (table 3), higher inflation begins to slow down real growth in the economy of model B relative to that of model A. That seems fairly clear, and the authors make some effort to trace down the source of the extra price-level response in model B. A clue to where the extra inflation comes from is in the behavior of the unemployment rate. Despite smaller real growth in model B, the unemployment rate is at the same level as in model A. Thus, productivity behavior must be worse in model B, which leads eventually to a higher inflation rate. Note that the lower productivity growth which appears to exist in model B must be purely a data-revision phenomenon, since model B has the same terminal estimation date as model A—1974.4 at the latest.

What about forecasting performance? The first conclusion which seems clear from the reported results is that the within-sample forecasting properties of the BEA system are better than the postsample forecasting properties. This is never a surprising conclusion; it's even predicted by theory whenever forecasting accuracy is measured by mean squared error–type statistics. Further, for reasons well-documented by the authors, the post-1974 period is a particularly severe test of the system.

As to whether model A with unrevised initial conditions (A^u), or model A with revised initial conditions (A^r), or model B wins the horse race—the answer is that for within-sample forecasting there is no simple verdict: A^r is unambiguously the worst at forecasting real GNP within sample for any horizon, A^r is unambiguously best at forecasting the price level, A^u and B are about equally good or bad when A^r is either the best or the worst. The way I read the results, no reasonable aggregation would produce a significant ordering of the models—it's all in where and when you want to make your errors.

The forecasting results are quite different for the postsample case. What distinguishes between the models in postsample forecasting is the time horizon. For two-year-ahead forecasts, the results are absolutely unambiguous: B is the best, A^r is the second-best, and A^u is the worst. That conclusion is independent of whether one gauges the forecast on real GNP, the rate of growth of real GNP, the price level, or the unemployment rate, and whether the gauge is absolute error, bias, or Theil's U-statistic. The results are in the same direction for one-year-ahead forecasts, though the weight of the evidence is not nearly so overwhelming as in the two-year-ahead case, and for some measures of accuracy and some variables the rank-ordering of the models would differ. For forecasting over a short horizon, one to two quarters ahead, there is simply no defensible rank ordering of the models, much as in the within-sample analysis. To be honest, as a model builder, I find the results of these forecasting experiments to be encouraging.

Let me close with a criticism of what I find generally to be a solid and useful paper. I would like a more complete reporting and evaluation of the forecasting results. Error statistics are useful, but they can easily hide the richest information. The authors, for example, provide a very limited analysis of the question of which version of the model better traces a path that is qualitatively like the 1974–76 period. How about the matter of lead time and how well turning points are identified? Many important questions related to short-term dynamics could have been addressed and might well have provided more complete information regarding the value of an improved data base.

8 The GNP Data Improvement Project (The Creamer Report)

In 1973, the Statistical Policy Division of the Office of Management and Budget formed an advisory committee to investigate the quality and timeliness of the data underlying the national economic accounts and to make specific recommendations for data improvement. The late Daniel Creamer was chairman of the committee, which consisted of five outside experts and a small staff.* The committee issued a preliminary report in the fall of 1977 and a final report around the time of the Income and Wealth Conference in the spring of 1979.† That report—whether preliminary or final is immaterial—was the subject of the last session of the conference.

Since the report covers a vast amount of very detailed material pertaining to the underlying statistics, it was decided to organize the session along lines of general interest to economists: the business cycle, long-term growth, price measurement, and the flow-of-funds accounts of the Federal Reserve. Each brief critique is accompanied by a rejoinder from a member of the committee or from a person who assisted the committee. Also, Robert Parker, chief of the National Income and Wealth Division of the Bureau of Economic Analysis, was asked by the conference chairman to provide some remarks.

---

*Other committee members were: Rosanne E. Cole, Edward F. Denison, Raymond W. Goldsmith, Alan Greenspan, and John W. Kendrick.

†U.S. Department of Commerce, Office of Federal Statistical Policy and Standards, *Gross National Product Data Improvement Project Report*, Report of the Advisory Committee on Gross National Product Data Improvement (Washington, D.C.: Government Printing Office), 1977.

Overview and Business Cycle Perspective
Morris Cohen

The Creamer Report represents the first full-scale outside review of the statistical adequacy of the national income and product accounts (NIPAs). True, over 20 years ago the National Accounts Review Committee appraised the accounts, but the emphasis then was on concepts. The Creamer Committee made no attempt to get involved in the conceptual framework. Rather, it concentrated on data improvement.

As everyone knows, the report would have been impossible without the full and what appears to be the complete cooperation of all the involved government agencies. The report shows so much comprehension of the ins and outs of this complicated system that, as an outside reviewer, I can only salute the small staff who drafted the report. The publication will, I am sure, make possible a better understanding of the strengths and weaknesses of the accounts under review. However, the long delay between the writing of the report and the final publication is deplorable from the point of view of those outside the process. The various government agencies, of course, have had access to it and indeed have been acting on its recommendations for some time. The Office of Federal Statistical Policy and Standards, now in the U.S. Commerce Department, has reported on the actions taken in the 1980 statistical budget in following the recommendations.[1]

It is quite clear from what I have already said and what I am about to say that I am highly enthusiastic about the thrust of the Creamer Report. To be sure, I would have preferred the report to be in the public domain for some time now. I assume that the review took so long and that the further time lag from report to the present conference, at least in part, stems from the huge tasks undertaken. After all, the committee was established in 1973, worked for 4½ years, and set forth a time frame for recommendations that go through 1983. Rather than wait another 10 years for a succeeding full-scale, perhaps gargantuan, review, I would urge that in the future these reviews or audits take place on a more timely basis, perhaps every five years at the minimum, perhaps even more frequently than that. If such a shortened schedule were followed, the report would not have to be so overwhelming, and a timely check could be undertaken between what was recommended and what did or did not take place and, particularly, the reasons why it did not take place. Above all, now that the first big review is finished, I again urge that subsequent reviews take less time from inception to public birth.

The scope of the report can be realized when one examines the over 150 recommendations which represent the focus of all the work and the suggested year-by-year timetable. I am tempted to close these remarks

Morris Cohen is professor of economics and finance at Long Island University.

with the flat statement that the estimated $25 million cost to the government (in 1976 prices) seems a pittance in light of the expected benefits to be gained, and, therefore, the report should be endorsed by the conference, of course after due deliberation. Seriously, though, it must be recognized what we are talking about. We are talking about a program of improved data gathering by the decentralized statistical agencies of the U.S. government. The purpose is to make the national income and product accounts (including flow of funds, balance of payments, etc.) even more useful and trustworthy than they already are. In somewhat different language, while the various statistical reports, say, for example, the monthly manufacturers' shipments, orders and inventory series, will be improved, what really counts even more is the contribution that these improved statistics will make to the national accounts. As the report itself notes, the committee was concerned with the statistical shortcomings of the GNP estimates. This conference should reinforce the emphasis on a fully articulated system of national accounts broadened, of course, to include flow of funds, balance of payments, etc., as the keystone for a better comprehension of a modern industrialized economy on a national basis, and eventually on an international scale.

I want to say some more about costs of data improvement, particularly the cost to the respondents. It is one thing for the committee to urge the government, which after all asked it to do just that, to add to the statistical budget. It is another thing to realize what the costs to the respondents might be. I found very little of this in the Creamer Report. I do believe that it has to be considered and strategies developed which would improve cooperation between the business community and the federal statistical agencies. The Census Bureau in recent years has begun a major effort to inform data users about what the census does, and this operation, with field representatives in major cities across the country, is bound to help bring about a better understanding of what the census tries to do and what it means for respondents. Perhaps now is the time to raise such a question about the national income accounts. We should try to bring this home to the people who fill out all the forms, as well as to the executives who approve the spending of company funds for the bigger and better statistical reports that we all seem to want so much. Perhaps the Commerce Department, through its various field offices, could also begin the educational task of explaining the significance of the national accounts to the ordinary accountant or statistical clerk at the company level. The recent expansion of the regional accounts, prepared by the Bureau of Economic Analysis, might be the mechanism whereby local interest could be attracted in the first place. Everyone in the business knows how important the cooperation offered by the reporting business firms can be in improving the accounts. Let us spend at least some time and effort in working together for this needed cooperation.

Turning to the report itself, there is no useful purpose to be gained by reviewing in detail the long list of carefully prepared recommendations for improvement. I do want to make some general observations on statistical methodology. In fact, I am compelled to make them since I did not realize that important if not key surveys underlying the national accounts were characterized by what I would insist is faulty methodology. I assume that, since I did not know this, then many other interested users of the national accounts did not know this either. All this, in passing, points up the great usefulness of the Creamer Committee's deliberations and report, particularly since most users of the statistical data do not have a full handbook on how the national accounts are prepared. Without this, one has to dig deeper, and that is the great service the Creamer Committee performed.

I was surprised to learn that the BEA survey of plant and equipment does not ask for revised data for prior times periods. The report also stated that this was true for the Census Bureau monthly survey of manufacturers' shipments, inventories, etc., but the bureau's own survey forms suggest that the report is in error. In any event, anyone who has ever conducted a continuing survey of business reporting knows how important such revisions can be.

I would like to underscore one of the general recommendations which calls upon the major federal statistical agencies to prevent deterioration in the quality of existing data in some of the sample surveys. I shall have more to say later about one of these surveys in particular. Perhaps the recommendation should have been broadened to establish review proceedings for some of the principal sampling surveys that involve experts outside the government itself. The National Bureau of Economic Research report on inventories, still unpublished, came into being after the fiasco of 1973–74 when inventory change was vastly understated in the preliminary GNP estimates. The lesson clearly is to stay ahead of the problems, not to react to them. While the Creamer Committee from time to time tries to do this, I would have preferred greater emphasis on the prevention of problems. True, there is a recommendation, which I heartily endorse, which calls for setting up the capability in the Federal Statistical System for quick surveys.

We should reflect for a moment why we need this capability. In a dynamic society that is growing more internationalized, sampling frames and survey questions based on knowledge, that is, benchmarks five to ten years old, and sometimes even older, can often fail to capture big shifts in behavior. Sampling surveys can tire with age just as humans do. Retraining sometimes helps to refreshen careers. New surveys, not in the mainstream of established procedures, might be able to capture some dynamic changes before the results of existing statistical samples that may be asking the wrong people, or not asking the right people, or asking the wrong questions become invalidated. As part of the review procedure, therefore, and without waiting for the next big formal review, there should be a mechanism which would enable the questioning of current samples and methodology. This could be concentrated in areas where there may be a suspicion that something is awry without it being a crisis. To quote the report: "Most users of the national income accounts need to be reminded that gains in firmly grounded statistics are not always held. That is, the quality of a particular statistical series can deteriorate and the trend may not be easily reversed. This is illustrated by the deterioration in the early 1970's of the currency of the survey sample of monthly retail trade statistics."

There is a minor gap in the Creamer Report which I suggest might be of assistance on this point. Throughout, the suggestions and recommendations are made in the name of the distinguished body of experts that comprised the committee. May I suggest that, in the future, more experts get involved in the process of improving the statistical methodology underlying the national accounts. These experts could also be outside the membership of the Conference on Research in Income and Wealth. Take the case of retail sales, surely a major component of current GNP estimation and a series already referred to earlier and which receives much attention in the Creamer Report. Why don't we have an advisory committee drawn from leading retailers, trade associations, professors of marketing, etc., who might be more aware of current institutional developments than senior civil servants have time to be. Some small investment in perhaps a half dozen such committees could possibly produce a big payout.

Improving the data base for the national accounts involves many statistical agencies besides the Bureau of Economic Analysis. The activities of two agencies in particular deserve comparison and hope for the future. I refer to the Bureau of Labor Statistics and the Census Bureau. My main point is that statistical agencies must themselves get involved in the analysis of the data they produce. In recent years, the Bureau of Labor Statistics has been doing this, and in my view this shows up in an improvement in their price information. While no one can say that the millennium is here on price statistics, no one can deny that major steps have been taken in improving price statistics, with the Producer Price Index a big forward step. I shall have more to say about prices later, but improvement should be recognized, and in particular the link with internal analysis of the home-grown statistics should be applauded. By comparison, the Census Bureau has yet to begin this process. Their search for personnel has begun, but the internal research effort of the Census Bureau is not yet off the ground. As an outside reviewer, I can urge that this be done and regret the fact that the Creamer Committee failed to mention this point at all. It is one thing for outside experts, including experts in allied agencies like BEA, to lecture census officials; it is another for one census employee, a research analyst, to talk over a luncheon table with another census employee, a sampling statistician, about the significance of collecting certain data in a certain way. I believe that with time such an internal research effort could have a potentially giant payoff.

Let me turn now to my main function, namely, to appraise the Creamer Report from the perspective of business-cycle analysis. As a general proposition, I would urge that as much attention as possible be paid to measuring current developments at the time they occur. The basic philosophy of the GNP system goes back to Simon Kuznets who was always very interested in basic long-term economic trends. His emphasis on the commodity-flow method of calculating the national income accounts has carried over to the present. I would add, of course, that the integration of the input/output tables into the estimation process represents a postwar development that still has a long way to go. Nevertheless, I am afraid that the present system as I understand it still tends to make the long term the basic point of reference. No one is at fault when I make this charge. Clearly, the accounts have to be heavily dependent on the quinquennial census benchmarks. These economic censuses, now taken every five years, comprise the heart of the GNP system. The younger members of the profession should be reminded that, prior to World War II, the manufacturing census was taken every two years. So we must now make do with benchmarks that are five years apart, not two as in Kuznets's day, and the Creamer Committee has a number of fine suggestions for improving the current economic censuses. The report also recommends several new censuses to plug up major information gaps and calls for special studies of construction, still a field that requires much more work.

The problem as I see it with the national accounts is the effect that benchmarking procedures have on the history of business cycles. After all, the more complete data are available only once every five years. As the five-year benchmarks are put into place, and typically, as we have observed, this means upward revisions despite recognition of the problem of births and deaths of companies, the business-cycle developments in between are not refurbished with new information. I am afraid that this process has a tendency to distort the historical pattern of business cycles as they are reflected in the national accounts. To be sure, the cycle has other dimensions as well, as many business-cycle indicators are independent of the national accounts. Yet I wonder at times about the significance of business-cycle developments that are measured with national account sectors including percentage changes from peak to trough in a wide variety of sector subcomponents.

All of this means that a great deal of emphasis should be placed on measuring the current changes in the economy as they take place. As the report notes: "Even annual estimates are too infrequent for developing fiscal, monetary, and income policies associated with pursuing the employment and purchasing power goals of the Employment Act of 1946. Satisfaction of this very legitimate need led to the development of monthly estimates of personal income and quarterly estimates of NIPA with the explicit understanding that the estimates would have far less published detail than the annual estimates and were bound to be subject to larger estimating errors, a necessary consequence of trading timeliness for accuracy." I would go on to add that the tradeoff in terms of money might be somewhat greater emphasis on more accuracy for the contemporary short term, perhaps at the expense of greater accuracy for the long term. I know this is controversial, but perhaps we have not spent enough time and money in bolstering the short-term and have worried too much about the long term. It is one thing for scholars, like Kuznets, to be concerned with depicting major secular changes in the economy. It is another for government policymakers, and, may I add, private sector decision makers as well, to depend heavily on short-term changes in the national accounts which get revised rather drastically when the benchmarks become available many years later. One wonders, at times, what the history actually has been.

The most important point I want to make about the usefulness of the national income accounts for the business-cycle watcher has to do with the question of how to appraise the current strength or weakness of the economy. This is a question that interests not only policymakers in Washington but private persons throughout corporate America, and indeed throughout the world. I take it for granted that on a contemporary basis it is always going to be difficult to be highly confident about any particular set of statistics, even the highly massaged current GNP estimates in real terms. I think this is going to be true even after every one of the over 150 Creamer recommendations is carried out through 1983.

I want to urge a higher priority than the committee gives to the proposition that a great deal of attention should be paid to the comparison of the current behavior of the national income accounts and the Federal Reserve Board's Index of Industrial Production. The committee does recommend that the BEA and FRB should get together on this issue and that periodic reports be published. I would go much further. To be sure, some work has already been done on this comparison, and more references can be seen in the publications of the BEA. I have not yet seen publications from the FRB staff written from their perspective. I would urge strongly that they begin to do this. I would go on to urge that some neutral organization bring together these two proud agencies in an attempt to grapple with the problem of measuring contemporary economic activity. Somewhere in the government, there should soon be a regular report which compares these and other measures of economic activity, points up the differences, reviews the similarities, and then concludes what is known or not known about the business cycle.

A quick review of the quarterly patterns of economic activity in 1978 shows some major differences in the two measures. For example, the economy in the third quarter of 1978 was a lot stronger according to the production index than according to the national accounts; the reverse was true of the fourth quarter. If one assumes, merely for the sake of argument, that the production index is closer to the truth than the national accounts, then it would follow that inventory accumulation was a lot stronger than the national accounts are presently showing. Thus the important question gets highlighted quite quickly. How accurate are the current inventory statistics, adjusted for inflation? Is this something public and private authorities should worry about? I would argue that it is, given the experience of 1973–74. That is only one example, and there are others, one of which I shall highlight later on, namely, the question of capital spending estimates. I am pleased that this comparison has begun to be taken seriously in recent years. I want very much to speed up this process, and on this point I view the Creamer Report as too conservative in its approach. They took a traditional tack, listing a wide variety of needed improvements. I want very much to upgrade the problem and its potential solution, so that by the time the next data improvement report is written it will include a section on how the comparison strengthened estimates all around.

The interchange between the Creamer Committee and the BEA, which has already resulted in important changes in procedure, must be commended highly. There is no question in my mind that the BEA is very much interested in the current business cycle, and this shows up in their highly illuminating commentaries in the *Survey of Current Business*. The fact that the allied publication, *Business Conditions Digest*, now emanates from the same agency may be having an impact. Therefore, among the mild brickbats being tossed out in this paper, there has to be very strong approval of two innovations which came about with the Creamer Committee. First, there is now being published on a contemporary basis the judgments made in quantitative terms about the unavailable data for the so-called 15-day estimate that plays such an important role in appraisals of current overall business activity. Second, the newly instituted 75-day estimate now means that users have access to all the current information articulated in contemporary estimates, without having to wait for the annual figures that come out the following July.

What still remains, unfortunately, are sizable historical revisions that obviously present great processing problems and thus have to be postponed. It so happens that prior to the publication of the 75-day estimate of fourth quarter 1978 GNP, in March 1979, the Census Bureau released a major revision of retail sales and inventories, but the effect of this on the national accounts was postponed to the annual revisions in July 1979.

One can understand why this was done, but perhaps someday it will be possible to incorporate such major revisions into the data when they become available. As a general proposition, all known information should be incorporated into the national accounts when available, and the sooner the better. Such a principle leads me to support the Creamer Committee recommendation, for example, that calls for use of special reports prior to the full-scale benchmark revisions. This means in effect that I give higher priority to current and recent information even if the trade-off is some distortion in secular patterns.

At times, the profession can get so concerned about all the details that it can overlook the main point, that continues to elude us, namely, a better understanding of the current business cycle as it unfolds. True, the Creamer Report has served a useful purpose in highlighting the errors revealed by the 1963 and 1967 benchmark estimates. It also usefully pointed up the frequent errors in the quarterly estimates for inventories, inventory valuation, net exports, farm and nonfarm residential construction, and many of the components of producers' durable equipment. I want to express a very important personal judgment that the biggest lack in the national accounts today is their failure to reveal fully the true nature of consumer behavior. Once upon a time, it was believed that the consumption function was written in concrete and that it could be depended upon in all seasons. Today, all of us know a lot better. Even though the Creamer Report devotes much attention to the various pieces of the consumption function, I would add the following major recommendation. As part of the data improvement project, there is an overwhelming need for an ongoing and continuing quarterly consumer survey that attempts to measure income, spending by broad categories, and hopefully saving. To be sure, such a survey is under study today and is mentioned in the report as something that will be put into place some day. I would argue that such a survey is long overdue.[2] It would enable analysts to make better judgments about consumer behavior. Even five years after the event, no one really understands why consumption expenditures collapsed in the fourth quarter of 1974.

Such a survey, which I would put at the top or close to the top of the list of recommendations for overall data improvement, might even prove to be helpful in buttressing the national accounts. Indeed, scattered throughout the report are references to what such a continuing survey could do to plug up some existing information gaps. At present, great reliance has to be placed on the personal saving estimates, which everyone knows leave much to be desired. This has long been the case, and it is not surprising considering its residual nature. I am on the side of the Denison dissent about the recommendation for monthly estimates of personal saving. This recommendation evidently is about to be implemented, and I agree with him that monthly estimates will not help since the quarterly ones are subject to such substantial errors. What could help and what is required, given the historical development of the accounts, would be a greater concern about a formal reconciliation between the flow-of-funds estimates of individual saving and the national income counterpart of personal saving.[3] As matters stand now, these two parallel series exist side by side with very little attention paid by anybody to this fact. This has been true for decades. On a personal note, when the author was a junior economist at what was then the Office of Business Economics he had a hand in one of the first attempts to reconcile saving as measured in the national accounts and saving as measured directly from the financial side. Little progress has been accomplished on this front over the ensuing three decades, and the problem cries out for some solution.

It is one thing to note the discrepancies that exist between the national income accounts and the flow-of-funds accounts, which the appendix to the flow-of-funds chapter in the report dutifully lists; it is another to put together a program that forces these two approaches to a reconciliation. Assuming that the flow-of-funds measure of individual savings can be strengthened, it might be a worthwhile goal to introduce a direct measure of savings into the national accounts and show a statistical discrepancy between it and the personal saving residual. My main point is the urgent need to improve understanding of consumer behavior. Clearly, the personal saving estimates currently cannot be relied upon for this purpose. New and perhaps revolutionary approaches may be required.

The Creamer Committee's chapter on data improvement for the national accounts in constant prices deserves some comment from the point of view of business-cycle developments, and perhaps even more so for the purpose of the whole game. It is now axiomatic that what counts for measuring economic activity in an age of inflation is real, not nominal, GNP. The great bulk of the report necessarily dealt with the nominal accounts. The chapter on prices was easy to write. All one can say, and the committee said it quite succinctly, is that the Bureau of Labor Statistics should have every opportunity to prepare price indexes that are meaningful. It took many years to get around to such a state, but the process has begun. My main concern is to be sure that the relevant price indexes fully reflect transaction prices. The appendix to the chapter on prices takes the novel form of a submission in 1978 to the appropriations committee for the comprehensive revision of the industrial price program. I can only say "amen" and wonder what has been happening all these years. My answer has to be that the problem has to become very serious before people will be forced to act in a meaningful way. The inflation rate, which has been accelerating over the past decade, has a bright side when viewed by technicians; it is bound to spur long-needed improvement, and it is coming.

As everyone knows, the most important single variable in economic analysis, if one is forced to pick just one, is real GNP. Today it is commonplace to begin the description of any industrialized economy in terms of real growth rates and in terms of the inflation rate. The best nominal GNP possible will prove worthless in an age of inflation if the estimates of prices used to yield real economic activity are faulty. Many, including the author, believe that current price data, apart from the revised Consumer Price Index, leave a great deal to be desired. Improvement is possible. Take the Census Bureau's price index of new home construction. In a field which is still marked by many problems, outlined by the Creamer Committee, this index has shown what can be done with some imagination. The committee obviously suggests that this principle be extended to other sectors of construction.

I hesitate to bring up some new questions about prices at a time when the long-needed improvement project is finally getting underway. I worry a bit about the report now almost two decades old, in which the Stigler Committee made many recommendations for improved price data.[4] Here we are almost 20 years later, and we are still talking about many of the same things. Yet, one of the key sectors of the economy is capital goods, and the price adjustments needed for this sector are difficult at best. The Creamer Committee supports the BLS plan to collect prices of industrial goods at time of shipment. One wonders about the kind of prices BLS has been collecting, and one worries about the distinction between shipment prices and order prices. The price-adjusting of capital spending includes many categories of capital goods that have fairly long lead times between order and data and delivery date. Like the Creamer Committee, I would argue that shipment prices are much more relevant for national accounts purposes. But for a better understanding of the inflation process all by itself—aside from deflation—the distinction between the two time perspectives should always be made quite sharply.

One has to take notice of price adjustments in other sectors as well—foreign, and particularly the government. I have long argued that the government has a major responsibility of keeping track of its own activities since it wants other sectors to do the same. Thus the proposed programs for prices in the state and local government area cannot get started too soon as far as I am concerned. Even more important, however, is the responsibility the federal government must have for tracking the inflation rate in its own purchases. This area has not been neglected by the BEA in recent years, and I must commend them for their vigorous research and the very important start they have made in the deflation of national defense purchases. The committee also supports the Federal Procurement Data System. All of us should stand behind their recommendation that constant-dollar national defense spending estimates become a part of the regular quarterly accounts. Eventually, it is hoped, there will be federal government procurement price indexes. The government itself could afford to be lethargic about price data for its own activities at a time of low inflation rates. It cannot afford to be lethargic today.

The subject of capital goods receives considerable attention in the Creamer Report. It is noted, and I was deeply disturbed by the fact, that of the 22 types of producers' durable equipment, nearly two-thirds had unacceptable (i.e., over 7.5%) errors in the first and second July estimates for 1967 compared to the actual benchmarks. The committee went on to note that, even for the third July estimate, 45% were still unreliable. I also take cognizance of the fact that the Creamer Committee chose not to include any discussion of the capital stock estimates. I wonder whether such errors had anything to do with this decision. In any event, I would strongly urge that, in subsequent reviews of the national accounts, the capital stock estimates be carefully studied. For many students of the economy, in academia, in research institutes, and in business, estimates of the capital stock play a critical role in evaluating the capital spending sector.

Attention was paid to the BEA Quarterly Plant and Equipment Survey. This was a proper judgment since the survey plays an important role in current estimates of nonresidential fixed investment. Many suggestions were made by the committee, and the BEA has been very cognizant of the issues involved. In the March 1979 *Survey of Current Business*, they reported three projects underway for reevaluating this important sector. The extension of the survey to cover the private nonfarm economy simply corrects an oversight that has long been a nuisance and is noncontroversial. The breakdown between plant and equipment would represent a major improvement, and it will help to provide the basis for a closer reconciliation with other measures of activity such as the business equipment component of the production index. This will also be helped by a second project, which will provide constant-dollar investment by industry. Third, there will finally be a detailed formal reconciliation between investment as shown by the plant and equipment survey and investment as estimated by the commodity-flow method. These projects are highly welcome and are awaited with great interest.

What still concerns me, however, is the failure to update the survey on a more regular basis. BEA notes, as other private analysts have, that starting with 1976 the survey and the commodity-flow methods have diverged, with the survey lagging, and the differences grew with each year. Consideration is also given to the business equipment component of the FRB production index, and it is again recognized that it corresponds quite close to the commodity-flow method and, therefore, suggests that the survey is in error. True, it may not be, but I would move the updating and basic revision of the survey right to the top of the heap in proposed recommendations.

The importance of investment in the economy is widely recognized. The sooner the survey is re-benchmarked and improved along the lines suggested by the committee, the better many of us will feel about it. The survey provides a major dimension to analysis and understanding of investment since it provides industry detail on a current basis. The national accounts tend to underplay the industry dimension, a deficiency which input-output tables help in part to correct. It is absolutely essential that there be accurate industry information on capital spending which can be tied into the national accounts with some confidence. Surely errors will persist, but a sharply rising discrepancy between two major data sources for current estimation provides a laboratory experiment of what to do about continually refreshing the national accounts and how the statistical system will respond to the challenge.

The Creamer Committee had so much ground to cover and has made so many fine suggestions for improving the national accounts that it may sound churlish to raise some issues they did not. An important part of the national accounts depends upon reports from business which, after all, are accounting reports required under law for all sorts of purposes. For publicly held corporations, it is a serious matter, for example, if an accounting firm publishes a qualification to the company's annual report. It is not clear from what the Creamer Committee reported, or in reading descriptions of how the various survey takers actually collect data from business, what is done about the adjustments that are typically made in year-end business-accounting statements. When benchmarks are established, such matters are taken care of. For the quarterly and annual estimates prior to benchmarks, however, one has the suspicion that little, if any, of these year-end adjustments get into the data. At times, these can be substantial. Thus, when the accountants review the annual figures for an enterprise, they are supposed to revise prior data if the discovered differences are material. Further, just to indicate the treacherous nature of the terrain I am looking at, economic statisticians should not necessarily assume that company figures are sacrosanct. We all know that IRS audits can uncover substantial changes in some cases, but it takes years to incorporate such new information into the accounts. Meanwhile, I would urge that there be a greater dialogue between the accounting profession and our profession. We should learn a lot more about what is being reported by business. I have the distinct impression that the accounting profession would be interested. I have the greater impression that newly minted accountants might welcome the dialogue. In case you were not aware of it, current CPA examinations in some states now include questions on macroeconomic policy. And students in schools of business are now required to take courses in macroeconomics to obtain the MBA degree, and in many cases they seem quite interested in the subject.

There is a second area not covered by the Creamer Report, which has been discussed in the past from time to time and which certainly deserves current attention. Specifically, there should be a better reconciliation between profits reported to shareholders and profits reported to the IRS. With much greater emphasis placed today on the Quarterly Financial Report as a major source of contemporary information, the basic ingredients are present for such a reconciliation. Indeed, I would imagine that this is precisely how the national income statisticians have to get the estimates they put into the accounts since this quarterly report is probably getting information that is also reported to shareholders. In appraising business decision making, it can be argued that perhaps the more relevant variable is profits reported to shareholders rather than to the government. A simple table, if need be quite condensed, could become a part of the accounts, and it might provide new insights into contemporary business decision making.

In summary, congratulations are in order for the Washington statistical establishment that originated the Creamer Committee and for the staff and members of the committee for the authoritative report they have issued. I trust that the recommendations of the report will have a better record of fruition than prior reports which have attempted to influence government statistics. My reading of what has already happened, and what is in prospect for the 1980 budget, offers ground for hope. My one final plea, fully recognizing its parochial character, is to lean toward the contemporary recording of economic events, even if the trade-off is a somewhat less accurate measurement of secular trends. The original stimulus for the Creamer investigation came from what was viewed as deficiencies in data measuring short-run developments. The national income accounts have their greatest usefulness and are worth considerable public sums only if they satisfy the requirements of policymakers in and out of the government.

Notes

1. Frumkin, Norman. 1979. Progress report on implementation of the GNP data improvement project recommendations. *Statistical Reporter* (March), pp. 181–87.

2. Such a survey is evidently now underway. "Work has begun on the Continuing Consumer Expenditure program—an effort to provide timely data on family expenditures. To be initiated in late 1979, the new survey program is being developed by the Bureau of Labor Statistics, contracting with the Bureau of the Census. . . . Following a 12- to 18-month startup period, data should be published on a regular basis—approximately 6 to 9 months after the collection period" (Eva Jacob, "Family Expenditure Data to Be Available on a Continuing Basis," *Monthly Labor Review* [April 1979], pp. 53–54).

3. See comments by John Gorman and response by Stephen Taylor, Chap. 8.
4. Price Statistics Review Committee, *The Price Statistics of the Federal Government*
(New York: National Bureau of Economic Research, 1961).

Comment   Rosanne Cole

The paper is generally sympathetic to the Creamer Report. There are
some good suggestions. For example, I think the reminder that the costs
and benefits to respondents merit more attention when considering the
costs and benefits of additional data collection is a point well taken.

There is also some criticism. If I understand it correctly, Prof. Cohen's
main objection has to do with what he considers to be the long-term focus
of the report's recommendations. His concerns can be put in the following way:

> There is implicit, both in the report and in the present system, a
> tendency to make accurate measurement of long-term economic trends
> the basic point of reference. As a consequence, the report implicitly
> accepts the current terms of the trade-off between timeliness and
> accuracy, and the revisions, both because of the nature of the new
> information and of the benchmarking procedures, have a tendency to
> distort the historical pattern of business cycles as they are reflected in
> the national accounts.
>
> The basic point of reference, or focus, should be the accurate
> measurement of current economic developments at the time they
> occur. Much more emphasis, therefore, should have been given in the
> report to improving the data underlying the current quarterly esti-
> mates—even at the expense of greater accuracy for the long-term.

In my judgment, the report's recommendations are well balanced
between those data improvements designed to enhance the current
quarterly estimates and those aimed at strengthening the benchmarks.
The criticism implies that there is much more of a choice, or trade-off,
than in fact exists between the accuracy with which short-term and
long-term economic changes can be measured. The real trade-off is
between the timeliness and the accuracy of the underlying data. For
example, there would be no loss in the accuracy with which long-term
changes are measured if, at the extreme, the data underlying each
quarterly estimate were augmented to equal that available for benchmark
periods. The resulting gain in accuracy in measuring the short-term
changes would simply be achieved at the expense of timeliness.

Similarly, improving the data used for the benchmark estimates is not
at the expense of accuracy in the quarterly estimates. The benchmarks

Rosanne Cole is manager, Economic Research and Forecasting, International Business
Machines Corp. Armonk, New York.

provide a check on the adequacy of the less complete, but timely, data underlying the current estimates. Proposing to neglect or even to do away with this check is in the vein of proposing to maim or kill the messenger—even though it is certainly true that he makes a very late appearance.

I wholeheartedly agree with Prof. Cohen that it is vexing indeed to users to realize the extent to which the revisions have altered the characteristics of postwar cyclical changes as they are depicted in the national accounts. Tables 8.1 and 8.2 provide an illustration of the magnitude of these changes for postwar cyclical contractions in GNP. Characteristics of the contractions in nominal GNP are shown in table 8.1; table 8.2 shows this information for constant-dollar GNP. Estimates of constant-dollar GNP have been available on a current quarterly basis only since 1959. Consequently, the mild recession beginning in 1960 was the first to be seen in the accounts at the time in terms of the impact on the course of both real and nominal GNP and the components. The earlier postwar recessions were shown, at the time they occurred, only in nominal magnitudes. There was no decline in nominal GNP during the 1969–70 and 1973–75 recessions, and they therefore do not appear in table 8.1.

Except for the 1980 contraction, the first estimates available—and, to the extent that the accounts are used, these are the data on which policy decisions would be based—make the contraction appear much more severe than it is subsequently seen to be in the revised data. The first estimates show declines in nominal GNP that are 1½ to 3 times larger than the declines now recorded. Constant-dollar GNP estimates differ by a slightly smaller amount. The initial figures show falls in real GNP during recessions that are 1¼ to nearly two times those now carried in the revised accounts.

Revised estimates show the 1980 real decline to be slightly more severe. The first estimates showed no decline in nominal GNP.

The uncertainty surrounding the amplitude of cyclical declines in GNP is also present with respect to specific turning-point dates. The timing of peaks has rarely been revised, but the dates of the low points in five of the seven postwar recessions have been changed. Only the dates of the troughs in 1958 and 1980 remain the same throughout the initial and successively revised estimates.

The peak of the expansion ending in 1960 and the troughs of the declines beginning in 1948, 1953, 1960, 1970, and 1973 are not marked by a single quarterly turning point but by a leveling-off period, or turning zone. In these cases, even small revisions are sufficient to shift the high or low point by one or even two quarters. Extreme cases are the troughs of the 1953–54 decline in nominal GNP and the 1969–70 decline in real GNP. The low point for these recessions has changed by as much as three quarters in various vintages of the estimates.

Yet what can be concluded from these comparisons? It would be a mistake, I believe, to suppose that the revisions distort cyclical patterns such that the early estimates of cyclical decline are in some sense more "correct" and closer to the truth than the revised estimates, even though some of the procedures used to obtain revised estimates may involve an element of oversmoothing.

One aspect of oversmoothing relates to the seasonal adjustment procedures. There is some evidence that the revised estimates have on occasion been overadjusted for seasonal movements such that the peak to trough decline is understated (Cole 1970, pp. 215–16).

The opposite effect has been present in the early estimates. There is some evidence that the factors used to adjust the early figures tend to understate the seasonal movements and this at times has been a source of the early estimates' persistent tendency to overstate cyclical declines in GNP. Further, it has been shown that revisions in the seasonal factors have accounted for the differences in the turning-point dates between the early and revised nominal GNP estimates (Cole 1969, chap. 4).

Finally, it may be that insufficient attention has been given to the possible consequences of the fact that benchmark years may occur at different stages of the business cycle or to the consequences of the shifts in weights that occur with the re-basing of price indexes and the constant-dollar estimates.

The Creamer Committee deliberately chose to separate the problem of source data adequacy from the problem of estimating procedures. In some respects this may be an artificial separation, but it certainly was an operational one. Perhaps the time has now come to provide the resources for the BEA to undertake a major review of their estimating procedures with an eye to the impact of the seasonal adjustment, deflation, and benchmarking procedures on short-term changes. (It should be noted, however, that major benchmarking cannot have been the source of any revisions in the cyclical amplitudes since 1972.)

Unless the data underlying the benchmarks and the data underlying the series used to interpolate between benchmarks and extrapolate the last benchmark have deteriorated over time, there are strong grounds for presuming the revised estimates to be more accurate than the earlier figures.

In some instances, as the Creamer Report documents, sources have deteriorated, and the report contains specific recommendations for strengthening them. Many of these recommendations refer to the benchmarks, yet I would contend that more accurate benchmarks, ceteris paribus, are directly associated with more accurate current quarterly estimates. This is because the current estimates are extrapolations of the benchmark estimates. The extrapolations are made by means of related series—and many of the report's recommendations are designed to bolster the quality of these series.

The report's recommendations are therefore better viewed as an integrated and concerted effort to improve the accuracy of the current quarterly estimates rather than as two separate efforts—one designed for students of long-term trends, and the other for users whose interests are short-term changes.

References

Cole, Rosanne. 1969. *Errors in provisional estimates of gross national product.* New York: Columbia University for National Bureau of Economic Research.

———. 1970. Some problems in estimating short term changes in GNP. *American Statistical Association 1970 Proceedings*, pp. 214–25.

Table C8.1   Postwar Cyclical Contractions in Current-Dollar GNP

Contractions[a]	Source and Date of Estimate[b]	Timing and Duration			Amplitude and Severity	
		Peak Quarter	Trough Quarter[c]	Number Quarters Decline	% Decline	% Decline per Quarter at Annual Rates
1948–49:						
First estimate	*EI* Jan. 1950	1948-IV	(1949-IV)			
	SCB Feb. 1950		1949-III	3	−5.6	−7.4
Revised estimate	*SCB* Dec. 1980	1948-IV	1949-IV	4	−3.4	−3.4
1953–54:						
First estimate	*EI* July 1954	1953-II	(1954-II)			
	SCB Aug. 1954		1954-I	3	−3.8	−5.0
Revised estimate	*SCB* Dec. 1980	1953-II	1954-II	4	−1.9	−1.9
1957–58:						
First Estimate	*EI* July 1958	1957-III	1958-I	2	−4.1	−8.0
Revised Estimate	*SCB* Dec. 1980	1957-III	1958-I	2	−2.8	−5.5
1960–61:						
First estimate	*EI* July 1961	1960-II	1961-I	3	−1.0	−1.3
Revised estimate	*SCB* Dec. 1980	1960-I	1960-IV	3	−0.4	−0.5
1980:						
First estimate	*SCB* July 1980	No decline				
Revised estimate	*SCB* July 1982	1980-I	1980-II	1	−0.1	−1.4

[a]There was no decline in nominal GNP during the 1969–70 and 1973–75 business-cycle contractions.

[b]*EI* denotes *Economic Indicators* and *SCB* denotes *Survey of Current Business.*

[c]Dates in parentheses indicate the given quarter was lower than the preceding quarter. Since data for the succeeding quarter were not available, the designation of a trough is uncertain.

Table C8.2   Postwar Cyclical Contractions in Constant-Dollar GNP

		Timing and Duration			Amplitude and Severity	
Contractions	Source and Date of Estimate[a]	Peak Quarter	Trough Quarter[b]	Number Quarters Decline	% Decline	% Decline per Quarter at Annual Rates
1948–49:						
First estimate[c]	*SCB* July 1958	1948-IV	1949-II	2	−2.4	−4.7
Revised estimate	*SCB* Dec. 1980	1948-IV	1949-II	2	−1.5	3.0
1953–54:						
First estimate[c]	*SCB* July 1958	1953-II	1954-II	4	−3.7	−3.7
Revised estimate	*SCB* Dec. 1980	1953-II	1954-II	4	−3.2	−3.2
1957–58:						
First estimate[c]	*SCB* Feb. 1959	1957-III	1958-I	2	−5.3	−10.3
Revised estimate	*SCB* Dec. 1980	1957-III	1958-I	2	−3.3	−6.6
1960–61:						
First estimate	*SCB* Aug. 1961	1960-II	1961-I	3	−2.3	−3.1
Revised estimate	*SCB* Dec. 1980	1960-I	1960-IV	3	−1.2	−1.5
1969–70:						
First estimate	*SCB* Apr. 1971	1969-III	1970-IV	5	−1.4	−1.2
Revised estimate	*SCB* Dec. 1980	1969-III	1970-I	2	−1.0	−1.9
1973–75:						
First estimate	*SCB* July 1975	1973-IV	(1975-II)	5	−7.8	−6.2
	SCB Aug. 1975	1973-IV	1975-I	5	−4.8	−3.8
Revised estimate	*SCB* Dec. 1980	1973-IV	1975-I	5		
1980:						
First estimate	*SCB* July 1980	1980-I	1980-II	1	−2.3	−9.1
Revised estimate	*SCB* July 1982	1980-I	1980-II	1	−2.5	−9.6

[a]See n.[b], table 8.1
[b]See no.[c], table 8.1
[c]Constant-dollar GNP estimates were not available on a current quarterly basis.

The GNP Data Improvement Report from the Perspective
of Its Use to Measure Economic Growth
Ronald E. Kutscher

I was asked to discuss the Creamer Report from the point of view of someone who is interested in data for measuring real economic growth. My particular orientation reflects a concern not only for the measurement of economic growth but also for the usefulness of these data in developing and operating a long-range economic model. Our BLS model is employed in making projections with a 5–15-year time horizon. It is not only a macromodel but, in addition, it has an industry orientation derived from an input-output model, so my remarks will reflect this further bias. I would further describe the interest of those concerned with measurement of economic growth and of long-term modelers as more directed toward annual data. Thus, emphasis on revisions of quarterly estimates and their tracking record is of lower priority to a long-term modeler. A long-term modeler would, in most instances, be satisfied with data published only after moderately final data are available (although certainly not waiting until benchmark data are available).

The long-range modeler not only emphasizes the macro GNP accounts but has an interest in bringing together the macro and the micro or industry modeling. From this developing horizon in modeling, another view of the GNP Data Improvement Project is possible. For example, are the changes recommended in this report of assistance in the integration of macro- and microsectors of a model? If not, what changes would make the accounts more useful? As an example, the interaction of wages and other factor payments, prices, and incomes not only at the macrolevel but also at the microlevel are important in tracking, modeling, and assessing the interactions of resource use, distribution of factor payments, and prices. Linking the micro- to the macroportion of models takes on increased significance in an economy with rapidly changing prices. It is only at the microlevel that most supply constraints can be handled—another element of increasing concern to analysts and modelers. Thus, in this paper I will stress the continued development of a fully integrated macro- and microdata base. For it is only at the industry level that one can really begin to deal with the interaction of energy, environment, or supply constraints. In fact, as the issues dealt with extend to such questions as the environment, it is even doubtful that many questions can be treated adequately in any comprehensive way short of subnational data.

Ronald E. Kutscher is assistant commissioner with the Office of Economic Growth and Employment Projections, Bureau of Labor Statistics.

In reviewing the report of the Data Improvement Project, I found much with which I could agree. I would support the recommendations that could be termed expanding the nonmanufacturing data base, the present weaknesses in which are well known.

A further set of recommendations that I support deals with expanding the data base on government procurement of goods and services from the private sector. I also agree and endorse the thrust of the recommendations concerning price needs of the national accounts. Finally, I am sure all would agree with the recommendation to provide an updated methodological handbook on the national accounts.

In reading this document, I had no disagreements with any of the explicit recommendations made by the Data Improvement Project except for several very trivial items. My criticism is more directed at the charges to the committee rather than at the committee's work. From my perspective, I wish the committee had dealt with a number of other subjects which are listed below.

1. The need for input-output tables to be fully integrated into the national accounts. While all new input-output tables in current prices are consistent with the new national accounts, the conceptual and statistical changes are not made in tables for earlier years nor are constant dollar input-output tables for earlier years prepared consistent with the new national accounts. As an example, the conceptual and statistical changes introduced into the 1967 input-output table were not made in the 1963 input-output table. For many purposes, such as most analyses of economic growth and its structural characteristics, consistent input-output tables over time are very important. This should be done not only for the earlier benchmark years but also for the annual estimates between benchmark years. This development of consistent input-output tables should be done not only in current dollars but also in constant dollars. This would require BEA to develop historical constant-dollar detailed input-output tables consistent with each new benchmark table.

2. The Data Improvement Project notes that annual adjustments in the second and third July revisions in many instances made the data no better when compared to final benchmarks, and in a distressing number of instances it was worse. If this experience is repeated with the 1972 benchmark, I would argue that BEA should give serious thought to putting more resources into producing the benchmark sooner rather than into the production of annual updates. Clearly one of the current difficulties with the GNP data base is the very long lag in introducing the benchmarks.

A second observation in this regard concerns the nature of the benchmark process. Any benchmark should assess, to the maximum extent feasible given resource constraints, whether estimates of the basic level and structure of the economy require modification. While BEA now does that in the case of current-dollar GNP, this is not true of real GNP, since the deflation takes place with the same price data. Since it seems very unlikely to get an independent check on prices in the forseeable future, perhaps an additional approach is worth considering (see item 3).

3. In modeling, particularly, as the modeling moves toward multifactor production functions, new data requirements are raised. One of these is in the measure of output. Currently, in many models where the macro GNP accounts are combined with a microdata base, this is done through the use of gross product originating as the measure of an industry's (or sector's) output. However, the measure of output that is more appropriate in multifactor analyses, which include intermediate materials as one of the factors, is a gross output concept rather than the net or gross product originating concept. Consequently, I would like to see developed a time series of gross output measures by industry that is conceptually linked to the input-output measures and through them to GNP. These gross output measures would need to be developed in current and constant dollars. Closely related to that would be total material and service inputs consumed by industry over time (perhaps broken into major categories such as energy, manufactured goods, etc.)—again linked to the input-output and GNP data base. This latter data need relates to the need to isolate intermediate along with other inputs such as capital or labor as an explanatory factor in output changes. While the Office of Economic Growth in BLS is developing some of the data series noted in items 3 and 4 listed here, it seems preferable for these to be developed and fully integrated into the national accounts.

Another independent check to benchmarking GNP might be to explore the use of industry data. This approach would aggregate GNP by industry to ascertain if that aggregate could be used as an independent check on the level of GNP. Such a check might be useful in the benchmarking process, even though of necessity it would not replace current procedures of reconciling income and product.

4. There is need for a national data base that includes estimates of capital stock by industry; these estimates were not recommended because of time constraints. This is one of the more important elements in linking the macro- and the microelements in economic models. An industry capital stock system is important in analyzing resource requirements and is needed in analyzing trade-offs with other resources such as labor or energy. Currently, gross private domestic investment in the national accounts is used by BEA to develop capital stock estimates for the total private economy and for a few major sectors. This data base needs to be disaggregated to provide capital stock by industry, the industry classification for which should be as close as possible to that in the data base described in item 3.

An adjunct to the industry capital stock data base would be an annual capital flow table. A capital flow table shows transactions between purchasers and producers of capital goods. If annual capital flow tables were available, it would be possible to relax the assumption that the industry pattern of capital expenditures is constant between benchmark years.

Capital investment in the accounts now covers investment for many purposes. Some developments on the part of BEA to divide investment by purpose is already underway, that is, investment for pollution purposes. This should be encouraged and expanded into other similar fields such as safety and health, noise and other standards. Further, I think it would be worthwhile to examine other divisions of capital. I have felt one of the difficult elements of investment for model builders is that one is attempting to explain something as diverse in purpose as rugs in the executive suite and rolling mills, or warehouses and religious buildings. These further divisions of capital investment would be especially useful if done by industry. Finer breakdowns of investment would not be directed toward a new definition of GNP but would simply introduce divisions which could be helpful in analyzing and explaining investment behavior.

5. An annual time series on income by industry, by type of income integrated with the input-output and national income data base, should be developed. As industry models are linked with macromodels, the need is increased for a time series on income or factor payments that has been fully integrated with the input-output and the GNP accounts. This recommendation is not to deny the many data problems that this would entail, such as estimates of profits by establishments classified by industry. However, such a development would be a great asset—for modeling and understanding the economy.

6. I feel analysis would be greatly aided by a disaggregation of the state and local government sector of the GNP accounts. This disaggregation would be such that state governments would be distinct from local governments. To continue to treat this as a single sector of demand must ignore the tremendous growth of these governments over the last three decades. Such a division should be especially helpful to government policymakers.

One cannot but be impressed with the thoroughness and detail with which the committee carried out its review of the GNP accounts. However, as I read the report I was struck by an analogy that may have some relevance here. Suppose an automobile is disassembled and every nut, bolt, screw, rivet, and panel is examined to determine if it has been made of the right metal, has been correctly machined, and coated with the best coating. Although this would constitute an extremely useful examination, I also felt I should have asked whether this auto was the correct form of transportation. Thus, I feel another conference could be built around the question of whether other measures of GNP might be useful. Of course you must realize that coming from an agency with seven versions of the unemployment rate, two consumer price indexes, and two employment series, I can naturally ask, "How long can we exist with only one GNP measure?"

Comment   John W. Kendrick

I have little to quarrel with in Ronald Kutscher's paper since he agreed with most of the recommendations relevant to growth analysis and had no significant disagreements. His chief comments related to areas of omission in the GNP Data Improvement Project (DIP) report, to which I had a few reactions.

He suggests that BEA shift resources from the annual revisions of GNP estimates, which apparently result in little net improvement over the initial July estimates, to speeding up preparation of the benchmark revisions. I doubt if the resources are fully transferable. Even if they were, I would still favor trying to make improvements on both fronts. If the annual revisions can be improved, which I believe they can, it would really be helpful for *both* short- and long-run analyses not to have to wait five years for improved interim estimates. If BEA can accelerate publication of the benchmark estimates and still mine the richer body of quinquennial census data called for by the DIP report, so much the better. But I would argue that any trade-off between quality and timeliness of the benchmark estimates should be tilted toward quality.

Kutscher would like to see BEA publish industry estimates of gross output (i.e., real value of total production), together with estimates of real intermediate product costs to reconcile the gross output estimates with the real gross product (i.e., net output) estimates now published. That would indeed be a most useful expansion of the available estimates, making possible broader analyses of production and productivity with respect to all inputs, both factor and intermediate. I hope the expansion of Census data on intermediate purchases of services as well as goods called for by DIP will make this possible.

I would, however, take issue with Kutscher that the industry gross output estimates will provide an additional means of benchmarking or checking the GNP estimates through production measures based on physical volume data. It seems to me that the benchmarking process must rely to a major extent on the current values, in terms of which economic transactions are carried on. The physical volume data may occasionally provide a convenient supplement to deflated value estimates. But in general I would trust price data more than the unit value data which

John W. Kendrick is professor of economics, George Washington University.

Kutscher implies might be used for checking the price data, and thus the real GNP series. Use of the quantity and value data for this purpose would be very limited, as I see it, unless Census attempted a major expansion of its quantity data collection in a degree of product detail which would, I believe, be unacceptable to budgeteers in government and industry alike.

Kutscher would like to have an annual capital flow table, in part as a basis for estimates of capital stocks, by industry. For purposes of productivity and growth analysis, I can heartily endorse his recommendation and note with satisfaction that BEA is now in process of developing its capital stock estimates on an industry basis.

Kutscher would also like to see the investment and stock estimates broken down by at least some broad categories, such as productive and "nonproductive." Dividing lines are difficult to draw, but I am sympathetic to the notion. I might note that the Wealth Inventory Planning Study, which I directed over 15 years ago, made a similar recommendation, but went further in urging that certain types of investment and capital of a functional nature that cut across industry lines, such as transportation equipment and power-generating equipment, should also be broken out.

Kutscher advocates annual estimates of national income by industry on an establishment definition consistent with the input-output tables. I would not object, so long as users recognize that conventions had to be used to a considerable extent to allocate overhead factor costs and profits among the establishments of mutliplant firms.

Finally, Kutscher regrets that the DIP project and report omit consideration of regional accounts, wealth statements, and possibilities of restructuring economic accounts to make them more useful, particularly for growth analysis and projections. I wish we had had the time and resources. Certainly, restructuring of the accounts to provide sector capital accounts and wealth statements, together with broader and more meaningful definitions of investment and wealth, would be of great value for growth analysis, projections, and as background for policy formulation.

I am convinced that in the decade ahead we will hear much more about the need for mechanisms within the federal government for giving greater emphasis to formulation of policies to promote productivity advance and economic growth, both as an anti-inflationary force and as a means to resuming historical rates of increase in real income per capita. One of the few good features of the Humphrey-Hawkins Act was the stress it puts on longer-range policy formulation. The productivity slowdown of the past decade underscores the need for this, as contrasted with short-run stabilization policy which seems to absorb most of the energies of our economic policymakers. By the time the NIA have become a better tool for long-run as well as short-run analyses, I hope government officials will be paying more attention to both categories of policy.

Data Needs in Flow of Funds
John A. Gorman

I am very glad that the report includes a discussion of the data needs in flow of funds (F/F) (U.S. Department of Commerce 1977, chap. 9). I am especially heartened because I observe very little familiarity with the F/F's on the part of many users of the national income and product accounts (NIPAs), and perhaps the inclusion of this chapter will help make the profession more aware of the F/F data.

One illustration of the limbo into which the profession has relegated the F/F's is the widespread preoccupation with the saving rate as measured in the NIPAs, to the exclusion of the conceptually equivalent, but statistically different, saving rate computable from the F/F's. The two saving rates are compared on table 8.3. Note that they tell quite different stories: the F/F saving rate is considerably higher than the NIPA saving rate; the saving rates move in different directions in 1972; and even though they move in the same direction in 1969, 1970, 1973, and 1975, the first differences in the movement of the saving rates differ by more than one-half a percentage point.

Both estimates of saving are derived as residuals: the NIPA saving is derived as personal income less personal taxes and outlays; the F/F saving is derived as persons' acquisition of physical and financial assets less capital consumption allowances and borrowing. Further, the allocations of many financial assets and liabilities to the household sector are also based on residual calculations. The existence of a large discrepancy between the two saving measures is evidence of a disturbing disharmony between the statistics entering the two sets of accounts.

One speculation on the nature of this discrepancy at the end of chapter 9 is that "methods for distributing production put too much into consumption and not enough into corporate business investment" (U.S. Department of Commerce 1977, p. 189). We have just gone through the preparation of the input-output table for 1972, and nothing we have learned in that process supports this speculation. While our benchmarking procedure is still far from complete, a preliminary analysis of the revised data for 1972 indicates an upward revision in NIPA personal saving, but not enough to eliminate the large discrepancy between the NIPA and F/F personal saving measures.

The chapter makes nine recommendations for improving the data for flow of funds. Only one of the nine recommendations gives any promise of help in reducing the discrepancy in the personal saving measures and in the sectors of the flow-of-funds accounts—the recommendation that

John A. Gorman is assistant chief, National Income and Wealth Division, Bureau of Economic Analysis.

"basic research be conducted on the measurement of land values with respect to use, ownership, encumbrances, and intangibles related to natural resources and leases" (U.S. Department of Commerce 1977, p. 187). Even if this research were undertaken in the near future, this research will take a long time to pay off in regular statistics, so the net result of the implementation of the recommendations in chapter 9 of the Data Improvement Report will be to leave us with an unacceptably large discrepancy between personal saving in the NIPAs and the F/F's for the forseeable future.

What of the recommendations in chapter 9, apart from improving the discrepancies? I will now go through them in order.

The first recommendation is that "the Bureau of Economic Analysis should provide current quarterly seasonally unadjusted data for all components on the product side and as many components as feasible for the income side of the national economic accounts" (U.S. Department of Commerce 1977, p. 184).

It is difficult to be against the provision of unadjusted numbers except on the basis of cost and feasibility. In this connection I should like to point out that approximately one-fifth of retailers do not maintain inventory accounts on a monthly basis; even the unadjusted numbers for such firms are imputations and need not give information on what actually happened. To obtain true unadjusted numbers for such firms, we would first have to induce them to keep books.

Even when firms keep books, they may record transactions inconsistently: for example, a borrower may accrue interest monthly; a lender might only record it semiannually when received. Unadjusted numbers in such cases would lead to an intensification, not a mitigation, of transaction discrepancies.

In any event, truly unadjusted data do not exist for all components of the NIPAs, even on the product side. If any unadjusted series is cooked up with imputations for transactions not actually measured, I do not understand how "a clear accounting relation be established on a quarterly basis between the NIPA receipts and expenditures and independently derived financial transactions" (U.S. Department of Commerce 1977, p. 183).

The Bureau of Economic Analysis (BEA) does provide unadjusted estimates for the product side of the accounts, corporate profits, and items entering the government accounts on a retrospective basis as part of the July revision. BEA has asked for funds to develop current quarterly measures on the product side and research the ability to estimate unadjusted income estimates. BEA hopes to have these sometime in the next five years, depending on funding. My personal view is that this will do little to improve the sectoral discrepancy problem in the flow of funds, which is indicated in table 8.3 is in the annual numbers.

The report points out, "Consistency in timing is a problem mainly in bank-related claims" (U.S. Department of Commerce 1977, p. 184), but it makes no proposals regarding any new data programs to improve bank-related statistics. I believe the absence from chapter 9 of a recommendation to improve bank data to be a major lost opportunity for the report. In effect, chapter 9 diagnoses an illness and then fails to recommend a therapy.

With respect to corporations, chapter 9 recommends, "The Securities and Exchange Commission should explore the feasibility of tabulating the quarterly and annual reports filed by all registered large nonfinancial corporations to provide an integrated statement income, balance sheets and sources of financing" (U.S. Department of Commerce 1977, p. 185). I have no quarrel with such a recommendation, if considered in isolation. However, I think it is a retrogression in the context of the statistical system as a whole. There has been a distinct tendency to withdraw coverage of small firms in our statistical system as evidenced by (1) the cuts in sample size suffered by the Statistics of Income program of the Internal Revenue Service in recent years, (2) the Federal Trade Commission's elimination of manufacturing firms with assets under $250,000 from the Quarterly Financial Report sample, and (3) the general propaganda blitz against federal paperwork burdens on business. In these circumstances I view as distinctly unhelpful a suggestion that the major data improvement for nonfinancial corporations in the F/F accounts be limited to registered companies only. Such an approach would be justified only if small firms were either negligible or behaved the same as large firms. Neither is the case.

If I were asked for recommendations in this areas, I would suggest the Federal Trade Commission resume sampling births and small firms, add a sources-and-uses-of-funds schedule to their questionnaire, and expand their industrial coverage. I would also urge the systematic editing and tabulation of Schedule M of the corporate tax return, which reconciles the income tax return with the company balance sheets. I believe this program would reduce the large corporate sector discrepancy in the F/F's, which in 1978 exceeded in amount 22 of the 27 financial transaction categories shown in the F/F statement for nonfinancial corporate business. A reduction in the corporate sector discrepancy will be matched by a similar reduction in the household sector discrepancy, given the residual nature of the allocation process.

With respect to state and local governments, chapter 9 recommends that "the Census Bureau should collect quarterly data on cash and security holdings of State and local governments" (U.S. Department of Commerce 1977, p. 185). I agree with this, and would also collect the liability side of the balance sheet. I would do so because in some years there have been large differences between the data on state and local bond issues and retirements used in the F/F's, and changes in outstanding debt collected by the Census Bureau. Collecting the outstanding debt quarterly would outflank the problem of combining data for disparate fiscal year-ends and provide a better control on the bond issue and, particularly, the bond retirement data.

The next recommendation is that "the Bureau of Economic Analysis should provide quarterly measures of fixed capital outlays, stocks, and capital consumption charges by sector and by type of capital as part of the national income and product accounts" (U.S. Department of Commerce 1977, p. 186).

BEA already supplies capital consumption charges by F/F sector on a quarterly basis. We allocate investment and estimate stocks annually. I view this suggestion as relating to providing investment by F/F sector quarterly. I think this could be done as part of the forthcoming benchmark revision by an adaptation of our annual method.

I have already commented on the recommendation with respect to land.

With respect to disaggregation of households, chapter 9 recommends: (1) speeding up tabulation and refining classification of trust fund survey, (2) exploiting nonprofit data from 1977 census, and (3) separation of wealthy individuals (U.S. Department of Commerce 1977, p. 187). In principle I have no difficulty with these recommendations. I suggest the Federal Reserve should take the lead in urging the other two bank supervisory agencies to join in improving the trust fund survey. Further, I am surprised that no reference is made to the forthcoming IRS tabulations on nonprofit institution information returns. Finally, I have always been skeptical of the imputation of the portfolios of the dead to those of the living, which is inherent in the estate tax procedure. Perhaps a better approach to disaggregating the personal sector would be to use the planned Survey of Income and Program Participation, although this too will have problems in getting data for the wealthy.

The next recommendation is, "The OMB Statistical Policy Division should establish an interagency task force to reconcile operational definitions on international transactions used by The Bureau of Economic Analysis, Treasury Department, and The Federal Reserve System" (U.S. Department of Commerce 1977, p. 188). I understand that this recommendation has been satisfied by the format changes introduced recently in the International Transaction tables.

Finally, the report recommends that "the Bureau of Economic Analysis should prepare a time series on the U.S. international investment position from 1948 forward" (U.S. Department of Commerce 1977, p. 188).

This is a good recommendation. It should be noted, however, that it involves reformating the investment position data for years prior to 1971 in order that the presentation from 1948 through 1969 agree with the quarterly statement of international transactions. This is a sizable operation for which BEA requested funding and which has been denied. Furthermore, this effort will not change the statistical discrepancy in the International Transaction table, since there are no new data for the 1948–69 period, and thus will not contribute to the resolution of the discrepancy problem in the F/F's.

Chapter 9 concludes with a description of the large offsetting discrepancies in the household and business sector. As I mentioned earlier, nothing in this chapter will lead to an early resolution of this.

In this section the report says, "Another possible source of discrepancies is through incorporation of noncorporate business or, statistically the same thing, purchases of noncorporate businesses by corporations" (U.S. Department of Commerce 1977, p. 189). Data on depreciation claimed on tax returns casts some doubt on this hypothesis. In table 8.4, the corporate share in tax return depreciation fell from 1968 to 1974, while the partnership share increased. This is not conclusive evidence on which way the legal form of organization has shifted: if partnerships were increasing the use of accelerated depreciation methods more than corporations were, or investing in assets with shorter lives than corporations were, the increase in the share of partnership depreciation would be consistent with a shift toward the corporate legal form. Nonetheless, I find it difficult to believe that these shifts are a major source of the statistical discrepancy in the household and corporate sectors, at least in the past decade or so.

To summarize, this chapter of the report makes only one recommendation for data improvement that gives any hope of resolving the statistical discrepancy problem—research on land. It omits three others that I think would give some hope of resolving the problem—expansion of the Quarterly Financial Report, tabulating schedule M, and improved reporting of bank data. It is true that the tabulation of schedule M is recommended elsewhere in the report (U.S. Department of Commerce 1977, p. 47), but I think the recommendation should also have been referenced in chapter 9 because of the strategic role data from schedule M could play in reducing the statistical discrepancy in the nonfinancial corporate sector of the F/F's.

Reference

U.S. Department of Commerce, Office of Federal Statistical Policy and Standards. 1977. *Gross National Product Data Improvement Project Report*. Report of the Advisory Committee on Gross National Product Data Improvement. Washington, D.C.: Government Printing Office.

Table C8.3   **Comparison of Personal Saving Rate in NIPAs with the Flow of Funds, 1968–78**

Year	Personal Saving as Percent of Disposable Personal Income[a] NIPA	F/F	Disposable Personal Income ($Billions)	Personal Saving ($Billions) NIPA	F/F
1968	7.1	8.2	593.4	41.9	48.8
1969	6.4	6.5	638.9	40.6	41.8
1970	8.0	9.0	695.3	55.8	62.5
1971	8.1	9.0	751.8	60.7	67.4
1972	6.5	9.4	810.3	52.6	75.9
1973	8.6	10.3	914.5	79.0	94.4
1974	8.5	10.0	998.3	85.1	99.5
1975	8.6	11.1	1,096.1	94.3	122.1
1976	6.9	9.8	1,194.4	82.5	117.5
1977	5.9	8.3	1,314.0	78.0	109.0
1978	6.1	8.1	1,474.0	89.4	119.6

Source: U.S. Department of Commerce, Bureau of Economic Analysis, *Survey of Current Business*, July 1982; U.S. Department of Commerce, Bureau of Economic Analysis, *The National Income and Product Accounts of the United States*, 1929–76, statistical tables, September 1981; Federal Reserve Board, *Flow of Funds Accounts, Second Quarter 1981*.
[a]The saving rate with F/F data was computed with F/F personal saving in the numerator and NIPA disposable personal income in the denominator. An alternative saving rate could be computed using the F/F personal saving in the numerator but adding the excess of F/F saving over NIPA saving to NIPA disposable personal income in the denominator; this alternative would be lower than the F/F personal saving rate column by .1 or .2 percentage points. The F/F personal saving is F/F individuals' saving adjusted to NIPA concepts.

Table C8.4   **Depreciation Reported on Business Income Tax Returns: Percent Reported by Legal Form of Organization, by Selected Industries, 1968 and 1974**

	Sole Proprietorships		Partnerships		Corporations	
	1968	1974	1968	1974	1968	1974
All nonfarm industries	9.5	8.0	5.7	8.4	84.9	83.6
Agriculture services, forestry, and fisheries	51.9	49.1	11.8	13.6	36.2	37.3
Mining	10.6	8.5	7.3	10.0	82.1	81.5
Contract construction	26.0	26.8	9.0	5.8	65.0	67.4
Manufacturing	1.4	1.3	.8	.7	97.8	97.9
Transportation	11.5	14.2	1.3	3.0	87.1	82.8
Communication, and electric gas, and sanitary services	.4	.3	.2	.4	99.4	99.3
Wholesale trade	14.3	10.7	5.0	3.1	80.7	86.1
Retail trade	28.5	21.2	6.8	4.8	64.7	74.0
Finance and insurance	4.4	2.1	2.7	2.0	92.9	95.9
Real estate	5.5	5.4	39.1	63.4	55.3	31.3
Services	29.7	22.4	10.3	15.1	60.0	62.5

Note: Computed from data published by the Internal Revenue Service in *Statistics of Income*

Comment   Stephen Taylor

It is gratifying to see John Gorman's concern about statistical discrepancies stated in public and discussed at some length. Users of statistical systems tend to find the discrepancies a nuisance to be set aside and often cannot understand the attention put to them by producers of the systems, such as BEA, or, for the flow-of-funds accounts, the Federal Reserve. Discrepancies are nevertheless prima facie evidence of inconsistency, and therefore of error, and they provide at least a starting agenda for further statistical research. Lack of discrepancy, incidentally, does not demonstrate the converse case of lack of error or even lack of inconsistency and is not an occasion for complacency, but in the real world of national financial accounts that is not a problem: the flow-of-funds system has 20 or more separate discrepancy accounts that lead active lives and that must be watched constantly for their rather complicated interactions with one another. They give almost no occasion for complacency.

The data improvement projects for flow-of-funds in chapter 9 that John Gorman discusses are not aimed solely at reducing discrepancies, but he is too hard on them when he says that only one is directed at improving

Stephen Taylor is with the Federal Reserve Board.

the household discrepancy. As Gorman points out, all of the household items are measured in the system as residuals by use of reported information from other groups in the economy. As a result, data improvements over a very wide range of activities redound to better measures of household transactions and condition, and the proposals in chapter 9 deserve more credit for this purpose than Gorman gives them. Recommendations for both more current state and local government figures and more standardized international flow categories go directly toward better household estimates. The request for more complete NIPA data in seasonally unadjusted form also goes in this direction, since a large part of what is not known in actual quarterly form is household income and consumption.

The obviously largest problem in household discrepancies is in business data, as mentioned both in chapter 9 and in Gorman's discussion. Almost any improvement in measures of business activity can be expected to raise the quality of household residuals, through direct or indirect channels, and Gorman mentions this. He disagrees, however, with the chapter 9 recommendation to mine SEC-mandated financial statements for a better picture of large corporations, feeling instead that more weight should be put into measuring small business.

This seems to be primarily a disagreement in strategy. Data on small business activity is unquestionably deplorable and deteriorating, but the chapter 9 proposal was made in a climate of rising protest against the paperwork burden of reporting to Washington and of tightening budget constraints on all types of statistical work in the federal government. The SEC reports already exist and would require zero additional paperwork by business, whereas the route that Gorman prefers would involve more reporting and more statistical work. There is considerable question whether the SEC reports can be applied meaningfully to national accounts, but with the commercial development of computerized versions of those data on a company basis it has become even easier to explore the possibility now than at the time the chapter 9 recommendation was first written.

In closing, a comment on Gorman's table 8.4: the statistical discrepancy that arises for incorporation of existing noncorporate businesses is a continuing condition if there is in fact a tendency for new enterprises to start in unincorporated form and to become corporations once they are well underway. The table 8.4 figures on distribution of business by form of organization say nothing about whether there is such a continuing flow of enterprises from one form to another but only that if there is it is a relatively stable process over the period in the table.

The Improvement of Price Data
Albert Rees

The National Income and Product Accounts use price data to deflate expenditures measured in current dollars and thus to estimate changes in real output. Deflation procedures are of greater importance when the price level is changing rapidly, as in the past decade, than when it is relatively stable. For this reason interest in the proper measurement of prices has never been greater than it is now.

Price data used for deflation can be improved in two basic ways. First, the coverage of the price series can be broadened by pricing additional kinds of goods and services, so that the movements of one set of prices need not be inferred from the movements of another. Second, the quality of existing price series can be improved.

Chapter 7 of the Report of the Advisory Committee on Gross National Product Data Improvement concentrates on the first of these two basic kinds of improvements. For example, it recommends the development of separate rent indexes for single-family homes and for units in multiple-unit structures: these could be used to improve the imputation of rent for owner-occupied housing. The report also recommends that the Producer Price Index (formerly the Wholesale Price Index) improve its coverage of equipment items, such as large aircraft, ships and boats, and computers, which would greatly strengthen the deflator for producers' durable equipment. It further recommends exploration of the feasibility of developing new price indexes covering the construction of various kinds of industrial facilities, for which output price data are now based in substantial part on input prices.

All of these recommendations, and several others like them, seem to me to be sound and important. However, the focus of chapter 7 on broadening the coverage of price indexes has led to a relative neglect of improvements in the quality of the price series already included. To be sure, the report cites several earlier studies that deal with this issue, specifically the report of the Stigler Committee (*Price Statistics* 1961), the Ruggles study (1977) of the Wholesale Price Index, and the forthcoming book on the prices of durable goods of Robert J. Gordon (forthcoming). It also recommends in general terms support of the ongoing efforts of the Bureau of Labor Statistics (BLS) to improve its price indexes. But it does not lend its authority to those detailed recommendations of the Stigler Committee, Ruggles, or Gordon that are still relevant for the improvement of pricing in areas now covered by price indexes.

Most existing price indexes used in deflation are components of either the Consumer Price Index (CPI) or the Producer Price Index (PPI)

Albert Rees is president of the Alfred P. Sloan Foundation, New York.

produced by the Bureau of Labor Statistics. Both indexes have recently undergone extensive revisions resulting in substantial improvements. The CPI now has weights based on a much broader universe of consumers than the old index. Many of the improvements in both indexes result from the introduction of probability sampling of vendors and products. This should deal adequately with one major past complaint about these indexes, which was that their vendor and product samples used to remain unchanged for long periods, a situation that could create substantial biases in estimates of price change. Finally, the new Producer Price Index has eliminated the double-counting of items that characterized the old Wholesale Price Index. The meaningless overall index for all commodities has been discontinued (see Early 1978)

A number of other issues have not yet been dealt with or are under study. The staff of BLS is well aware of these issues, and the purpose of raising them here is *not* to call them to the attention of BLS. It is to help make others aware of them so that the research community can support BLS when it seeks authorization and funding to implement further changes.

One of the principal issues raised in the Stigler Report (*Price Statistics* 1961) and by Stigler and Kindahl (1970) concerns the difference between list prices and actual transactions prices. Transactions prices may include discounts from list or other concessions to buyers that vary with the tightness of the market. As the Report of the Advisory Committee notes, list prices are therefore stickier than transactions prices. When used as deflators, they will tend to overstate the fall in real output during a recession. The Consumer Price Index has long collected transactions prices for goods where discounts are important, such as automobiles and major appliances. The Producer Price Index now includes some transactions prices, particularly for metals and chemicals. It may be desirable to extend the use of transactions pricing to additional areas of the PPI.

It will, of course, never be possible to capture in a price index all of the varied and ingenious changes in terms of sale that affect the true prices of commodities and services. Such cleverly disguised changes in transactions prices are particularly likely in periods of substantial excess supply or excess demand at posted prices. For example, the Council on Wage and Price Stability (COWPS) was told by aluminum fabricators that, during the aluminum shortages of 1973, fabricators were expected to resell their scrap to primary aluminum producers as an implicit condition of receiving continued supplies of primary metal. One efficient fabricator who generated less scrap than was expected of him told COWPS that he felt he had to buy scrap for resale on the open market at prices above those paid to him by his supplier of primary aluminum.

The same industry provides evidence of opposite kinds of price behavior. In 1975, when major producers of primary aluminum were producing at about 75% of capacity, a few small producers were operating at much higher levels, although their posted prices were the same. One may surmise that their transactions prices were not the same without knowing how this was arranged.

A second major issue affecting price indexes concerns the timing aspects of price quotations. Ruggles has produced valuable data showing the distribution of PPI price series by whether the series refers to the time of order or the time of shipment. The report supports BLS plans to move more price quotations to a time of shipment basis, which is the appropriate basis for deflators. However, series on prices at the time of order are also of interest for other purposes. They will serve as a better leading indicator of general price changes than will prices at time of shipment.

I should like to point out that the distinction between time of order and time of shipment is only one of the timing issues that need to be considered. Another major distinction is between prices under new contracts and prices under continuing contracts. This issue affects both commodities sold under long-term contract, such as steam coal to utilities or crude petroleum to refiners, and payments for services such as rent and mortgage interest rates. Studies of the cyclical behavior of prices will find the movements of prices on new contracts of greatest interest. On the other hand, the average price under all contracts in force is clearly the relevant measure for deflators, and the same is true for the use of price indexes in cost-of-living escalator clauses.

The BLS practice on this issue is not consistent. At the time data were collected for the Ruggles report, coal was priced on the basis of average realized unit selling price, which includes prices under old contracts. Domestic crude petroleum was priced on the basis of spot prices posted by buyers, which presumably reflects short-run demands for quantities in excess of any being received under contracts. In a Laspeyres price index, it would be consistent to have separate series on spot prices and average existing contract prices, together with base-period data for use as weights on the fraction of output sold on each basis. Data on average realized sales prices from sellers who sell on both bases will reflect the movements of both kinds of prices, but they will also reflect shifts in the relative importance of the two arrangements. This is consistent with the use of current value weights in the broad construction of deflators, although deflators are generally based on Laspeyres price indexes at the item level.

A much more important example of the timing problem concerns the pricing of rent and mortgage interest in the CPI. Rent has always been priced as the average monthly rental under existing leases or unwritten commitments, the appropriate concept for deflation and escalation. Changes in mortgage interest, however, are based on the rates quoted on new mortgages beginning in a given month. The effect of this is to give fluctuations in mortgage interest rates a disproportionate effect on the

CPI. When interest rates rise, there will then be a corresponding tendency of cost-of-living adjustment clauses in collective bargaining agreements and the legislated formulas that govern transfer payments to overcompensate the average recipient of such income. This issue deserves attention both from BLS and from the Council on Wage and Price Stability. One solution to the problem would be for BLS to collect and publish mortgage interest rates on both bases, but not to include the separate series on rates on new mortgages in more aggregative indexes. The problem in this instance does not affect the deflator for personal consumption expenditures, since the imputed rent on owner-occupied housing is based on the rent of rental housing.

The final issue I should like to mention concerns adjustment for quality change. The present practice of the Bureau of Labor Statistics and the Bureau of Economic Analysis (BEA) is to make an adjustment in a price series for quality improvement in a product when data can be obtained on the cost to the producer of making the improvement. The Report of the Advisory Committee quotes a BEA paper which states that such data are not always available, and that quarterly movements in the affected series will therefore appear as price changes rather than as output changes. Presumably we can all agree that more data on the costs to producers of quality improvement would be desirable.

There is, however, a much more important aspect of quality change that the report does not consider. This is what may be called "costless" quality improvement resulting from technical change. Of course, such improvement is not really costless, since it usually results from prior investment in research and development. But it is "costless" as BLS and BEA use the term if it does not cost the manufacturer more to make the improved product.

These issues are being considered at much greater depth at other sessions of this conference, and their further exploration here would not be appropriate.

The Advisory Committee on Gross National Product Data Improvement was asked to consider improvements within the framework of the existing National Income and Product Account rather than to consider changes in that framework. Given this charge, chapter 7 of their report does a very good job. Its sins, if there are any, are all sins of omission rather than commission. Its recommendations are sound and pertinent and should be carried out to the extent that available resources permit.

References

Early, John F. 1978. Improving the measurement of producer price change. *Monthly Labor Review* 101 (April): 7–15.

Gordon, Robert J. *The measurement of durable goods prices*. New York: National Bureau of Economic Research (forthcoming).

Stigler, George J., and Kindahl, James K. 1970. *The behavior of industrial prices*. New York: National Bureau of Economic Research.
The price statistics of the federal government. 1961. The Stigler Committee Report. New York: National Bureau of Economic Research.
Richard Ruggles. 1977. *The Wholesale Price Index* (Washington, D.C.: Council on Wage and Price Stability [June].

Some Comments on Papers on
the Creamer Report
Daniel Creamer

Murray Foss gave me two directives: (1) to be a discussant of that part of Morris Cohen's paper dealing with the "overview" and of Alfred Rees's paper on "The Improvement of Price Data," and (2) to respond to anything else that moves me to comment. I interpret the latter as an invitation to ramble, which at my age comes naturally.

The practice of attaching the chairman's name to the sort of report we have prepared certainly fails to be fully informative and seriously slights the contribution of others. I should like to emphasize that the writing of the report was a staff effort. Norman Frumkin made the single largest contribution in the research, the drafting of chapters, and overseeing the final draft through publication. La Verne Collins's contribution was also a major one in the preparation of report materials and in writing. Lou Weiner prepared the chapter on price data and, before ill health overtook him, he further assisted us by persuading Stephen Taylor to take responsibility for the chapter on flow-of-funds estimates. Needless to say, the members of the advisory committee provided guidance throughout, saved us from numerous (but, as Morris Cohen has demonstrated, not from all) errors, and were fully supportive. We also appreciate their forbearance from complaining when their one-year commitment was stretched to four-and-one-half years.

The last point leads directly to Morris Cohen's first remark. He refers to the four-and-one-half years from the inception of the project to the completion of the report and the additional lapse of 18 months until publication. This delay is characterized as "deplorable." Since I have no responsibility for the printing delay, I agree with Morris that that delay is certainly deplorable.

The matter of the four-and-one-half years to prepare the report, I think, is worth a few comments. Certain features of the original design of the project meant delays were inevitable. The budget of $80,000, even in 1973 prices, is not a generous sum. In addition to myself, there was to be a

The late Daniel Creamer was an economist with The Conference Board.

staff of three who were to be on half-time loan (not reimbursable) from regular full-time employment in federal agencies. My own input was also restricted to half-time. Until mid-1975 this was necessary because of my continuing commitment to the Conference Board. After that date a half-time schedule just about matched my energy level. Having my base in New York City was the source of some inefficiencies. This experience suggests to me, and this is my reason for dwelling on it, that, if sponsoring agencies are to avoid deplorable delays, they should provide budgets adequate for full-time staff and direction and not entrust the project to a nonresident who does not have the energy for a full-time commitment.

Beyond the sponsors' mistakes must be mentioned the approach that I imposed on the project. To carry out the assignment, it seemed to me that it was essential to deal with the nuts and bolts of a vast network of interlocking estimates. To master these details on a half-time basis is time-consuming, especially since the last detailed description of the construction of the national accounts published in 1954 was obsolete. Another necessary step was the review of each proposed recommendation by the appropriate data-collecting agency in order to have the benefit of their judgments on relevancy, feasibility, and cost. This too is time-consuming. Perhaps one may argue that we overwhelmed ourselves by concerning ourselves with so much detail. Less detail would have shortened the time required. However, to have done so would have probably undercut another objective of the project, namely, to provide the Office of Federal Statistical Policy and Standards with a management tool to assist in further developing the economic statistics of the federal statistical system. This objective, it seems to me, is better served by the degree of detail that we attempted to provide.

Now for a few remarks on more serious matters. There are three or four points in Morris Cohen's paper to which I would like to respond. Morris notes correctly that there is no mention in the report of capital stock estimates. I had every intention of addressing the subject, in part because this has been a subject of special interest to me. Despite the four-and-one-half-year interval, time was up before I got around to it.

There is one aspect of the subject that seems to have escaped attention. It relates to the measurement of increments to capital stocks in short time periods, say, up to one year. For such intervals, capital expenditures are an inadequate basis for estimates of increments to gross capital stocks if the estimates are to be used for measurement of capital productivity, capacity, and capacity utilization. Capital expenditures as a concept is weak in that they include progress payments for capital items not only not yet installed but not yet completed or received. Much more relevant are "additions to depreciable assets" in a given period. This statistic, I should think, is readily available from enterprise accounts. If I were asked for another recommendation, without benefit of review by the advisory committee, it would be for BEA to add a question on its company plant and equipment survey on additions to depreciable assets in each quarter. A similar recommendation would be relevant to the Census Bureau for its Annual Survey of Manufactures.

Since shipments are a closer proxy for gross additions than capital expenditures, it occurs to me now that BEA might want to review its current methodology in estimating quarterly producers' durable equipment by type. For most of the items the procedure entails an averaging of shipments and expenditures.

This distinction may explain the difference between the movement of commodity-flow estimates (essentially shipments) and survey estimates based on expenditures. This seems to puzzle Morris Cohen. In a given quarter they need not show the same relative movements. Both concepts should be measured since they serve different analytical uses.

The second point that I have selected from Morris's paper is his concern over the estimator's failure to make explicit use of year-end business accounting adjustments. These adjustments Morris points out can make a "whale of a difference" in a company's reported profits. The effect of this failure, I should think, is much less serious than Morris suggests. NIPA estimates depend on aggregates of company reports, and this allows for the possibility of adjustment errors being offsetting to a significant degree.

The third item is his final plea "to lean toward the contemporary recording of economic events, even if the trade-off is a somewhat less accurate measurement of secular trends." May I suggest the trade-off may be more costly than stated. This is particularly true if among the requirements for achieving more accurate recording of the recent past is to have larger samples and higher response rates. This typically means less timeliness. Are users ready to accept this? Of course, advances in enterprise use of computer technology for record keeping and reporting may change this.

Alfred Rees, as is Morris Cohen, is a gentle critic of our report, or more specifically in Rees's case, of our chapter 7 on "Improving Price Data." He seems to agree with what we said but mildly chides us about what was left unsaid, our sins of omission. Clearly his points are valid, and we do confess to the sins. The inclusion of the specific points noted in his paper certainly would have made for a more balanced discussion. My only response is a rationalization developed in retrospect. The reason for the omissions, I suppose, is that we were much impressed by the revision plans of the BLS both for the CPI (then in progress) and for the Producer Price Index. The perceptive and imaginative character of the planned revisions suggested to us that our most helpful course was to recommend as strongly as we could that BLS be given the resources to implement its plans with all due speed. If this were done, we were confident the more glaring deficiencies of the price indexes (mentioned and unmentioned) would be eliminated. Still fuller discussion might have undercut the degree of emphasis we wanted to place on this major recommendation.

In Ronald Kutscher's paper, our errors of omission from the perspective of measuring economic growth are for the most part requests for new aggregates and for finer sets of disaggregation. These specifics are one with his final observation that in addition to examining whether the auto parts were the best available we should also have explored whether this auto was the correct form of transportation. (Is there not another question implied: From where to where do you want to travel?) I understand Kutscher's sense of dissatisfaction with our report on this score. However, our report seemed required and feasible with reference to the quality of the auto parts that we were directed to scrutinize and to suggest specifics for improving. To deal with the proper form of transportation was stipulated as being out-of-scope.

Nonetheless, I should mention that our outlines for the final report at one time provided for an epilogue on the probable new data needs for the NIPA accounts over the next 10 years—an attempt at a forward look. The long struggle to complete what has now been published precluded the preparation of the epilogue. But all that happens is for the best. We now have Richard Ruggles's perceptive analysis of new directions for the national accounts together with those of Ronald Kutscher from a more limited perspective. I am sure these statements give us a better start on new directions than any statement I might have completed.

And now a concluding word to say we much appreciate that the Income and Wealth Conference took our report seriously, virtually unseen—at least seriously enough to have placed it on the agenda. We hope you conclude that a fair number of the objectives expected of the report have indeed been met.

A Bureau of Economic Analysis Perspective
Robert P. Parker

I would like to say a few words about the Creamer Report from a BEA perspective. Clearly, the preparation of this report has been beneficial to BEA. Specific changes that have resulted from the report have been enumerated in an article that appeared in the March 1979 issue of the *Statistical Reporter*. Although I won't repeat the listing of improvements already in place or shortly forthcoming, there has been definite progress. BEA already has adopted some of the recommendations. For example,

Robert P. Parker is chief, National Income and Wealth Division, Bureau of Economic Analysis.

BEA now makes available at the time of the release of the preliminary GNP estimate its projection of key series for which data for the quarter are missing. The published monthly personal income series has been expanded to include personal taxes, outlays, and saving. Also, funds to prepare constant-dollar defense purchases are now part of BEA's budget, and the resulting series have been incorporated into the published GNP estimates. Work also is progressing at BEA on many of the other Creamer Report recommendations. These projects include the reconciliation of the GNP and the FRB industrial production index, improving the Plant and Equipment Expenditures Survey, introduction of BLS price data into the deflation of exports and imports, and the estimation of capital stock by industry.

The process of preparing the report and the steps taken to implement its recommendations also have had other impacts on BEA. There has been some improvement in the communication of our needs to other agencies—both those with which we have had limited or no contact in the past as well as those with which we have had continuing relations. The improved communications have increased not only the level of understanding of the role of each agency's data in preparing the NIPA estimates but also the number of people at these agencies who understand our needs. Furthermore, at BEA there has been increased awareness of the role of other agencies in providing our source data and the problems—financial and others—of these agencies in obtaining additional data. This expansion of the understanding of mutual needs and problems in my opinion also will lead to improved NIPA estimates.

While I don't want to diminish in any way the pluses of the Creamer Report for BEA, it also is necessary to consider its minuses. As has been implied by other speakers at the conference, the report itself really has few or no minuses—only limitations. Thus, I would like to discuss the limitations of the report itself and some problems that have arisen in the process designed to implement the report's recommendations.

First, the implementation plan did not take into account the maintenance of the status quo with regard to source data, especially with regard to the sample size underlying key NIPA source series. For example, at the same time the IRS was being asked to increase its budget for certain improvements, they were significantly cutting back on the size of the sample used to prepare the *Statistics of Income* reports. Similar situations developed with regard to the Federal Trade Commission and the *Quarterly Financial Report* and the Department of Agriculture and the *Farm Production Expenditure Survey*.

Second, the implementation plan focuses attention on the recommended improvement items at the individual agency level and not at the total level. Thus, one agency may add to its budget proposal a $50,000 improvement item that is far less important to improving the quality of the NIPA estimates than a comparably priced recommendation to an agency that decides not to push this latter item and request the necessary funding. In other words, the additional money being spent on improvement items is not always being spent for the highest priority items. This development may be occurring because the report did not provide priorities for its recommendations.

Third, the report does not seem to have influenced the level of scrutiny in the forms clearance function performed in accordance with the Federal Reports Act for potential sources of NIPA improvement. This situation is especially true in the case of information collected in interview surveys from which microdata files are created—such as the *Current Population Survey* and the *Survey of Income Program Participants*. This lack of concern for NIPA improvement increases the problems of integrating these microdata files with the macroestimates prepared by BEA.

As for the report itself, I have a few comments. It would have been better had the report provided for an annual or less frequent updating. As it now stands, as we identify new needs for data, there is no provision to supplement the recommendations.

Another problem with the report is that it might have been better had the report emanated from the Office of Management and Budget (OMB) rather than the Commerce Department. Although the Office of Federal Statistical Policy and Standards has been diligent in its efforts to implement the recommendations, OMB, because of its clout with the budget, may have had more success in gaining agency cooperation.

Finally, the report did not sufficiently deal with potential problems facing the statistical agencies who must collect the additional data. There are two specific problems that we see in this area. The first is the pressure to reduce reporting burden; the second, the role of the standards-setting bodies of the accounting profession.

The pressure to reduce the reporting burden runs opposite to the recommendations of the Creamer report to collect more data. It seems to us that something needs to be done to counter the pressure to reduced reporting burden, since the successful collection of additional data can only proceed with the support of the business community. With regard to the accounting profession, the rules underlying "generally accepted accounting principles" do determine the kind of data easiest to collect. Rule changes—such as those affecting leasing and capitalization of interest—can create serious problems in collecting data conceptually consistent with the BEA's needs. What is needed is for the data needs of national income accounting to be seriously considered in the process of formulating accounting rules, as I understand is done in some European countries. While BEA has written position papers on various proposals of the Financial Accounting Standards Board, we see no indication of any recognition that our concerns are legitimate. We feel that the communication of the importance of the NIPAs, imput-output tables, and International Transaction Accounts to both the business community and the accounting profession is vital to improving the ability of the federal government to collect data to improve the quality and timeliness of BEA's work. A proposal dealing with these problems in the Creamer Report would have been most welcome.

The last topic I'd like to discuss deals with the potential improvement to GNP that will come from the expanded Producer Price Index program of BLS. Several conference speakers have applauded this work, which is designed primarily to generate industry net output prices. The deflation of GNP will benefit from this effort in several ways: more transaction prices, better information on the timing of prices on a delivery basis, and more commodity prices. However, BEA's needs are for commodity and not industry prices. In the short run, BEA would benefit the most by the immediate development of prices for such commodities as ships, computers, and large aircraft, as recommended in the Creamer Report. We hope that BLS will be able to help in this area sooner than is called for in their present plans.

In closing, the Creamer Report has focused widespread attention on BEA's work. Its recommendations will point the way toward improving the statistics underpinning this effort. We see the report as emphasizing, clarifying, and justifying our long-standing quests for more and better data.

Contributors

V. Lewis Bassie
David Kinley Hall
Box 38
University of Illinois
Urbana, Illinois 61801

Morris Cohen
Morris Cohen & Associates
241 Main Street
Hackensack, New Jersey 07601

Rosanne Cole
Economic Research and Forecasting
International Business Machines
    Corporation
Old Orchard Road
Armonk, New York 10504

Daniel Creamer
Deceased

Edward F. Denison
The Brookings Institution
1775 Massachusetts Avenue, N.W.
Washington, D.C. 20036

John F. Early
General Research Corporation
7655 Old Springhouse Road
McLean, Virginia 22102

Otto Eckstein
Data Resources, Inc.
29 Hartwell Avenue
Lexington, Massachusetts 02173

Robert Eisner
Department of Economics
Northwestern University
Evanston, Illinois 60201

Murray F. Foss
American Enterprise Institute
1150 17th Street N.W.
Washington, D.C. 20036

Karl D. Galbraith
Bureau of Economic Analysis
U.S. Department of Commerce
Washington, D.C. 20230

Robert J. Gordon
Department of Economics
Northwestern University
2003 Sheridan Road
Room 6180
Evanston, Illinois 60201

John A. Gorman
National Income and Wealth Division
Bureau of Economic Analysis
U.S. Department of Commerce
Washington, D.C. 20230

Alan Greenspan
Townsend-Greenspan & Co., Inc.
1 New York Plaza
New York, New York 10004

Zvi Griliches
Department of Economics
Harvard University
125 Littauer Center
Cambridge, Massachusetts 02138

Bruce T. Grimm
Bureau of Economic Analysis
U.S. Department of Commerce
Washington, D.C. 20230

Albert A. Hirsch
Econometric Studies Branch
Bureau of Economic Analysis
U.S. Department of Commerce
Washington, D.C. 20230

Saul H. Hymans
Department of Economics
University of Michigan
Ann Arbor, Michigan 48104

John W. Kendrick
Department of Economics
George Washington University
Washington, D.C. 20006

Lawrence Klein
Department of Economics
Wharton School
University of Pennsylvania
3718 Locust Street
Philadelphia, Pennsylvania 19174

Ronald E. Kutscher
Office of Economic Growth and Employment Projections
Bureau of Labor Statistics
U.S. Department of Labor
441 G. Street N.W.
Washington, D.C. 20212

Marilyn E. Manser
Mathematica Policy Research, Inc.
600 Maryland Avenue, S.W.
Suite 550
Washington, D.C. 20024

Arthur M. Okun
Deceased

Robert P. Parker
National Income and Wealth Division
Bureau of Economic Analysis
U.S. Department of Commerce
Washington, D.C. 20230

Albert Rees
Alfred P. Sloan Foundation
630 Fifth Avenue
Room 3550
New York, New York 10020

Richard Ruggles
Department of Economics
Yale University
New Haven, Connecticut 06520

Stanley J. Sigel
Division of Research and Statistics
Federal Reserve Board
Washington, D.C. 20551

James H. Sinclair
Division of Industrial Prices and Price Indexes
Office of Prices and Living Conditions
Bureau of Labor Statistics
U.S. Department of Labor
441 G. Street N.W.
Washington, D.C. 20212

Stephen Taylor
Division of Research and Statistics
Federal Reserve Board
Washington, D.C. 20551

Helen Stone Tice
Bureau of Economic Analysis
U.S. Department of Commerce
Washington, D.C. 20230

Jack E. Triplett
Office of Research and Evaluation
Bureau of Labor Statistics
U.S. Department of Labor
441 G. Street, N.W.
Washington, D.C. 20212

Richard C. Ziemer
Bureau of Economic Analysis
U.S. Department of Commerce
Washington, D.C. 20230

Author Index

Subject Index